Keys to Success

IN COLLEGE, CAREER, AND LIFE

How to Achieve Your Goals

FOURTH EDITION

Carol Carter

Joyce Bishop

Sarah Lyman Kravits

Editorial Consultant

Richard D. Bucher

*Professor of Sociology,
Baltimore City Community College*

Prentice Hall

Library of Congress Cataloging-in-Publication Data

Carter, Carol.
    Keys to success in college, career, and life : how to achieve your goals / Carol Carter,
Joyce Bishop, Sarah Lyman Kravits ; editorial consultant, Richard D. Bucher.—4th ed.
    p. cm.
    Rev. ed. of: Keys to success. 3rd ed. c2001.
    Includes bibliographical references and index.
    ISBN 0-13-094765-2
    1. College student orientation—United States—Handbooks, manuals, etc.   2. Study
skills—Handbooks, manuals, etc.   3. College students—United States—Life skills guides.
4. Career development—United States—Handbooks, Manuals, etc.   I. Title: Keys to
success. II. Bishop, Joyce (Joyce L.). III. Kravits, Sarah Lyman. IV. Bucher,
Richard D. V. Carter, Carol. Keys to success. VI. Title.

LB2343.32 .C37 2003
378.1'98—dc21
                                                     2002016929

Vice President and Publisher: Jeffery W. Johnston
Senior Acquisitions Editor: Sande Johnson
Assistant Editor: Cecilia Johnson
Production Editor: Holcomb Hathaway
Design Coordinator: Diane C. Lorenzo
Cover Designer: Thomas Borah
Cover Photos: Corbis Stock Market
Production Manager: Pamela D. Bennett
Director of Marketing: Ann Castel Davis
Director of Advertising: Kevin Flanagan
Marketing Manager: Christina Quadhamer

This book was set in Sabon by Aerocraft Charter Art Service. It was printed and
bound by Banta Book Group. The cover was printed by The Lehigh Press, Inc.

Pearson Education Ltd., *London*
Pearson Education Australia Pty. Limited, *Sydney*
Pearson Education Singapore Pte. Ltd.
Pearson Education North Asia Ltd., *Hong Kong*
Pearson Education Canada, Ltd., *Toronto*
Pearson Educación de Mexico, S.A. de C.V.
Pearson Education–Japan, *Tokyo*
Pearson Education Malaysia Pte. Ltd.
Pearson Education, *Upper Saddle River, New Jersey*

10 9 8 7 6 5 4 3 2 1
ISBN 0-13-094765-2

Photo Credits, by page

p. 2, Dynamic Graphics; p. 23, Breton Littlehales; p. 24, Lonnie Duka/Index Stock Imagery, Inc.; p. 56, Tomi/Getty Images, Inc./PhotoDisc, Inc.; p. 58, D. Berry/Getty Images, Inc./PhotoDisc, Inc.; p. 68, Dynamic Graphics; p. 74, Mary Kate Denny/PhotoEdit; p. 85, Tim Schaffer; p. 89, Gabe Palmer/Corbis/Stock Market; p. 106, Tom Hauck/Getty Images, Inc.; p. 110, Dynamic Graphics; p. 121, Robert Harbison; p. 131, Jeff Greenberg/PhotoEdit; p. 148, Dynamic Graphics; p. 153, Dynamic Graphics; p. 176, Mark Richards/PhotoEdit; p. 190, Copyright Images 100 LTD; p. 198, Doug Menuez/Getty Images, Inc./PhotoDisc, Inc.; p. 212, Gary Conner/PhotoEdit; p. 224, Dynamic Graphics; p. 228, Chip Henderson/Index Stock Imagery, Inc.; p. 235, Bruna Stude/OmniPhoto Communications, Inc.; p. 266, Corbis Images; p. 270, Kevin Horan/Getty Images, Inc.; p. 283, Ulrike Welsch/PhotoEdit; p. 287, Jared Leeds, 2001; p. 299, Getty Images, Inc.; p. 302, Dynamic Graphics; p. 308, Gallaudet University; p. 321, Tony Freeman/PhotoEdit; p. 340, PhotoDisc, Inc.; p. 346, Ryan McVay/Getty Images, Inc./PhotoDisc., Inc.; p. 353, Stewart Cohen/Getty Images, Inc.; p. 376, Copyright Images 100 LTD; p. 389, Jack Star/Getty Images, Inc./PhotoDisc, Inc.; p. 392, Michal Heron/PH College; p. 414, Dynamic Graphics; p. 427, Bob Daemmrich/The Image Works; p. 429, David Sailors/Corbis/Stock Market; p. 441, Getty Images, Inc. All other photographic images © Hemera Technologies, Inc.

Dedication

HEALING OUR HEARTS

We dedicate this edition to the lives and the loved ones of those lost in the terrorist attacks on America on September 11, 2001. We ask that all of us remember that day by taking more time to be with those we care about, by living our lives to the fullest, and by replacing hatred with kindness in our neighborhoods, our country, and the world. We ask that you keep your spirit strong in times of adversity and be true to the resources, talents, and greatness within you.

WITHDRAWN

Mission Statement

Our mission is to help students know and believe in themselves, take advantage of resources and opportunities, set and achieve their goals, learn throughout their lives, discover careers that fulfill and support them, build fruitful and satisfying relationships with others from all backgrounds and walks of life, and experience the challenges and rewards that make life meaningful.

Brief Contents

Contents

Part I
Defining Yourself and Your Goals   1

Part II
Developing Your Learning Skills   109

NOTE: Every effort has been made to provide accurate and current Internet information in this book. However, the Internet and information posted on it are constantly changing, so it is inevitable that some of the Internet addresses listed in this textbook will change.

Foreword

Certainly college is a wonderful key to opportunities never imagined! I had great expectations before my entrance into the "Inferno." The most important aspect of attending college seemed to be the Spirit of Success. Yet, I could not feel this spirit without the costs of failure. My first days as a college student were extremely difficult to cope with academically and socially. The Herculean workload weighed me down. Getting help seemed like the best answer, but talking did not bring solutions. I had to get involved.

The contents of *Keys to Success* made learning personal, providing insight into the obstacles that confronted me. The "learn-by-doing" emphasis took me from the trenches of failure and turned me into a student who could set priorities and manage time. Writing definitely brought abundance to my table in note taking and studying. Curriculum planning, cultural issues, and wellness are topics I found useful due to personal stuggles in these areas.

Self-awareness, confidence, and responsibility are three pillars that support a life I can call my own. I have been provided "keys" to set goals in areas I never imagined embarking upon, such as research in gender studies, taking courses in multiple intelligences, and continuing Model United Nations. Once I had organized my academic life, my social life returned again, and the task of lifelong learning evolved into a goal I seek today.

As you embark on your journey to success, know that the tools in *Keys to Success* can assist you not only in college, but for a lifetime. Pay attention to the information on technology because it connects you with peers, instructors, and the resources of the world. Check out issues on sexual decisions and substance abuse, diversity, and managing finances; these will be helpful long after graduation. Information on goal setting and critical thinking will inspire you to grow into a responsible and well-organized individual. *Keys to Success* reveals the extraordinary through the practical. It is certainly a book that I will refer to often for the rest of my life.

My goal as student editor is to inspire you to aim for goals compassionately and extraordinarily. You, too, can be successful with this book! All that you need to succeed in college is available within it. Opportunities are all around you, and *Keys to Success* will help you unlock the benefits of these opportunities. So have a look for yourself. A warm thank you goes out to the authors and editors; and to the reader, my best to you in all your endeavors.

Jason Kim

Undergraduate student,
The Johns Hopkins University

No matter how well you perform in school, there is always something more that can be done to improve the way you learn. *Keys to Success* will equip you with learning strategies designed to produce success not only in school but also in life. Time management, for example, is a skill that nourishes and sustains our accomplishments; it is the gateway to personal satisfaction and workplace innovation.

As a senior majoring in English at Northwestern University, I've found that applying the strategies found in *Keys to Success* promotes facility in learning and even improves the general quality of my life. The learning skills described in this book have helped me to study more efficiently, and thereby create time for my passions in life—literature, music, and writing. I'm confident they will do the same for you.

Alexander Stacey

Undergraduate student,
Northwestern University

My decision to go back to school after 18 years has been a hard one and I have had to overcome a lot of inner obstacles. I was worried about having enough time to study as well as taking care of my three children. After finishing *Keys to Success,* I have come to realize that once you set a goal for yourself there is nothing you can't achieve.

The confidence and knowledge I have gained after reading *Keys to Success* have been immeasurable and have seeped into every aspect of my life. I have learned that I'm a visual learner, which has helped me with the way I take my class notes as well as the way I study for my tests. The straightforward format made it easy to read and understand. At my community college, I'm enrolled in a 2 + 2 program that will let me get my AA degree here and then transfer to Florida Atlantic University to finish my bachelor's degree in Elementary Education.

Coming back to school has been a positive and enriching life experience and has shown my children how important it is to have an education. I am very proud to have been a part of the revision process for *Keys to Success.*

Patricia Wright

Undergraduate student,
Indian River Community College

Preface

Owner's Manual

PLEASE READ THIS FIRST

Y ou are living in a world of enormous change, a world where technology turns dreams into reality, where people from every land and culture communicate and interrelate—often for the first time—and where new opportunities are created as quickly as old ones fade away. The world may seem bright with promise, even as the choices you face feel overwhelming—what to study, what career to pursue, what lifestyle to adopt, what to believe.

Two keys will help you get where you want to go. The first is *an open mind*—being a receptive learner. Only when you are open to information, choices, and situations can you hope to see the possibilities that are often right in front of you. The second is *motivation*. Throughout life, you will need the determination and drive to take advantage of those possibilities and achieve your goals.

Open Your Mind to *Keys to Success*

Start by opening your mind to the many features in this text and to the resources available in your course. *Keys to Success* is filled with tools that will help you to develop the attitudes, ideas, and skills that are the building blocks of future success. Among the tools you will encounter are:

A college primer. Because there's so much to know right off the bat, *Quick Start to College* has been added at the beginning of this text. *Quick Start* helps you get a feel for the structure of your college, the people who can help you with academic and life issues, the resources available to you, and expectations from instructors, administrators, and fellow students.

Skills that prepare you for college, career, and life. The ideas and strategies that help you succeed in college also take you where you want to go in your career and personal life. The three parts of this text help you develop a firm foundation for lifelong learning.

- *Part I: Defining Yourself and Your Goals.* **Chapter 1** provides an **overview** of today's college experience and an opportunity to evaluate your personal starting point. **Chapter 2** helps you identify complementary aspects of your **learning style**—your Multiple Intelligences and your Personality Spectrum profile—and choose strategies that make them work for you. **Chapter 3** helps you master valuable **goal-setting and time-management** skills that keep you moving forward.

- *Part II: Developing Your Learning Skills.* **Chapter 4** puts your learning into action, introducing you to an array of **critical-thinking skills**—how to take in, question, and use information so that you can solve problems, make decisions, and plan strategically. The remaining chapters in Part II build crucial skills for the classroom and beyond—**Reading and Studying (Chapter 5), Listening, Note Taking, and Memory (Chapter 6), Research and Writing (Chapter 7), and Test Taking (Chapter 8).**

- *Part III: Creating Success.* Recognizing that success includes more than academic achievement, **Chapter 9** focuses on developing the **interpersonal and communication skills** you need in a diverse society. **Chapter 10** helps you to manage the **stress and wellness** issues that so many college students face, while **Chapter 11** helps you develop the **money-management and career-planning** skills that you need in college and beyond. Finally, **Chapter 12** helps you **think expansively:** What path have you traveled during the semester? What plans do you have for your future?

Skill-building exercises. Today's graduates need to be effective thinkers, team players, writers, and strategic planners. The set of exercises at the end of each chapter—"Building Skills for College, Career, and Life Success"—encourages you to develop these valuable skills and to apply thinking processes to any topic or situation:

- *Critical Thinking: Applying Learning to Life.* These exercises encourage you to apply critical thinking to chapter topics in ways that take your personal needs and goals into account.
- *Teamwork: Combining Forces.* This exercise gives you a chance to interact and learn in a group setting, building your teamwork and leadership skills in the process.
- *Writing: Discovery Through Journaling.* This journal exercise provides an opportunity to express your thoughts and develop your writing skills.
- *Career Portfolio: Charting Your Course.* This exercise helps you gather evidence of your talents, skills, interests, qualifications, and experience. At the end of the semester, you will have created a portfolio of information and insights that will help you find the right career and job.

Exercises appearing at the end of each part help you to develop other important skills:

- *Becoming a Better Test Taker.* This feature tests you on material from three or four different chapters, using multiple-choice, fill-in-the-blank, and essay questions.
- *Web Connection.* Using the Prentice Hall Student Success Supersite and other on-line resources, this exercise helps you apply and build your knowledge through the medium of the Internet.

Diversity of voice. The world is becoming increasingly diverse in ethnicity, perspective, culture, lifestyle, race, choices, abilities, needs, and more. In recognition of this fact, many voices speak to you from these pages, through the following features:

- *Personal Triumph* presents a real-life story of a person who has overcome difficult circumstances in the pursuit of education and fulfillment. You may relate personally to the people profiled, but even if you don't, you will be inspired by their stories. What you read of their courage and perseverance will motivate you to step up your personal efforts to succeed. You will find a Personal Triumph story in each chapter and at the end of each part.

- *Chapter opening Q & As* highlight questions posed by actual students as they begin college. Each question is answered by another person who has had similar experiences.

- *Text examples* deal with the realities that students face—balancing school with work; returning to school as an older student; dealing with financial needs, parenting, supporting various lifestyles and schedules; and so on.

- *Chapter summaries* introduce a word or phrase from a language other than English and suggest how you might apply the concept to your own life.

What's new in this edition. As we revise, we are in constant touch with students and instructors who tell us how we can improve. For this edition we worked with student editors and contributors gathered from all over the country. Some provided the real-life stories for Personal Triumph and chapter opening Q & As; others read our manuscript in detail and gave us honest and valuable feedback. More than ever before, this edition contains what students taking this course have told us that they want and need—and it reflects their hard work and dedication.

In addition to the personal stories found throughout the text, other new elements include:

- Multiple Intelligence charts throughout the text that demonstrate, in specific, concrete ways, how to apply MI strategies to chapter topics.
- Expanded discussion of academic integrity (Chapter 1).
- Expanded discussion of choosing a major (Chapter 2).
- Strategies for finding the main idea in reading (Chapter 5).
- A primer on doing Internet research (Chapter 7).
- A look at the unique choices faced by minority students (Chapter 9).
- Strategies to maintain ideal body weight and avoid obesity (Chapter 10).

- Increased focus on stress management (Chapter 10).
- Expanded coverage of the pitfalls of credit card debt (Chapter 11).

Be Motivated to Achieve Your Goals

Now that you are open to what is available to you within these pages, the next step depends on your motivation—your ability to get yourself moving toward your goal. In this case, being motivated means studying *Keys to Success* and taking specific actions to use what you learn to create options and opportunities.

You are responsible for your education and your future. We can offer helpful suggestions, strategies, and ideas, but ultimately it's up to you to use them. We challenge you to start now to make the most of the opportunities before you. If you know yourself, choose the best paths available to you, and follow them with determination, you will earn the success that you deserve. You've made a terrific start by choosing to pursue an education—now you can build the future of your dreams.

Students and instructors: Send your questions, comments, and ideas about *Keys to Success* to us at www.caroljcarter.com. We look forward to hearing from you.

Acknowledgments

This book has come about through a heroic group effort. We would like to take this opportunity to acknowledge the people who have made it happen. Many thanks to:

- Our savvy student editors, for their wisdom and guidance. They read manuscript in detail, gave us the benefit of their best instincts, and even got advice from friends. Their high level of constructive criticism has made this edition stronger than ever. Student editors are: Jason Kim, The Johns Hopkins University; Alexander Stacey, Northwestern University; Patricia Wright, Indian River Community College

- Other helpful student contributors include: Jemma Erikson, Pepperdine University; Jeremy Hawn, University of Denver; Elena Rodriguez, University of Colorado at Boulder; Sandi Armitage; Marisa Connell; Jennifer Moe; Alex Toth

- Our esteemed reviewers, whose input has made an incalculable difference.

Fourth edition reviewers: Fred Amador, Phoenix College; Leslie Chilton, Arizona State University; Jim Coleman, Baltimore City Community College; Sara Connolly, Florida State University; Skye Gentile, California State University, Hayward; Karen Hardin, Mesa Community College; Patricia Hart, California State University, Fresno; Laura Kauffman, Indian River Community College; Kathy Masters, Arkansas State University; Sue Palmer, Brevard Community College; Marsha Walden, Valdosta State University; Angela Williams, The Citadel

Reviewers from previous editions: Manual Aroz, Arizona State University; Glenda Belote, Florida International University; Todd Benatovich, University of Texas at Arlington; John Bennett, Jr., University of Connecticut; Ann Bingham-Newman, California State University–LA; Mary Bixby, University of Missouri–Columbia; Barbara Blandford, Education Enhancement Center at Lawrenceville, NJ; Jerry Bouchie, St. Cloud State University; Mona Casady, SW Missouri State University; Kara Craig, University of Southern Mississippi; Janet Cutshall, Sussex County Community College; Valerie DeAngelis, Miami-Dade Community College; Rita Delude, NH Community Technical College; Marianne

Edwards, Georgia College and State University; Judy Elsley, Weber State University in Utah; Bob Gibson, University of Nebraska–Omaha; Sue Halter, Delgado Community College; Suzy Hampton, University of Montana; Maureen Hurley, University of Missouri–Kansas City; Karen Iversen, Heald Colleges; Kathryn K. Kelly, St. Cloud State University; Nancy Kosmicke, Mesa State College; Frank T. Lyman, Jr., University of Maryland; Marvin Marshak, University of Minnesota; Barnette Miller Moore, Indian River Community College; Rebecca Munro, Gonzaga University; Bobbie Parker, Alabama State University; Virginia Phares, DeVry of Atlanta; Brenda Prinzavalli, Beloit College; Jacqueline Simon, Education Enhancement Center at Lawrenceville, NJ; Carolyn Smith, University of Southern Indiana; Joan Stottlemyer, Carroll College; Thomas Tyson, SUNY Stony Brook; Eve Walden, Valencia Community College; Rose Wassman, DeAnza College; Don Williams, Grand Valley State University; William Wilson, St. Cloud State University; Michelle G. Wolf, Florida Southern College

• The PRE 100 instructors at Baltimore City Community College, Liberty Campus, for their ideas, especially college President Dr. Jim Tschechtelin, Co-ordinator Jim Coleman, and Sonia Lynch, Jack Taylor, and Peggy Winfield. Thanks also to focus group participants Stan D. Brown, Frederick W. Campbell, Jr., James E. Coleman, Joseph A. Faw, Lyllis M. Green, and Marjorie E. Hunt. Special thanks to the late Rita Lenkin Hawkins for her support.

• Those who generously contributed personal stories, exhibiting courage in being open and honest about their life experiences:

Beverly Andre, Triton College; Edhilvia Campos, Parkland Community College; Chip Case, Piedmont Virginia Community College; Shera Chantel Caviness, University of Memphis; Peter Changsak, Sheldon-Jackson College; Rosalia Chavez, University of Arizona; Carol Comlish, University of Alabama; Brett Cross, University of Washington; Dani E. Day, Community College of Denver; Darrin Estepp, Ohio State University; Katherine Freeman, University of Akron; Chris Wong Sick Hong, Texas A & M; Erin Hughey-Commers, St. John's College;

Susie Ivy, Dominican University; Kevin Leman, Psychologist, Speaker, and Author; Ramona Z. Locke, Vice President Senior Financial Consultant, Merrill Lynch Private Client Group; Joe A. Martin, Jr., Professor of Communications, University of West Florida; Matt Millard, University of Wyoming; Gustavo Minaya, Essex Community College; Todd Montalbo, University of Alaska; Raymond Montolvo, Jr., University of Southern California; Julia Nolan, University of California, Davis; Michael Nolan, Oregon State University; Tim Nordberg, Chicago Youth Project; Morgan Paar, Academy of Art College; Morgan Packard, Tulane University; Richard Pan, Columbia University; Nathalie Piraino, Essex Community College; Gloria Finn Porter, Attorney at the Center for Justice; Jo Anne Roe, Instructor, Oak Park–River Forest High School; Norma Seledon, Director, Las Mujeres en Accion; Carlos Vela Shimano, ITESM Campus, Mexico; Tim Short, Washington State University; Litzka Stark, Sarah Lawrence College; Randy Ust, University of Mary; Tracy Ust, St. Cloud University

• The instructors at DeVry, especially Susan Chin and Carol Ozee, for their suggestions.

• The folks at California State University at Fresno, for their support and ideas: Patricia B. Hart, Phyllis Khuen, Scott Sailor, and Timothy Stearns. Special thanks to Candace Lee Egan for her work on the Keys to Lifelong Learning Telecourse and Marie E. Provencio for her help with the instructor's manual.

• Vikki and Eric Mayberry, Jeff and Margo McIlroy, Kate Lareau, Carol Abolafia, and Sue Bierman for their invaluable assistance.

• Cynthia Nordberg, for her work with contributors and her particular talent in gathering true and important stories.

• Michael Jackson for his writing samples and advice.

• Our editorial consultant Rich Bucher, professor of sociology at Baltimore City Community College, who provided important advice and consultation on diversity.

• Dr. Frank T. Lyman, Jr., educational consultant and innovator, for his invaluable advice on the text and for his generous permission to use and adapt his Thinktrix critical thinking system. Dr. Lyman is nationally recognized for innovations in curriculum and instruction including Think-Pair-Share and the Thinktrix.

• Marjorie Freilich-Den, Sheri Garrou, Ross T. Labaugh of California State University at Fresno, and Bobbie Stevens of University of Texas at Arlington, for their reviews of the revised material on library research.

• Our terrific editor Sande Johnson and assistant editor Cecilia Johnson for their hard work, candid comments on the manuscript, and belief in the cause.

• Those who reviewed and contributed to the instructors' manual, for their insight:

Todd Benatovich, University of Texas at Arlington; Amy Bierman, student, Old Dominion University; Jennifer Cohen; Jodi Levine, Temple University; Geri MacKenzie, Southern Methodist University; Gene Mueller, Henderson State University; Tina Pitt, Heald College; Dan Rice, Iowa State University; Michael and Frances Trevisan, Washington State University; Karen Valencia, South Texas Community College; Eve Walden, Valencia Community College; Don Williams, Grand Valley State University; William Wilson, St. Cloud State University; Nona Wood, North Dakota State University

• Sara Stensgaard of the University of Buffalo, for her work in integrating Web activities.

• Our fabulous production team, especially Gay Pauley.

• Our marketing gurus, especially Christina Quadhamer and Barbara Rosenberg.

• Jeff Johnston, Robin Baliszewski, Gary June, Jim Bozik, Will Ethridge, and Rit Dojny, for their vision and commitment to these books and to the success of all students.

• The Prentice Hall representatives and the management team led by David Gillespie, who, since getting his masters in student affairs, has always had a passion for student success and communicates that passion to those with whom he works.

• Our families and friends, who have encouraged us and put up with our commitments. Special thanks to Josephine Kravits for accommodating her mother's work schedule.

• We extend a very special thanks to Judy Block, whose research, writing, and editing work was essential and invaluable.

Finally, for their ideas, opinions, and stories, we would like to thank all of the students and professors with whom we work. Joyce in particular would like to thank the thousands of students who have allowed her, as their professor, the privilege of sharing part of their journey through college. We appreciate that, through reading this book, you give us the opportunity to learn and discover with you— in your classroom, in your home, on the bus, and wherever else learning takes place.

About the Authors

Carol Carter is founder and president of LifeBound, which provides seminars, coaching and resources for high school and college students. In addition, as Director of Faculty Development at Prentice Hall, Carol puts together and runs faculty symposia and workshops in student success across the country.

She has written *Majoring in the Rest of Your Life: Career Secrets for College Students* and *Majoring in High School*. She has also co-authored *Keys to Preparing for College, Keys to College Studying, The Career Tool Kit, Keys to Career Success, Keys to Study Skills, Keys to Thinking and Learning,* and *Keys to Success*. She has taught welfare-to-work classes, team taught in the La Familia Scholars Program at Community College of Denver, and has conducted numerous workshops for students and faculty around the country. She is the host of the Keys to Lifelong Learning Telecourse, a 26- episode telecourse to help students at a distance prepare for college, career, and life success. In addition to working with students of all ages, Carol thrives on foreign travel and culture; she has been fortunate enough to have been a guest in more than 40 countries. Please visit her website and write her at www.caroljcarter.com.

Joyce Bishop holds a Ph.D. in psychology and has taught for more than 20 years, receiving a number of honors, including Teacher of the Year for 1995 and 2000. For five years she has been voted "favorite teacher" by the student body and Honor Society at Golden West Col-

lege, Huntington Beach, CA, where she has taught since 1987 and is a tenured professor. She has worked with a federal grant to establish Learning Communities and Workplace Learning in her district, and has developed workshops and trained faculty in cooperative learning, active learning, multiple intelligences, workplace relevancy, learning styles, authentic assessment, team building, and the development of learning communities. She is currently teaching on-line and multimedia classes, and training other faculty to teach on-line in her district and region of 21 colleges. She also co-authored *Keys to College Studying, Keys to Success, Keys to Thinking and Learning,* and *Keys to Study Skills*. Joyce is the lead academic of the Keys to Lifelong Learning Telecourse, distributed by Dallas Telelearning.

Sarah Lyman Kravits comes from a family of educators and has long cultivated an interest in educational development. She co-authored *Keys to College Studying, The Career Tool Kit, Keys to Success, Keys to Thinking and Learning,* and *Keys to Study Skills* and has served as Program Director for LifeSkills, Inc., a nonprofit organization that aims to further the career and personal development of high school students. In that capacity she helped to formulate both curricular and organizational elements of the program, working closely with instructors as well as members of the business community. She also gives faculty workshops in student success and in critical thinking. Sarah holds a B.A. in English and drama from the University of Virginia, where she was a Jefferson Scholar, and an M.F.A. from Catholic University.

Quick Start to College

A Guide to Knowing *What* to Do, *How* to Do It, and *Where* to Get Help

Quick Start to College will help you explore the following topics:

- How colleges are structured
- How to get academic help
- What your college expects of you

From your first day of school, you face the challenge of adjusting to the realities of college, which may be nothing like you've ever encountered. It may help you to know that nearly every college student—no matter age or experience—feels overwhelmed as college begins. It is hard to feel at ease when you literally don't know where you are going, whom you will meet, and what you will be asked to do.

Quick Start to College will help you feel in control right away as you begin the most important educational journey of your life. Use this material as a guide to help you explore your college and the specific resources available to you. Keep in mind that the names of offices and personnel titles may vary, so if a term mentioned here is not used at your school, simply replace it with the correct language. Also, keep in mind that some colleges do not offer every resource.

No matter whom you meet in college—instructors, advisors, administrators, support personnel, and fellow students—you are a full participant in the educational process. This brings with it responsibilities that include:

- Envisioning what you want to accomplish during college and then making it happen
- Taking an active role in your courses from the first day of class
- Taking personal responsibility for learning, which involves setting goals, managing your time, completing assignments on schedule, and seeking help, if necessary
- Striving to do your best
- Being an advocate for yourself in all your interactions with others
- Taking care of yourself—your mind, body, and relationships
- Getting involved in activities and student organizations that you like and that will help you develop as a person and a team member
- Exploring different majors and deciding what you want to study
- Pursuing academic goals that are meaningful to you (honors or awards, involvement in academic organizations, internships or other work experiences that support your academic path)

Taking responsibility for your success does not imply that you are on your own. On the contrary, you will be surrounded by people who are eager to help—if you are willing to ask and be persistent.

How colleges are
structured

Think of your college as a large organization made up of arms that perform specific functions and that are run by hundreds and sometimes thousands of people. The two primary functional arms of your college focus on teaching and administration.

Teaching Takes Center Stage

The primary mission of most colleges and universities is teaching—communicating to students the knowledge and thinking skills needed to become lifelong learners. Although the term "instructor" is used in this text, teachers have official titles that show their rank within your college. Instructors with the highest status are *full professors*. Moving down from there are *associate professors, assistant professors, lecturers, instructors*, and *assistant instructors*, more commonly known as *teaching assistants* or *TAs*. (Remember that titles may vary from school to school.) *Adjuncts* may teach several courses, but are not official staff members. Later in *Quick Start*, you will see how to communicate with and get help from your instructors.

Administrators Provide Support

The administrative staff enables your college—and the student body—to function. As Figure QS.1 shows, *vice presidents* deal with the nuts and bolts of operations; they make sure buildings are repaired, instructors are hired, students are registered, tuition is collected. *Deans*, in contrast, are in charge of operations and issues that directly involve students—for example, a Dean of Student Affairs and a Dean of Admissions. (These divisions and titles do not always apply, so learn the system at your college.)

Large universities may be divided into *schools* that have separate administrative structures and staffs—for example, a School of Business or a School of Social Work. Each school normally has its own dean, and each department has a *chair* or *chairperson*—an instructor named to head the department.

One of the most important administrative offices for students is the *Office of the Dean of Student Affairs*, which, in many colleges, is the center for student services. Staff members try to answer your questions or direct you to others who can help. Learn how the student-help system works so you can identify specific people to turn to in case of a problem.

Administrative Offices Dealing with Tuition Issues and Registration

Among the first administrators you will meet are those involved with tuition payments, financial aid, and registration.

The *bursar's office* (also called the *office of finance*, the *accounting office*, and *cashiering services*) issues bills for tuition and room and board and collects payments from students and financial aid sources. Direct your questions about tuition payments to this office.

The *financial aid office* helps students apply for financial aid and understand the eligibility requirements of different federal, state, and private programs. The three main sources of

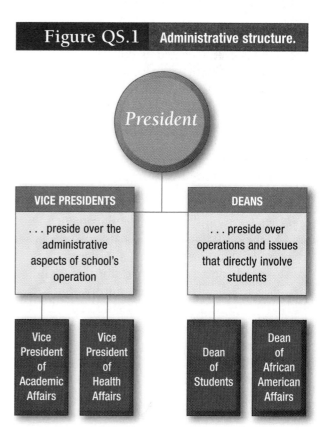

Figure QS.1 Administrative structure.

President

VICE PRESIDENTS
...preside over the administrative aspects of school's operation

DEANS
...preside over operations and issues that directly involve students

Vice President of Academic Affairs

Vice President of Health Affairs

Dean of Students

Dean of African American Affairs

financial aid are student loans, grants, and scholarships. You will learn more about these sources below.

The *registrar's office* (also called the *admissions office* in many two-year colleges) handles course registration, sends grades at the end of the semester, and compiles your official transcript, which is a comprehensive record of your courses and grades. Graduate schools require a copy of your official transcript before considering you for admission, as do many employers before considering you for a job. Transcripts are requested through the registrar's office.

Administrative Services for Students

A host of services are designed to help students adjust to and succeed in college and to deal with problems that arise. Here are some services you are likely to find:

Academic enhancement centers, including reading, writing, math, and study-skills centers. These centers offer consultations and tutoring to help students improve skills at all levels and become more confident.

Academic computer center. Most schools have sophisticated computer facilities equipped with computers, software, printers, and other equipment. At many schools, these facilities are open every day, and are staffed by technicians who can assist you with computer-related problems. Many facilities also offer training workshops.

Student housing or commuter affairs office. Residential colleges provide on-campus housing for undergraduate students, with many schools requiring lower classmen to live on campus rather than off. The housing office handles room and roommate placement, establishes behavioral standards, and deals with special situations (e.g., an allergic student's need for a room air conditioner) and problems. Schools with commuting students may have programs to assist students with transportation and parking.

Health services. Your college health center is staffed with medical professionals who may include physicians, nurse practitioners, registered nurses, and support staff. If you are not feeling well, visit the clinic for help. Available services generally include prescriptions for common medicines, routine diagnostic tests, vaccinations, and first aid. All clinics are affiliated with nearby hospitals for emergency care. In addition, psychological counseling is sometimes offered through the health clinic, or it may have a separate facility. Remember that although services are available, it is up to you to seek them out. Many colleges require proof of health insurance coverage at the time of registration. (Students under the age of about 23 are generally covered under a parent's policy.) You'll need health insurance if you are hospitalized or need to see a specialist not affiliated with the college health office.

Career services. This office helps students find part-time and full-time jobs, as well as summer jobs and internships. Career offices have reference files on specific careers and employers. They also introduce students to the job-search process, helping them learn to write a résumé and cover letter and use the Internet to find job opportunities. Career offices often invite employers to interview students on campus and hold career fairs to introduce different companies and organizations. Summer internships and jobs are snapped up quickly, so check the office early and often to improve your chances. Visit the career office during your freshman year to begin developing an effective long-term career strategy.

Services for students with disabilities. Colleges must provide disabled students with full access to facilities and programs. For students with documented disabilities, federal law requires that assistance be provided in the form of appropriate accommodations and aids. These range from interpreters for the hearing-impaired to readers and note takers for the visually impaired to ramps for students in wheelchairs. If you have a disability, visit the Office of Students with Disabilities to learn what is offered. Remember, also, that this office is your advocate if you encounter problems.

Veteran affairs. The Office of Veteran Affairs provides veterans with various services, including academic and personal counseling and current benefit status, which may affect tuition waivers.

Parking. Campus parking spaces can be scarce, with the best choices often going to students with seniority. (Disabled students are always given priority privileges.) Students with cars are generally required to register vehicles annually with campus security and get a parking sticker.

How to get academic *help*

A ttending college is one of the best decisions you've made. However, deadlines, academic and social pressures, and simply being in new surroundings can make the experience stressful at times. (Chapter 10 talks more about stress management.) Understanding that help is available is the first step in helping yourself. Step two is actually *seeking* help from those who can give it. This requires knowing where to go and what assistance you can reasonably expect.

Before turning to others, try to find the answers you need on your own. For general guidance, check your college catalog, handbook, and Web site.

Help from Instructors and Teaching Assistants

When you want to speak personally with an instructor for longer than a minute or two, choose your time carefully. Before or after class is usually not the best time for anything more than a quick question—instructors may be thinking about their lecture or be surrounded by other students with questions. When you need your instructor's full attention, there are three ways to communicate effectively—make an appointment during office hours, send e-mail, and leave voice-mail messages.

Office hours. Instructors are required to keep regular office hours during which students can schedule personal conferences. Generally, these are posted during the first class, on instructors'

office doors, and on instructors' or departmental Web pages. Always make an appointment for a conference; if you show up unannounced, there's a good chance your instructor will be busy. Face-to-face conferences are ideal for working through ideas and problems—for example, deciding on a term paper topic. Conferences are also the best setting to ask for advice—if, for example, you are considering majoring in the instructor's field and need guidance on courses.

E-mail. Use e-mail to clarify assignments and assignment deadlines, to ask specific questions about lectures or readings, and to clarify what will be covered on a test. Try not to wait until the last minute to ask test-related questions; your instructor may not have time to respond. Instructors' e-mail addresses are generally posted on the first day of class and may also be found in your student handbook or syllabus, which is a detailed description of what you will learn in the course. Links may also be available on the college home page.

Voice mail. If something comes up at the last minute, you can also leave a message in your instructor's office voice-mail box. Make your message short, but specific. Tell the instructor your reason for calling *("This is Rick Jones from your ten o'clock Intro to Psychology class. I'm supposed to present my project today, but I'm sick in bed with a fever.")* and avoid general messages *("This is Rick Jones from your ten o'clock class. Please call me at 555-5555.").* Avoid calling instructors at home unless they give specific permission to do so.

If you are taking a large lecture course, you may have a primary instructor plus a teaching assistant (TA) who meets with a small group of students on a regular basis. It is a good idea to approach your TA with course-related questions and problems before approaching the instructor. Because TAs deal with fewer students, they have more time to devote to specific issues.

Help from Academic Advisors

In most colleges, every student is assigned an advisor who is the student's personal liaison with the college. (At some schools, students receive help at an advising center.) Your advisor will help you choose courses every semester, plan your overall academic program, and understand college regulations including graduation requirements. He or she will point out possible consequences of your decisions (*"If you put off taking biology this semester, you're facing two lab courses next semester."*), help you shape your educational goals, and monitor your academic progress. Your advisor also knows about tutoring and personal counseling programs and may write recommendations when you are searching for a job.

It is important to remember that you, not your advisor, are responsible for your progress—for fully understanding graduation requirements, including credit requirements, and choosing the courses you need. Your advisor is there to help you with these critical decisions.

Help from a Mentor

If you are fortunate, you will find a mentor during college—a trusted counselor or guide who takes a special interest in helping you reach your goals. Mentoring relationships demand time and energy on both sides. A mentor can give you a private audience for questions and problems, advice tailored to your needs, support, guidance, and trust. A mentor cares about you enough to be devoted to your development. In return, you owe it to a mentor to be open to his or her ideas and, respectfully, to take advice into consideration. You and your mentor can learn from each other, receive positive energy from your relationship, and grow together.

Your mentor might be your faculty advisor, an instructor in your major or minor field of study, or an academic support instructor. You may also be drawn to someone outside school—a longtime friend whose judgment and experience you admire or a supervisor at work. Some schools have faculty or peer mentoring programs to match students with people who can help them. Check your student handbook or Web site or ask your faculty advisor if this is offered at your school.

Help from Learning Specialists

Almost everyone has difficulty in some aspect of learning, and you may view your struggles as simply an area of weakness. In contrast, people with diagnosed learning differences have conditions that make certain kinds of learning difficult. Some learning disabilities cause reading problems, some create difficulties in math, and still others make it difficult for students to process the language they hear.

If you have a learning disability, know that you are one of many. Colleges are filled with students with diagnosed learning problems who get help, develop coping skills, and excel in their chosen fields. To succeed on your own terms, you have a responsibility to understand your disability, to become an advocate for your rights as a student with special needs, and to do your best to overcome your condition. Consider the following strategies.

Be Informed About Your Disability

In Public Law 94-142, the federal government defines a learning disability as follows: "a disorder in one or more of the basic psychological processes involved in understanding or in using language, spoken or written, which may manifest itself in an imperfect ability to listen, think, speak, read, write, spell, or to do mathematical calculations. The term includes such conditions as perceptual handicaps, brain injury, minimal brain dysfunction and dyslexia." A learning disability diagnosis involves specific testing done by a qualified professional, and it may also involve documentation from instructors and family.

Identify Your Needs and Seek Assistance

If you are officially diagnosed with a learning disability, you are legally entitled to aid, and, in fact, the law requires colleges to hire specialists to help you one-on-one. Armed with your test results and documentation, speak with your advisor about getting support that will help you learn. Among the services that may be available are testing accommodations (e.g., having extended time, working on a computer, or taking oral rather than written exams); books on tape; note-taking assistance (e.g., having a fellow student take notes for you or having access to the instructor's notes); taking a reduced course load; and auditing a course before you take it for credit.

What your college *expects* of you

You are a full participant in your relationship with your college. Much is expected of you, and you have the right to expect much in return. The specific expectations described in this section involve understanding financial aid and curriculum and graduation requirements, choosing and registering for classes, following procedures, pursuing academic excellence, understanding and following your school's honor code, learning your college's computer system, and getting involved in extracurricular activities. Do your best to understand how to proceed in all these areas and, if you still have problems, ask for help—from instructors, administrators, advisors, mentors, experienced classmates, and family members.

Understand and Apply for Financial Aid

The average cost in the United States for a year's full-time undergraduate tuition, including room and board, in 1999–2000 ranged from $7,302 at public colleges to $20,277 at private colleges. Moreover, the total cost for an undergraduate's yearly tuition, room and board increased 22 percent at public colleges and 27 percent at private colleges in the last decade, far outpacing inflation. As a result, nearly half of all students receive some kind of aid.[1]

Most sources of financial aid don't seek out recipients. It is up to you to learn how you (or you and your parents, if they currently help support you) can finance your education. Visit your school's financial aid office, research what's available, weigh the pros and cons of each option, decide what works best, then apply early. Above all, think critically. Never assume that you are *not* eligible for aid. The types of aid available are student loans, grants, and scholarships.

Student Loans

As the recipient of a student loan, you are responsible for paying back the amount you borrow, plus interest, according to a predetermined payment schedule that may stretch over a number of years. The amount you borrow is known as the loan *principal,* and *interest* is the fee that you pay for the privilege of using money that belongs to someone else. During 2000, the annual percentage rate on direct government loans was 6.92 percent. Loan payments usually begin soon after graduation, after a "grace period" of between six months and a year, and last no more than 10 years.

The federal government administers or oversees most student loans. To receive aid from any federal program, you must be a citizen or eligible non-citizen and be enrolled in a program that meets government requirements. Individual states may differ in their aid programs, so check with the financial aid office for details.

Table QS.1 describes the main student loan programs to which you can apply. Amounts vary according to individual circumstances. In most cases, loans are limited to tuition costs minus any other financial aid you are receiving. (The information presented here on federal loans and grants is from *The 2001–2002 Student Guide to Financial Aid,* published by the U.S. Department of Education.)

There are many helpful on-line references for student loans, some of which enable you to apply on-line.

Grants and Scholarships

Unlike student loans, neither grants nor scholarships require repayment. Grants, funded by federal, state, or local governments as well as private organizations, are awarded to students who show financial need. Scholarships are awarded to students who show talent or ability in specified areas and may be financed by government or private organizations, schools, or individuals. Table QS.2 describes federal grant programs.

Even if you did not receive a grant or scholarship as a freshman, you may be eligible for opportunities as a sophomore, junior, or senior. These opportunities are often based on grades and campus leadership and may be given by individual college departments.

Additional information about federal grants and loans is available in the current version (updated yearly) of *The Student Guide to*

LOAN	DESCRIPTION
Table QS.1	**Federal student loan programs.**
Perkins	Low, fixed rate of interest. Available to those with exceptional financial need (determined by a government formula). Issued by schools from their allotment of federal funds. Grace period of up to nine months after graduation before repayment, in monthly installments, must begin.
Stafford	Available to students enrolled at least half-time. Exceptional need not required, although students who prove need can qualify for a subsidized Stafford loan (the government pays interest until repayment begins). Two types of Staffords: the direct loan comes from federal funds, and the FFEL (Federal Family Education Loan) comes from a bank or credit union. Repayment begins six months after the student graduates, leaves school, or drops below half-time enrollment.
PLUS	Available to students enrolled at least half-time and claimed as dependents by their parents. Parents must undergo a credit check to be eligible, or may be sponsored through a relative or friend who passes the check. Loan comes from government or a bank or credit union. Sponsor must begin repayment 60 days after receiving the last loan payment.

Financial Aid. This publication can be found at your school's financial aid office, or you can request it by mail or phone. The publication is also available on-line.

Address:
Federal Student Aid Information Center
P.O. Box 84
Washington, DC 20044-0084

Phone: 1-800-4-FED-AID
        (1-800-433-3243)

TTY for the hearing impaired:
        1-800-730-8913

Internet address:
www.ed.gov/prog_info/SFA/StudentGuide/

If you are receiving aid from your college, follow all the rules and regulations, including meeting application deadlines and remaining in academic good standing. In most cases, you will be required to reapply for aid every year.

Scholarships. Scholarships are given for various abilities and talents. They may reward academic achievement, exceptional abilities in sports or the arts, citizenship, or leadership. Certain scholarships are sponsored by federal agencies.

If you display exceptional ability and are disabled, female, of an ethnic background classified as a minority (e.g., African American or American Indian), or a child of someone who draws government benefits, you might find federal scholarship opportunities geared toward you.

All kinds of organizations offer scholarships. You may receive scholarships from individual departments at your school or from your school's independent scholarship funds, local organizations such as the Rotary Club, or privately operated aid foundations. Labor unions and companies may offer scholarships for children of employees. Membership groups, such as scouting organizations or the YMCA/YWCA, might offer scholarships, and religious organizations, such as the Knights of Columbus and the Council of Jewish Federations, are another source.

A relatively new federal program, known as the HOPE Scholarship, gives eligible students a tax credit worth up to $1,500, which reduces the amount of taxes you owe on a dollar for dollar basis. Say, for example, your federal tax bill is $1,800. As a HOPE Scholarship recipient, you deduct $1,500 from the $1,800 you owe, which leaves you with a tax bill of only

Table QS.2	Federal grant programs.
GRANT	**DESCRIPTION**
Pell	Need-based; the government evaluates your reported financial information and determines eligibility from that "score" (called an expected family contribution or EFC). Available to undergraduates who have earned no other degrees. Amount varies according to education cost and EFC. Adding other aid sources is allowed.
Federal Supplemental Educational Opportunity (FSEOG)	Need-based; administered by the financial aid administrator at participating schools. Each participating school receives a limited amount of federal funds for FSEOGs and sets its own application deadlines.
Work-study	Need-based; encourages community service work or work related to your course of study. Pays by the hour, at least the federal minimum wage. Jobs may be on-campus (usually for your school) or off (often with a nonprofit organization or a public agency).

$300. Students are eligible during their first two years of post-secondary education.

Researching grants and scholarships. It can take work to locate scholarships and work-study programs because many aren't widely advertised. Start digging at your financial aid office and visit your library, bookstore, and the Internet. Guides to funding sources, such as *College Financial Aid for Dummies* by Herm Davis and Joyce Lain Kennedy, catalog thousands of organizations. Check out on-line scholarship search services.

Use common sense when applying for aid. Fill out applications as neatly as possible and submit them on time or early. You can access the Free Application for Federal Student Aid (FAFSA) form at your library, the Federal Student Aid Information Center, through your college financial aid office, or via the U.S. Department of Education's Web site—www. ed.gov/finaid.html. Finally, be wary of scholarship scam artists who ask you first to pay a fee before they will help you find aid.

Understand Curriculum and Graduation Requirements

Every college has requirements for a degree that are stated in the catalog or on a Web site. Among the requirements you may encounter at your college are the following:

- Number of credits needed to graduate, including credits required in major and minor fields.
- Curriculum requirements, including specific course requirements. A liberal arts college, for example, may require a specified number of course hours in the humanities, social sciences, and natural sciences, plus a foreign language and a computer-literacy course.
- Departmental major requirements, including the cumulative average needed for acceptance as a major in the department. For example, you may be automatically accepted if your grade point average is at least 2.7 out of 4. Those with a lower average may require special approval and may be turned down.

Your goal is to remain in *good academic standing* throughout your college career as you pursue your degree. Among the degrees granted by different two-year and four-year colleges are Bachelor of Arts, Bachelor of Science, Associate of Arts, Associate of Science, and Associate of Applied Science.

Choose and Register for Classes

Choosing and registering for classes is challenging, especially the first time. Among the things you should consider as you scan the college catalog and make your course selections are the following:

- Core/general requirements for graduation. You have to take these classes no matter your major.

- Your major or minor or courses in departments you are considering as a major or minor.

- Electives you want to take because they sound interesting, even though they are out of your field. These include classes and teachers that the grapevine says are not to be missed.

In most schools, you can choose to attend a class without earning academic credit by *auditing* the class. Because tuition and fees are generally the same and seats are given on a space-available basis, why would you make this choice? The main reason is to explore different areas without worrying about a grade. Usually, students audit during their junior or senior year.

Once you decide on courses, but before you register, create a schedule that shows daily class times. If the first class meets at 8:00 A.M., ask yourself if you will be at your best at that early hour. It is always a good idea to create a back-up schedule, or even several alternatives, because you may be closed out of some classes. Show your ideas to your advisor for input and approval.

Actual course registration varies from school to school. Registration may take place through your school's computer network, via touch-tone phone, or in the school gym or student union. When you register, you may be asked to pay your tuition and other fees. If you are receiving financial aid, it is up to you to make sure that checks from all aid sources have arrived at the college before registration. If they haven't, you'll probably need to get on the phone to expedite the payment.

Follow Procedures

Your college is a bureaucratic organization, which means that you have to follow established rules and regulations. Normally, procedures are clear and not excessively burdensome, but they can still seem stressful the first time you do them. Among the most common procedures you will encounter are the following:

- *Adding or dropping a class.* This should be done within the first few days of the semester if you find that a course is not right for you or that there are better choices. Your advisor can tell you how to follow your school's drop/add procedures, which involve completing a form. Late-semester unexcused withdrawals (i.e., any withdrawal after a predetermined date) receive a failing grade. However, course withdrawals that are approved for medical problems, a death in the family, or other special circumstances have no impact on your grade point average.

- *Taking an Incomplete.* If you can't finish your work due to circumstances beyond your control—an illness or injury, for example— many colleges allow you to take a grade of *Incomplete* and make the work up at a later, specified time. You'll need approval from your instructor, and you'll also need to commit to making up the work during vacation or semester break.

- *Transferring schools or moving from a two-year to a four-year college.* If you are a student at a community college and intend to transfer to a four-year school, be sure to take the courses required for admission to that school. In addition, be sure all your courses are transferable, which means they will be counted toward your degree at the four-year school. Community colleges generally have advisors to help students work through this process. If you are unhappy at a four-year college and want a change, it is up to you to check out the degree requirements of the new college (you can do this by browsing through the college catalog) and complete an application.

- *Taking a leave of absence.* There are many reasons students take a leave of absence for a semester or a year and then return. You may want time away from academics to think through your long-term goals, or you may be needed for a family emergency. If you are in good standing at your college, leaves are generally granted in consultation with your dean and advisor. In contrast, students with academic or disciplinary problems who take a leave may have to reapply for admission when their leave is complete. Check with your advisor regarding details.

Read your college handbook about the various procedures used at your school. If you still have questions, speak with your advisor.

Pursue Academic Excellence

Your instructors expect you to do your best in their classes. Doing your best means that you attend every class with a positive attitude, arrive on time, complete assignments on schedule, listen attentively and participate in discussions, value honest scholarship, and seek help if you need it. In return for your efforts, you will learn a great deal and you will receive a course grade. Think of your instructor as the manager of a company. If you want to get the best performance review and the highest pay raise, you'll need to over-deliver on his or her expectations of you.

It is important to remember that your *work*—and not *you*—receives the grades. A *D* or an *F* does not diminish you as a person, but rather tells you that your efforts or work products are below what the instructor expects. Similarly, an *A* does not inflate your value as a person, but recognizes the superb quality of your academic performance.

Most schools use grading systems with numerical grades or equivalent letter grades (see Table QS.3). The highest course grade is an *A*, or 4.0, and the lowest is an *F*, or a 0.0. When all numerical grades are averaged together and multiplied by the number of semester hours per course, they form your *grade point average*, or *GPA*. In every course, you earn a certain number of college credits, called *semester hours*. For example, Accounting 101 may be worth 3 hours, and Physical Education may be worth 1 hour. These numbers generally refer to the number of hours the course meets per week.

Learn the minimum grades that you need to remain in good standing at your school and to be accepted and continue in your departmental major. At some schools, for example, grades below 2.0 may not be counted toward your major requirement. Figure QS.2 shows you how to calculate your GPA.

Table QS.3	Letter grades and equivalent numerical grades per semester hour.										
Letter Grade	A	A-	B+	B	B-	C+	C	C-	D+	D	F
Numerical Grade	4.0	3.7	3.3	3.0	2.7	2.3	2.0	1.7	1.3	1.0	0.0

Figure QS.2	Calculating your GPA.		
COURSE	**SEMESTER HOURS**	**GRADE**	**GRADE POINTS**
Chemistry 1	4	C	4 credits x 2 points = 8
Freshman Writing	3	B+	3 credits x 3.3 points = 9.9
Spanish I	3	B-	3 credits x 2.7 points = 8.1
Introduction to Statistics	3	C+	3 credits x 2.3 points = 6.9
Social Justice	2	A-	2 credits x 3.7 points = 7.4
Total semester hours: 15 Total grade points for semester: 40.3			
GPA for semester (total grade points divided by semester hours): 40.3 divided by 15 = 2.68 Letter equivalent grade: C+/B-			

Learn the Honor Code

Your school's code of honor, or academic integrity policy, should be printed in your student handbook. This code defines the standards of ethical behavior that are expected of you in your academic work and in your relationships with faculty, administrators, and fellow students. As you will see in Chapter 1, academic integrity is a commitment to five fundamental values: honesty, trust, fairness, respect, and responsibility. As a student enrolled in your school, you have agreed to abide by your school's honor code.

You have also agreed to suffer the consequences should you be discovered violating a core value. Different schools have different ways of dealing with alleged violations. In most cases, students are brought before a committee of instructors or a jury of students to determine whether the offense actually occurred. What happens to a student found guilty varies from school to school. The University of Virginia expels any student found guilty of an honor code violation. North Carolina State University may require participation in an academic integrity seminar. Other schools use suspension, grade reduction, or course failure, depending on the offense.

Master the College Computer System

A large part of the communication and work that you do in college involves the computer. Here are just some examples:

- Registering for classes
- Accessing a Web-based course syllabus and required-readings list
- E-mailing instructors and students for assignment clarification; receiving e-mail responses
- Tapping into library databases and the Internet for research
- Completing assignments and writing papers on your word processor
- Submitting papers via e-mail to instructors
- Creating spreadsheets for math and science classes
- E-mailing classmates to schedule group/team meetings

- Receiving school-wide announcements via the college computer network
- Taking interactive quizzes
- Downloading the latest plane/train/bus schedule via the Internet as you plan your trip home during a school break

In most colleges, it is no longer possible to manage without a computer—either your own, one borrowed from school, or one accessed in computer labs. According to a recent survey, 75 percent of college students own a computer.[2] Most dorm rooms are now wired for computers, which gives students access to the campus network, including the library database.

Here are some suggestions for using your computer effectively:

- *Get trained.* Start by getting help to connect to your college network. Then, take training classes to master word processing, data and spreadsheets, and the Internet. In some schools, these classes are required. If your typing skills are weak, take a course or use a software program to develop your skills.

- *Use computers to get information.* If you have specific questions about your school, check for answers on the college Web site. You may find the information or the e-mail address of a contact person. You must also learn to use the Internet for academic library research (see Chapter 7 for more information).

- *Be a safe and cautious user.* Although computers seem to be the answer to everything, they sometimes fail. To safeguard your work, use your computer carefully and with respect, especially if it belongs to someone else or your school. Second, create regular back-ups by saving your work onto the computer hard drive every few minutes. In addition, don't just rely on the hard drive; periodically back up your work in a secondary location such as on a diskette, a CD, or a Zip disk.

- *Use computers for appropriate tasks.* A quick diversion to Internet surfing or a computer game can help refresh you, but it can get out of hand. Try to stay away from these distractions altogether during study time and set strict time limits at other times to keep your academic focus. Remaining focused is especially important when you are using the computer lab and others are waiting their turn.

- *Protect yourself from trouble.* The following strategies will help:
  - Run virus checks on your personal machine and install and update an antivirus program.
  - Don't reveal personal data, including financial data, to strangers you meet on the Internet.
  - Be reluctant to take part in chat rooms that are not part of your school's network. Locate chat rooms made up of fellow students and spend down time visiting with others in cyberspace.
  - If you encounter a technical problem, talk to technicians in the computer lab. Their help can save you hours of time and frustration.

A Special Word About E-mail

You may be required to communicate with your instructor, submit homework, and even take exams via e-mail. Every student who has access to e-mail should spend time becoming proficient in electronic communication. Following are some important suggestions:

- *Use your college's e-mail system.* Register for an e-mail account at your school as soon as possible, even if you have a personal e-mail address through America Online or another Internet service provider. Without this connection, you may not be able to receive school-wide e-mails or access electronic files at the college library.

- *Be careful of miscommunication.* Body language (vocal tone, facial expression, body position) can account for over 75 percent of what you communicate face-to-face. With e-mail, however, your words stand alone, forcing you to be careful about your content and tone. Try to be diplomatic and pleasant, and think before you respond to messages that upset you. If you write back too quickly, you may be sorry later.

- *Use effective writing techniques.* Your e-mail tells a lot about you. To make the best impression—especially when communicating with an instructor or administrator—take the time to find the right words. Organize your thoughts and use proper spelling, punctuation, and grammar. Here are some additional tips that will make your e-mails easy to read: get to the point in the first paragraph, use short paragraphs, use headings to divide long e-mails into digestible sections, and use numbered and bulleted lists. Always proofread before hitting "send."

- *Rein in social e-mailing.* Prioritize your e-mailing. Respond to the most important and time-sensitive requests first, especially school-related ones. Save personal and conversational e-mail for when you have down time.

The computer skills you learn in college will be invaluable at work and in your personal and community activities. Most of today's jobs require computer literacy, as well as the ability to continue to learn as technology changes.

Get Involved

College gives you the opportunity to become involved in activities outside of class. These activities enable you to meet people who share your interests and to develop teamwork and leadership skills. They also give you the chance to develop skills that may be important in your career. For example, you might join the Spanish Club to improve your language skills if you expect to work in Arizona, where there is a large Spanish-speaking population, after graduation. Being connected to friends and a supportive network of people is one of the main reasons people stay in school instead of dropping out.

Choose activities you genuinely enjoy, and then decide on your level of involvement. Do you want to attend meetings from time to time or become a group leader? As a freshman, you may want to try several activities before deciding on those that are right for you. Figure QS.3 shows a sample of the activities that are available at Southern Connecticut State University in New Haven, Connecticut. Your school may offer hundreds of similar choices.

Some freshmen take on more than they can comfortably handle and neglect their studies. If you see that your grades are dropping, it may be time to reduce your activities and focus on your work. As you seek the right balance, consider this: Studies have shown that students who join organizations tend to persist in their educational goals more than those who don't branch out.[3]

Figure QS.3	A sampling of activities offered at college.	
Accounting Society	Earth Science Club	National Student Nurses Association
Art League	Finance Club	Orchestra
Asian Academic Society	Foreign Language Clubs	Psychology Club
Band	Habitat for Humanity	Society of Professional Journalists
Biology Club	Intercollegiate Sports	Sports Medicine Club
Business Administration Club	Intramural Sports	Student Government
Cheerleaders	Mathematics Club	Veterans Association
Choir	Minority Pre-Law and Business Association	WOWL Radio Station
Computer Club	National Organization for Women (NOW)	Yearbook

Source: Southern Connecticut State University: Student Services Website, May 1, 2001.

You are beginning the journey of your college education. The work you do in this course and in the remaining pages of *Keys to Success* will help you achieve your goals in your studies and in your personal life and career. As you move forward, think about the words Josh Billings, a nineteenth-century American writer, said over 100 years ago: *"Everyone who does the best he can do is a hero."* From this day forward, be your own personal hero.

 ## uggested Readings

Baker, Sunny, and Kim Baker. *College After 30: It's Never Too Late to Get the Degree You Need!* Holbrook, MA: Bob Adams, 1992.

Gottesman, Greg, Daniel Baer, et. al. *College Survival: A Crash Course for Students by Students,* 5th ed. New York: Macmillan, 1999.

Jeffers, Susan. *Feel the Fear and Do It Anyway.* New York: Fawcett Columbine, 1992.

Light, Richard J. *Making the Most of College: Students Speak Their Minds.* Cambridge, MA: Harvard University Press, 2001.

Rozakis, Laurie. *The Complete Idiot's Guide to College Survival.* New York: Alpha Books, 2001.

Shields, Charles J. *Back in School: A Guide for Adult Learners.* Hawthorne, NJ: Career Press, 1994.

Weinberg, Carol. *The Complete Handbook for College Women: Making the Most of Your College Experience.* New York: New York University Press, 1994.

 ## nternet Resources

Prentice Hall Student Success Supersite (information about student life, student-to-student bulletin boards, personal stories, opinion polls, and more): **www.prenhall.com/success**

ndnotes

1. Statistics in this paragraph from U.S. Department of Education, National Center for Education Statistics, Digest of Educational Statistics 2000. From Web site http://nces.ed.gov/pubs2001/digest/ch3.html, May 7, 2001.

2. Lisa Guernsey, "For the New College B.M.O.C., 'M' Is for 'Machine.'" *The New York Times,* August 10, 2000, p. G7.

3. Alexander W. Astin, *Preventing Students from Dropping Out.* San Francisco: Jossey-Bass, 1976.

Defining Yourself and Your Goals

CHOOSE

1

IN THIS CHAPTER

In this chapter you explore answers to the following questions: • How will college change your life? • How do you make a successful transition to college? • How can you get motivated? • Why is academic integrity important? • What is the connection between college and lifelong learning?

*W*elcome to college

WELCOME—or welcome back—to your education. Like Matt Millard (see next page), you are embarking on a new phase of life that may bring all kinds of questions and concerns. This chapter will preview the changes ahead and inspire you to manage your transition successfully. You will explore specific strategies that will help motivate you to succeed. Finally, you will see how the skills you build in college can help you learn throughout your life—and why that means greater success for you.

opening doors

Matt Millard, University of Wyoming, Laramie, Wyoming

Todd Montalbo, University of Alaska, Anchorage, Alaska

How can I get the most out of college?

I think it's very important to do what you love.

I decided to attend college so I could have a job doing what I really like instead of just doing it for the money. Even though I haven't decided what I want to do when I graduate, I know that I want to continue learning for a long time. I'd even like to continue on to get a Masters and maybe even a Ph.D. someday. So far, I'm mainly interested in the theater and English, but I'm not quite sure where to go with it.

I try to take steps to better myself. Even though I'd like it to be more often, I work out at racquetball a couple of times a week. I also think it's important to help other people, so I make time to help my friends with their homework and stuff like that. My grades are average so I'd like them to get better. I'd also like to get a little more focused on what I want to declare as a major. What steps do you think I need to take in order to get the most out of my learning?

I think it's very important to do what you love. That will really help your goal of lifelong learning. Even though having money is important, it's more important to enjoy what you're doing and feel like you're making a difference. I chose education as my major because I really like being with young people and feel I can influence their lives in a positive way. Plus, my mother is a teacher. After going to her classes and seeing her teach, I decided it was something I'd enjoy. I've changed my major twice, though, since I started school. I tried the business department, but realized after taking an economics class that I just wasn't that interested.

It might be beneficial for you to try different classes in the subjects that really interest you. That way you'll know if you're on the right track. Another suggestion is to join a drama club or try out for a local theater production. You might want to get to know someone who makes a living teaching English. He may be able to help you decide if it's the career for you. I also recommend that you try to have balance in your life. I'm a member of the ski team at my school. Whenever I come back from skiing and sit down to study, I feel like I'm more focused and I feel like my whole life isn't just studying. I'm more motivated that way. I also get a lot more done in a shorter time because I have more energy.

Your first year can be a big adjustment. I can guarantee you, it will get better. You can help make it easier by exploring different professions, changing some of your normal routines, and trying classes that other students say are interesting or exciting.

How will college *change* your life?

In choosing to pursue an education, you are building your power to create a better world. But what does that mean for you? In what new direction are you sending your life through this decision to become more educated? You need to know that what you do today—in a writing classroom, a study session, a conference with an instructor, or other educational setting—will bring positive changes.

Education Means Striving for New Goals

Begin to realize what education will mean for you by looking at your reasons for starting, or returning to, college. One or more of the following reasons might come to mind:

- I want to earn a better living.
- I want to build marketable skills in a particular career area.
- Getting a higher education degree will help me move ahead in my career.
- I want to be a student and learn all that I can.
- I am recently divorced and must develop skills that will help me earn a living.
- Everybody in my family goes to college; it's expected.
- I got a scholarship.
- My friend loves her job and encouraged me to take courses in the field.
- My parent (or spouse or partner) pushed me to go to college.
- I have to increase my skills so that I can provide for my kids.
- I don't really know.

All of these answers are legitimate. It isn't easy to enroll in college, cover tuition, sign up for classes, and show up at class. Your reasons have been compelling enough to get you here. Be honest with yourself about why you are here, and you will have a realistic picture about your expectations as you begin.

Next, begin to think about your educational goals in more detail. You don't need answers right now—what's important is that you start thinking. What courses do you want to take? What kind of schedule do you want? What degree or certificate are you shooting for? Think also about academic excellence and whether honors and awards are important goals. If you are aiming for a particular career, consider what may be required (e.g., degrees, certificates, postgraduate education, internships). Finally, and most importantly, think about what you want in terms of learning, relationships, and personal growth.

After you have a solid idea of what you want out of your college experience, you can begin your biggest and most rewarding job— to stick with it and reap the benefits.

Education Promotes Success

Your education consists of far more than the accumulation of credit hours. If you take advantage of all your college has to offer, you will develop the skills and talents you need to succeed in your career and life. What will your education do for you?

Education prepares you for career success. This happens in two ways. First, education expands your career choices by teaching you, through your courses and the people you meet, more about potential careers and jobs than you ever imagined. Second, your day-to-day course work gives you the hands-on skills you need to achieve the career goals you choose. Education makes you a more *literate* person—able to use written and mathematical skills to learn and to improve your life.

Education improves your employability and earning potential. Although education doesn't automatically guarantee a high-level, well-paying job, it greatly increases the probability you will find one (see Figure 1.1 and Figure 1.2 for details). Having a college degree makes an impression on potential employers and makes you eligible for higher-salaried positions. In basic terms, there is a significant wage gap between high school and college graduates, and you want to be on the winning side of it.

Education affects both community involvement and personal health. Education prepares you to become involved in your community by helping you understand political, economic, and social conditions and how they affect people's lives. Education also increases health knowledge, motivating you to practice good health habits and to make informed decisions about your physical and mental health.

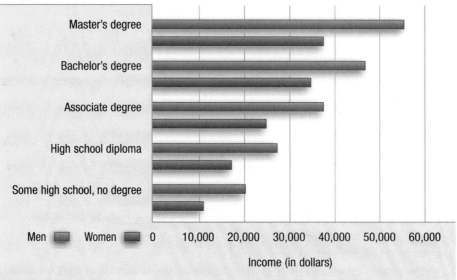

| Figure 1.1 | Education and income. |

Median annual income of persons with income 25 years old and over, by highest degree attained and gender, 1998.

Source: U.S. Department of Commerce, Bureau of the Census, *Current Population Reports,* Series P-60, Money Income in the United States: 1998.

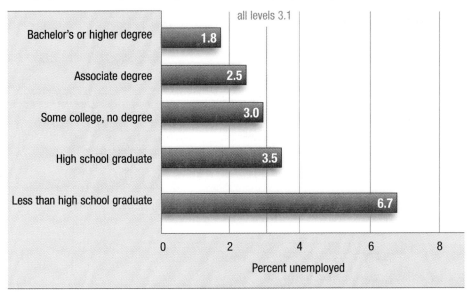

Figure 1.2 Education and employment.

Unemployment rates of persons 25 years old and over, by highest degree attained.*

all levels 3.1

	Percent unemployed
Bachelor's or higher degree	1.8
Associate degree	2.5
Some college, no degree	3.0
High school graduate	3.5
Less than high school graduate	6.7

Source: U.S. Department of Labor, Bureau of Labor Statistics, Office of Employment and Unemployment Statistics, *Current Population Survey,* 1999.

Education broadens your worldview. As it introduces you to new ways of learning, doing, being, and thinking, education increases your understanding of diversity and your appreciation of areas that affect and enrich human lives, such as music, art, literature, science, politics, and economics.

How do you make a *successful transition* to college?

Beginning college is a significant transition for anyone. Introducing such a responsibility into your life is both exciting and stressful. For most students, it takes time to feel comfortable. To begin, spend some energy knowing your situation and connecting with others.

Know Your Situation

If you feel like you are about to go down the first hill on a roller coaster, you are not alone. Students face all kinds of challenges as they begin college. Look at Table 1.1 for some examples.

How do you face these challenges and come out on the other side of the transition feeling ready to achieve? Reading this book and taking this

Table 1.1	Different students face different challenges.
IF YOU ARE:	**THEN YOU MIGHT BE:**
Eighteen years old and right out of high school	■ More responsible for yourself than ever before ■ Facing a much bigger course load
Returning to college after five or more years out	■ Concerned that you can't remember how to deal with tests and studying ■ Worried that you won't be able to relate to the younger crowd
Juggling college with a full- or part-time job	■ Apprehensive about balancing your schedule ■ Worried that you won't accomplish your goals in either work or school
Going to college as a parent	■ Wondering how you'll manage child care ■ Concerned about achieving your academic goals while taking care of your children
Moving away from parents to a new residence on or near campus	■ Living away from home for the first time and taking care of your own needs ■ Interacting with new people, perhaps as roommates or housemates ■ Adjusting to a new part of the country
Commuting	■ Rearranging your schedule to accommodate your travel ■ Budgeting for commuting costs
Living with parents while in school	■ Struggling to become independent ■ Adjusting to feeling unconnected to other students who live at school
Living with a physical or learning disability	■ Worried about how to manage your disability while in school ■ Concerned about tapping into all the help your college offers for students with disabilities

course will help you tremendously. The following are the transition-busting tools that you will gather as you move through the semester:

- Investigating the resources available to you in college (Quick Start to College)
- Discovering your learning style (Chapter 2)
- Learning to manage your time and set the goals that are right for you (Chapter 3)
- Building critical-thinking skills (Chapter 4)
- Solidifying study skills such as reading, note taking, and test taking (Chapters 5, 6, 7, and 8)
- Building solid, beneficial relationships with others (Chapter 9)
- Maintaining your mental and physical health (Chapter 10)
- Keeping your career plans and financial picture in mind (Chapter 11)
- Focusing on your life's mission (Chapter 12)

Because so much of what you do in college involves others, teamwork is a special focus. Improving your ability to work as part of a team is crucial to your successful transition.

Build Teamwork Skills in a Diverse World

Think of your accomplishments and you will find that rarely do you achieve anything alone. Your success at school and at work depends on your ability to cooperate in a team setting. Such cooperation includes communicating well, sharing tasks, and developing a common vision. For example:

- You learn, complete projects, and pass courses as part of an *educational* team, with instructors, fellow students, tutors, administrators, and advisors.
- You deal with the challenges of day-to-day life in a *family* or *community* team, with the help of parents, siblings, relatives, and friends.
- You achieve work goals in a *work* team, with supervisors, coworkers, and consultants.

Teams gain strength from the diversity of their members. A study group for a course, for example, may have a mix of men and women who differ in age, race, culture, stage of life, learning styles, and academic abilities. By combining abilities, the students build a base of knowledge and skills that they cannot achieve alone. *The greater the diversity of a team, therefore, the greater the number of choices or solutions when problem solving.*

The needs of an increasingly diverse student body have molded a new educational experience. So-called "traditional" students—18 years old, just out of high school, and living in on-campus dorms—now often share classrooms with less traditional students. The following observations, illustrated in Figures 1.3, 1.4, and 1.5, indicate how the student population has changed since the 1980s:

- Students are more diverse in all ways: age, gender, ethnicity.
- Students are older and many have family responsibilities.
- Students are following less traditional educational paths. For example, more students attend two-year colleges, attend school part-time, and work while attending school.

Furthermore, diversity is part of the reality of living in the United States today. The year 2000 census reports that one in four Americans is a member of a minority group as compared to 1980, when only one in five reported minority status. The nation's diversity is expected to grow.

What does this mean for you? In order to succeed postgraduation in a world where you will almost certainly be working in a diverse environment, you have to be able to team up successfully with all kinds of people. Throughout this book, you will find references to a diverse mixture of people in different life circumstances. Chapter 9 goes into more detail about communicating across lines of difference.

Opening your mind to differences is crucial now as you enter a new college environment where you are meeting and working

Figure 1.3

Students are more diverse.

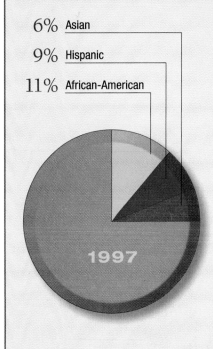

6% Asian
9% Hispanic
11% African-American

1997

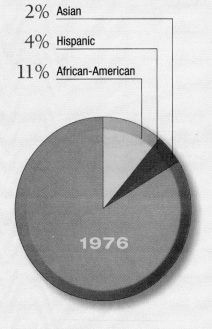

2% Asian
4% Hispanic
11% African-American

1976

Source: U.S. Department of Education, National Center for Educational Statistics, *Digest of Education Statistics 2000*, NCES 2001–034, by Thomas D. Snyder. Washington D.C.: U.S. Government Printing Office, 2001, pp. 194–195.

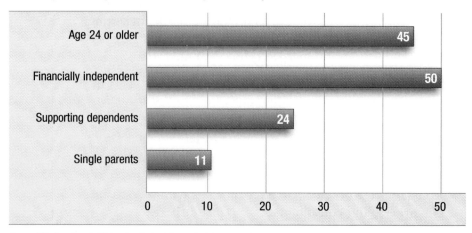

Figure 1.4 | Students are older and have varied responsibilities.

Percentage of undergraduate student body, academic year 1995–1996

Age 24 or older	45
Financially independent	50
Supporting dependents	24
Single parents	11

Source; U.S. Department of Education, National Center for Educational Statistics, *Digest of Education Statistics 2000,* NCES 2001–034, by Thomas D. Snyder. Washington D.C.: U.S. Government Printing Office, 2001, pp. 274, 374; and U.S. Department of Education, National Center for Education Statistics, *Profile of Undergraduates in U.S. Postsecondary Education Institutions: 1995–96,* NCES 98-084, by Laura J. Horn, Jennifer Berktold, and MPR Associates, Inc. Washington D.C.: U.S. Government Printing Office, 1998, p. 77.

with people you never met before, and in the future, where that exposure to new people will continue. The more open you are to diverse views, ways of conduct, and methods of thought, the more capable you will become of making the most out of every challenging situation in your life. Take classes like sociology and ethics that will help you to stretch your comfort zone—to understand, accept, and embrace diverse ways of thinking and doing.

As you make your transition, remember that you are responsible for examining your unique challenges and seeking out the educational opportunities that help you meet them. How can you motivate yourself? Particular strategies help you build and maintain your drive to learn and succeed.

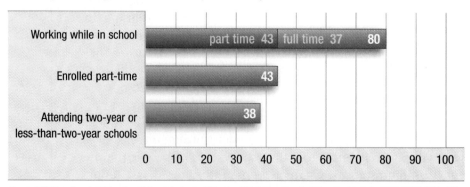

Figure 1.5 | Students are following less traditional educational paths.

Percentage of undergraduate student body, academic year 1995–1996

Working while in school	part time 43 full time 37 80
Enrolled part-time	43
Attending two-year or less-than-two-year schools	38

Source; U.S. Department of Education, National Center for Educational Statistics, *Digest of Education Statistics 2000,* NCES 2001–034, by Thomas D. Snyder. Washington D.C.: U.S. Government Printing Office, 2001, pp. 234–235; and U.S. Department of Education, National Center for Education Statistics, *Profile of Undergraduates in U.S. Postsecondary Education Institutions: 1995–96,* NCES 98-084, by Laura J. Horn, Jennifer Berktold, and MPR Associates, Inc. Washington D.C.: U.S. Government Printing Office, 1998, p. 5.

How can you get *motivated?*

Success is a process, not a fixed mark—and (motivation) is what keeps the process in motion. Motivation is the energy that fuels your drive to achieve. Successful people are those who can consistently motivate themselves to learn, grow, and work toward goals.

[handwritten margin note:] MOTIVATION — A force that moves a person to action; often inspired by an idea a fact, an event, a goal.

College provides an opportunity for you to discover the goals most important to you and build the motivation it takes to achieve them. Wherever you start, and whatever obstacles you encounter on the way, your motivation can help lead you to the future you envision. Tom Bradley, son of a Texas sharecropper, became the first African-American mayor of Los Angeles in 1973 and served five successive terms. Ruth Bader Ginsberg, originally rejected as a Supreme Court clerk because Justice Felix Frankfurter didn't hire women, became a Supreme Court justice herself 30 years later.

What motivates you? People have all kinds of different *motivators*—goals or ideas that move them forward. For example, some potential motivators for attending school could be learning a marketable skill, supporting a family, or self-improvement. Furthermore, motivators can change with time or with different situations. A student might begin work on a course feeling motivated by a desire to earn a particular grade, and later, becoming interested in the subject, he becomes motivated by a desire to master the material.

From time to time, everyone experiences a loss of motivation, whether short term or for a longer spell. How can you build motivation or renew lost motivation? First, start on the path. Just beginning makes you feel better as you work toward your goals. Newton's first law of motion, a law of physics, says that things in motion tend to stay in motion and things at rest tend to stay at rest. Be a thing in motion.

> "A journey of a thousand miles begins with a single step."

LAO TZU

Second, explore the following motivation-boosting strategies—making a commitment, developing positive habits, being responsible, building self-esteem, and facing your fears. Explore them, and experiment to see what helps most. You might use them in combination, focus on the ones that have the most positive effects on you, or try them out one by one.

Finally, reading and thinking about the Personal Triumph stories in each chapter and in the Part review sections will give you real-world insight into what it takes to sustain motivation in the face of difficult obstacles. Even if you have never experienced such obstacles, let the courage of the people profiled inspire you to confidence about your own life. If they can leap their hurdles successfully, so can you.

Make a Commitment

How do you focus the energy of motivation? Make a commitment. Commitment means that you do what you say you will do. When you honor a commitment to an academic goal, a career dream, or a self-improvement task, you prove to yourself and others that your intentions can be trusted. Commitment often stretches over a period of time; you hold yourself to a promise for as long as necessary to reach your goal.

How do you go about making and keeping a commitment?

- *State your commitment concretely.* Set a clear goal and break it into manageable pieces. Be specific; for example, "I'm going to turn in the weekly essay assignments on time," rather than "I'm going to do my best work in this course." Emphasize to yourself what you will gain from this commitment.
- *Take the first step.* Sometimes feeling overwhelmed can immobilize you. Decide on the first step of your commitment and take it today. Then continue a day at a time, breaking tasks into small steps.
- *Stay aware of each commitment.* Keep a list of commitments in your planner, on your refrigerator, or on your computer. If they involve events or projects that take place on specific dates, note them on a calendar. Talk about them with someone you trust to help you stay on track.
- *Keep an eye on your progress.* You're not a failure if you lose steam; it's normal. Recharge by reflecting on the positive effects of your commitment and what you have already achieved.
- *Reward yourself as you move ahead.* Rewards help you feel good about what you've accomplished so far and can help keep you going. Treat yourself to dinner with a friend, a new CD, a movie night.

For example, you might make this commitment: "I will write in my journal every night before going to sleep." You make journal entries for two weeks and then evaluate what positive effects this daily practice has had on your writing ability. If you were to stop writing for a time, you can renew your commitment by reminding yourself of how keeping a journal has improved your writing ability and relieved stress. You might boost your commitment by telling a partner or housemate to check on you.

Making commitments helps you keep a steady focus on your most important goals. It gives you a sense of accomplishment as you experience gradual growth and progress.

Develop Positive Habits

People have all kinds of habits; some you may consider "bad" and others "good." Bad habits stall motivation and prevent you from reaching important goals. Some bad habits, such as chronic lateness, cause obvious problems. Other habits, such as surfing the Internet, may not seem bad until you realize that you needed to spend those hours studying.

Good habits are those that bring the kind of positive effects that keep motivation high. You often have to wait longer and work harder to see a reward for good habits, which makes them harder to maintain. If you reduce your nights out to gain study time, for example, your grades won't improve in a week. Changing a habit is a process; trust that the rewards are somewhere down the road.

Look at the positive and negative effects of your habits to decide which you want to keep and which you need to change or improve. Take the following steps to evaluate a habit and, if necessary, make a change (if the habit has more negative effects than positive ones). Don't try to change more than one habit at a time—trying to reach perfection in everything all at once can overwhelm you.

1. *Define and evaluate the habit.* Name your habit and look at the negative and positive effects. If there are more negatives than positives, it is most likely a habit worth changing.

2. *Decide to keep or change the habit.* Until you are convinced that you will receive a benefit, efforts to change will not get you far. Commit to a change if you see too many negative effects.

3. *Start today—and keep it up.* Don't put it off until after this week, after the family reunion, or after the semester. Each day gained is a day you can benefit from a new lifestyle. To have the best chance at changing a habit, be consistent for at least three weeks so that you become accustomed to the new habit.

4. *Reward positive steps.* Choose a reward that encourages you to stay on target. If you earn a good grade, for example, treat yourself to one night out instead of slacking off on studying the following week.

Finally, don't get too discouraged if the process seems difficult. Rarely does someone make the decision to change and do so without a setback or two. Take it one step at a time; when you lose steam, reflect on what you stand to gain. With persistence and positive thinking, you can reach your goal.

Be Responsible

In college, you are in charge of your life in a way that you may never have been before. Even if you have lived on your own and held a job, helped raise a family, or both, college adds greatly to that responsibility. You are responsible for making decisions that keep you in motion and avoiding choices that stall you in your tracks. You are your own manager.

Taking responsibility is all about living up to your obligations, both those that are imposed on you and those that you impose on yourself. Through action, you prove that you are responsible—"response-able"—able to respond. When something has to be done, a responsible person does it—as efficiently as possible and to the best of his or her ability.

Responsibility Means Action

Taking responsibility is taking action—and doing it reliably. In college, responsible people can be trusted to live up to obligations like these:

- Attending class and participating in activities and discussions
- Completing reading and assignments on time
- Communicating with instructors and fellow students

These actions may sound mundane to you, everyday requirements that don't have much bearing on the greater goals in your life. However, they are the building blocks of responsibility that get you where you want to go. Here's why:

- *Everyday responsibilities get you in the action habit.* As with any other habit, the more you do something, the more it becomes second nature. The more often you complete and turn in assignments on time, for example, the more likely you are to stay on top of your job tasks down the road when you are on a tight deadline.

- *The small accomplishments make a big impression.* When you show up to class, pay attention, contribute, and work hard, you send a message. An instructor who observes these behaviors is more likely to trust and respect you. People who trust you may give you increasing power and opportunities for growth because you have shown you are capable of making the best of both.

- *Fulfilling day-to-day responsibilities gives you freedom.* The more responsible you are, and the more responsibilities you take on, the more those around you will give you the freedom to handle situations and problems on your own. You will be perceived as a fully functioning team member who can be counted on to pull his or her share of the load, no matter the circumstances.

Responsibility Means Initiative

INITIATIVE

The power to begin or to follow through energetically with a plan or task; determination.

When you show initiative, you push yourself to take that first, often difficult, step. Initiative is the spark plug of responsibility—it jump-starts you into action. By taking initiative, you respond quickly and continually to changes that occur.

Initiative means that you make a move on your own instead of waiting for people, rules, requirements, or circumstances to push you. You show initiative when you go to a counselor for help with a problem, make an appointment with an instructor to discuss a paper, talk to a friend about a conflict, speak up in class, find a better way to do a task at work, vote, or start an exercise program. Once you take that first step, it is often easier to keep your momentum going and continue to act responsibly.

Responsibility can take enormous effort. Remember that you gain self-respect when you prove that you can live up to your promises.

Face Your Fears

Everyone experiences fear. Anything unknown—new people, experiences, challenges, situations—can be frightening. The changes involved in pursuing an education, for example, can inspire fear. You may wonder if you can handle the work, if you have chosen the right school or program, or if your education will prepare you to find a job you like and that pays well.

If your fears become overwhelming, they can derail your motivation. Some people give in to fear because they feel safer with the familiar, even if it doesn't make them happy. Ultimately, though, giving in to fear by giving up on your motivation may keep you from living the life you have envisioned.

The challenges you face as you work toward your goals demand a willingness to face your fears and push your limits. The following steps will help you work through fear with courage:

1. *Acknowledge fears.* The act of naming your fear begins to lessen its hold on you. Be specific. Knowing that you fear taking a biology course may not inspire you to action; whereas, focusing on your fear of working with live mice in biology lab gives you something tangible to deal with.

"He has not learned the lesson of life who does not every day surmount a fear."

RALPH WALDO EMERSON

2. *Examine fears.* Sometimes one fear hides a larger one. If you fear a test, determine whether you fear the test itself or the fact that if you pass it, you will have to take a tougher class next. If you fear the test, take steps to prepare for it. If you fear the next class, you might talk with your instructor about it.

3. *Develop a plan of attack.* Evaluate what will help you overcome your fear. For example, if you are scared of reading Shakespeare, help yourself by asking your instructor for advice, going over assigned plays with a study group, and watching a Shakespeare movie.

4. *Move ahead with your plan.* Courage is the key to moving ahead. Take the steps that help you to confront and move beyond your fears.

As you work through your fears, talk about them with people you trust. Everyone has fears, and when people share strategies, everyone benefits.

Build Self-Esteem

When people believe in their value and capabilities, their self-esteem fuels their motivation to succeed. Belief, though, is only half the game. The other half is the action and effort that help you feel that you have earned your self-esteem. Rick Pitino, a highly successful basketball coach, discusses developing self-esteem in his book *Success Is a Choice*: "Self-esteem is directly linked to deserving success. If you have established a great work ethic and have begun the discipline that is inherent with that, you will automatically begin to feel better about yourself. It's all interrelated. You must deserve victory to feel good about yourself."[1]

Building self-esteem, therefore, involves both *thinking positively* and *taking action.* Together, they help you generate the belief in yourself that keeps you motivated.

SELF-ESTEEM

A strong and deeply felt belief that you as a person have value in the world.

Think Positively

Attitudes influence your choices and affect how you perceive and relate to others. A positive attitude can open your mind to learning experiences and inspire you to action. If, for example, you keep an open mind in a course that at first seems like a waste of time, you might discover that the course teaches you something valuable. You have the power to create your own reality, and with a positive attitude you can make it a positive one.

One way to create a positive attitude is through **positive self-talk.** When you hear negative thoughts in your mind ("I'm not very smart"), replace them with positive ones ("It won't be easy, but I'm smart enough to figure it out"). You would probably never criticize a good friend in the same way that you sometimes criticize yourself. These hints will help you put positive self-talk into action:

- *Stop negative talk in its tracks.* If you catch yourself thinking, "I can never write a decent paper," stop and say to yourself, "I can write better than that and next time I will." Then think about some specific steps you can take to improve your writing.

- *Pay yourself a compliment.* Note your successes. Be specific: "I have really improved my spelling and proofreading." Some people keep a list of positive statements about themselves in a notebook or use calendars with daily affirmations. These are great reminders of positive self-talk.

- *Replace words of obligation with words of personal intent.*

I should	*becomes*	I choose to
I'll try	*becomes*	I will

Words of intent give you power and control because they imply a personal decision to act. For example, when you say, "I have to be in class by 9:00," you're saying that someone else has power over you and has handed you a required obligation. When you say, "I want to be in class by 9:00 because I don't want to miss anything I need to learn," you're saying that the choice is yours.

It can sometimes be difficult to think positively. If you have a deep-rooted feeling of unworthiness, you may want to see a counselor. Many people have benefited from skilled professional advice.

Take Action

Although thinking positively sets the tone for success, it cannot get you there by itself. You have to take action. Without action, positive thoughts become empty statements or even lies.

Consider, for example, a student in a freshman composition class. This student thinks every possible positive thought: "I am a great student. I know how to write well. I can get a B in this class. I will succeed in school." And so on. She even writes her thoughts down on notes and posts them where she can see them. Then, during the semester, she misses about one-third of the class meetings, turns in some of her papers late, and completely forgets a couple of assignments. She doesn't make use of opportunities to work with her study partner. At the end of the course, when she barely passes the class, she wonders how things went so wrong when she had such a positive attitude.

+ + +
POSITIVE
SELFTALK

Supportive and positive thoughts and ideas that a person communicates to himself or herself.

This student did not succeed because she did not earn her belief in herself through action and effort. By the end of a semester like this, positive thoughts look like lies. "If I can get a B, why did I get a D? If I am such a great student, why did I barely make it through this course?" Eventually, with nothing to support them, the positive thoughts disappear, and with neither positive thoughts nor action, a student will have a hard time achieving any level of success.

Following are some ways to get moving in a positive direction:

- *Build your own code of discipline.* Develop general guidelines to follow, based on what actions are important to your success. Perhaps your top priorities are personal relationships and achievement in school. Construct each day's goals and actions so that they help you achieve your larger objectives.

- *Make action plans and follow through.* Figure out how you plan to take action for any situation, so that, for example, "I am a great student" is backed up by specific actions to ensure success. When you have a plan, just do it. Only after taking action can you reap the benefit.

- *Acknowledge every step.* Even the smallest action is worth your attention because every action reinforces a positive thought and builds self-esteem. First you believe that you are a good student, then you work hard in class, then you do well on a test, then you believe more emphatically that you are a good student, then you complete a successful group project, then you feel even better about yourself, and so on.

The process of building and maintaining self-esteem involves many successes and disappointments. Only by having a true sense of self-esteem, though, can you achieve your dreams. You are in control of your self-esteem because you alone are ultimately responsible for your thoughts and actions. Do what it takes to both believe in yourself and take the action that anchors and inspires that belief.

Believing in yourself helps you make good choices. When your self-esteem is strong, you are more likely to choose actions that you can be proud of.

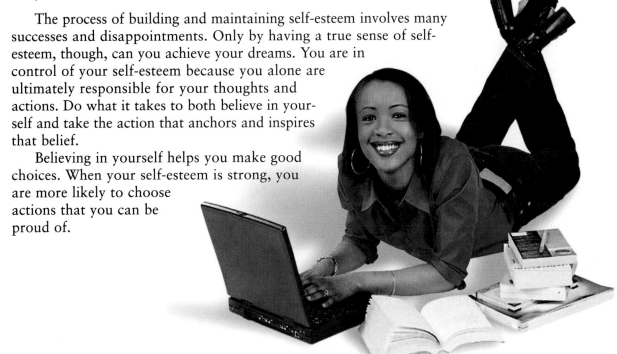

Why is academic integrity *important?*

INTEGRITY

Adherence to a code of moral values; incorruptibility, honesty.

Integrity is at the heart of your actions as a member of your academic community. Having academic integrity implies that you adhere to a code of moral values, prizing honesty and fairness in all aspects of academic life: classes, assignments, tests, papers, projects, and relationships with students and faculty.

When you register for college, you agree, either implicitly or explicitly, to a code of academic conduct consisting of positive actions as well as actions to avoid. Following this code—doing what is asked of you honestly and in a manner that promotes learning—ensures a quality education based on ethics and hard work.

Positive Actions that Define Academic Integrity

The Center for Academic Integrity, part of the Kenan Institute for Ethics at Duke University, defines academic integrity as a commitment to five fundamental values: honesty, trust, fairness, respect, and responsibility.[2] These values form the basis of acceptable behaviors for students and instructors.

- *Honesty.* The most fundamental value in college is honesty. Honesty defines the pursuit of knowledge and implies a search for truth in your class work, papers and lab reports, and teamwork with other students.

- *Trust.* Mutual trust—between instructor and student, as well as among students—forms the basis for the free exchange of ideas that is fundamental to learning. Trust means that you are true to your word.

- *Fairness.* Instructors must create a fair academic environment in which students are judged against clear standards and in which procedures are well defined.

- *Respect.* In a respectful academic environment, both students and instructors accept and honor a wide range of opinions, even if the opinions are contrary to core beliefs.

- *Responsibility.* You are responsible for your own choices in school and in striving for the best education. Personal responsibility implies a commitment to choices that reflect fairness and honesty.

Table 1.2 links the core values of academic integrity to expectations for students and instructors.

Violations of Academic Integrity

The principles of academic integrity are frequently violated on college campuses:[3]

- In a recent survey, three out of four college students admitted to cheating at least once during their undergraduate careers.

Table 1.2	Values are at the core of academic integrity.	
CORE VALUE	**IMPLICATIONS FOR STUDENTS**	**IMPLICATIONS FOR INSTRUCTORS**
Honesty	Avoid cheating on tests and experiments, lying to instructors and classmates, promising work and failing to deliver, plagiarizing, or damaging the reputations of fellow students.	Provide students with honest feedback about their work; avoid changing expectations for assignments, tests, and papers without notifying students.
Trust	Deliver honest, thoughtful work and create an environment in which work can be shared freely without fear that it will be stolen.	Set clear guidelines for assignments and for evaluating work.
Fairness	Give instructors the benefit of the doubt before judging them. Give reading assignments the benefit of the doubt before judging their value and relevance. Give fellow students the benefit of the doubt before judging their contributions.	Set clear expectations that enable students to prepare adequately for exams. Grade exams against a uniform standard. Be just in the face of dishonesty, acting to uphold standards followed by the vast majority of students.
Respect	Attend class on time, pay attention, listen with an open mind to divergent points of view, participate in discussions, meet deadlines, credit sources in your papers, and commit to do your best.	Recognize each student as an individual with something to offer; take students' views and opinions seriously; provide honest and complete feedback on assignments; answer questions about course requirements and content.
Responsibility	Do your best and make sure that you do not help others abuse academic standards. Cover your answers during tests, refuse to help friends complete independent projects, and never sell your work to others.	Be a role model as you demonstrate standards of academic integrity by crediting the work of others. Promote students' sense of responsibility by being there for them to clarify concepts and assignments.

- Nearly 80 percent of high-achieving, college-bound high school graduates believe that cheating is commonplace.
- A Web site providing free term papers averages more than 80,000 hits a day.
- When a neurobiology professor at the University of California at Berkeley used anti-plagiarism software, he discovered that 15 percent of his students had copied at least part of their term papers from the Internet.[4]

Many students convince themselves that they are not violating their school's code of academic integrity when they "bend the rules." However, such violations—turning in work previously submitted in another class, using unauthorized devices during an exam, misusing library materials, providing unethical aid to another student, or getting help with a project when you are supposed to be working alone—still constitute a sacrifice of ethics that isn't worth the price.

Your School's Code

Explore your school's specific requirements. Your school's code of honor, or academic integrity policy, should be printed in your student handbook. Read it; when you enrolled, you agreed to abide by it.

You have also agreed to bear the consequences should you be discovered violating any of your school's policies. In most cases, students are brought before a committee of instructors or a "jury" of students to determine whether the offense has occurred. Consequences vary from school to school. The University of Virginia, for example, expels any student found guilty of an honor code violation. North Carolina State University requires some students to participate in an academic integrity seminar. Other schools use suspension, grade reduction, or course failure, depending on the offense.

The Benefits of Following Accepted Standards

Having academic integrity has important positive effects on the following:

Your behavior patterns. When you condition yourself to play fair now, you set a pattern that follows you on the job and in your personal relationships. Your friends, associates, and employers value someone who is honest, trustworthy, fair, respectful, and responsible.

Your knowledge level. If you cheat on a test you might pass the test—and the course—but what do you remember after you receive your grade? The point of college is to acquire knowledge and skills that you will use long after you graduate. Retaining knowledge leads to obtaining—and retaining—jobs.

Your interaction with others. When you act with academic integrity, you show respect for the work of others. In turn, you earn trust and respect from them, which may lead to friendships and opportunities.

Your self-esteem. Remember that self-esteem is tied to action. The more you act in respectful and honorable ways, the better you feel about yourself, and the more you are able to succeed. You earn satisfaction from doing it on your own without cheating yourself or the system.

Your rewards. People who live by a solid ethical code tend to value the activities they pursue and look to them for satisfaction, rather than focusing on secondary rewards such as grades (at school) or money (at work). If you pursue knowledge for the sake of knowledge, the grades will likely follow.

The academic integrity you demonstrate in college reflects your personal value system. You are responsible for thinking through your values and for taking actions that reflect your core beliefs. Chapter 3 takes you through the process of values clarification and linking values to actions.

Above all, you are responsible for your own integrity. You can choose actions that build your confidence, ability, knowledge, and reputation. Make choices that serve you well. With a strong sense of integrity, you are able to learn throughout your life and use what you learn to adapt to change.

What is the connection between college and *lifelong learning?*

n his book *TechnoTrends—24 Technologies That Will Revolutionize Our Lives,* futurist Daniel Burns describes a tomorrow that is linked to continuing education: "The future belongs to those who are capable of being retrained again and again," he says. "Think of it as periodically upgrading your human assets throughout your career. . . . Humans are infinitely upgradeable, but it does require an investment" in lifelong learning.[5] College is the ideal training ground for learning skills that will serve you throughout your life.

College Prepares You to Learn from Failure and Celebrate Success

Every life has problems to be solved and difficult decisions to be made. Even the most successful people and organizations make mistakes and experience failures. There is a lot to be gained from failing. In fact, failure is one of the greatest teachers. Failure is an opportunity to realize what you didn't know so that you can learn and improve. What you learn from a failure will most likely stay with you more intensely and guide you more effectively than many other things you learn.

College brings new challenges and with them come situations in which you may fail. When you face difficult obstacles, let yourself down or disappoint others, or make mistakes, what is important is how you deal with the situation. Although it's human to pretend a failure didn't happen, blame yourself, or blame someone else, choices like these can deny you valuable lessons. If you can accept failure as part of life, forgive yourself, and learn from it, you will be able to pick yourself up and keep improving.

Learning from Failure

Learning from your failures and mistakes involves careful thinking. One useful course of action is to first look at what happened, then make any improvements that you can, and finally decide how to change your action or approach in the future. For example, imagine that after a long night of studying for a test, you forgot that you had a deadline for a five-page paper the next day.

Look at what happened. Your exhaustion and concern about the test caused you to forget to check your planner to see what else was on your plate. Now you may face a lower grade on your paper if you turn it in late, plus you may be inclined to rush it and quickly turn in a paper that isn't as good as it could be.

Make any possible improvements on the situation.
You could visit your instructor during office
hours, or send an e-mail, explain the situation
and ask if you can have a brief extension on the
paper.

Make changes for the future. You can set a goal to
note deadlines in a bright color and to check
your planner more often. You can also try
arranging your study schedule so that you will
be less exhausted.

Facing failure can be hard. Here are some
ways to boost your outlook when failure gets
you down:

- *Stay aware of the fact that you are a capable, valuable person.* Focus your energy on
  your best abilities and know that you have
  the strength to try again.
- *Share your thoughts and disappointment
  with others.* Exchange creative energy that
  can help you learn from failures rather than
  having a mutual gripe session.
- *Look on the bright side.* At worst, you
  flunk the test or paper. At best, you have
  learned a lesson that will help you avoid
  similar situations in the future. There might
  even be other positive results.

Finally, remember that your value as a human
being does not diminish when you make a mistake. Expect that you always will do the best
that you can, knowing that just getting through
another day as a student, employee, or parent is
a success. In addition, because failure is a frequent result of risk taking, people who can
manage failure show that they have the courage
to take risks and learn. Employers often value
risk takers who sometimes fail more than people who avoid failure by never going beyond
the status quo.

Celebrating Success

Success is being who you want to be and doing
what you want to do. You may not feel successful until you reach an important goal you have
set for yourself. However, success is a process.
Each step along the way to improvement and
growth, no matter how small, is a success
worth acknowledging. If you received a C on a
paper and then earned a B on the next one, for

PERSONAL TRIUMPH

*y*ou have begun a journey of self-discovery
that will help you define who you are and
what you want out of life. What Bryan M.
Johnson has learned about himself and
the world from his own journey has led him to
goals that have great meaning for him.

I still remember a good friend's concern when I
joined the Navy a year out of high school. I
understood his sentiments. I thought of military enlistment as custom-made for boneheads
not bright enough to further their education or
talented enough to do anything else.

If that was the case, then I fit the mold at
19. I barely graduated from high school with an
abysmal 1.8 GPA; my most formidable accomplishment was holding the senior-year record
for skipping classes. After high school, I drove
a patio furniture delivery van. I had "quit" my
other job as a cashier after being accused of fin-
gering money from the register (truthfully, I
just couldn't add or subtract). Faced with a life
of delivering windproof side tables, I decided to
give the military a shot. When I bid farewell at
the patio store, the manager laughed. "You'll be
back," he said. I walked out thinking he was
probably right.

After naval boot camp, I was assigned on a
destroyer, my days filled with backbreaking
hours of sanding and painting in a never-ending
battle to preserve the ship's exterior. I learned
the value of an honest day's work, but soon
began looking for a way out of a dull, weary
routine. I found it that first Christmas home,
when I spent my stocking money on remedial
math and reading texts. I returned to the ship
with a backpack full of scholarly spoils, and the
tiny bulb over my rack burned every night for
almost a year. My hard work paid off when I
landed a position standing navigation watch.

As he showed me how to plot our destroyer's
course, my new supervisor said something that
made a lasting impression. "If you don't do your
job right, don't pay attention, people could die."
Lives were at stake and someone was trusting
me to make good decisions. I was honored.

Bryan M. Johnson, medical student,
Uniformed Services University, Bethesda, Maryland

What an odd yet wonderful feeling that was. More important, a fire had ignited inside me. I now rose to challenges instead of avoiding them, and loved the sense of self-worth I felt at a job well done.

To fill in dozens of empty hours at sea, crew members talked with one another. I learned that a person's skin color, or where he came from, wasn't a very good indicator of his character. I also realized that my preconceived notion of a military consisting of losers was completely unfounded. I knew one sailor, for instance, who joined the Navy because he cherished his country's freedom and wanted to give his time and energy in return.

Despite a worthwhile four years, I decided not to re-enlist and to give college a try. I diligently pursued a B.S. degree, and graduated with honors and hopes of attending medical school. Yet something was missing. I recalled the pride I had felt in my uniform, a symbol of something greater than myself. I applied to the United States' only military school of medicine and started classes.

Going home these days is a bit like winding back the clock 10 years—old friends look bewildered when I mention that I've rejoined the service. Don't think I'm offended: I belong to an organization that defends the rights of Americans to have their own opinions.

Although I've put the past behind me, I often wonder what the manager would say if I dropped by the patio store. But then he'd be right: I would be back—but only to buy a ceramic yard frog.

Take a moment to consider . . .

- *What you feel has been the most significant learning experience in your life so far.*
- *What you would like to be most proud of when you graduate from college.*

Source: Bryan M. Johnson, "How the Navy Changed My Life," from *Newsweek*, August 3, 1999, p. 12. All rights reserved. Reprinted by permission.

example, your advancement is successful. When you are trying to drop a harmful habit, each day you stay on course is a victory.

Here are some ways to celebrate successes big and small:

- *Appreciate yourself.* Take time to congratulate yourself for a job well done—whether it is a good grade, an important step in learning a language, a job offer, or a personal victory over substance abuse.

- *Build your confidence for future challenges.* Let this experience help you to solidify your confidence. Show yourself and others that you are capable of building on and continuing your success.

- *Stay sensitive to others.* Some people around you may not have been as successful. Remember that you have been in their place and they in yours. Enjoy what you have and support others as they need it.

Both failure and success will be a bottomless source of learning as you move through college and beyond. The better coping skills you build now, the more you benefit in the future.

College Provides an Opportunity to Examine Your Life

Making the commitment to work toward a college education means putting energy into thinking about yourself on a big-picture level. What do you do well? What do you want out of life? What can you improve? College gives you the chance to evaluate where you are and to make some concrete decisions about how to get to where you want to be.

This course is an ideal opportunity to kick off this exploration, and one place to begin is with The Wheel of Life, an assessment that helps you get an idea of your starting point. The image of the wheel has been used for centuries as a way to help people understand themselves and their world. Some Native American cultures, for example, use the "medicine wheel" to reflect the life cycle. In different regions (North, South, East, and West), qualities represented by colors and animals, seasons,

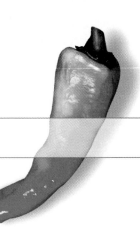

and stages of life are honored on the wheel, providing a way to understand each experience as one progresses through life.

Think of the wheel in Figure 1.6 as a circle of your lessons and growth areas at this time in your life. Look at each area on the wheel and ask

"If you don't risk anything, you risk even more."

ERICA JONG

yourself where you feel accomplished and where you would like to improve. At the end of this course, you will do this exercise again. This wheel is based on one used by an organization that trains personal coaches. You can create a similar wheel at different stages throughout your life, determining your set of categories based on your goals, values, and needs at any given time.

College Builds a Foundation for Learning Throughout Life

As a student just beginning a college career, you may have so much on your plate that you can't imagine thinking past next month, never mind what you need to learn throughout life. However, you are investing time, money, and energy in your education—and you should know that the learning skills you are developing now will bring you success far beyond graduation.

The importance of being a lifelong learner is linked to the enormous change taking place in the world. Changes like the following demand continued learning in the years ahead.

- *Knowledge in nearly every field is doubling every two to three years.* That means that if you stop learning, for even a few years, your knowledge base will be inadequate to keep up with the changes in your career.
- *Technology is changing how you live and work.* The Internet and technology will shape communications and improve knowledge and productivity during the next 20 years—and will require continual learning.
- *Our economy is moving from a product and service base to a knowledge and talent base.* Jobs of the past are being replaced by knowledge-based jobs that ask workers to think critically to come up with solutions.
- *Workers are changing jobs and careers more frequently.* The National Research Bureau reports that currently the average employee changes jobs every three to four years, and it is estimated that a 22-year-old college graduate in the year 2000 will have an average of 8 employers in his or her first 10 years in the workplace.[6] Every time you decide to start a new career, you need new knowledge and skills.

All of these signs point to the need to become *lifelong learners*—individuals who embrace learning as a mechanism for improving their

Figure 1.6   The wheel of life.

Rate yourself in each area of the wheel on a scale of 1 to 10, 1 being least developed (near the center of the wheel) and 10 being most developed (the outer edge of the wheel). In each area, at the level of the number you choose, draw a curved line to create a new outer edge for that segment of the chart. Remember, this is for your benefit only, so be honest. Finally, look at your wheel as a whole. What does it say about the balance in your life? If this were a real wheel, how well would it roll?

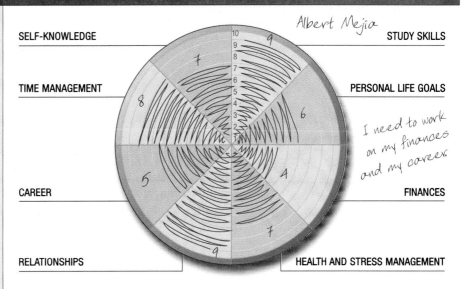

Sample Wheel

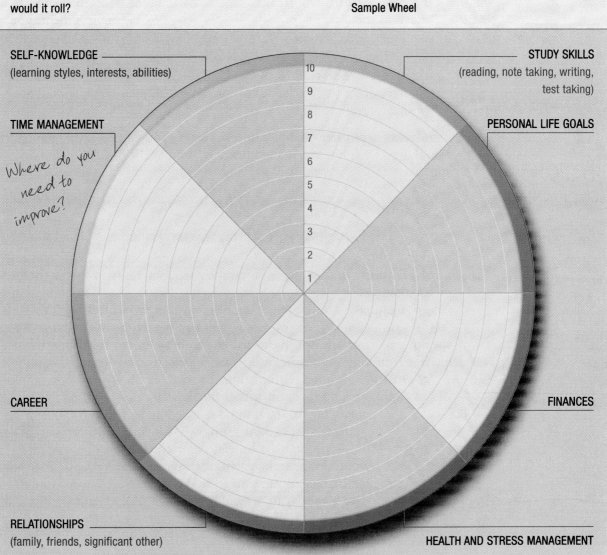

SELF-KNOWLEDGE
(learning styles, interests, abilities)

STUDY SKILLS
(reading, note taking, writing, test taking)

TIME MANAGEMENT

PERSONAL LIFE GOALS

CAREER

FINANCES

RELATIONSHIPS
(family, friends, significant other)

HEALTH AND STRESS MANAGEMENT

Source: Based on "The Wheel of Life" model developed by the Coaches Training Institute, © Co-Active Space 2000.

lives and careers. Developing flexibility helps you keep an open mind and learn throughout your life.

Change—in College and Beyond—Demands Flexibility

The vast majority of Americans see lifelong learning as important in their own lives. In a recent survey of workers, ages 18–24, conducted by the country's leading labor union, the American Federation of Labor and Congress of Industrial Organizations (AFL-CIO), 85 percent of respondents viewed education and training as the nation's top economic priority, and 9 out of 10 believed that the key to career advancement is ongoing education and training.[7]

Lifelong learning requires *flexibility*—an attitude that defines how you approach the challenge of change and continual learning in school and at work. Flexibility implies that you:

- *Embrace change, responding to it with anticipation.* Risk taking is necessary for personal growth and success. By entering college, you have accepted the challenges and risks of college in order to succeed.
- *Become self-directed.* Realize that you will guide yourself through much of the learning process. In this new, flexible environment, you are in charge.
- *See yourself as part of a bigger picture.* Change is happening to everyone. In addition to the technological, economic, and personal changes described earlier, it is happening on a cultural, social, and business level.

Change will often throw you for a loop. You cannot stop change from happening, but you can embrace it and benefit from it by making conscious choices about how to handle changes.

Be an Agent of Change

Being an *agent of change* means being aware of change, adjusting to what it brings, and sometimes even instigating change yourself. Every choice now will affect what happens down the road. Start now to be in charge of your choices.

For example, say that your school is planning to cancel a number of sections of a course that you need. You can be an agent of change by speaking to your advisor about using another class to fulfill the requirement, petitioning with other students to keep sections open, talking to the instructor about getting admitted to an existing section, or finding an internship that substitutes for the class.

Having an open mind is essential to being responsive to change. You cannot know what lies in store for you in life—who you will meet, what challenges you will face, what circumstances will affect you. Staying open to what life brings allows you to make the most of each change that comes your way, whether it is global (a downturn in world economic health) or personal (a health crisis of your own).

Seek continual change and improvement in your education. Take to heart this quotation from a student in Mississippi: "Without an education in the [new millennium], we the people will be in serious trouble. Because now everything is moving forward fast and without an education you will be moving nowhere."[8] Let your ability to make change happen keep you on the move.

In Chinese writing, this character has two meanings: One is "chaos"; the other, "opportunity." The character communicates the belief that every chaotic, challenging situation in life also presents an opportunity. By responding to challenges actively, you can discover the opportunity within the chaos.

Let this concept reassure you as you begin college. You may feel that you are going through a time of chaos and change. Remember that no matter how difficult the obstacles, you have the ability to persevere. You can create opportunities for yourself to learn, grow, and improve.

Building Skills
FOR COLLEGE, CAREER, AND LIFE SUCCESS

Critical Thinking *Applying Learning to Life*

IDENTIFY YOURSELF. Where do you fit in today's student population? Make a brief "sketch" of yourself in words—describe your particular circumstances, opinions, and needs in a short paragraph. Here are some questions to inspire thought:

- How do you describe yourself—your culture, ethnicity, gender, age, lifestyle?
- How long are you planning to be in college?
- How do you describe your family?
- What is your work situation, if you work?
- What is your current living situation?
- What do you feel are your biggest challenges right now?
- What qualities make you special?

Activate Your Self-Esteem

Use the two aspects of building your self-esteem to move yourself toward one important school-related goal for this semester. Make your goal as specific as possible. For example, "I want to find a job that allows me to work at night and still have time to study for my day classes."

Your goal: _____

_____

_____

_____

_____

THINK POSITIVE. What *positive thoughts* about yourself and your abilities will help you achieve your goal? List them here:

_____

_____

_____

_____

_____

_____

_____

_____

_____

_____

_____

TAKE ACTION. Be specific about the *actions* you will take to back up your positive thoughts and achieve your goal. List them here:

_____

_____

_____

_____

_____

_____

_____

_____

_____

_____

The last step is up to you: *Just do it.*

Facing Your Fears[9]

One valuable solution to any fear is to let go of the need to be perfect that often prevents people from doing anything at all, and to *do something*. The easiest way to do this is to break the task into manageable units and do one step at a time. First, think of an activity you have been postponing because of fear (fear of success, of failure, of the task, of perfectionism). Describe it here.

_____

_____

Now, list four small activities that get you closer to working through that fear. If you don't want to start a major project, for example, you can read a book on the subject, brainstorm what you already know about it, or just write one page about it.

1. _____

2. _____

3. _____

4. _____

Commit yourself to one small step that you will take within the next two days. State it here.

_____

_____

List the time you will begin the activity and how much time you will spend doing it.

_____

_____

What reward will you give yourself for having taken that step?

_____

_____

After taking the step, describe how it felt.

_____

_____

Affirm that you have taken that first step and are on the way to success by signing your name here and writing the date. Use the motivation strategies from the text to make sure you continue on the road toward conquering your fear.

Signature _____ *Date* _____

Teamwork *Combining Forces*

MOTIVATORS. Gather in a group of three to five students. Each person should take out a blank sheet of paper and write at the top what he or she thinks is his or her biggest motivation problem; that is, the situation or thing that most often kills that person's motivation. Don't include names on the pages. When everyone is finished, each person should pass his or her page to the person to the left. On the page you receive, you should list one idea you have about fighting the particular motivation problem that is at the top of the page. Again, when everyone is finished, pass the pages to the left. Continue until your page comes back to you.

Then, discuss the ideas together. Offer thoughts about which ideas might work better than others. Add other ideas to the list if you think of them. You may want to combine everyone's lists together so that each group member has a copy. You may also want to share your ideas with the class if you have time.

Writing *Discovery Through Journaling*

To record your thoughts, use a separate journal or the lined page at the end of the chapter.

REASONS FOR COLLEGE. Think back to the section describing various reasons that people decide to go to college. Now describe your own: Why are you here? How do you feel about your reasons for being here? Next, describe your educational goals: What do you want out of college?

Career Portfolio *Charting Your Course*

SETTING CAREER GOALS. Whether you have a current career, have held a few different jobs, or have not yet entered the workplace, college is an ideal time to take stock of your career goals. Even if you won't enter the workplace for a few years, now is not too early to consider what you might like to do after you have finished school. The earlier in your college education that you consider your career goals, the more you can take advantage of how college can help prepare you for work, in both job-specific and general ways.

Take some time to think about your working life. Spend 15 minutes brainstorming everything that you wish you could be, do, have, or experience in your career—the career area, finances, benefits, experiences, travel, anything you can think of. List your wishes on a blank piece of paper, draw them, depict them using cutouts from magazines, or combine these ideas—whatever you like best.

Now, look at your list. To discover how your wishes relate to one another, group them in order of priority. Take three pieces of paper and label them Priority 1, Priority 2, and Priority 3. Write each wish on the piece of paper where it fits, with Priority 1 being the most important, Priority 2 the second most important, and Priority 3 the third.

Look at your priority lists. What do they tell you about what is most important to you? What wishes are you ready to work toward right now? Circle the three highest-priority wishes that you want to achieve with your entry into a new career.

Assess Yourself *Student Success Strategies*

If you have access to the CD-ROM Strategies for Success, *use the following questions to assess your thoughts and enhance your understanding of the chapter. The questions below represent only some of the activities provided on the CD for the chapter topics—try others if you have time.*

Click on the Where Are You Now? bookmark. Use the following activities to prime your mind for making the most of your education:

1. Take the pre-assessment to consider how you believe education is involved in your drive toward success.

2. Watch the video and think about education's six areas of influence: lifelong learning, self-concept, extended possibilities, community service, personal health and well-being, and quality of life. In the field provided, type these in priority order from most important to least important.

3. Click on Activity One: Educational Contract. Fill in the Educational Contract and experience the clarity and motivation that often come from putting your thoughts down on paper. Print it out to keep in your portfolio.

4. Take the post-assessment to clarify what you know about how education can help you achieve your goals.

SUGGESTED READINGS

Baker, Sunny and Kim Baker. *College After 30: It's Never Too Late to Get the Degree You Need!* Holbrook, MA: Bob Adams, 1992.

Cobb, Joyanne. *Learning How to Learn: A Guide for Getting Into College with a Learning Disability, Staying In, and Staying Sane.* Washington, DC: Child Welfare League of America, 2001.

Evers, Frederick T., James Cameron Rush, and Iris Berdow. *The Bases of Competence: Skills for Lifelong Learning and Employability.* San Francisco, CA: Jossey-Bass, 1998.

Jeffers, Susan. *Feel the Fear and Do It Anyway.* New York: Fawcett Columbine, 1992.

Lewis, Erica-Lee and Eric L. Lewis. *Help Yourself: Handbook for College-Bound Students with Learning Disabilities.* New York: Princeton Review, 1996.

Shields, Charles J. *Back in School: A Guide for Adult Learners.* Hawthorne, NJ: Career Press, 1994.

Weinberg, Carol. *The Complete Handbook for College Women: Making the Most of Your College Experience.* New York: New York University Press, 1994.

INTERNET RESOURCES

Student Center: www.studentcenter.org

Student.Com: College Life Online: www.student.com

National Attention Deficit Disorder Association: www.add.org

National Center for Learning Disabilities: www.ncld.org

Prentice Hall Student Success Supersite: Student Union: www.prenhall.com/success/StudentUn/index.html

Success Stories: www.prenhall.com/success/Stories/index.html

ENDNOTES

1. Rick Pitino, *Success Is a Choice.* New York: Broadway Books, 1997, p. 40.

2. Center for Academic Integrity, Kenan Institute for Ethics, Duke University. A Report from the Center for Academic Integrity, October 1999. Downloaded March 19, 2001 from www.academicintegrity.org.

3. Cited in Center for Academic Integrity, Kenan Institute for Ethics, Duke University. A Report from the Center for Academic Integrity, October 1999. Downloaded March 19, 2001 from www.academicintegrity.org.

4. Verne G. Kopytoff, "Brilliant or Plagiarized? Colleges Use Sites to Expose Cheaters." *The New York Times,* January 20, 2000, p. G7.

5. Cited in Colin Rise and Malcolm J. Nicholl, *Accelerated Learning for the 21st Century.* New York: Dell, 1997, pp. 5–6.

6. Jay Palmer, "Marry Me A Little," *Barron's,* July 24, 2000, p. 25.

7. Study cited in Susan Rosenblum, "Young Workers Name Lifelong Learning As Top Need for Economy of Future," *Nation's Cities Weekly,* September 6, 1999, p. 1.

8. National Institute for Literacy Web site: www.nifl.gov/reders/!intro.htm#C

9. Rita Lenken Hawkins, Baltimore City Community College, 1997.

JOURNAL

name   date

visit: www.prenhall.com/carter NY Times link for this chapter

In this chapter you explore answers to the following questions: • **What is a learning style?** • **How can you discover how you learn?** • **Why is it important to know how you learn?** • **How can you start thinking about choosing a major?**

IN THIS CHAPTER

Self-awareness

MANY STUDENTS do what they have to do in school without any idea of how they learn best. What Michael Nolan (see next page) already knows about himself serves as an excellent jumping-off point for his exploration of the college courses and the major that will make sense for him. Combining what you already know about yourself with the two different learning-style assessments in this chapter will help you further clarify your personal path. You can then apply what you have discovered as you consider your major and what it means for your life.

EXPLORE

knowing how you learn and how to choose a major

Michael Nolan, Oregon State University, Corvallis, Oregon

Julia Nolan, University of California, Davis, California

How can I find the right major for me?

I encourage you to take internships in your field . . .

I have loved sports as long as I can remember. I love the strategy, the thought, and the decisions involved as much as I do the athletics. In fact, to me, the creation of a winning team from a jumble of talented players is often more interesting than the game itself.

Because of this, the business of sports is fascinating to me. One problem is that it's hard to get experience in as competitive a field as sports business. Also, there aren't a lot of sports business programs in the country, particularly at schools that interest me and have strong sports programs. Ideally, I'd also like to have a major that could be used somewhere else, in case I can't find a job in sports.

How can I find a major that appeals to my interests and that leads to a good career? How can I make sure that I like my chosen occupation and test its compatibility with me at school? And how can I learn what classes I should take to learn the most about sports business and excel in my field?

From early childhood, I wanted to be a scientist. I lived for the day when I'd be able to go to a *real* university and do *real* research in a *real* lab and contribute to the growing body of scientific knowledge. So, when one of my professors asked me to work for him on some antibiotics research at the end of my freshman year, I was ecstatic. After years of anticipation, I'd finally get to do what I'd dreamed of.

And I found that I hated it. Most of what I did was repetitive, such as reacting the product, identifying the product, purifying the product; all in long, laborious tasks for which I couldn't see the end result. Even worse, even if what I was working on did turn into a lifesaving antibiotic, it would likely take decades before anyone could use it. I found I just didn't have the patience for research. I don't like long hours of repetitive lab work and I don't want to wait for decades for a theory to become useful.

So, I discovered engineering. And I found a career that seems perfect for me, even though I couldn't have imagined myself as an engineer when I started college. Yet, the irony is that I only discovered that I love engineering and don't adore scientific research because I did an internship.

Had I not decided to do research in college, I'd probably be looking for a good Ph.D. program now, rather than doing something I love. I still like research and I still love reading about what's on the cutting edge of technology, but I also realize that a life of pure research isn't for me. That's probably the most important thing that I learned from my internship. I encourage you to take internships in your field because it was a lot better for me to learn that I didn't like lab work in college than it would have been several years into my first job.

What is a *learning style?*

It happens in nearly every college course: Students listen to lectures throughout the semester. Each student hears the same words at exactly the same time and completes the same assignments. However, after finals, student experiences with the course range from fulfillment and high grades to complete disconnection and low grades or withdrawals. Many causes may be involved—different levels of interest and effort, different levels of ability, outside stresses. Another major factor that often is not considered is learning style.

Although presentation styles vary, the standard lecture is still the norm in the majority of classrooms. This might lead you to assume that most students learn best in a lecture setting. Unfortunately, this is not the case, and students who don't learn as well from a lecture course may develop doubts about their competence. However, there are many different and equally valuable ways to learn. To succeed in any kind of course—and in life—you have to know how you learn, understand the strategies that heighten your strengths and boost your weaknesses, and know when to use them.

LEARNING STYLE

A particular way in which the mind receives and processes information.

The Two Parts of Learning Style

Students process information in different ways and have varied styles of interaction with others. Say, for example, that a group of students is taking a freshman composition class that is broken up into study groups during two out of three class meetings. Students who are comfortable working with words or happy when engaged in discussion with a study group may do well in the course. Students who are more mathematical than verbal, or who prefer to work alone, might not do as well. The learning-style factor results in different levels of success with the course.

This example shows that learning style is about more than just what kinds of courses or topics you prefer. Learning style can be seen as having two equally important aspects:

- Learning preferences—what abilities and areas of learning interest you and come most easily to you
- Personality traits—how you interact with information and with others

These two aspects are important partners in defining how you learn—and how you succeed in college and beyond. Neither one gives you a complete picture without the other. Imagine that a freshman composition instructor discovers that her entire class has strong verbal learning preferences. Thrilled, she proceeds with her group discussion-based course, figuring that the students will continue to do well. After finals, she is surprised to find a wide array of grades. A possible reason: Not everyone functions well in small group discussions.

Likewise, suppose another instructor chances on a course section composed entirely of students who love the experience-based, hands-on style of his biology course. He assumes that everyone will pass with flying colors. They don't, however—because, of course, not everyone has a natural learning preference in the sciences, no matter how much they like the style of interacting with the course material.

Getting Perspective on Learning Style

What you find out about your learning style through the assessments in this chapter can help you manage yourself effectively at school, work, and home. However, no assessment has the final word on who you are and what you can and cannot do. It's human to want an easy answer—a one-page printout revealing the secrets of your identity—but this kind of quick fix does not exist.

Your thinking skills—your ability to evaluate information—enable you to see yourself as a whole, including your strengths and weaknesses. Your job is to analyze the information you gain from the assessments in this chapter to arrive at an accurate self-portrait. Before you get into the heart of the assessments and what they mean, consider how to best use what you learn from them.

Using Assessments for Reference

Approach any assessment as a tool with which you can expand your idea of yourself. There are no "right" answers, no "best" set of scores. Think of it in the same way you would a new set of eyeglasses for a person with somewhat blurred vision. The glasses will not create new paths and possibilities, but will help you see more clearly the ones that already exist.

You continually learn, change, and grow throughout your life. Any evaluation is simply a snapshot, a look at who you are in a given moment. Your answers can, and will, change as you change and as circumstances change. They provide an opportunity for you to look at the present moment by asking questions: Who am I right now? How does this compare to who I want to be?

Using Assessments for Understanding

Understanding your preferred learning styles helps to prevent you from boxing yourself into categories that limit your life. Instead of saying, "I'm no good in math," someone who is not a natural in math can make the subject easier by tapping into learning style-related strategies. For example, a learner who responds to visuals can learn better by drawing diagrams of math problems; a learner who benefits from discussing material with others can improve comprehension by talking out problems with a study partner.

Most people have one or two dominant learning styles. In addition, you may change which abilities you emphasize, depending on the situation. For example, a student with a highly developed visual sense might find it easy to take notes in think link style (see Chapter 6 for an explanation of different note-taking styles). However, if an instructor writes an outline on the board as a guide to a detailed topic, the same student might work with the outline. The more you know yourself, the more you are able to assess and adapt to any situation.

Facing Challenges Realistically

Any assessment reveals areas of challenge as well as ability. Rather than dwelling on limitations (which often results in a negative self-image) or ignoring them (which often leads to unproductive choices), use what you know from the assessment to face your limitations and work to improve them.

> "To be what we are, and to become what we are capable of becoming, is the only end of life."

ROBERT LOUIS STEVENSON

In any area of challenge, look at where you are and set goals that help you reach where you want to be. If a class is difficult, examine what improvements to make in order to succeed. If a work project involves tasks that give you trouble, face your limitations head-on and ask for help. Exploring what you gain from working on a limitation helps you build the motivation you need to move ahead.

How can you *discover* how you learn?

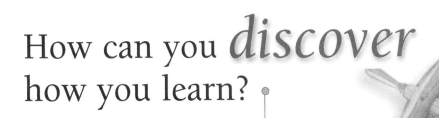

This chapter presents two assessments that help you discover your style of learning and personality traits. View these as two equally important halves that help you form a whole picture of who you are as a learner.

The first assessment focuses on learning preferences and is called *Multiple Pathways to Learning*. It is based on the Multiple Intelligences Theory developed by Howard Gardner.

The second assessment is geared toward personality analysis and is based on the Myers-Briggs Type Inventory® (MBTI). The assessment is called *Personality Spectrum* and helps you evaluate how you react to people and situations.

Multiple Intelligences

There is a saying, "It is not how smart you are, but how you are smart." In 1983, Howard Gardner, a Harvard University professor, changed the way people perceive intelligence and learning with his theory of Multiple Intelligences. This theory holds that there are at least eight distinct intelligences possessed by all people, and that every person has developed some intelligences more fully than others. According to the Multiple Intelligences Theory, when you find a task or subject easy, you are probably using a more fully developed intelligence; when you have more trouble, you may be using a less developed intelligence.[1]

Gardner believes that the way you learn is a unique blend of intelligences, resulting from your distinctive abilities, challenges, experiences, and training. In addition, how you learn isn't necessarily set in stone—particular levels of ability in the intelligences may develop or recede based on changes in your life. Traditionally, the notion of intelligence has been linked to tests such as the Stanford-Binet IQ test and others like it that rely on mathematical, logical, and verbal measurements. Gardner, however, thinks that this doesn't accurately reflect the entire spectrum of human ability:

> I believe that we should . . . look . . . at more naturalistic sources of information about how peoples around the world develop skills important to their way of life. Think, for example, of sailors in the South Seas, who find their way around hundreds, or even thousands, of islands by looking at the constellations of stars in the sky, feeling the way a boat passes over the water, and noticing a few scattered landmarks. A word for intelligence in a society of these sailors would probably refer to that kind of navigational ability.[2]

Table 2.1 offers brief descriptions of the focus of each of the intelligences. You can find information on related skills and study techniques on page 46. The Multiple Pathways to Learning assessment helps you determine the levels to which your intelligences are developed.

Personality Spectrum

Personality assessments indicate how you respond to both internal and external situations—in other words, how you react to information, thoughts, and feelings, as well as to people and events. Employers may give such assessments to employees and use the results to set up and evaluate teams.

The Myers-Briggs Type Inventory is one of the most widely used personality inventories in both psychology and business, and was one of the first instruments to measure psychological types. Katharine Briggs and her daughter, Isabel Briggs Myers, together designed the MBTI. Later, David Keirsey and Marilyn Bates combined the 16 Myers-Briggs types into four temperaments and developed an assessment called the Keirsey Sorter based on those temperaments.

INTELLIGENCE

As defined by H. Gardner, an ability to solve problems or fashion products that are useful in a particular cultural setting or community.

Table 2.1	Multiple intelligences.	43
INTELLIGENCE	**DESCRIPTION**	
Verbal–Linguistic	Ability to communicate through language (listening, reading, writing, speaking)	
Logical–Mathematical	Ability to understand logical reasoning and problem solving (math, science, patterns, sequences)	
Bodily–Kinesthetic	Ability to use the physical body skillfully and to take in knowledge through bodily sensation (coordination, working with hands)	
Visual–Spatial	Ability to understand spatial relationships and to perceive and create images (visual art, graphic design, charts and maps)	
Interpersonal	Ability to relate to others, noticing their moods, motivations, and feelings (social activity, cooperative learning, teamwork)	
Intrapersonal	Ability to understand one's own behavior and feelings (self-awareness, independence, time spent alone)	
Musical	Ability to comprehend and create meaningful sound and recognize patterns (music, sensitivity to sound and patterns)	
Naturalistic	Ability to understand features of the environment (interest in nature, environmental balance, ecosystem, stress relief brought by natural environments)	

Derived in part from the Myers-Briggs and Keirsey theories, the Personality Spectrum assessment adapts and simplifies their material into four personality types—Thinker, Organizer, Giver, and Adventurer—and was developed by Dr. Joyce Bishop in 1997. The Personality Spectrum gives you a personality perspective on how you can maximize your functioning at school and work. For each personality type, you'll see techniques that improve work and school performance, learning strategies, and ways of relating to others. Page 48 gives you more details about each type.

Scoring the Assessments

The assessments follow this section of text. As you complete them, try to answer the questions objectively—in other words, answer the questions to best indicate who you are, not who you want to be (or who your parents or instructors want you to be). Then, enter your scores on page 49. Don't be concerned if some of your scores are low—that is true for almost everyone.

Following each assessment is information about the typical traits of, and appropriate study strategies for, each intelligence or spectrum dimension. You have abilities in all areas, though some are more developed than others. Therefore, you may encounter useful suggestions under any of the headings. During this course, try a large number of new study techniques and keep what works for you.

Remember, also, that knowing your learning style is not only about guiding your life toward your strongest abilities; it is also about using other strategies when you face challenges. No one goes through life always able to find situations where strengths are in demand and weaknesses are uninvolved. Use the strategies for your weaker areas when what is required of you involves tasks and academic areas that you find difficult. For example, if you are not characteristically strong in logical–mathematical intelligence and have to take a required math or science course, the suggestions geared toward logical–mathematical learners may help you build what skill you have.

IMPORTANT NOTE *about scoring...*

The two assessments are scored *differently.* For *Multiple Pathways to Learning,* each intelligence has a set of numbered statements, and you consider each numbered statement on its own, giving it the number you feel best suits your response to it. You will, therefore, have any combination of numbers for each intelligence, from all 4s to all 1s or anywhere in between.

For *Personality Spectrum,* you rank order the four statements that complete each statement, giving a 4 to the one most like you, a 3 to the next most, a 2 to the next, and a 1 to the one least like you. You will, therefore, have a 4, 3, 2, and 1 for each of the eight numbered questions.

MULTIPLE PATHWAYS TO LEARNING

Directions: Rate each statement as follows. Write the number of your response (1–4) on the line next to the statement and total each set of six questions.

| ① rarely | ② sometimes | ③ usually | ④ always |

1. _____ I enjoy physical activities.
2. _____ I am uncomfortable sitting still.
3. _____ I prefer to learn through doing.
4. _____ When sitting I move my legs or hands.
5. _____ I enjoy working with my hands.
6. _____ I like to pace when I'm thinking or studying.
_____ **TOTAL for Bodily–Kinesthetic**

7. _____ I enjoy telling stories.
8. _____ I like to write.
9. _____ I like to read.
10. _____ I express myself clearly.
11. _____ I am good at negotiating.
12. _____ I like to discuss topics that interest me.
_____ **TOTAL for Verbal–Linguistic**

13. _____ I use maps easily.
14. _____ I draw pictures/diagrams when explaining ideas.
15. _____ I can assemble items easily from diagrams.
16. _____ I enjoy drawing or photography.
17. _____ I do not like to read long paragraphs.
18. _____ I prefer a drawn map over written directions.
_____ **TOTAL for Visual–Spatial**

19. _____ I like math in school.
20. _____ I like science.
21. _____ I problem solve well.
22. _____ I question how things work.
23. _____ I enjoy planning or designing something new.
24. _____ I am able to fix things.
_____ **TOTAL for Logical–Mathematical**

25. _____ I listen to music.
26. _____ I move my fingers or feet when I hear music.
27. _____ I have good rhythm.
28. _____ I like to sing along with music.
29. _____ People have said I have musical talent.
30. _____ I like to express my ideas through music.
_____ **TOTAL for Musical**

31. _____ I need quiet time to think.
32. _____ I think about issues before I want to talk.
33. _____ I am interested in self-improvement.
34. _____ I understand my thoughts and feelings.
35. _____ I know what I want out of life.
36. _____ I prefer to work on projects alone.
_____ **TOTAL for Intrapersonal**

37. _____ I like doing a project with other people.
38. _____ People come to me to help settle conflicts.
39. _____ I like to spend time with friends.
40. _____ I am good at understanding people.
41. _____ I am good at making people feel comfortable.
42. _____ I enjoy helping others.
_____ **TOTAL for Interpersonal**

43. _____ I enjoy nature whenever possible.
44. _____ I think about having a career involving nature.
45. _____ I enjoy studying plants, animals, or oceans.
46. _____ I avoid being indoors except when I sleep.
47. _____ As a child I played with bugs and leaves.
48. _____ When I feel stressed I want to be out in nature.
_____ **TOTAL for Naturalistic**

Developed by Joyce Bishop, Ph.D., and based upon Howard Gardner's *Frames of Mind: The Theory of Multiple Intelligences.*[2]

MULTIPLE INTELLIGENCES

Skills

VERBAL–LINGUISTIC

- Analyzing own use of language
- Remembering terms easily
- Explaining, teaching, learning, using humor
- Understanding syntax and meaning of words
- Convincing someone to do something

MUSICAL–RHYTHMIC

- Sensing tonal qualities
- Creating or enjoying melodies and rhythms
- Being sensitive to sounds and rhythms
- Using "schemas" to hear music
- Understanding the structure of music

LOGICAL–MATHEMATICAL

- Recognizing abstract patterns
- Reasoning inductively and deductively
- Discerning relationships and connections
- Performing complex calculations
- Reasoning scientifically

VISUAL–SPATIAL

- Perceiving and forming objects accurately
- Recognizing relationships between objects
- Representing something graphically
- Manipulating images
- Finding one's way in space

BODILY–KINESTHETIC

- Connecting mind and body
- Controlling movement
- Improving body functions
- Expanding body awareness to all senses
- Coordinating body movement

INTRAPERSONAL

- Evaluating own thinking
- Being aware of and expressing feelings
- Understanding self in relationship to others
- Thinking and reasoning on higher levels

INTERPERSONAL

- Seeing things from others' perspectives
- Cooperating within a group
- Communicating verbally and nonverbally
- Creating and maintaining relationships

NATURALIST

- Deep understanding of nature
- Appreciation of the delicate balance in nature

Study Techniques

VERBAL–LINGUISTIC

- Read text and highlight no more than 10%
- Rewrite notes
- Outline chapters
- Teach someone else
- Recite information or write scripts/debates

MUSICAL–RHYTHMIC

- Create rhythms out of words
- Beat out rhythms with hand or stick
- Play instrumental music/write raps
- Put new material to songs you already know
- Take music breaks

LOGICAL–MATHEMATICAL

- Organize material logically
- Explain material sequentially to someone
- Develop systems and find patterns
- Write outlines and develop charts and graphs
- Analyze information

VISUAL–SPATIAL

- Develop graphic organizers for new material
- Draw mind maps
- Develop charts and graphs
- Use color in notes to organize
- Visualize material

BODILY–KINESTHETIC

- Move or rap while you learn
- Pace and recite
- Move fingers under words while reading
- Create "living sculptures"
- Act out scripts of material, design games

INTRAPERSONAL

- Reflect on personal meaning of information
- Visualize information/keep a journal
- Study in quiet settings
- Imagine experiments

INTERPERSONAL

- Study in a group
- Discuss information
- Use flash cards with others
- Teach someone else

NATURALIST

- Connect with nature whenever possible
- Form study groups of people with like interests

Adapted by Dr. Joyce Bishop from David Lazear, *Seven Pathways of Learning,* 1994.

PERSONALITY SPECTRUM

STEP 1. Rank order all four responses to each question from most like you (4) to least like you (1). Use the circles next to the responses to indicate your rankings.

4	**3**	**2**	**1**
most like me	more like me	less like me	least like me

1. I like instructors who
   a. ○ tell me exactly what is expected of me.
   b. ○ make learning active and exciting.
   c. ○ maintain a safe and supportive classroom.
   d. ○ challenge me to think at higher levels.

2. I learn best when the material is
   a. ○ well organized.
   b. ○ something I can do hands-on.
   c. ○ about understanding and improving the human condition.
   d. ○ intellectually challenging.

3. A high priority in my life is to
   a. ○ keep my commitments.
   b. ○ experience as much of life as possible.
   c. ○ make a difference in the lives of others.
   d. ○ understand how things work.

4. Other people think of me as
   a. ○ dependable and loyal.
   b. ○ dynamic and creative.
   c. ○ caring and honest.
   d. ○ intelligent and inventive.

5. When I experience stress I would most likely
   a. ○ do something to help me feel more in control of my life.
   b. ○ do something physical and daring.
   c. ○ talk with a friend.
   d. ○ go off by myself and think about my situation.

6. I would probably not be close friends with someone who is
   a. ○ irresponsible.
   b. ○ unwilling to try new things.
   c. ○ selfish and unkind to others.
   d. ○ an illogical thinker.

7. My vacations could be described as
   a. ○ traditional.
   b. ○ adventuresome.
   c. ○ pleasing to others.
   d. ○ a new learning experience.

8. One word that best describes me is
   a. ○ sensible.
   b. ○ spontaneous.
   c. ○ giving.
   d. ○ analytical.

STEP 2. Add up the total points for each letter.

TOTAL for a. ○ Organizer   TOTAL for c. ○ Giver

TOTAL for b. ○ Adventurer   TOTAL for d. ○ Thinker

STEP 3. Plot these numbers on the brain diagram on page 49.

PERSONALITY SPECTRUM

Skills

Study Techniques

THINKER

- Solving problems
- Developing models and systems
- Analytical and abstract thinking
- Exploring ideas and potentials
- Ingenuity
- Going beyond established boundaries
- Global thinking—seeking universal truth

THINKER

- Find time to reflect independently on new information
- Learn through problem solving
- Design new ways of approaching issues
- Convert material into logical charts and graphs
- Try to minimize repetitive tasks
- Look for opportunities where you have the freedom to work independently

ORGANIZER

- Responsibility, reliability
- Operating successfully within social structures
- Sense of history, culture, and dignity
- Neatness and organization
- Loyalty
- Orientation to detail
- Comprehensive follow-through on tasks
- Efficiency

ORGANIZER

- Try to have tasks defined in clear, concrete terms so that you know what is required
- Look for a well-structured, stable environment
- Request feedback
- Use a planner to schedule tasks and dates
- Organize material by rewriting and organizing class or text notes, making flash cards, or carefully highlighting

GIVER

- Honesty, authenticity
- Successful, close relationships
- Making a difference in the world
- Cultivating your own potential and that of others
- Negotiation; promoting peace
- Communicating with others
- Openness
- Helping others

GIVER

- Study with others
- Teach material to others
- Seek out tasks, groups, and subjects that involve helping people
- Find ways to express thoughts and feelings clearly and honestly
- Put energy into your most important relationships

ADVENTURER

- High ability in a variety of fields
- Courage and daring
- Approaching problem solving in a hands-on fashion
- Living in the present
- Spontaneity and action
- Ability to negotiate
- Nontraditional style
- Flexibility
- Zest for life

ADVENTURER

- Look for environments that encourage nontraditional approaches
- Find hands-on ways to learn
- Seek people whom you find stimulating
- Use or develop games and puzzles to help memorize terms
- Fight boredom by asking if you can do something extra or perform a task in a more active way

Personality Spectrum: Place a dot on the appropriate number line in the brain diagram for each of your four scores from p. 47; connect the dots; then shade each section using a different color. Write your scores in the four circles just outside the diagram. See information regarding scores below.

Multiple Pathways to Learning: In the vertical bars below the brain diagram, indicate your scores from p. 45 by shading from the bottom going up until you reach the number corresponding to your score for that intelligence. See information regarding scores below.

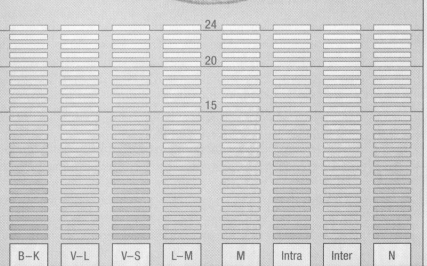

THINKER

Technical
Scientific
Mathematical
Dispassionate
Rational
Analytical
Logical
Problem Solving
Theoretical
Intellectual
Objective
Quantitative
Explicit
Realistic
Literal
Precise
Formal

GIVER

Interpersonal
Emotional
Caring
Sociable
Giving
Spiritual
Musical
Romantic
Feeling
Peacemaker
Trusting
Adaptable
Passionate
Harmonious
Idealistic
Talkative
Honest

ORGANIZER

Tactical
Planning
Detailed
Practical
Confident
Predictable
Controlled
Dependable
Systematic
Sequential
Structured
Administrative
Procedural
Organized
Conservative
Safekeeping
Disciplined

ADVENTURER

Active
Visual
Risking
Original
Artistic
Spatial
Skillful
Impulsive
Metaphoric
Experimental
Divergent
Fast-paced
Simultaneous
Competitive
Imaginative
Open-minded
Adventuresome

Left Brain   Right Brain

17   19   26   18

24

20

15

B–K   V–L   V–S   L–M   M   Intra   Inter   N

For the Personality Spectrum, 26–36 indicates a strong tendency in that dimension, 14–25 a moderate tendency, and below 14 a minimal tendency.

For Multiple Pathways to Learning, 21–24 indicates a high level of development in that particular type of intelligence, 15–20 a moderate level, and below 15 an underdeveloped intelligence.

Source for brain diagram: Understanding Psychology, 3/e, by Morris, © 1996. Adapted by permission of Prentice-Hall, Inc., Upper Saddle River, NJ.

Why is it *important* to know *how* you learn?

The knowledge you have gained by taking the assessments in this chapter can guide you to smart choices that will bring success in your studies, the classroom, and the workplace.

Study Benefits

Knowing how you learn helps you choose techniques that maximize what you do best *and* find strategies that help you improve when you have trouble. Say you have discovered that you respond best to information presented in a linear, logical way. You can use that knowledge to select areas of study or courses that have the presentation you like. When you must take a course that doesn't suit you as well, you can find ways to convert the material so that it better matches your learning style.

This text helps you apply what you learn about your learning style to other important topics, in two different ways. First, with the exception of Chapter 12, each of the following chapters has a feature, Multiple Intelligence Strategies, that shows how to improve your mastery of different skill areas through strategies specific to each of the Multiple Intelligences. Second, in the discussion of careers in Chapter 11, a special segment applies the Personality Spectrum to both career choice and work success strategies.

Classroom Benefits

Knowing your learning style can help you make the most of the teaching styles of your instructors (an instructor's teaching style often reflects his or her learning style). Your particular learning style may work well with the way some instructors teach and be a mismatch with other instructors. Occasionally, you may be able to choose an instructor who teaches in a way that maximizes how you learn. Class schedules, however, usually don't make such choices possible.

After several class meetings, you should be able to assess the instructor's teaching styles (it's common for instructors to have more than one). Figure 2.1 sets forth some common styles. If your style doesn't match up well with that of your instructor, you have a number of options.

Bring extra focus to your weaker areas. Working on your weaker points helps you break new ground in your learning. For example, if you're a verbal person in a math- and logic-oriented class, increase your focus and concentration during class so that you get as much as you can from the presentation. Then spend extra study time on the material, ask others

Figure 2.1	Teaching styles reflect instructor learning styles.
LECTURE	Instructor speaks to the class for the entire period, little to no class interaction.
GROUP DISCUSSION	Instructor presents material but encourages class discussion throughout.
SMALL GROUPS	Instructor presents material and then breaks class into small groups for discussion or project work.
VISUAL FOCUS	Instructor uses visual elements such as diagrams, photographs, drawings, transparencies.
VERBAL FOCUS	Instructor relies primarily on words, either spoken or written on the board or overhead projector.
LOGICAL PRESENTATION	Instructor organizes material in a logical sequence, such as by time or importance.
RANDOM PRESENTATION	Instructor tackles topics in no particular order, jumps around a lot, or digresses.

from your class to help you, and search for additional supplemental materials and exercises to reinforce your knowledge.

Ask your instructor for additional help. For example, a visual person might ask an instructor to recommend visuals that help to illustrate the points made in class. Take advantage of your instructor's office hours to talk one-on-one about what's giving you trouble—especially in a large lecture, your instructor won't know what's going on with you unless you speak up.

"Convert" class material during study time. For example, an interpersonal learner takes a class with an instructor who presents big-picture information in lecture format. This student might organize study groups and talk through concepts with other group members while filling in the factual gaps. Likewise, a visual student might rewrite notes in different colors to add a visual element—for example, using one color for central ideas, another for supporting examples.

Instructors are as unique as students, and no instructor can fulfill the particular needs of a whole classroom of individuals. You often have to shift elements of your habitual learning approach to better mesh with how your instructor presents material. Being flexible in this way benefits you throughout life. Just as you can't hand-pick your instructors, in the workplace you are rarely, if ever, able to choose your boss or change his or her style.

Career Benefits

Because different careers require different abilities, there is no one "best" learning style for the workplace. Knowing how you learn brings you the following key benefits on the job:

- *Better performance.* Because so much of what you do at school (e.g., interacting with others, reading, taking notes) is what you do on the job, it follows that your learning style is essentially the same as your working style. If you know how you learn, you can look for a career, position, and environment that suits you best. You can perform at the top of your ability if you work at a job in which you feel competent and happy.

"They are able because they think they are able."

VIRGIL

- *Better teamwork.* Teamwork is a primary feature of the modern workplace. The better your awareness of your abilities and personality traits, the better you are able to communicate with others and identify what tasks you can best perform in a team situation.
- *Better self-awareness.* Knowing how you learn helps you pinpoint roadblocks. This helps you to work on difficult areas; plus, when a task requires a skill that is tough for you, you can either take special care with it or suggest someone else whose style may be better suited to it.

All three of these areas of benefit—study, classroom, and career—come into play as you begin to consider how to focus your studies in college. Take what you have learned about yourself into account when thinking about your choice of a major.

How can you start thinking about *choosing a major?*

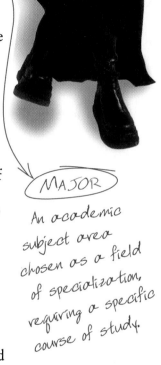

Sometime during the first half of your time in college, after you complete your general education courses, you will be asked to declare an academic major. Choosing a major is one of the biggest decisions you make in college. It determines many of the courses you take, much of what you learn, many of the people with whom you interact, and often your future career.

First, though, remember that you don't have to decide your future in the next five minutes. Most students come to college with little idea of what they want to study or do for a living. Furthermore, you learn about yourself and make changes as you explore. Many students change their majors one or more times during their college career. And, as career expert and professor Dr. Randall Hansen notes, "Your major in college is important for your first job after graduation, but studies show that most people will change careers about four or five times over the course of their lives."[4]

The key is to *start* now, even though you probably don't have to make a decision right away. It takes time to think through options and get an idea of what is required for different majors and careers. Think of choosing a major as a multistep process that starts with knowing your interests and abilities, continues with looking into career areas, moves to exploring academic options, and concludes with making the choice that is right for you.

MAJOR

An academic subject area chosen as a field of specialization, requiring a specific course of study.

Identify Interests and Abilities

The best majors and careers for you are ones that involve your interests and abilities. You already have some strong clues from the work you have done in exploring how you learn. Take those into consideration and continue the process of learning about yourself by concentrating on your academic interests, abilities, and skills. Asking questions like the following helps to pinpoint your areas of interest and—just as importantly—areas to avoid:

- What courses have I enjoyed the most? What might these courses have in common?
- What subjects are interesting to me when I read and study?
- What school- or career-related activities do I look forward to most?
- In what skills or academic areas do I perform best?
- What areas are most difficult for me? What do I struggle with?
- When I open the college catalog, what areas of study or courses am I drawn to?
- Do I consider myself to be a "natural" in any particular area?

- Am I focused on taking courses that will prepare me for a particular career or is my goal to become well rounded through a broad education?
- Am I willing to go to graduate or professional school to become qualified in a particular field?

In today's flighty economy, it can be hard to take your interests into account if they don't seem to lead you to a well-paying, stable career. Considering your interests, however, can lead you to an area of study or a job that you love—and that won't leave you bored or unfulfilled. Here are three positive effects of focusing on what interests you:

- *You have more energy.* When you're doing something you like, time seems to pass quickly. Contrast this with how you feel about disagreeable activities. You accomplish much more in a subject or career area that you enjoy.
- *You perform better.* When you were in high school, you probably got your best grades in your favorite classes. That doesn't change as you get older. The more you like something, the harder you work at it—and the harder you work, the more you improve and the more job and financial success you have. Do something you love, say career experts, and the money will follow.
- *You have a more positive attitude.* A positive attitude contributes to your success in areas in which you lack natural ability or experience.

Link Interests and Abilities to Careers

The point of declaring and pursuing a major is to help you reach a significant level of knowledge in one subject, often in preparation for a particular career area. So, before you focus on majors, think broadly about the career areas that interest you. Having some idea of career interests helps you narrow the field when looking more carefully at potential majors.

Many students select a major because it prepares them to find work in a particular field after they graduate. An education major, for example, is able to teach in elementary school after fulfilling the departmental requirements

PERSONAL TRIUMPH

*S*ome of the most significant lessons you learn about yourself come from getting through difficult times. Gloria Finn Porter had the drive to succeed, and inspiring mentors helped her find a path that felt right for her.

At an early age, I learned that life can appear unfair. My mother was married seven times, and my father was her third husband. When my mother was 35, she started drinking and was an alcoholic almost immediately. When I was 14, I quit school, left home, and got a job at a fast-food restaurant. My girlfriend had been kicked out of her house, so we rented an apartment together. We drank alcohol and did drugs. I attempted suicide several times.

When I hit my 20s, I picked up a DUI. Getting arrested, however, was the catalyst for change in my life. To expunge the DUI from my record, I went into six months of treatment for alcohol abuse at a halfway house in Wisconsin and earned my G.E.D. When I completed the program, I was sober, but I had no money and no clear idea of what I wanted to do.

On a whim, I decided to move to my grandmother's home in Tennessee and try to start school. I walked into Cumberland University in Lebanon and told them that I wanted to go to school, but couldn't pay for it. Between student loans, grants, and scholarships, it all worked out. I also worked at an all-night truck stop, which was a lot of fun.

Before graduating, I started applying to law schools. I believe that if you keep putting one foot in front of the other, and if you have good motives, you will run into your future. During law school, I volunteered with the Public Defender's office. It was there that I met Jim Sheehan, a veteran public defender, who would teach me not only about the law, but about compassion for others, including those with whom I do not agree.

In 1999, Jim Sheehan founded the Center for Justice. I feel privileged to have been a part of that start-up process. We manage a wide range

Gloria Finn Porter, Cofounder and Attorney
at the Center for Justice, Spokane, Washington

of cases including family law, civil rights, environmental, and landlord–tenant issues. Our passion is helping people with modest incomes who are caught in unfair legal situations.

I have learned that to achieve anything, I must ignore the negative voices. When someone says that I can't do something, I see myself achieving that goal. I actually see it; I hold that vision and revisit it each and every day. When someone told me that I would be 35 when I graduated law school, I thought, "Well, I am going to be 35 regardless of what I do—I might as well be a lawyer." I just kept thinking of the little engine that could.

I have also learned to ask for help. No one does it alone. I received so much help from family, friends, counselors, professors, fellow attorneys, my therapist, and mentors and supervisors at the Public Defender's office. People want to help those who want to help themselves.

Last, I have learned to have compassion for those who have harmed me and others. While my mother and father caused us pain, they also loved us very much. They simply did not have the ability to be stable and healthy. It is true that I still see unfairness, but I understand the bigger picture now. It is not about my childhood anymore; it is about me making positive choices and being grateful for my life.

My story was written for those of you who have struggled. You can do anything you want to do—just have faith, get in your little train, and go.

Take a moment to consider . . .

- *How getting through something difficult has fueled your drive to succeed.*
- *A person whose help and attention have helped you learn about yourself and discover goals that feel right to you.*

for undergraduate study. Similarly, an accounting major is prepared for an entry-level job in the accounts payable department of a major corporation.

For many career-oriented majors, students need graduate or professional school to achieve their career goal. For example, in the health sciences field, students who hope to become physicians, physicians' assistants, or dentists have to attend a professional school and be licensed by the state in which they practice. Their undergraduate major is just the beginning of a long journey of learning.

Other undergraduates are looking for intellectual growth and a field that interests them, and they don't focus specifically on a direct career link. These students often gravitate to the liberal arts, which includes departments like English, philosophy, comparative literature, and art history. Although these courses generally do not prepare students for specific jobs when they graduate, they help develop analytic and decision-making skills that are invaluable over a lifetime. Liberal arts majors often go on to a graduate or professional school and wind up in a variety of professions including law, business management, and publishing.

Ultimately, only you can decide how important the career connection is to you. Use the following strategies as you explore what's out there.

Use resources. Visit the career center to take a career assessment or to find out what career areas currently have the best long-term prospects. Talk to people who have jobs that interest you. Read current media to keep up with where the best prospects are.

Explore the educational requirements of different careers. Your choice of a major may be more or less crucial depending on the career area. For example, pursuing a career in medicine almost always requires a major in some area of the biological sciences, whereas aspiring writers may have majored in anything from political science to philosophy.

Consider learning style. Technological and scientific careers demand strength in logical–mathematical thinking, for example, and educational careers often involve extensive interpersonal interaction.

Look at your stronger and weaker areas and see what careers are likely to make the most of what you do well. Chapter 11 goes into more depth on the topic of career exploration.

Try hands-on exploration. Extracurricular activities and volunteering opportunities might give you particular insight into what works well for you. For example, a student interested in architecture may volunteer with a group building houses for the disadvantaged, or a student considering social work can join a service fraternity.

Keep values in mind. What you think you want in a career might not always go along with your most closely held values. Ask yourself what careers support the principles that guide your life choices. How important to you are service to others, financial security, a broad-based education, time for family? Where do you stand on political and moral issues? Think carefully about how your values are supported by any career you consider.[5] Chapter 3 has more information on exploring your values.

Finally, when exploring careers, avoid assumptions about what is available to you. Every career area has job options that aren't obvious right away. For example, a student working toward a teaching certification doesn't have to teach in a public school. This student can develop curricula, act as a consultant for businesses, develop an on-line education service, teach overseas for the Peace Corps, or create a public television program. The sky's the limit.

Explore Academic Options

Once you have a good idea of who you are and what interests you in the working world, the next step is to find out as much as you can about the academic choices open to you. This helps you narrow down possible majors until you find one that works. The following suggestions will help you explore. Some suggestions involve your contact with others. As you read, keep in mind the importance of establishing a support network early on. Advisors, instructors, tutors, classmates, RAs (resident assistants), and others can give you important advice and feedback all along the path.

Read the college catalog to learn your parameters. Every school has its own set of rules that govern the declaration (and changing) of majors. Your catalog tells you what you need to know (some schools may even have their catalogs available on-line). Right from the start, examine what your school requires of you. Find answers to these general questions first:

- When do I have to declare a major? (generally at the end of the second year for four-year programs; earlier for associate or certificate programs)
- What majors are offered at my school?

- What are my options in majoring? (double majors, minors, or interdisciplinary majors)

Once you have this basic information, take time during your first semester to review the majors your school offers. If a major looks interesting, read the detailed course descriptions and learn the departmental requirements you have to meet. Then, for each major you want to explore further, look for answers to the following questions:

- What minimum grade point average, if any, does the department require before it will accept me as a major?
- What preparatory courses (prerequisites) are required?
- What courses (within or without the department) am I required to take? How many credits do I need to graduate in the major?
- Do I have to take courses according to a prescribed sequence—and if so, what is the recommended order of courses?
- Will I have to write a thesis to graduate in this major?
- Who are the departmental advisors?

Work closely with your advisor. Don't make decisions in a vacuum. Begin discussing your major early on with your advisor, even if you don't intend to declare right away. For any given major, your advisor may be able to tell you about the course work and career possibilities. Your advisor can help you evaluate what's available and together you can find the best options.

Visit the department. Ask the department secretary for information (in print form or on the Web) about majors offered by that department (most academic departments compile information to help students make an informed decision about requirements). Then, ask about sitting in on several classes to get a first-hand introduction to the instructors and the work. If, after this experience, you continue to be interested, consider asking an instructor for an appointment to discuss becoming a major.

Speak to people with experience in the major. This includes both current majors and alumni. Ask students who are a year or two ahead to describe their experiences with the courses, the workload, and the professors. Ask them about the link between their career goals and their major. Ask, also, if there is a special club for student majors. For example, a student attending a meeting of the Psi Chi Club for psychology majors might pick up valuable information about courses, instructors, department requirements, and career paths.

Think out of the box—look at creative options for majoring. Don't limit your choices before you have to. Schools often have one or more of the following open to you:

- *Double majors.* Say, for example, you are interested in majoring in English and philosophy. Ask your academic advisor if it is possible to meet the requirements for both departments. Double majors are encouraged for committed students capable of handling the increased workload.

- *Interdisciplinary majors.* If what you want to major in isn't listed in the college catalog, don't immediately assume it's impossible. Talk with your academic advisor. Some schools allow certain students to design their own majors with help and approval from their advisors and instructors. In such a case, you and your advisor work together to come up with a unique list of courses. An example is a course load that combines biology, chemistry, and political science for a career path into public policy medicine.

- *Minors.* A minor also involves a concentration of courses in a particular department, but has fewer requirements than a major. As a sociology major, for example, you can satisfy your career goal to become a social worker by minoring in Spanish, an important second language in the region you hope to work. Or you can use your minor to pursue a lifelong interest—to study the trombone, learn about archeology, learn about world religions.

- *Majors involving courses outside your school.* Some schools may have study abroad programs (spending a semester or a year at an affiliated college in a different country) or opportunities to take courses at nearby schools. Such courses might apply to a major that interests you.

Plan your curriculum. Although you won't necessarily want to plan out your entire college course load at the beginning of your first semester, planning a tentative curriculum—both within and without your major—can help to give you a clearer idea of where you are heading. It can also help you avoid pitfalls, such as not being able to get into a course you need. Here are some tips:

CURRICULUM
The particular set of courses required for a degree.

- *Fulfill core requirements.* Make time for your core courses in the beginning of your college career. The sooner you complete them, the sooner you can focus your studies on the areas that interest you most. Plus, you cannot graduate without fulfilling these requirements, no matter how distinguished your performance in your major.

- *Use electives to branch out.* Prior to declaring your major, choose electives in your areas of interest. Enlarging the scope of your knowledge helps to improve your critical thinking, broaden your perspectives, and perhaps introduce you to career possibilities you have never considered.

- *Register early.* When students wait until the last minute to register for the following semester, some courses they want have already been filled; as a result, they may have to take courses they would not necessarily have chosen. In a worst-case scenario, you may have to delay your graduation in order to fit in a required course.

- *Stay flexible.* Even as you plan, know that your goals, available courses, and other factors may change anytime. One of the advantages of having a plan is that you have something concrete to turn to and adjust when change comes your way.

Be open to changing majors. Some students may change their minds one or more times before finding a major that fits. For example, a pre-med student taking a course in medical ethics might find that his true passion lies in philosophy and religion. You have a right to change your mind; each detour along the way helps to guide you to a path that feels like home. Just act on your new decision right away by informing your advisor and planning a schedule linked to your new choices. Some courses you've taken may even apply to your new major.

No matter what path you choose, working toward any major helps you to develop your most important skill—knowing how to use your mind. More than anything, your future success in school and career depends on your ability to contribute to the workplace through clear, effective, and creative thinking.

Follow Your Passion

It is tempting to tailor your major and career to an area that seems like a sure success. Friends or parents may have warned you against certain careers, encouraging you to stay with "safe" careers that seem socially acceptable or that pay well. In many cases, family and financial circumstances lead students to choose a major that leads directly to well-paying job opportunities and to avoid areas that don't seem to have a clear-cut path to a stable job.

"Great minds have purposes; others have wishes."

WASHINGTON IRVING

Prestige and money may be important—but they usually are not viable replacements for deep personal satisfaction. Furthermore, your major, important as it is, might not ultimately be strongly linked to your career. The Penn State University Web site article "Major Decisions," reports:

> Studies have shown that within ten years after graduation most people are working in careers that are not directly connected to their undergraduate majors. . . . Many jobs that exist today will be performed in very different ways five years from now or may even be obsolete by then. New types of jobs are emerging every year, and most of us have no way of knowing what those jobs will be or what type of education will be needed in order to qualify for them. Consequently, the current emphasis in career planning at the undergraduate level is on the development of general, transferable skills (writing, speaking, computer, problem-solving, team-building) that employers want and that graduates will need in order to adjust to rapidly-changing careers.[6]

Think carefully about your courses, your major, and your career. If your true passion takes you off what seems like a safer path, the choice may be very challenging. However, you are the one who has to live with your decision. Make a choice that leads you toward the life you have dreamed of. Make a choice that makes the most of the real you.

sabiduría

In Spanish, the term *sabiduría* represents the two sides of learning: knowledge and wisdom. Knowledge—building what you know about how the world works—is the first part. Wisdom—deriving meaning and significance from knowledge and deciding how to use it—is the second. As you continually learn and experience new things, the *sabiduría* you build will help you make knowledgeable and wise choices about how to lead your life.

Think of this concept as you discover more about how you receive knowledge in all aspects of your life—in school, work, and personal situations. As you learn how your unique mind works and how to use it, you can more confidently assert yourself. As you expand your ability to use your mind in different ways, you can create lifelong advantages for yourself.

Building Skills

FOR COLLEGE, CAREER, AND LIFE SUCCESS

Critical Thinking *Applying Learning to Life*

LEARNING ABOUT HOW YOU LEARN. Knowing how you learn can provide insight that will help you make the best possible decisions about your future. List your two strongest intelligences.

_____

_____

Describe a positive experience at work or school that you can attribute to these strengths.

_____

_____

_____

_____

_____

Name your two least-developed intelligences.

_____

_____

What challenge do you face that may be related to your least-developed intelligences?

_____

_____

_____

_____

_____

Making School More Enjoyable

Name a required class that you are not necessarily looking forward to taking this year. How does your feeling about the class involve what you know about your learning style? Name three study techniques from the chapter that may help you get the most out of the class and enjoy it more.

_____

_____

_____

_____

_____

_____

_____

_____

_____

_____

_____

_____

Interests, Majors, and Careers

Start by listing activities and subjects you like.

1. _____

2. _____

3. _____

4. _____

5. _____

Thinking about your interests and learning style, name two majors that might suit you.

1. _____

2. _____

For each major, name a corresponding career area you may want to explore.

1. _____

2. _____

Keep these majors and career areas in mind as you gradually narrow your course choices in the time before you declare a major.

Teamwork *Combining Forces*

IDEAS ABOUT PERSONALITY TYPES. Divide into groups according to the four types of the Personality Spectrum—Thinker-dominant students in one group, Organizer-dominant students in another, Giver-dominant students in a third, and Adventurer-dominant students in the fourth. If you have scored the same in more than one of these types, join whatever group is smaller. With your group, brainstorm four lists for your type:

the **strengths** of this type

the **struggles** it brings

the **stressors** (things that cause stress) for this type

career areas that tend to suit this type

If there is time, each group can present this information to the entire class to enable everyone to have a better understanding and acceptance of one another's intelligences. You might also brainstorm strategies for dealing with your intelligence's struggles and stressors, and present those ideas to the class as well.

Writing *Discovery Through Journaling*

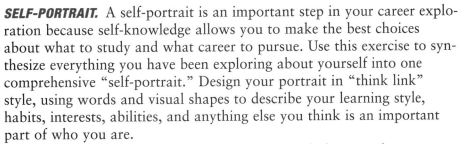

To record your thoughts, use a separate journal or the lined page at the end of the chapter.

YOUR LEARNING STYLE. Discuss the insights you have gained through exploring your multiple intelligences and personality spectrum. What strengths have come to your attention? What challenges have been clarified? Give some specific ideas of how you might use your strengths and address your challenges in the courses you are taking this semester.

Career Portfolio *Charting Your Course*

SELF-PORTRAIT. A self-portrait is an important step in your career exploration because self-knowledge allows you to make the best choices about what to study and what career to pursue. Use this exercise to synthesize everything you have been exploring about yourself into one comprehensive "self-portrait." Design your portrait in "think link" style, using words and visual shapes to describe your learning style, habits, interests, abilities, and anything else you think is an important part of who you are.

A think link is a visual construction of related ideas, similar to a map or web, that represents your thought process. Ideas are written inside geometric shapes, often boxes or circles, and related ideas and facts are attached to those ideas by lines that connect the shapes. See the note-taking section in Chapter 6 for more about think links.

Use the style shown in the example in Figure 2.2 or create your own. For example, in this exercise you may want to create a "wheel" of ideas coming off your central shape, entitled "Me." Then, spreading out from each of those ideas (interests, learning style, etc.), draw lines connecting all of the thoughts that go along with that idea. Connected to "Interests," for example, might be "singing," "stock market," and "history." You don't have to use the wheel image. You might want to design a treelike think link or a line of boxes with connecting thoughts written below the boxes, or anything else you like. Let your design reflect who you are, just as the think link itself does.

Figure 2.2   Sample self-portrait think link.

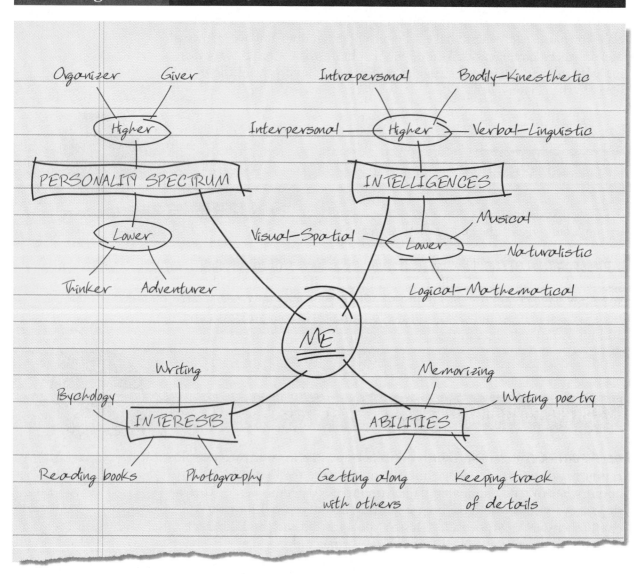

If you have access to the CD-ROM Strategies for Success, *use the following questions to assess your thoughts and enhance your understanding of the chapter. The questions below represent only some of the activities provided on the CD for the chapter topics—try others if you have time.*

Click on the **Learning Styles** bookmark. From completing the Multiple Intelligences assessment in the chapter, recall your two strongest intelligences and your two weakest.

1. Scroll ahead to each of your two strongest intelligences. Read the descriptions and consider how they suit you. Click on the heading showing study strategies; from what you know about what works for you, create two new strategies for each of the two intelligences and write them down on a separate sheet of paper.

2. Scroll to each of your two weakest intelligences. Note the study strategies. For each intelligence, choose two strategies that you plan to use the next time you are in a study situation that requires you to use this intelligence. Evaluate later to see if the strategies you chose helped to boost your ability and confidence.

S uggested Readings

Barger, Nancy J., Linda K. Kirby, and Jean M. Kummerow. *Work Types: Understand Your Work Personality—How It Helps You and Holds You Back, and What You Can Do to Understand It.* New York: Warner Books, 1997.

College Board, ed. *The College Board Index of Majors and Graduate Degrees 2001.* New York: College Entrance Examination Board, 2000.

Gardner, Howard. *Intelligence Reframed: Multiple Intelligences for the 21st Century.* New York: Basic Books, 2000.

Harrington, Paul, et al. *The College Majors Handbook: The Actual Jobs, Earnings, and Trends for Graduates of 60 College Majors.* Indianapolis, IN: Jist Works, 1999.

Keirsey, David. *Please Understand Me II: Temperament, Character, Intelligence.* Del Mar, CA: Prometheus Nemesis Book Company, 1998.

Pearman, Roger R. and Sarah C. Albritton. *I'm Not Crazy, I'm Just Not You: The Real Meaning of the 16 Personality Types.* Palo Alto, CA: Consulting Psychologists Press, 1997.

Phifer, Paul. *College Majors and Careers: A Resource Guide for Effective Life Planning, 4th ed.* Chicago: Ferguson Publishing, 1999.

I nternet Resources

Keirsey Sorter and other Myers-Briggs information: www.keirsey.com

Prentice Hall Student Success Supersite Majors Exploration: www.prenhall.com/success/MajorExp/index.html

Exploring Multiple Intelligences: www.multi-intell.com

E ndnotes

1. Howard Gardner, *Multiple Intelligences: The Theory in Practice.* New York: Harper-Collins, 1993, pp. 5–49.

2. Ibid, p. 7.

3. Developed by Joyce Bishop, Ph.D., Psychology faculty, Golden West College, Huntington Beach, CA. Based on Howard Gardner, *Frames of Mind: The Theory of Multiple Intelligences.* New York: Harper-Collins, 1993.

4. Hansen, Randall S., Ph.D. (January 2001). "Choosing a College Major: How to Chart Your Ideal Path" [on-line]. Available at www.quintcareers.com/choosing_major.html (March 2001).

5. Leonard, Michael J. (January 1996). "Major Decisions: For Students Who Are Exploring Majors" (Division of Undergraduate Studies, The Pennsylvania State University) [on-line]. Available at www.psu.edu/dus/md/ (July 2001).

6. Ibid.

JOURNAL

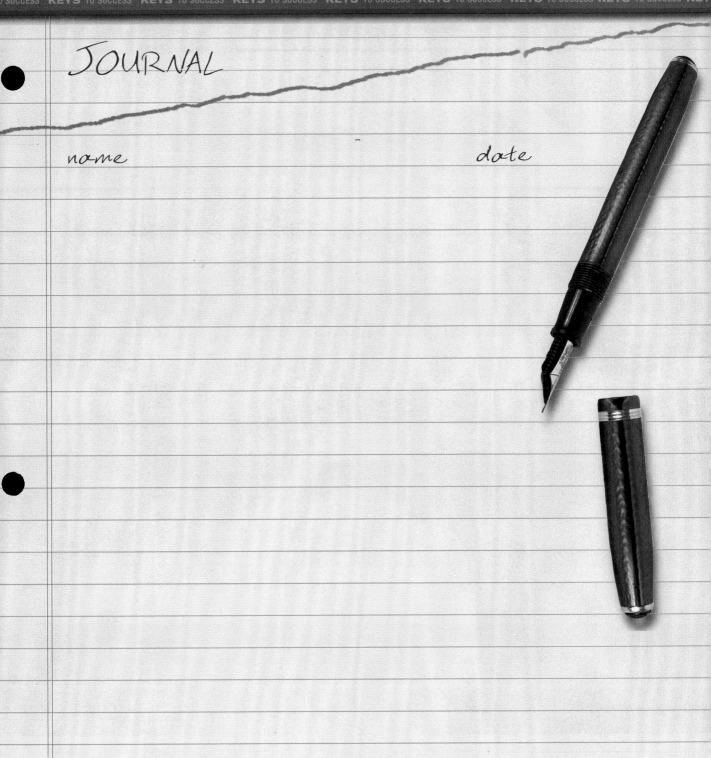

name   date

visit: www.prenhall.com/carter NY Times link for this chapter

IN THIS CHAPTER

In this chapter you explore answers to the following questions:

- What defines your values? • How do you set and achieve goals? • How can you manage your time? • Why is procrastination a problem?

Goal setting and time management

PEOPLE DREAM of what they want out of life, but as Rosalia Chavez (see next page) has experienced, obstacles can interfere with those dreams. However, when you set goals, prioritize, and manage your time effectively, you can develop the kind of "big picture" vision that gets you moving. This chapter explains how defining your values and taking specific steps toward goals can help you turn your dreams into reality. The section on time management discusses how to translate your goals into daily, weekly, monthly, and yearly steps. Finally, you explore how procrastination can derail your dreams and how to avoid it.

using values to map your course

Rosalia Chavez, University of Arizona, Tucson, Arizona

Norma Seledon, Las Mujeres en Accion, Chicago, Illinois

How can I stay focused on my school goals?

Your desire to learn and grow . . . will fuel your efforts.

I married at 18 and didn't finish high school. After our two sons were born, I decided to get my G.E.D., but my husband didn't want me to. At this point, I knew I had to start making opportunities for myself. Shortly after I had begun to further my education, my husband died. I am now taking classes full-time and I work part-time in the Chicano/Hispano Student Affairs Office. I would like to empower future generations of Hispanic women to follow their dreams by telling them my story.

I have to make daily decisions about priorities, and my life situations often get in the way of my schoolwork. Recently, I had to drop a class because my children were sick and I couldn't keep up. My son, who is 11, has ADHD (attention deficit hyperactivity disorder). I can no longer afford his medicine because I was denied state medical assistance. Can you offer suggestions about how I can manage my life and stay focused on my school goals?

Your story is not atypical. Your taking control of your life is, however, exemplary. As director of an organization whose primary focus is Latina leadership and working with survivors of domestic violence, I am aware that setting and sticking to your goals is not easy, particularly when you have cultural and societal factors working against you. With many higher education programs designed for those without families, it is challenging to meet the demands of school and parenting. Your desire to learn and grow, not only for yourself but for your family and community, will fuel your efforts.

I recognize some of your challenges. In my last year of college I had a newborn, was pregnant, worked full-time, and attended school full-time. You must prioritize and pace yourself so that you find a balance. It may help to speak to professors about your situation. My daughter was due at the middle of my last semester, and some professors were flexible with my assignments. My son is also diagnosed with ADHD. I demand periodic meetings with a team of school officials so that we may approach my son's education from a team perspective.

With patience and perseverance, you will achieve your current goals and set more for yourself. Continue to develop a support system and to share your story. We must all continue to figure out how to distill the beauty and strength of our culture and traditions. Felicidades!

What defines your *values?*

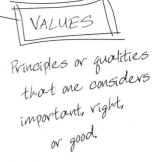

VALUES

Principles or qualities that one considers important, right, or good.

Y our personal **values** are the beliefs that guide your choices. As a group, they constitute your *value system*. For example, your values may include strength of family, being educated, living independently, and seeking worthwhile employment. Each person has a unique value system that sets the foundation for action.

You demonstrate your particular value system in the priorities you set, how you communicate with others, your family life, your educational and career choices, and even the material things with which you surround yourself. Take a look at yourself and your choices: What do they say about you? Going all-out to be on time to appointments and classes shows that you value punctuality. Making time for music, movies, and museums shows that you value the arts. Driving your grandfather to his doctor visits shows that you value family—and health. Fitting school into your busy life shows that you value education.

Here are some reasons why examining your values is a useful first step in goal setting.

- *Self-understanding.* You cannot create a clear picture of what you want out of life until you understand what is truly important to you. You can achieve what you value with the help of goals tailored to those values.

- *Relating to the world around you.* Understanding what you value helps you choose your relationships with people (e.g., family, friends, instructors, supervisors) and organizations (e.g., schools, companies, political or charitable groups) according to how their values compare to yours.

- *Building a personal foundation.* Having a strong set of values gives you a foundation to return to when difficulty in achieving a goal forces you to reevaluate what you want and what is possible.

Values are the foundation on which to build your goals. Start exploring your values by looking at their sources.

Sources of Values

Values are choices. People often choose values based on what others seem to value. A value system is constructed over time, using information from many different sources, including:

- parents, guardians, siblings, and other relatives
- friends and peers
- religious beliefs
- instructors, supervisors, mentors, and others

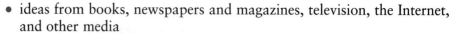

- ideas from books, newspapers and magazines, television, the Internet, and other media
- workplace and school

A particular value may come from one or more sources. For example, a student may value education (primary source: parents), sports (primary sources: media and friends), and a spiritual life (primary sources: religious organization and grandparents). Another student may have abandoned many of the values that he or she grew up with and adopted the values of a trusted mentor. Still another may find that adopting certain values became important in order to succeed in a particular career area. Being influenced by the values of others is natural, although you should use critical thinking to make sure your choices are right for you.

Choosing and Evaluating Values

Examining the sources of your values can help you define what you believe in. Sources, however, aren't as important as evaluating how your choices fit into your total value system. Your responsibility is to make value choices based on what is right for you and those involved with you. Think through the following when considering your values:

Be wary of setting goals according to other people's values. Friends or family may encourage you to strive for what they think you should value. You may, of course, share their values. If you follow advice that you don't believe in, however, you may have a hard time sticking to your path. For example, someone who attends school primarily because a parent thought it was right may have less motivation than someone who made an independent decision to become a student. Staying in tune with your own values helps you to make decisions that are right for you.

Evaluate your values carefully to determine if they are right for you. Although some values may seem positive on the surface, they may actually have a negative impact on you and others. For example, you might consider it important to keep up with the latest technologies, but continually buying computers, software, CD players, cell phones, and pagers might jeopardize your finances. Ask yourself: How will adopting this value affect my life?

Reevaluate your values periodically as you experience change. Life changes and new experiences may alter your values. For example, a student may have loved growing up in a small town where everyone shared similar backgrounds. However, starting college exposes him, for the first time, to people from different ethnic, racial, and religious backgrounds, and he realizes how much he can benefit from knowing them. This exposure creates a change in values that leads to his decision to live and work in a large, diverse city after graduation. Similarly, people who survive near-fatal car accidents often place greater value after the accident on time spent with friends and family. Your values grow and develop as you do if you continue to think them through.

The goals that you set for yourself express your values and translate them into action. You experience a strong drive to achieve if you build goals around what is most important to you.

How do you set and *achieve* goals?

A **goal** can be something as concrete as buying a health insurance plan or as abstract as working to control your temper. When you set goals and work to achieve them, you engage your intelligence, abilities, time, and energy in order to move ahead. From major life decisions to the tiniest day-to-day activities, setting goals helps you define how you want to live and what you want to achieve.

Like learning a new physical task, setting and working toward goals takes a lot of practice and repeated efforts. As long as you do all that you can to achieve a goal, you haven't failed, even if you don't achieve it completely or in the time frame you had planned. Even one step in the right direction is an achievement. For example, if you wanted to raise your course grade to a B from a D, and you ended up with a C, you have still accomplished something important.

Paul Timm, an expert in self-management, believes that focus is a key ingredient in setting and achieving goals: "Focus adds power to our actions. If somebody threw a bucket of water on you, you'd get wet. . . . But if water was shot at you through a high-pressure nozzle, you might get injured. The only difference is focus."[1] Focus your goal-setting energy by defining a personal mission, placing your goals in long-term and short-term time frames, evaluating goals in terms of your values, setting priorities, and exploring different types of goals.

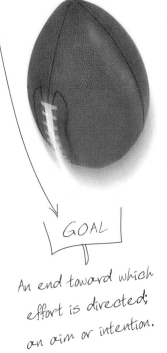

GOAL

An end toward which effort is directed; an aim or intention.

Identifying Your Personal Mission

How often do you step back and look at where you are, where you've been, and where you want to be? Life moves fast, and it's easy to get caught up in just getting through each day. Not having a big-picture view, however, may leave you feeling empty, not knowing what you've done or why. You can avoid that emptiness by periodically thinking carefully about your life's mission and most far-reaching goals.

Where do you start? One helpful way to determine your general direction is to write a personal mission statement. Dr. Stephen Covey, author of *The Seven Habits of Highly Effective People,* defines a mission statement as a philosophy outlining what you want to be (character), what you want to do (contributions and achievements), and the principles by which you live (your values). Dr. Covey compares the personal mission statement to the Constitution of the United States, a statement of principles that guides the country: "A personal mission statement . . . becomes a personal constitution, the basis for making major, life-directing decisions, the basis for making daily decisions in the midst of the circumstances and emotions that affect our lives."[2]

Your personal mission shouldn't be written in stone. What you want out of life changes as you move from one phase to the next—from single person to spouse, from student to working citizen. Stay flexible and reevaluate your personal mission from time to time.

Here are some examples of mission statements. The following personal mission statement was written by Carol Carter, one of the authors of *Keys to Success*.

> My mission is to use my talents and abilities to help people of all ages, stages, backgrounds, and economic levels achieve their human potential through fully developing their minds and their talents. I also aim to balance work with people in my life, understanding that my family and friends are a priority above all else.

A company, like a person, has to establish standards and principles that guide its many activities. Companies often have mission statements so that each member of the organization clearly understands what to strive for. Here is a mission statement from the company that publishes this text:

> To provide the most innovative resources—books, technology, programs—to help students of all ages and stages achieve their academic and professional goals inside the classroom and out.

If you are not sure how to start formulating your mission statement, look to your values to guide you. Define your mission based on what is important to you. For example, if you value service to others, your mission statement might focus on choosing a service-oriented career path.

You have an opportunity to write your own personal mission statement at the end of this chapter. Thinking through your personal mission can help to put you in control of your life instead of allowing circumstances and events to control you. If you frame your mission statement carefully so that it truly reflects your goals, it can be your guide in everything you do.

Placing Goals in Time

Everyone has the same 24 hours in a day, but it often doesn't feel like enough. Have you ever had a busy day flash by so quickly that it seems you accomplished nothing? Have you ever felt that way about a longer period of time, like a month or even a year? Your commitments can overwhelm you unless you decide how to use time and plan your steps toward goal achievement.

"Obstacles are what people see when they take their eyes off the goal."

NEW YORK SUBWAY BULLETIN BOARD

If developing a personal mission statement establishes the big picture, placing your goals within particular time frames allows you to bring individual areas of that picture into the foreground. Planning your progress, step by step, helps you maintain your efforts over the extended time period often needed to accomplish a goal. There are two categories: long-term goals and short-term goals.

Setting Long-Term Goals

Establish first the goals that have the largest scope, the *long-term goals* that you aim to attain over a lengthy period of time, up to a few years or more. As a student, you know what long-term goals are all about. You have set yourself a goal to attend school and earn a degree or certificate. Getting an education is a significant goal that often takes years to reach.

Some long-term goals are lifelong, such as a goal to continually learn more about yourself and the world around you. Others have a more definite end, such as a goal to complete a course successfully. To determine your long-term goals, think about what you want out of your professional, educational, and personal life. Here is Carol Carter's long-term goal statement:

> To accomplish my mission through writing books, creating an Internet Web site, giving seminars, and developing programs that create opportunities for students to learn and develop. To create a personal, professional, and family environment that allows me to manifest my abilities and duly tend to each of my responsibilities.

For example, you may establish long-term goals such as these:

- I will make the effort, while in school, to develop my technological skills so that I am comfortable with computers and other technology when I graduate.
- I will use my current and future job experience to develop practical skills that will help me get a satisfying, well-paying job.

Long-term goals don't have to be lifelong goals. Think about your long-term goals for the coming year. Considering what you want to accomplish in a year's time gives you clarity, focus, and a sense of what needs to take place right away. When Carol thought about her long-term goals for the coming year, she came up with the following:

1. Develop books, Internet-based material, and programs to provide internships, scholarships, and other quality initiatives for students.
2. Allow time in my personal life to eat well, run five days a week, and spend quality time with family and friends. Allow time daily for quiet reflection and spiritual devotion.

In the same way that Carol's goals are tailored to her personality and interests, your goals should reflect who you are. Personal missions and goals are as unique as each individual. Continuing the previous example, you might adopt these goals for the coming year:

- I will learn to navigate the Internet and research topics on-line.
- I will look for a part-time job with a local newspaper or newsroom.

Setting Short-Term Goals

When you divide your long-term goals into smaller, manageable goals that you hope to accomplish within a relatively short time, you are setting *short-term goals*. Short-term goals narrow your focus, helping you to maintain your progress toward your long-term goals. Say you have set the long-term goals you just read in the previous section. To stay on track toward those goals, you may want to accomplish these short-term goals in the next six months:

- I will write an assigned paper using information found on the Internet.
- I will make an effort to ask instructors and advisors for advice on how to get into the news business.

These same goals can be broken down into even smaller parts, such as the following one-month goals:

- I will learn to do research on the Internet using search directories.
- I will have lunch with someone in the news business so that I can learn about his or her experience.

In addition to monthly goals, you may have short-term goals that extend for a week, a day, or even a couple of hours in a given day. Take the Internet research goal. Such short-term goals may include the following:

- By the end of today: Find out what the major search directories are.
- One week from now: Read an Internet guide book to learn how to use search directories effectively.
- Two weeks from now: Experiment with search directories to see which ones will be most useful to me.
- Three weeks from now: Research my topic using the two search directories that have the most helpful information.

As you consider your long- and short-term goals, notice how all of your goals are linked to one another. As Figure 3.1 shows, your long-term goals establish a context for the short-term goals. In turn, your short-term goals make the long-term goals seem clearer and more reachable.

Setting Different Kinds of Goals

People have many different goals, involving different parts of life and different values. School is currently a focus in your life, and when you read Chapter 1 you began to examine your educational goals. Because you are more than just a student, you have other kinds of goals as well. As you consider these goals, remember that many of your goals are interconnected—a school goal is often a step toward a career goal and can affect a personal goal as well.

Career Goals

Consider the following factors when thinking about career goals (you explore this topic in more detail in Chapter 11).

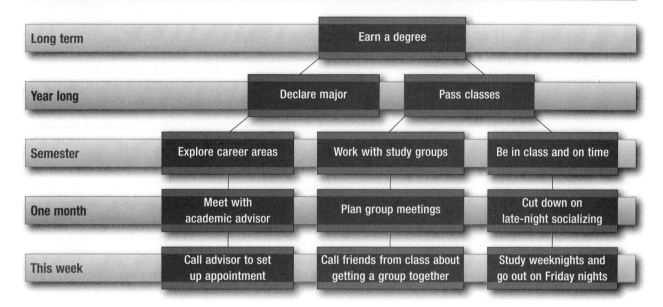

Figure 3.1 Goals reinforce one another.

Long term		Earn a degree	
Year long	Declare major	Pass classes	
Semester	Explore career areas	Work with study groups	Be in class and on time
One month	Meet with academic advisor	Plan group meetings	Cut down on late-night socializing
This week	Call advisor to set up appointment	Call friends from class about getting a group together	Study weeknights and go out on Friday nights

- The job you want after you graduate—duties and level of responsibility (e.g., manager, supervisor, independent contractor, business owner), hours, coworkers, salary, commuting distance, industry, company size, location.
- Career areas that reflect your strongest and most important values.
- Financial goals—how much money you are aiming for to pay your bills, live comfortably, and save for the future.

Personal Goals

Consider personal goals in terms of self, family, and lifestyle.

- Yourself—examine who you are and who you want to be (character, personality, health/fitness, values, and conduct).
- Family—whether you want to stay single, be married, be a parent, or increase a family you've already started, and what kind of relationship you want with family members.
- Lifestyle—where and with whom you want to live, in what kind of home, how you want to participate in your community, and what you want to do in your leisure time.

Even though your academic goals may seem like they take top priority at the moment, it's important to put them in the context of your goals in all life areas because goals are interconnected. You may want to graduate on a particular date—but not meeting a personal health goal may result in a problem that gets in the way. You might want to major in a particular subject—but thinking over your career goals may show you that your values and skills don't match up well with that subject. Keeping everything in mind helps you make better choices for yourself.

Achieving goals becomes easier when you are realistic about what is possible. Setting priorities helps you make that distinction.

Prioritizing Goals

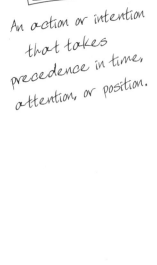

PRIORITY

An action or intention that takes precedence in time, attention, or position.

When you set a priority, you identify what's important at any given moment. Prioritizing helps you focus on your most important goals, especially when the important ones are the most difficult. Human nature often leads people to tackle easy goals first and leave the tough ones for later. The risk is that you might never reach for goals that are crucial to your success.

Consider the following when setting priorities:

- *Your values.* Think about your values and personal mission: Which major life goals are more important than all others? Look at your school, career, and personal goals. Do one or two of these paths take priority for you right now? In any path, which goals take priority?

- *Your relationships with others.* For example, if you are a parent, your children's needs are probably a priority. You may be in school so you can give them a better life, and you may arrange your schedule so that you can spend time with them. If you are in a committed relationship, you may arrange your work shifts so that you and your partner are home together as often as possible.

- *Your time.* The next section helps you get a handle on how to map out your days so that you accomplish as much as you can. Your schedule affects your priorities because some days you just won't have enough time to do all that you want to do. Depending on how much time that day's goals take, you might prioritize based on what you can fit in.

You are a unique individual, and your priorities are yours alone. What may be top priority to someone else may not mean that much to you, and vice versa. You can see this in Figure 3.2, which compares the priorities of two very different students. Each student's priorities are listed in order, with the first priority at the top and the lowest priority at the bottom.

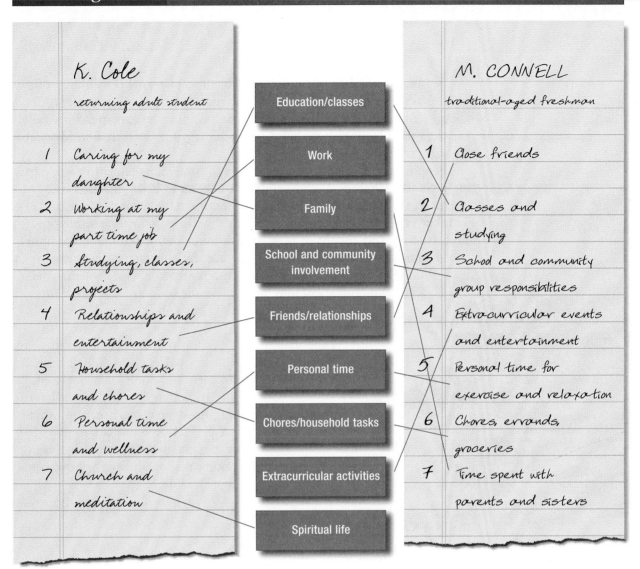

Figure 3.2 Different people, different priorities.

K. Cole
returning adult student

1. Caring for my daughter
2. Working at my part time job
3. Studying, classes, projects
4. Relationships and entertainment
5. Household tasks and chores
6. Personal time and wellness
7. Church and meditation

Education/classes

Work

Family

School and community involvement

Friends/relationships

Personal time

Chores/household tasks

Extracurricular activities

Spiritual life

M. CONNELL
traditional-aged freshman

1. Close friends
2. Classes and studying
3. School and community group responsibilities
4. Extracurricular events and entertainment
5. Personal time for exercise and relaxation
6. Chores, errands, groceries
7. Time spent with parents and sisters

Setting priorities moves you closer to accomplishing specific goals. It also helps you begin planning to achieve your goals within specific time frames. Being able to achieve your goals is directly linked to effective time management. In fact, the main goal of time management is to facilitate the achievement of your goals.

How can you *manage* your *time?*

Time is one of your most valuable and precious resources; your responsibility and potential for success lie in how you use yours. You cannot change how time passes, but you can spend it wisely. Efficient time management helps you achieve your goals in a steady, step-by-step process.

People have a variety of approaches to time management. Your learning style (see Chapter 2) can help you understand how you use time. For example, students with strong logical–mathematical intelligence and Thinker types tend to organize activities within a framework of time. Because they stay aware of how long it takes them to do something or travel somewhere, they are usually prompt. By contrast, Adventurer types and less logical learners with perhaps stronger visual or interpersonal intelligences may neglect details such as how much time they have to complete a task. They can often be late without meaning to be.

Time management, like physical fitness, is a lifelong pursuit. No one can plan a perfect schedule or build a terrific physique and then be "done." Throughout your life, your ability to manage your time will vary with your stress level, how busy you are, and other factors. Don't expect perfection—just do your best and keep working at it. Time management involves building a schedule, taking responsibility for how you spend your time, and being flexible.

Build a Schedule

Just as a road map helps you travel from place to place, a schedule is a time-and-activity map that helps you get from the beginning of the day (or week, or month) to the end as smoothly as possible. Schedules help you gain control of your life in two ways: They allocate segments of time for the fulfillment of your daily, weekly, monthly, and longer-term goals, and they serve as a concrete reminder of tasks, events, due dates, responsibilities, and deadlines.

Keep a Planner

Gather the tools of the trade: a pen or pencil and a planner (sometimes called a date book). A planner is indispensable for keeping track of your time. Some of you have planners and may have used them for years. Others may have had no luck with them or have never tried. Even if you don't feel you would benefit from one, try it. Paul Timm says, "Most time management experts agree that rule number one in a thoughtful planning process is: Use some form of a planner where you can write things down."[3]

There are two major types of planners. The day-at-a-glance version devotes a page to each day. Although it gives you ample space to write

These strategies help you find effective ways to tame your jumble of responsibilities through time management.

INTELLIGENCE	SUGGESTED STRATEGIES	WHAT WORKS FOR YOU? WRITE NEW IDEAS HERE
Verbal–Linguistic	■ Carry a small calendar and to-do list. Try carrying a small cassette recorder and dictate important scheduling. ■ Write out your main weekly priorities. Looking at what is stressful and what inspires confidence, make adjustments.	
Logical–Mathematical	■ Schedule time each day to organize and plan your tasks. Develop a logical system for indicating priority. ■ Compute how many hours a week you spend studying, working, having fun, and doing extracurricular activities. Evaluate the balance and make any necessary changes.	
Bodily–Kinesthetic	■ Schedule classes so that you have time in between to exercise or to take a long walk from one class to the next. ■ Create a schedule for the month. Take an exercise break. Come back and write your goals for this week and today.	
Visual–Spatial	■ Create your daily schedule and to-do lists using think links or other visual organizers. ■ Use wall calendars or charts to map out goals for the week and month, using different colors for different tasks/goals.	
Interpersonal	■ Involve someone in your goal achievement—make a commitment to someone to complete a step toward a goal. ■ Discuss monthly goals with friends. Ask them to evaluate whether they are too ambitious or not ambitious enough.	
Intrapersonal	■ Schedule quiet time each day to reflect on your priorities and upcoming tasks. ■ Each week, sit alone and write down that week's scheduling challenges. Brainstorm three productive ways you can deal with these challenges.	
Musical	■ Make time in your schedule for music—listen to CDs, go to a concert, play an instrument.	
Naturalistic	■ Try to schedule some time outside each day. ■ Sit outside where you feel relaxed. In this state of mind, plan out your schedule for the next week and month.	

the day's activities, it's harder to see what's ahead. The week-at-a-glance book gives you a view of the week's plans but has less room to write per day. If you write detailed daily plans, you might like the day-at-a-glance version. If you prefer to remind yourself of plans ahead of time, try the book that shows a week's schedule all at once. Some planners contain sections for monthly and yearly goals.

Another option is an electronic planner or personal digital assistant (PDA) that can hold a large amount of information. You can use it to schedule your days and weeks, make to-do lists, and create and store an address book. Electronic planners are powerful, convenient, and often fun. However, they certainly cost more than the paper version, and you can lose important data if something goes wrong with the computer inside. Evaluate your options and decide what works best for you.

Link Daily and Weekly Goals with Long-Term Goals

After you evaluate what you need to accomplish in the coming year, semester, month, week, and day to reach your long-term goals, use your schedule to record those steps. Write down the short-term goals that will enable you to stay on track. Here is how a student might map out two different goals over a year's time:

This year:	Complete enough courses to maintain class standing. Improve my physical fitness.
This semester:	Complete my biology class with a B average or higher. Lose 10 pounds and exercise regularly.
This month:	Set up biology study group schedule to coincide with quizzes. Begin walking and lifting weights.
This week:	Meet with study group; go over material for Friday's quiz. Go for a fitness walk three times; go to weight room twice.
Today:	Go over Chapter 3 in biology text. Walk for 40 minutes.

To manage your time so that you stay on top of your goals, you need to focus first on scheduling the most immediate, smaller goals—what you do on a daily and weekly basis. Scheduling daily and weekly goals, or tasks, that tie in to your long-term goals lends the following benefits:

- increased meaning for your daily activities
- a greater chance of achieving long-term goals
- a sense of order and progress

For college students, as well as working people, the week is often the easiest unit of time to consider at one shot. Weekly goal setting and planning allows you to keep track of day-to-day activities while giving you the larger perspective of what is coming up during the week. Take some time before each week starts to remind yourself of your long-term goals. Keeping long-term goals in mind helps you determine related short-term goals you can accomplish during the week to come.

Figure 3.3   Note daily and weekly tasks.

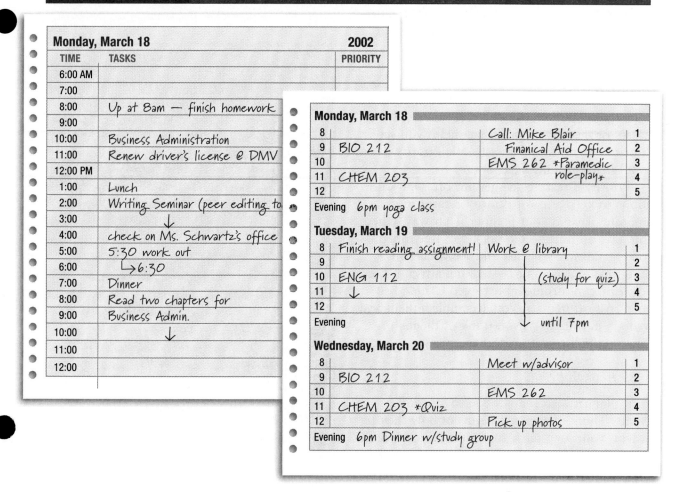

Figure 3.3 shows parts of a daily schedule and a weekly schedule.

Indicate Priority Levels

Prioritizing enables you to use your planner with maximum efficiency. On any given day, your goals have varying degrees of importance. Record your goals first, and then label them according to their level of importance using these categories: Priority 1, Priority 2, and Priority 3. Identify these categories by using any code that makes sense to you. Some people use numbers, as above. Some use letters (A, B, C). Some write activities in different colors according to priority level. Some use symbols (*, +, –).

- *Priority 1* activities are the most important and pressing things in your life. They may include attending class, completing school assignments, picking up a child from day care, and paying bills.

- *Priority 2* activities are part of your routine. Examples include a meeting of a school club, working out, a regular time you study at the library, grocery shopping, or cleaning. Priority 2 tasks are important but more flexible than Priority 1 tasks.

- *Priority 3* activities are those you would like to do but don't consider urgent, like a phone call or a night out. Many people don't enter Priority 3 tasks in their planners until they are sure they have time to get them done.

Prioritizing your activities is essential for two reasons. First, some activities are more important than others, and effective time management requires that you focus most of your energy on Priority 1 items. Second, looking at all of your priorities helps you plan when you can get things done. Often, it's not possible to get all of your Priority 1 activities done early in the day, especially if they involve scheduled classes or meetings. Prioritizing helps you set Priority 1 items and then schedule Priority 2 and 3 items around them as they fit.

Priority 3 tasks often get put off. One solution is to keep a list of Priority 3 tasks in a separate place in your planner. That way, when you have an unexpected pocket of free time, you can consult your list and see what you have time to accomplish—making a trip to the post office, returning a borrowed CD, and so on. Cross off items as you accomplish them and write in new items as you think of them. Rewrite the list when it gets too messy.

Keep Track of Events

Your planner also enables you to schedule events. Think of events in terms of how they tie in with your long-term goals, just as you would your other tasks. For example, being aware of quiz dates, due dates for assignments, and meeting dates helps reach your goals to achieve in school and become involved.

Note events in your planner so that you can stay aware of them ahead of time. Write them in daily, weekly, monthly, or even yearly sections, where a quick look will remind you that they are approaching. Writing them down also helps you see where they fit in the context of all your other activities. For example, if you have three big tests and a presentation all in one week, you'll want to take time in the weeks before to prepare for them.

Following are some kinds of events worth noting in your planner:

- due dates for papers, projects, presentations, and tests
- the details of your academic schedule, including semester and holiday breaks
- important meetings, medical appointments, or due dates for bill payments
- birthdays, anniversaries, social events, holidays, and other special occasions

PERSONAL TRIUMPH

*U*ncontrollable circumstances can lead to great obstacles. Scott Stoffel has found that such obstacles can be overcome with ambitious goals and enormous effort. Each person has a mountain to climb, and he is on the way to the top of his.

When it comes to his senses, Scott Stoffel is basically left with taste and smell. His parents discovered Scott was practically blind when he was 4 years old and kept getting hit in the face while playing catch. Fifteen years later, music became vague noise with no melody. The extremely rare genetic disorder that took most of his sight and hearing has also decreased the sensitivity in his fingers and his limbs; his thumbs hardly work, and he limps with a cane.

"Life is a testing ground—everyone has adversity to deal with," Mr. Stoffel, 32, wrote in an e-mail interview. "The point is to see who has the grit to overcome and who doesn't. And since my challenges seemed so indomitable, maybe that was a compliment, like saying I had something special down deep that could help me win a hopeless battle."

This month, Mr. Stoffel graduated, *magna cum laude*, from Temple University in Philadelphia, having pursued his degree in electrical engineering and computer science largely through independent study because he can neither see blackboards nor hear lectures. His senior project, a palm-read Braille device, is designed to help people who are deaf and blind with dull fingers like his own communicate better.

"I will never again look at a person with disabilities and say, you know what, I don't think he can do it," said John Helferty, Mr. Stoffel's mentor and department chairman.

"When the hearing caved in, it was like my whole life just came to an end," Mr. Stoffel recalled. So, he quit his job selling computers and hid out in his parents' basement in Connecticut for a few years, writing science fiction and designing computer games. In 1994, he started rehabilitation at the Helen Keller National Center on Long Island, and later he took writing classes at Hofstra University. In 1998, he switched to Temple, and to engineering, seeing technology as

Scott Stoffel, Graduate of Temple University, Philadelphia, Pennsylvania

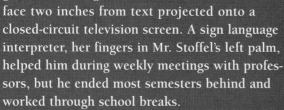

a potential savior for people with disabilities (and a lucrative profession for him).

He got migraines reading 15 hours a day, using large magnifying glasses or sitting with his face two inches from text projected onto a closed-circuit television screen. A sign language interpreter, her fingers in Mr. Stoffel's left palm, helped him during weekly meetings with professors, but he ended most semesters behind and worked through school breaks.

The palm-read Braille device is a 9-inch by 5-inch by 4-inch wooden box with six pins that pop up and down, controlled by a computer program to form Braille characters people can feel with body parts other than fingertips. It cost less than $400 to make.

Professor Helferty taught about half of Mr. Stoffel's courses himself, urged colleagues to accommodate him, and constructed the hardware for the Braille device because his student could not.

"When I see somebody with his aspirations, his commitment and his drive, I have to step up to the plate too and say we're in this journey together," Mr. Helferty said. "You're climbing Mount Everest and I'm your Sherpa guide and I'm going to go every inch with you."

Now Mr. Stoffel—who lives in North Wales, Pennsylvania, with his wife, Sandra, a woman he met at Helen Keller who also has limited sight and hearing—is job searching, eager to have his $474 monthly disability payments cut off and start working on his debt.

"Planting the flag at the top of the mountain," Mr. Helferty said, "will be getting the job."

Take a moment to consider . . .

- *How this story gives you perspective on your own abilities and limitations.*

- *What goal for you is worth a great deal of effort and difficulty to attain.*

- benchmarks for steps toward a goal, such as due dates for sections of a project

Take Responsibility for How You Spend Your Time

No matter what restrictions your circumstances create, you are in charge of choosing how to manage them. When you plan your activities with your most important goals in mind, you are taking responsibility for how you live. Use the following strategies:

Plan your schedule each week. Before each week starts, note events, goals, and priorities. Decide where to fit activities like studying and Priority 3 items. For example, if you have a test on Thursday, you can plan study sessions on the preceding days. If you have more free time on Tuesday and Friday than on other days, you can plan workouts or Priority 3 activities at those times. Looking at the whole week will help you avoid being surprised by something you had forgotten was coming up.

Make and use to-do lists. Use a *to-do list* to record the things you want to accomplish. If you generate a daily or weekly to-do list on a separate piece of paper, you can look at all tasks and goals at once. This helps you consider time frames and priorities. You might want to prioritize your tasks and transfer them to appropriate places in your planner. Some people create daily to-do lists right on their planner pages. You can tailor a to-do list to an important event, such as exam week, or an especially busy day. This kind of specific to-do list can help you prioritize and accomplish an unusually large task load.

Make thinking about time a priority. Take a few minutes a day to plan. Although making a schedule takes time, it can mean hours of saved time later. Say you have two errands to run, both on the other side of town; not planning ahead could result in driving across town twice in one day. Also, when you take time to write out your schedule, be sure to carry it with you and check it throughout the day. Find a planner size you like—there are books that fit into your briefcase, your bag, or even your pocket.

Post monthly and yearly calendars at home. Keeping a calendar on the wall helps you stay aware of important events. You can purchase one or draw it yourself, month by month, on plain paper. Use a yearly or a monthly version (Figure 3.4 shows a monthly calendar), and keep it where you can refer to it often. If you live with family or friends, make the calendar a group project so that you stay aware of each other's plans. Knowing each other's schedules can also help you avoid problems such as two people needing the car at the same time.

"Even if you're on the right track, you'll get run over if you just sit there."

WILL ROGERS

Schedule down time. When you're wiped out from too much activity, you don't have the energy to accomplish as much. For example, you've probably experienced one of those study sessions during which, at a certain point, you realize that you haven't absorbed anything for the last hour. Prioritize a little down time to refresh you and improve your attitude. Even half an hour a day helps. Fill the time with whatever relaxes you—reading, watching television, chatting on-line, playing a game or sport, walking, writing, or just doing nothing.

DOWN TIME

Quiet time set aside for relaxation and low-key activity.

Figure 3.4   Keep track with a monthly calendar.

APRIL

SUNDAY	MONDAY	TUESDAY	WEDNESDAY	THURSDAY	FRIDAY	SATURDAY
	1 WORK	2 Turn in English paper topic	3 Dentist 2pm	4 WORK	5	6
7 Frank's birthday	8 Psych Test 9am WORK	9	10 6:30 pm Meeting @ Student Ctr.	11 WORK	12	13 Dinner @ Ryan's
14	15 English paper due WORK	16 Western Civ paper—Library research	17	18 Library 6 p.m. WORK	19 Western Civ makeup class	20
21	22 WORK	23 2 p.m. meeting, psych group project	20 Start running program: 2 miles	25	26 WORK Run 2 miles	27
28 Run 3 miles	29 WORK	30 Western Civ paper due	31 Run 2 miles			

Be Flexible

No matter how well you plan your time, life changes can make you feel out of control. One minute you seem to be on track, and the next minute chaos hits. Coping with changes, whether minor (a room change for a class) or major (a medical emergency), can cause stress. As your stress level rises, your sense of control dwindles.

Although you cannot always choose your circumstances, you may have some control over how you handle them. Dr. Covey says that language is important when trying to take action. Using language like "I have to" and "They made me" robs you of personal power. For example, saying that you "have to" go to school can make you feel that others control your life. However, language like "I have decided to" and "I prefer" helps energize your power to choose. Then you can turn "I have to go to school" into "I choose to go to school rather than work in a dead-end job."

Use the following ideas to cope with changes large and small.

Day-to-Day Changes

Small changes can result in priority shifts that jumble your schedule. On Monday, a homework assignment due in a week might be Priority 2; then, if you haven't gotten to it by Saturday, it becomes Priority 1.

Think of change as part of life and you will be able to more effectively solve the dilemmas that come up. For changes that occur frequently, think through a backup plan ahead of time. For sudden changes, the best you can do is to keep an open mind about possibilities and to remember to call on your resources in a pinch. Your problem-solving skills (see Chapter 4) will help you build your ability to adjust to whatever changes come your way.

Life Changes

Sometimes changes are more serious than a class schedule shift. Your car breaks down; your relationship falls apart; you fail a class; a family member develops a medical problem; you get laid off. Such changes call for more extensive problem solving. They also require an ability to look at the big picture. Although a class change affects your schedule for a day, a medical problem may affect your schedule for much longer.

When life hands you a major curve ball, sit down (ideally with someone whose opinion you trust) and lay out your options. Explore all of the potential effects before making a decision (again, the problem-solving and decision-making skills in Chapter 4 will serve you well here). Finally, make full use of your school resources. Your academic advisor, counselor, dean, financial aid advisor, and instructors may have ideas and assistance to offer you—but they can only help if you let them know what you need.

No matter how well you manage time, you will have moments when it's hard to stay in control. Knowing how to identify and avoid procrastination and other time traps helps you get back on track.

Why is *procrastination* a problem?

Procrastination occurs when you postpone tasks. People procrastinate for different reasons. Having trouble with goal setting is one reason. People may project goals too far into the future, set unrealistic goals that are too frustrating to reach, or have no goals at all. People also procrastinate because they don't believe in their ability to complete a task or don't believe in themselves in general. Procrastination is human, and not every instance of procrastination means trouble. If it is taken to the extreme, however, procrastination can develop into a habit that causes problems at school, on the job, and at home.

PROCRASTINATION

The act of putting off a task until another time.

Jane B. Burka and Lenora M. Yuen, authors of *Procrastination: Why You Do It and What To Do About It,* say that habitual procrastinators are often perfectionists who create problems by using their ability to achieve as the only measure of their self-worth: "The performance becomes the only measure of the person; nothing else is taken into account. An outstanding performance means an outstanding person; a mediocre performance means a mediocre person."[4] For the procrastinator, the fear of failure prevents taking the risk that could bring success.

People also procrastinate in order to avoid the truth about what they are capable of achieving. "As long as you procrastinate, you never have to confront the real limits of your ability, whatever those limits are," say Burka and Yuen.[5] If you procrastinate—and fail—you can blame the failure on waiting too long or on other problems that crop up while you wait to act, not on any personal challenge or shortcoming. This might help you feel good about yourself in the short run. If you never give yourself the chance to succeed, however, you won't discover how to improve on your challenges in a lasting way—and, even more unfortunately, you will never find out how far your abilities can take you.

Anti-procrastination Strategies

Following are some ways to fight procrastination:

Look at the effects of procrastinating versus not procrastinating. What rewards lie ahead if you get it done? What are the effects if you continue to put it off? Which situation has better effects? Chances are you will benefit more in the long term from facing the task head-on.

Set reasonable goals. Plan your goals carefully, allowing enough time to complete them. Unreasonable goals can be so intimidating that you do nothing at all. "Pay off the credit card bill next month" could throw you. However, "Pay off the credit card bill in 10 months" might inspire you to take action.

Break the task into smaller parts. Look at the task in terms of its parts. How can you approach it step by step? If you can concentrate on achieving one small goal at a time, the task may become less of a burden. In addition, setting concrete time limits for each task may help you feel more in control.

Get started whether or not you "feel like it." Going from doing nothing to doing something is often the hardest part of avoiding procrastination. The motivation techniques from Chapter 1 might help you take the first step. Once you start, you may find it easier to continue.

Ask for help. You don't always have to go it alone. For example, if you avoid a project because you dislike the student with whom you have to work, talk to your instructor about adjusting tasks or group assignments. Once you identify what's holding you up, see who can help you face the task.

Shake off the judgments of others. A student who feels that her instructor doesn't like her, for example, might avoid studying for that course. Instead of letting judgments like these lead you to procrastinate, choose actions that put you in control. If you have trouble with an instructor, address the problem with that instructor directly and try to make the most of your time in the course.

Don't expect perfection. No one is perfect. Most people learn by starting at the beginning and wading through plenty of mistakes and confusion. It's better to try your best than to do nothing at all.

Reward yourself. The reward that lies at the end of a long road to a goal may be great, but while you are on the way, it may not always be enough to motivate you. Find ways to boost your mood when you accomplish a particular task along the way. Remind yourself—with a break, a movie, some kind of treat that you like—that you are making successful progress.

Procrastination can cause you problems if you let it get the best of you. When it does happen, take some time to think about the causes. What is it about this situation that frightens you or puts you off? Answering that question can help you address what causes lie underneath the procrastination. These causes might indicate a deeper issue that you can address.

Other Time Traps to Avoid

Procrastination isn't the only way to spend your time in less-than-productive ways. Keep an eye out for these situations too.

Saying yes when you don't have the time. First, think before you respond. Ask yourself what effects a new responsibility will have on your schedule. If it will cause you more trouble than it seems to be worth, say no graciously.

Studying at a bad time of day. When you are tired, you may need extra time to fully understand your material. If you study when you are most alert, you can take in more information in less time.

Studying in a distracting location. Find an environment that helps you maximize study time. If you need to be alone to concentrate, for example, studying near others might interfere with your focus. Conversely, people who require a busier environment to stay alert might choose a more active setting.

> "I have always thought that one man of tolerable abilities may work great changes, and accomplish great affairs among mankind, if he first forms a good plan."
>
> **BENJAMIN FRANKLIN**

Not thinking ahead. Forgetting important things is a big time drain. One book left at home can cost you extra time going back and forth. Five minutes of scheduling before your day starts can save you hours.

Not curbing your social time. You plan to make a quick telephone call, but the next thing you know you've been talking for an hour, losing sleep or study time. Don't cut out all socializing, but stay aware. Smart choices have results that boost your self-respect.

Taking on too many tasks and projects. You may feel overwhelmed by all that you want to accomplish in your life. See what tasks you can reasonably delegate to others. No one can take a test for you, but another day-care parent could pick up your child on a day when your time runs short.

Of course no one is going to be able to avoid all of these time traps all of the time. Do the best that you can. The first step is an awareness of your particular tendencies. Once you know how you tend to procrastinate and waste time, you can take steps to change your habits. Time is your ally—make the most of the time that you have.

In Hebrew, this word, pronounced "chai," means "life," representing all aspects of life—spiritual, emotional, family, educational, and career. Individual Hebrew characters have number values. Because the characters in the word *chai* add up to 18, the number 18 has come to be associated with good luck. The word *chai* is often worn as a good luck charm. As you plan your goals, think about your view of luck. Many people feel that a person can create his or her own luck by pursuing goals persistently and staying open to possibilities and opportunities.

Consider that your vision of life may largely determine how you live. You can prepare the way for luck by establishing a personal mission and forging ahead toward your goals. If you believe that the life you want awaits you, you will be able to recognize and make the most of luck when it comes around. *L'chaim*—to life, and good luck.

Building Skills
FOR COLLEGE, CAREER, AND LIFE SUCCESS

Critical Thinking *Applying Learning to Life*

Your Values

Begin to explore your values by rating the following values on a scale from 1 to 4, 1 being least important to you and 4 being most important. If you have values that you don't see in the chart, list and rate them in the blank spaces on the next page.

VALUE	RATING	VALUE	RATING
Knowing yourself		Mental health	
Physical health		Fitness/exercise	
Spending time with family		Close friendships	
Helping others		Education	
Being well paid		Being employed	
Being liked by others		Free time/vacations	
Enjoying entertainment		Time to yourself	
Spiritual/religious life		Reading	
Keeping up with news		Staying organized	
Financial stability		Intimate relationship	
Creative/artistic pursuits		Self-improvement	
Lifelong learning		Facing your fears	

(continued)

Considering your priorities, write your top five values here:

1. _____

2. _____

3. _____

4. _____

5. _____

Select one value and evaluate it in a few sentences. What is its main source? Do you feel it is a positive value for you, or not, and why? How does this value guide your choices?

_____

_____

_____

_____

_____

_____

_____

_____

_____

_____

Short-Term Scheduling

Take a close look at your schedule for the coming month, including events, important dates, and steps toward goals. On the calendar layout on the next page, check the name of the month and fill in appropriate numbers for the days. Then, record what you hope to accomplish, including the following:

- due dates for papers, projects, and presentations
- test dates
- important meetings, medical appointments, and due dates for bill payments
- birthdays, anniversaries, and other special occasions
- steps toward long-term goals

This kind of chart helps you see the monthly "big picture." To stay on target from day to day, check these dates against the entries in your date book and make sure that they are indicated there as well.

JANUARY FEBRUARY MARCH APRIL MAY JUNE JULY AUGUST SEPTEMBER OCTOBER NOVEMBER DECEMBER

Sunday	Monday	Tuesday	Wednesday	Thursday	Friday	Saturday

Discover How You Spend Your Time

In the table below, estimate the total time you think you spend per week on each listed activity. Then, add the hours. If your number is over 168 (the number of hours in a week), rethink your estimates and recalculate so that the total is equal to or below 168. Then, subtract your total from 168. Whatever is left over is your estimate of hours that you spend in unscheduled activities.

ACTIVITY	ESTIMATED TIME SPENT
Class	
Work	
Studying	
Sleeping	
Eating	
Family time/child care	
Commuting/traveling	
Chores and personal business	
Friends and important relationships	
Telephone time	
Leisure/entertainment	
Spiritual life	
Total	

Now, spend a week recording exactly how you spend your time. The chart on pages 96–97 has blocks showing half-hour increments. As you go through the week, write in what you do each hour, indicating when you started and when you stopped. Don't forget activities that don't feel like "activities" such as sleeping, relaxing, and watching TV. Also, be honest—record your actual activities instead of how you want to spend your time or how you think you should have spent your time. There are no wrong answers.

After a week, go through the chart and look at how many hours you actually spent on the activities for which you estimated your hours before. Tally the hours in the boxes in the following table using straight tally marks; round off to half hours and use a short tally mark for each half hour. In the third column, total the hours for each activity. Leave the "Ideal Time in Hours" column blank for now.

ACTIVITY	TIME TALLIED OVER ONE-WEEK PERIOD	TOTAL TIME IN HOURS	IDEAL TIME IN HOURS
Example: Class	⊪⊪⊪⊪⊪⊪ ⎮⎮	16.5	
Class			
Work			
Studying			
Sleeping			
Eating			
Family time/child care			
Commuting/traveling			
Chores and personal business			
Friends and important relationships			
Telephone time			
Leisure/entertainment			
Spiritual life			
Other			

Add the totals in the third column to find your grand total. Compare your grand total to your estimated grand total; compare your actual activity hour totals to your estimated activity hour totals. What matches and what doesn't? Describe the most interesting similarities and differences.

_____

_____

_____

What is the one biggest surprise about how you spend your time?

_____

_____

_____

Name one change you would like to make in how you spend your time.

_____

_____

_____

Monday		Tuesday		Wednesday		Thursday	
TIME	ACTIVITY	TIME	ACTIVITY	TIME	ACTIVITY	TIME	ACTIVITY
5:00 AM		5:00 AM		5:00 AM		5:00 AM	
5:30 AM		5:30 AM		5:30 AM		5:30 AM	
6:00 AM		6:00 AM		6:00 AM		6:00 AM	
6:30 AM		6:30 AM		6:30 AM		6:30 AM	
7:00 AM		7:00 AM		7:00 AM		7:00 AM	
7:30 AM		7:30 AM		7:30 AM		7:30 AM	
8:00 AM		8:00 AM		8:00 AM		8:00 AM	
8:30 AM		8:30 AM		8:30 AM		8:30 AM	
9:00 AM		9:00 AM		9:00 AM		9:00 AM	
9:30 AM		9:30 AM		9:30 AM		9:30 AM	
10:00 AM		10:00 AM		10:00 AM		10:00 AM	
10:30 AM		10:30 AM		10:30 AM		10:30 AM	
11:00 AM		11:00 AM		11:00 AM		11:00 AM	
11:30 AM		11:30 AM		11:30 AM		11:30 AM	
12:00 PM		12:00 PM		12:00 PM		12:00 PM	
12:30 PM		12:30 PM		12:30 PM		12:30 PM	
1:00 PM		1:00 PM		1:00 PM		1:00 PM	
1:30 PM		1:30 PM		1:30 PM		1:30 PM	
2:00 PM		2:00 PM		2:00 PM		2:00 PM	
2:30 PM		2:30 PM		2:30 PM		2:30 PM	
3:00 PM		3:00 PM		3:00 PM		3:00 PM	
3:30 PM		3:30 PM		3:30 PM		3:30 PM	
4:00 PM		4:00 PM		4:00 PM		4:00 PM	
4:30 PM		4:30 PM		4:30 PM		4:30 PM	
5:00 PM		5:00 PM		5:00 PM		5:00 PM	
5:30 PM		5:30 PM		5:30 PM		5:30 PM	
6:00 PM		6:00 PM		6:00 PM		6:00 PM	
6:30 PM		6:30 PM		6:30 PM		6:30 PM	
7:00 PM		7:00 PM		7:00 PM		7:00 PM	
7:30 PM		7:30 PM		7:30 PM		7:30 PM	
8:00 PM		8:00 PM		8:00 PM		8:00 PM	
8:30 PM		8:30 PM		8:30 PM		8:30 PM	
9:00 PM		9:00 PM		9:00 PM		9:00 PM	
9:30 PM		9:30 PM		9:30 PM		9:30 PM	
10:00 PM		10:00 PM		10:00 PM		10:00 PM	
10:30 PM		10:30 PM		10:30 PM		10:30 PM	
11:00 PM		11:00 PM		11:00 PM		11:00 PM	
11:30 PM		11:30 PM		11:30 PM		11:30 PM	

Friday		Saturday		Sunday		Notes
TIME	ACTIVITY	TIME	ACTIVITY	TIME	ACTIVITY	
5:00 AM		5:00 AM		5:00 AM		
5:30 AM		5:30 AM		5:30 AM		
6:00 AM		6:00 AM		6:00 AM		
6:30 AM		6:30 AM		6:30 AM		
7:00 AM		7:00 AM		7:00 AM		
7:30 AM		7:30 AM		7:30 AM		
8:00 AM		8:00 AM		8:00 AM		
8:30 AM		8:30 AM		8:30 AM		
9:00 AM		9:00 AM		9:00 AM		
9:30 AM		9:30 AM		9:30 AM		
10:00 AM		10:00 AM		10:00 AM		
10:30 AM		10:30 AM		10:30 AM		
11:00 AM		11:00 AM		11:00 AM		
11:30 AM		11:30 AM		11:30 AM		
12:00 PM		12:00 PM		12:00 PM		
12:30 PM		12:30 PM		12:30 PM		
1:00 PM		1:00 PM		1:00 PM		
1:30 PM		1:30 PM		1:30 PM		
2:00 PM		2:00 PM		2:00 PM		
2:30 PM		2:30 PM		2:30 PM		
3:00 PM		3:00 PM		3:00 PM		
3:30 PM		3:30 PM		3:30 PM		
4:00 PM		4:00 PM		4:00 PM		
4:30 PM		4:30 PM		4:30 PM		
5:00 PM		5:00 PM		5:00 PM		
5:30 PM		5:30 PM		5:30 PM		
6:00 PM		6:00 PM		6:00 PM		
6:30 PM		6:30 PM		6:30 PM		
7:00 PM		7:00 PM		7:00 PM		
7:30 PM		7:30 PM		7:30 PM		
8:00 PM		8:00 PM		8:00 PM		
8:30 PM		8:30 PM		8:30 PM		
9:00 PM		9:00 PM		9:00 PM		
9:30 PM		9:30 PM		9:30 PM		
10:00 PM		10:00 PM		10:00 PM		
10:30 PM		10:30 PM		10:30 PM		
11:00 PM		11:00 PM		11:00 PM		
11:30 PM		11:30 PM		11:30 PM		

Think about what kinds of changes might help you improve your ability to set and achieve goals. Ask yourself important questions about what you do daily, weekly, and monthly. On what activities do you think you should spend more or less time? Go back to the table on page 95 and fill in the "Ideal Time in Hours" column. Consider the difference between actual hours and ideal hours when you think about the changes you want to make in your life.

To-Do Lists

Make a to-do list for what you have to do tomorrow. Include all tasks—Priority 1, 2, and 3—and events. Use a coding system of your choice to indicate priority level of both tasks and events. Use this list to make your schedule for tomorrow in the date book, making a separate list for Priority 3 items. At the end of the day, evaluate this system—did the list make a difference? If you liked it, use this exercise as a guide for using to-do lists regularly.

TOMORROW'S DATE: _____

1. _____   7. _____
2. _____   8. _____
3. _____   9. _____
4. _____   10. _____
5. _____   11. _____
6. _____   12. _____

Your Procrastination Habits

Name one situation in which you habitually procrastinate.

_____

_____

_____

What are the effects of this procrastination? Discuss how it may affect the quality of your work, motivation, productivity, ability to be on time, grades, or self-perception.

_____

_____

_____

What you would like to do differently in this situation? How can you achieve what you want?

_____

_____

_____

Teamwork *Combining Forces*

INDIVIDUAL PRIORITIES. In a group of three or four people, brainstorm long-term goals and have one member of the group write them down. From that list, pick out five goals that everyone can relate to most. Each group member should then take five minutes alone to evaluate the relative importance of the five goals and rank them in the order that he or she prefers, using a 1 to 5 scale with 1 being the highest priority and 5 the lowest.

Display the rankings of each group member side by side. How many different orders are there? Discuss why each person has a different set of priorities and be open to different views. What factors in different people's lives have caused them to select particular rankings? If you have time, discuss how priorities have changed for each group member over the course of a year, perhaps by having each person re-rank the goals according to his or her needs a year ago.

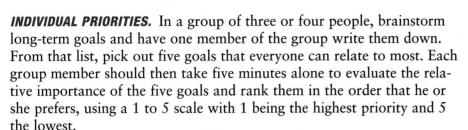

Writing *Discovery Through Journaling*

To record your thoughts, use a separate journal or the lined page at the end of the chapter.

PERSONAL MISSION STATEMENT. Using the personal mission statement examples in the chapter as a guide, consider what you want out of your life and create your own personal mission statement. You can write it in paragraph form, in a list of long-term goals, or in a visual format such as a think link (see Chapter 6 for information on think links). Take as much time as you need in order to be as complete as possible. Draft your statement on a separate sheet of paper and take time to revise it. If it is in written form, rewrite the final version on the journal page.

Career Portfolio *Charting Your Course*

CAREER GOALS AND PRIORITIES. The most reasonable and reachable career goals are ones that are linked with your school and life goals. First, name a personal long-term career goal.

_____

_____

_____

Then, imagine that you will begin working toward it. Indicate a series of smaller goals—from short-term to long-term—that you feel will help you achieve this goal. Write what you hope to accomplish in the next year, the next six months, and the next month.

_____

_____

_____

Now, explore your job priorities. How do you want your job to benefit you? Note your requirements in each of the following areas.

Duties and responsibilities

_____

_____

Salary and benefits

_____

_____

Hours (part-time vs. full-time)

_____

_____

Job requirements (e.g., travel, location)

_____

_____

Industry or field

_____

_____

Flexibility

_____

_____

Affiliation with school or financial aid program

_____

_____

What kind of job, in the career area for which you listed your goals, might fit all or most of your requirements? List two possibilities here.

1._____

2._____

If you have access to the CD-ROM Strategies for Success, *use the following questions to assess your thoughts and enhance your understanding of the chapter. The questions below represent only some of the activities provided on the CD for the chapter topics—try others if you have time.*

Click on the Goal Setting and Time Management bookmark. Use the following activities to hone your goal setting and time management skills:

1. Take the pre-assessment to see how you perceive yourself as a goal setter and time manager.

2. Click on Activity One: Your Personal Mission Statement. Making sure your computer is on-line, click on the Franklin Covey link and read the material. In the field provided, write—or revise, if you have already created one—your own personal mission statement based on what you have learned.

3. Click on Activity Two: Prioritizing. Complete your priority list and then analyze it on the next screen. Think about whether your priorities reflect the goals that you consider most important.

4. Click on Activity Three: Journal Reflections. Think about, and type your response to, journal question number two—procrastination.

Suggested Readings

Covey, Stephen. *The Seven Habits of Highly Effective People.* New York: Simon & Schuster, 1995.

Emmett, Rita. *The Procrastinator's Handbook: Mastering the Art of Doing It Now.* New York: Walker & Co., 2000.

Gleeson, Kerry. *The Personal Efficiency Program: How To Get Organized to Do More Work in Less Time, 2nd ed.* New York: John Wiley & Sons, 2000.

Lakein, Alan. *How to Get Control of Your Time and Your Life.* New York: New American Library, 1996.

McGee-Cooper, Ann with Duane Trammell. *Time Management for Unmanageable People.* New York: Bantam Books, 1994.

Sapadin, Linda and Jack Maguire. *Beat Procrastination and Make the Grade: The Six Styles of Procrastination and How Students Can Overcome Them.* New York: Penguin USA, 1999.

Timm, Paul R. *Successful Self-management: A Psychologically Sound Approach to Personal Effectiveness.* Los Altos, CA: Crisp Publications, 1996.

Internet Resources

Mind Tools (section on time management): www.mindtools.com/page5.html

Top Achievement—goal setting and self-improvement resources: www.topachievement.com

Endnotes

1. Paul R. Timm, Ph.D., *Successful Self-Management: A Psychologically Sound Approach to Personal Effectiveness.* Los Altos, CA: Crisp Publications, Inc., 1987, pp. 22–41.

2. Stephen Covey, *The Seven Habits of Highly Effective People.* New York: Simon & Schuster, 1989, pp. 70–144, 309–318.

3. Timm, pp. 22–41.

4. Jane B. Burka, Ph.D. and Lenora M. Yuen, Ph.D., *Procrastination.* Reading, MA: Perseus Books, 1983, pp. 21–22.

5. Ibid.

JOURNAL

name   date

visit: www.prenhall.com/carter NY Times link for this chapter

Part I

DEFINING YOURSELF AND YOUR GOALS

Becoming a Better Test Taker

MULTIPLE CHOICE. Circle or highlight the answer that seems to fit best.

1. A *motivator* is
   A. the ability to achieve a goal.
   B. progress toward a goal.
   C. a decision to take action.
   D. a want or need that moves a person to action.

2. The direct benefits of responsibility include
   A. earning the trust of others at school, work, and home.
   B. getting motivated to achieve study goals.
   C. improved ability to plan strategically.
   D. moving up at work.

3. A *learning style* is
   A. the best way to learn when attending classes.
   B. a particular way of being intelligent.
   C. an affinity for a particular job choice or career area.
   D. a way in which the mind receives and processes information.

4. The best way to use learning-style assessments is to see them as
   A. a reference point rather than a label; a tool with which to see yourself more clearly.
   B. a road map for your life; a message that shows the paths you must take in order to be successful.
   C. a lesson about group learning; a way to find the group of learners with whom you work best.
   D. a definitive label for your working style; a clear-cut category where you fit.

5. When choosing and evaluating your values, it is important to
   A. set goals according to what your friends and family value.
   B. keep your values steady over time.
   C. reevaluate values periodically as you experience change.
   D. set aside values that no one else seems to think are good for you.

6. It is important to link daily and weekly goals with long-term goals because
   A. the process will help you focus on the things that are most important to you.
   B. short-term goals have no meaning if they are not placed in a longer time frame.
   C. the process will help you eliminate frivolous activities.
   D. others expect you to know how everything you do relates to what you want to accomplish in life.

FILL-IN-THE-BLANK. Complete the following sentences with the appropriate word(s) or phrase(s) that best reflect what you learned in the chapter. Choose from the items that follow each sentence.

1. When you make a _____, you do what you say you will do. (initiative, motivation, commitment)

2. Showing _____ helps you to take that first step toward a goal and respond to changes in your life. (motivation, initiative, integrity)

3. One way to look at learning style is to divide it into two equally important aspects: _____ and _____. (learning preferences/personality traits, verbal/visual, interests/abilities)

4. The best careers and majors for you are ones that take into consideration your _____ and _____. (references/contacts, learning style/abilities, interests/abilities)

5. Your _____ is a philosophy outlining what you want to be, what you want to do, and the principles by which you live. (responsibility, mission, integrity)

6. Being _____ helps you cope with day-to-day changes and life changes. (organized, flexible, on time)

ESSAY QUESTIONS. The following essay questions will help you organize and communicate your ideas in writing, just as you must do on an essay test. Before you begin answering a question, spend a few minutes planning (brainstorm possible approaches, write a thesis statement, jot down main thoughts in outline or think link form). To prepare yourself for actual test conditions, limit writing time to no more than 30 minutes per question.

1. Discuss habits, both good and bad. What are the effects of each? Describe a useful plan for changing a habit that is having negative effects.

2. Define *values* and *value system*. How do values develop, and what effect do they have on personal choices? How are values connected to goal setting? Give an example from your life of how values have influenced a personal goal.

PERSONAL TRIUMPH

Orlando Hernandez, pitcher, Major League Baseball

*a*n exceptional love for a sport, a talent to match, and a limitless drive led Orlando Hernandez to find a way to play baseball on his own terms. Keeping his goal in mind, he overcame daunting obstacles and arrived in a world where he could create the life he had envisioned.

Orlando "El Duque" Hernandez was born on Oct. 11, 1969. in Villa Clara, Cuba. As children, he and his younger half-brother Livan became well known locally for their talents at pitching a baseball. After years of developing their skills in the sport, both brothers were named to the Cuban national team soon after they graduated from high school. In international play with the team, Orlando put up an impressive record of 129 wins and 47 losses, prompting his countrymen to give him the nickname "El Duque." Both brothers were lucky enough to play with the team in the 1996 Olympics in Atlanta in which Cuba won the gold medal. This was to be the last victory the two brothers would share.

In 1996, during a Cuban national team trip to Mexico, Livan Hernandez defected to the United States and signed a contract with the Florida Marlins, with whom he would win the World Series that same year. Fidel Castro then banned Orlando from playing baseball for fear that he too was planning a defection, though Hernandez had no such plans at that time. Unable to play the game he loved, Orlando became a rehabilitation therapist at a psychiatric hospital. Before long, however, he sought to leave Cuba so that he could pursue his dream. On December 26, 1997, after being banned from the sport for a year, Hernandez and seven other Cubans boarded a small boat and headed north toward the United States seeking political asylum. The U.S. Coast Guard picked up their boat three days after they landed on the Caribbean island of Aguilla Cay.

Too anxious to wait for a U.S. visa to get back to his sport and profession, Orlando gained legal

residence in Costa Rica and was allowed to become a legal free agent in professional baseball in January 1998. At that point, he was signed by the New York Yankees and made his major league debut on June 3, 1998. The Yankees won the World Series that same year, making it the first time in major league history that two brothers pitched for the championship team in consecutive years. After the season, Hernandez was honored by being presented the Thurman Munson Award for his charity work and courage in his personal life as well as on the baseball diamond.

Orlando has had much success on the playing field since his transition to baseball in the United States. In 1999, he was chosen as the starter for the first game of the World Series, which he won in part by posting the most strikeouts by a Yankee since 1958. The Yankees would go on to their second straight championship. In the 2000 season, Hernandez was named as the opening day starter for the Yankees, making him the first foreign-born pitcher to start the season in the team's long history. New York won its third straight championship that year—with Orlando Hernandez as a pivotal ingredient in the success of the team. With great perseverance, El Duque has made his dream come alive.

Take a moment to consider . . .

- *What you love to do most, and what you would do in order to pursue it.*

- *What goal might make use of your abilities if you were prevented from pursuing your most important dream.*

Sources: www.mlb.com, http://espn.go.com, www.cnnsi.com

The Prentice Hall Supersite has a section entitled Majors Exploration. Go to www.prenhall.com/success and click on the Majors Exploration button. Choose one major that interests you and use the site to answer the following questions on a separate sheet of paper. If you have time and are interested in more than one major, explore two or three.

1. Name and describe the major.

2. For what careers does this major prepare you?

3. What classes do students typically need to take in order to graduate with this major? If your school has a Web site, visit it to determine the specific course requirements for this major and anything else you need to be accepted into the major (e.g., a specific grade point average).

4. Describe how your learning style and personality make you a good candidate for this major.

5. Draw up a plan of short-term and long-term goals that would help you succeed in your major. Your plan might include:

   • Courses you need to take as part of your major and your schedule for taking these courses during your time in college

   • Minimum grade point average needed to qualify for your major

   • Meetings with academic advisors or instructors

   • Organizations you could join that are relevant to the major

   • Internships that complement your major

   • Evaluating whether graduate school is necessary to pursue your chosen career

6. As you consider your major, start to think about financing your education. Using a search engine, locate two scholarships or grants that are available to students with your interests. Is this money available to students in undergraduate programs? Is additional money out there for graduate students?

Developing Your Learning Skills

In this chapter you explore answers to the following questions: • What is critical thinking? • How does critical thinking help you solve problems and make decisions? • How do you reason? • How can you open your mind to new perspectives? • Why plan strategically?

IN THIS CHAPTER

Critical and creative thinking

THE PROBLEM of getting the classes you need is just one of many faced by Edhilvia Campos (see next page) and college students everywhere. Solving that problem requires thinking through the situation and taking the steps that will bring the most positive effects— an excellent example of critical thinking.

Through the essential task of asking important questions about ideas and information, critical thinking enables your mind to process, store, and create. This chapter shows you that you think critically every day, helps you learn how your mind works when you think critically, and gives you the power to use critical-thinking processes to help you manage whatever life brings.

becoming an active learner

Edhilvia Campos, Parkland Community College, Champaign, Illinois

Shera Chantel Caviness,
Graduate, University of Memphis

How do I decide which classes I need?

Find an academic counselor in your field who can guide you . . .

Every semester it's a challenge to figure out the classes I need. I am majoring in microbiology, but the science courses I need aren't always available. Also, I eventually want to transfer to the University of Illinois. The processes for registering and figuring out what credits will transfer seem complicated.

When I came to the States for college, only a few of my math credits transferred because the math classes I had taken in high school in Venezuela were not acceptable. My freshman year I took two algebra classes and later found out that they couldn't be applied to my major. I may want to go back to Venezuela during the summers. I've considered taking classes then, but the Venezuelan universities don't really offer my major. Do you have suggestions for what I can do to make this process more efficient?

First and foremost, hang in there. I know that things seem hard now, but your efforts will pay off. Attending college is similar to a "micro" real world. Throughout college, you will have to face problems that must be solved. I understand that you feel you wasted time and money taking certain classes. But some classes are not always transferable, and unfortunately money has to be spent to take certain courses before entering a degree program.

To prepare to transfer, find an academic counselor at the University of Illinois (preferably one in your major) who can tell you what will transfer so that you will not have to repeat or take unnecessary classes. While at Parkland, find an academic counselor in your field who can guide you toward appropriate courses for that degree, and use the undergraduate catalog to stay informed of the necessary classes for your major. Get to know the professors in your field because they can help. If some classes are not available for one semester, gather at least 8 to 10 students to voice concern about opening a section. Professors are often unaware of the demand for certain courses because students do not speak up.

If you do plan to return to Venezuela for the summer, only take courses that will apply to your degree or take some general lower-division classes that are transferable. Make sure you check with the counselors at Parkland and the University of Illinois before signing up. All in all, keep your determination alive and do not let things discourage you. Always find something valuable within each course you take because this will help you become more well rounded. Remember to think positive; this is only a "micro" real-world experience, helping to prepare you for the R-E-A-L world.

What is *critical thinking?*

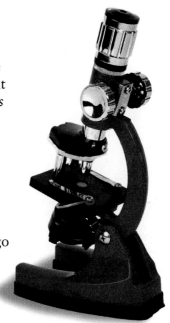

You may have heard the term "critical thinking" before. The meaning of "thinking" seems clear—so what, exactly, could "critical thinking" mean? Although you might assume that the word *critical* implies something difficult and negative, as it is used here it actually means "indispensable" and "important." *Critical thinking means finding that which is important.*

Consider the following definition of critical thinking:

> When you think critically, you take in information, examine its important aspects by asking questions about it, and then put what you have learned to use through thinking processes such as problem solving, decision making, reasoning, opening your mind to new perspectives, and planning strategically.

Questioning is at the heart of critical thinking because it allows you to go *beyond the basic recall of information.* When you think critically, you examine important aspects by asking questions.

Critical thinking brings you countless advantages, including:

- *Being able to apply knowledge.* Critical thinking moves you beyond repeating back what you know. For instance, it won't mean much for elementary education students to quote child development facts on an exam unless they can evaluate real children's needs in the classroom.

- *Being an innovator.* In class or on the job, you are valued if you look for ways to spur positive change and implement new ideas.

- *Building brain power.* Critical thinkers understand how their minds work—and they actively use their minds. Because thinking is a skill, the more you use it, the better you become.

You think critically now, in all kinds of ways—when you decide between two different courses by reading course descriptions and talking to your advisor, for example, or when you see that you need extra income and look for a job that fits your needs. You make these decisions by asking questions—What is the best course for me? What kind of job fits into my schedule?—and seeking answers.

The Path of Critical Thinking

Look at Figure 4.1 to see a visual representation of critical thinking. The critical-thinking path involves taking in information, examining it by asking questions, and then using it.

Taking in Information

Although most of this chapter focuses on questioning and using information, this first step is just as crucial. The information you receive and recall is your raw material. When you take in information accurately and without judgment, you have the best material with which to work as you think. Once you have clear, complete information, examine it through questioning.

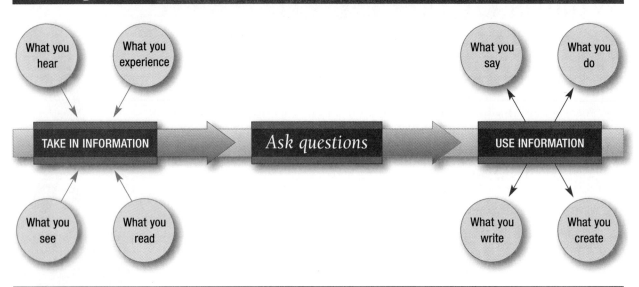

Figure 4.1 The critical-thinking path.

Questioning Information

A critical thinker asks many kinds of questions about a given piece of information, such as:

> Where did it come from? What could explain it? In what ways is it true or false? Do I consider it good or bad, and why? How is this information similar to or different from what I already know? What effects does it have?

Critical thinkers also ask whether information can help them solve a problem, for example, or make a decision. Questioning is the key to learning and to linking what you learn to other information.

Using Information

After taking in information, examining it by questioning, and transforming it into something they can use, critical thinkers put the information to work. Now comes the actual work of solving the problem, making the strategic plan, and so on. This last stage of the critical-thinking path is where new knowledge—inventions, ideas, creations—is born out of the mix of what you already know, what you have newly acquired, and the power of your mind.

Creativity and Critical Thinking

Critical thinking, especially the third stage of using information, is inherently creative because it involves the creation of something new from given information. Creativity goes beyond art and music; a creation can be a novel solution, idea, approach, tangible product, work of art, system, or program. Innovations created by all kinds of people continually expand and change the world. Here are some examples of creative innovations that have had an impact:

CREATIVITY

The ability to produce something new through imaginative skill.

- Jody Williams and the group she founded, International Campaign to Ban Landmines, have convinced nearly 100 countries to support a treaty that would end land mine production and sales.
- Art Fry and Spencer Silver invented the Post-it™ in 1980, enabling people to save paper and protect documents by using removable notes.
- Rosa Parks refused to give up her seat on the bus to a white person, setting off a chain of events that gave rise to the civil rights movement.
- Jim Henson revolutionized children's television, and the way children learn about the world, through his invention of the Muppets and development of *Sesame Street.*

Creativity is part of every thinking process. When you brainstorm potential problem solutions or possible decisions, you are being creative. When you come up with unique ways to challenge an assumption or achieve a strategic goal over time, you are being creative.

"The world of reality has its limits. The world of imagination is boundless."

JEAN-JACQUES ROUSSEAU

Creative and critical thinkers combine ideas and information in ways that form new solutions, ideas, processes, or products. "The hallmark of creative people is their mental flexibility," says creativity expert Roger von Oech. "Like race-car drivers who shift in and out of different gears depending on where they are on the course, creative people are able to shift in and out of different types of thinking depending on the needs of the situation at hand."[1] Figure 4.2 lists some primary characteristics of creative people. As you build critical-thinking skills, you will have opportunities to put these characteristics into play.

Figure 4.2	Characteristics of creative people.

CHARACTERISTIC	EXAMPLE
Willingness to take risks	Taking a difficult, high-level course.
Tendency to break away from limitations	Entering a marathon race.
Tendency to seek new challenges & experiences	Taking on an internship in a high-pressure workplace.
Broad range of interests	Inventing new moves on the basketball court and playing guitar at an open-mike night.
Ability to make new things out of available materials	Making curtains out of bedsheets.
Tendency to question norms & assumptions	Adopting a child of different ethnic background than the family's.
Willingness to deviate from popular opinion	Working for a small, relatively unknown political party.
Curiosity and inquisitiveness	Wanting to know how a computer program works.

Source: Adapted from T. Z. Tardif and R. J. Sternberg, "What Do We Know About Creativity?" in *The Nature of Creativity,* ed., R. J. Sternberg (London: Cambridge University Press, 1988).

		Table 4.1	Critical thinking involves a creative response.

YOUR ROLE	SITUATION	RIGID, NON-QUESTIONING RESPONSE	CREATIVE, QUESTIONING RESPONSE
Student	Instructor is lecturing on the causes of the Vietnam war.	You assume everything your instructor says is true.	You consider what the instructor says, write questions about issues you want to clarify and discuss them with the instructor or classmates.
Spouse/Partner	Your partner feels he/she does not have enough quality time with you.	You think he/she is wrong and defend yourself.	You ask your partner why he/she thinks this is happening, and together you come up with ways to improve the situation.
Employee	Your supervisor is angry with you about something that happened.	You avoid your supervisor or deny responsibility for the incident.	You determine what caused your supervisor to blame you; you talk with your supervisor about what happened and agree on a different approach in the future.

A creative, critical thinker is also an open-minded thinker, one who remains receptive to possibilities rather than accepting or rejecting information or ideas without examination. Table 4.1 illustrates this concept by comparing how critical and non-critical thinkers might respond to particular situations.

Think about responses you or others have had to different situations. Consider when you have seen people take the time to question, and when you haven't, and what resulted from each way of responding. This will help you begin to see what kind of an effect critical thinking can have on the way you live.

Learning How Your Mind Works

Start to put critical thinking into real-world perspective by imagining a specific scenario. You have an opening in your schedule and are trying to decide between two science courses—biology and biomedical ethics. As you work toward a decision, you might ask questions like the following:

- Do these courses have any prerequisites—and if so, what are they?
- What are the similarities in the subject matter between biology and biomedical ethics?
- How do the workloads for these two courses differ?
- How would the biology course fit into my existing schedule?
- Would biology or biomedical ethics fit a major or career that interests me? If so, how?

- How do I investigate the rumor that the biomedical ethics instructor is too tough on students?
- Which course is the best fit for me considering all that I have discovered?

When you ask important questions like these, your mind performs basic *actions*. Sometimes it uses one action by itself, but most often it uses two or more in combination. To know these actions is to have a fundamental understanding of thinking. These actions are the building blocks with which you construct the critical-thinking processes described later in the chapter.

Identify your mind's actions using a system originally derived by educators Frank Lyman, Arlene Mindus, and Charlene Lopez[2] and developed by numerous other instructors. Based on their studies of how people think, they named seven basic types of thought. These types, referred to here as actions, are not new to you, although some of their names may be. They represent the ways in which you think all the time.

Through exploring these actions, you go beyond just thinking in order to learn *how* you think. In a way, you are studying an instruction manual for your mind. Following are explanations of each of the mind actions, including examples (some from the questions you just read). Write your own examples in the blank spaces. Icons representing each action help you visualize and remember them.

The Mind Actions

Recall: *Facts, sequence, and description.* This is the simplest action, representing the simplest level of thinking. When you **recall,** you name or describe previously learned ideas, facts, objects, or events, or put them into sequence. *Examples:*

- Identifying the prerequisites for biology and biomedical ethics (you discover there are none).
- Naming the steps of a geometry proof, in order.

Your example: Recall two school-related events scheduled this month.

_____

_____

_____

The icon: Capital R stands for *recall* or *remembering.*

Similarity: *Analogy, likeness, comparison.* This action examines what is **similar** about one or more elements—situations, ideas, people, stories, events, or objects. *Examples:*

- Examining similarities in the subject matter between biology and biomedical ethics (both are based in the sciences, both involve biology-related material).
- Comparing class notes with another student to see what facts and ideas you both consider important.

Your example: State how your two favorite classes are similar.

_____

_____

_____

The icon: The Venn diagram illustrates the idea of similarity. The two circles represent the elements being compared, and the shaded area of intersection indicates that they have some degree of similarity.

Difference: *Distinction, contrast.* This action examines what is **different** about one or more elements. *Examples:*

- Looking at how the workloads for biology and biomedical ethics differ (biology has more assignments plus a lab component; biomedical ethics has less scientific work but more papers).
- Looking at differences between two of your instructors—one divides the class into discussion groups; the other keeps desks in place and always lectures.

Your example: Explain how one of your favorite courses differs from a course you don't like as much.

_____

_____

_____

The icon: Here the Venn diagram is used again to show difference. The nonintersecting parts of the circles are shaded, indicating that the focus is on what is not in common.

Cause and Effect: *Reasons, consequences, prediction.* Using this action, you look at what has **caused** a fact, situation, or event and what **effects** come from it. In other words, you look at why something happened and the consequence of its occurrence. *Examples:*

- Thinking through how taking the biology course would affect your existing schedule (it means moving or changing another class you've already registered for because it comes right after that class and is located across campus).
- Seeing how staying up too late causes you to oversleep, which causes you to be late to class, which results in missing material, which causes you to feel confused about course topics.

Your example: Write what causes you to become motivated in a class.

_____

_____

_____

The icon: The arrows, pointing toward one another in a circular pattern, show how a cause leads to an effect.

Example to Idea: *Generalization, classification.* From one or more known **examples** (facts or events), you develop a general **idea** or ideas. Grouping facts or events into patterns may allow you to make a general statement about several of them at once. This mind action moves from the known to the previously unknown and from the specific to the general. *Examples:*

- Exploring whether biology or biomedical ethics fits a major or career interest. (You start with the examples. You like biology; you aren't sure about a career in the sciences; you are intrigued by medicine; you have an interest in law; you are fascinated by ethics. These examples lead you to the idea—biomedical ethics would probably be a better fit.)
- From several successful experiences in classes where the instructor uses visuals to illustrate ideas, you conclude that your learning style has a strong visual component.

Your example: Name activities you enjoy. Using them, derive an idea of a class you want to take.

_____

_____

_____

The icon: The arrow and "Ex" pointing to a light bulb on their right indicate how an example or examples lead to the idea (the light bulb lit up).

Idea to Example: *Analysis, substantiation, proof.* In a reverse of the previous action, you take a known **idea** or ideas and think of **examples** (events or facts) that support or prove that idea. This mind action moves from the general to the specific, the reverse of example to idea. *Examples:*

- Investigating the rumor that the biomedical ethics instructor is too tough on students. (Starting with the idea that the instructor is too tough on students, you talk to five different students who have taken the class. Examples they give you lead you to believe that the instructor is indeed demanding.)
- You present an argument to your advisor regarding a change of major. (You start with the idea—you are a good candidate for a change of major—and support it with examples—you have worked in the field you want to change to, you have already fulfilled some of the requirements for the new major.)

Your example: Name an idea of a career path you would like to follow, and support this idea with examples of your interests and skills.

_____

_____

_____

The icon: In a reverse of the previous icon, this one starts with the light bulb and has an arrow pointing to "Ex." This indicates that you start with the idea and then move to the supporting examples.

Evaluation: *Value, judgment, rating.* Here you **judge** whether something is useful or not useful, important or unimportant, good or bad, or right or wrong by identifying and weighing its positive and negative effects (pros and cons). Be sure to consider the specific situation at hand (a cold drink might be good on the beach in August but not so good in the snowdrifts in January). With the facts you have gathered, you determine the value of something in terms of the predicted effects on you and others. Cause-and-effect analysis almost always accompanies evaluation. *Examples:*

- Looking at all that you have discovered—scheduling, relation to interests, difficulty, prerequisites, subject matter—about the potential effects of taking one of the two courses you are considering, you evaluate that biomedical ethics is your best bet.

- Someone offers you a chance to cheat on a test. You evaluate the potential effects if you are caught. You also evaluate the long-term effects of not actually learning the material and of doing something ethically wrong. You decide that it isn't right or worthwhile to cheat.

Your example: Evaluate your mode of transportation to school.

_____

_____

The icon: A set of scales out of balance indicates how you weigh positive and negative effects to arrive at an evaluation.

You may want to use a mnemonic device—a memory tool, as explained in Chapter 6—to remember the seven mind actions. You can make a sentence of words that each start with a mind action's first letter, such as "Really Smart Dogs Cook Eggs In Enchiladas."

Putting Mind Actions to Work

When you first learned to write, someone taught you how to create the shape of each letter or character. You slowly practiced each curve and line. Later you carefully put letters or characters together to form words. Now, much later, you write without thinking consciously about the individual units that make up your written thoughts. You focus primarily on how to express your ideas, not on creating proper letters; your words appear on paper as you work toward that goal.

The process of learning and using mind actions is similar. If you take time now to consciously think through the specific actions your mind uses when you think, they will eventually become second nature to you, a solid foundation for your thinking on which you can build productive skills.

Because you have been using these actions for a long time, developing a working understanding of your mind will take you far less time than it took to learn to write. As you work through the actions themselves and see how they combine to form thinking processes, you will build this crucial understanding. During the semester, as you work through other chapters in the book, you will see icons marking where particular mind actions are taking place. These will help you to more easily identify how your mind is working.

You rarely use the mind actions one at a time as they are presented here. Usually you combine them and repeat them. Sometimes they overlap. When you combine them in working toward a goal (a problem to solve, a decision to make), you are performing a *thinking process*. Following are explorations of several important critical-thinking processes: solving problems, making decisions, reasoning, opening your mind to new perspectives, and planning strategically. These thinking processes are similar in that they involve the steps of gathering, evaluating, and using information. As you will see, however, the sequence or combination of mind actions may vary considerably. Figure 4.7 on page 138 reminds you that the mind actions form the core of the thinking processes.

How does *critical thinking* help you solve problems and make decisions?

Problem solving and decision making are probably the two most crucial and common thinking processes. Each one requires various mind actions. The processes overlap somewhat because every problem that needs solving requires you to make a decision. However, not every decision requires that you solve a problem (e.g., not many people would say that deciding what to order for lunch is a problem).

Although both of these processes have multiple steps, you do not always have to work through each step. As you become more comfortable solving problems and making decisions, your mind automatically clicks through the steps. Also, you become more adept at evaluating which problems and decisions require serious consideration and which can be taken care of quickly and simply.

Problem Solving

Life constantly presents problems to be solved, ranging from common daily problems (how to manage study time) to life-altering situations (how to design a child-custody plan during a divorce). Choosing a solution without thinking critically may have negative effects. If you move through the steps of a problem-solving process, however, you have a good chance of coming up with a favorable solution.

Brainstorming

Brainstorming is a crucial element of problem solving. You are brainstorming when you approach a problem by letting your mind free-associate, coming up with as many possible ideas, examples, or solutions as you can without immediately evaluating them as good or bad. **Brainstorming** is also referred to as divergent thinking; you start with the issue or problem and then let your mind diverge, or go in many different directions, in search of ideas or solutions.

Following are some general guidelines for creative and successful brainstorming:[3]

Don't evaluate or criticize an idea right away. Write down your ideas so that you remember them. Evaluate them later, after you have had a chance to think about them. Try to avoid criticizing other people's ideas as well. Students often become stifled when their ideas are evaluated during brainstorming.

Focus on quantity; don't worry about quality until later. Generate as many ideas or examples as you can without worrying about which one is "right." The more thoughts you generate, the better the chance that one may be useful. Brainstorming works well in groups. Group members can become inspired by, and make creative use of, one another's ideas.

Let yourself play. People often hit on their most creative ideas when they are exercising or just relaxing. Often when your mind switches into play mode, it can more freely generate new thoughts. A thought that seems crazy might be a brilliant discovery. For example, the idea for Velcro came from examining how a burr sticks to clothing. Dreams can also be a source.[4]

Use analogy. Think of similar situations and write down what you remember; what ideas or strategies have worked before? *Analogy* puts the similarity mind action to work recalling potentially helpful ideas and examples and stimulating your mind to come up with new ones. For example, the Velcro discovery is a product of analogy: When trying to figure out how two pieces of fabric could stick to one another, the inventor thought of the similar situation of a burr sticking to clothing.

Don't fear failure. Even Michael Jordan got cut from the basketball team as a high school sophomore in Wilmington, North Carolina. If you insist on getting it right all the time, you may miss out on the creative path—often paved with failures—leading to the best possible solution.[5]

The Problem-Solving Process

When you have a problem to solve, taking the following steps will maximize the number of possible solutions and will allow you to explore each one carefully. Figure 4.3 demonstrates a way to visualize the flow of problem solving.

1. *Identify the problem accurately*. What are the facts? *Recall* the details of the situation. To define a problem correctly, focus on its *causes* rather than its effects. Consider the Chinese saying: "Give a man a fish, and he will eat for a day. Teach a man to fish, and he will eat for a lifetime." You may state the problem first as "The man is hungry." If you stay with this statement, giving him a fish seems like a good solution. Unfortunate-

Figure 4.3   Problem-solving plan.

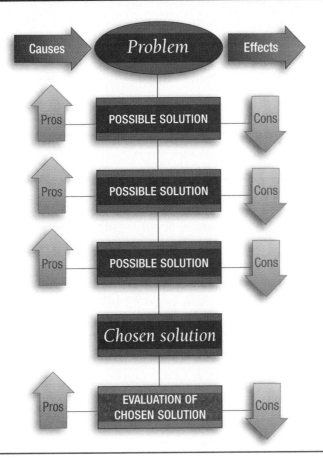

Source: © 1983 George Eley and Frank Lyman, University of Maryland.

ly, the problem returns—because hunger is an effect. Focusing on the probable cause brings a new definition: "The man does not know how to find food." Given that his lack of knowledge is the true cause, teaching him to fish truly solves the problem.

2. *Analyze the problem.* Analyze, or break down into understandable pieces, what surrounds the problem. What *effects* of the situation concern you? What *causes* these effects? Which causes are most powerful or significant? Are there hidden causes? Look at the causes and effects that surround the problem.

3. *Brainstorm possible solutions.* Brainstorming helps you to think of examples of how you solved similar problems, consider what is different about this problem, and come up with new possible solutions. Remember that to get to the heart of a problem, you must base possible solutions on the most significant causes instead of putting a bandage on the effects.

4. *Explore each solution.* Why might your solution work or not work? Might a solution work partially or in a particular situation? *Evaluate* ahead of time the pros and cons (positive and negative effects) of each proposed solution. Create a chain of causes and effects in your head, as far into the future as you can, to see where this solution might lead.

5. *Choose and implement the solution you decide is best.* Decide how you will put your solution to work. Then, carry out your plan.

6. *Evaluate the solution that you acted on.* What are the positive and negative *effects* of what you did? In terms of your needs and those of others, was it a useful solution or not? Could the solution use any adjustments to be more useful? In evaluating, you are collecting data.

7. *Refine the solution.* Problem solving is a process. You may have opportunities to apply the same solution again. Evaluate repeatedly, making changes that you decide make the solution better (i.e., more closely related to the causes of the problem).

The following example illustrates one way to use this plan to solve a problem.

- *Step 1: Identify.* A student is having trouble understanding course material.

- *Step 2: Analyze.* If some effects of not understanding include poor grades and lack of interest, some causes may include poor study habits, not listening in class, or lack of sleep.

- *Step 3: Brainstorm.* Seeing the most significant cause as being poor study habits, the student comes up with ideas such as seeking help from his instructor or working with a study group.

- *Step 4: Explore.* The student considers individually the effects of different solutions: improved study habits, more sleep, tutoring, or dropping the class.

- *Step 5: Choose.* The student decides on a combination of improved study habits and tutoring.

- *Step 6: Evaluate.* Evaluating his choice, the student may decide that the effects are good but that his fatigue still causes problems in understanding the material.

- *Step 7: Refine the solution.* The student may decide to continue to study more regularly but, after a few weeks of tutoring, could opt to trade in the tutoring time for some extra sleep. He may decide to take what he has learned from the tutor so far and apply it to his increased study efforts.

Using this process enables you to solve school, work, and personal problems in a thoughtful, comprehensive way. Figures 4.4 and 4.5 show two examples of how to use this plan to solve a problem. They represent the same plan as Figure 4.3, but include writing space for use during the problem-solving process.

Decision Making

Decisions are choices. Making a choice, or decision, requires thinking critically through the possible choices and evaluating which will work best for you, considering the situation.

Before you begin the process, evaluate what kind of decision you have to make. Some decisions, such as what books to bring to class, are little day-to-day considerations that you can take care of quickly. Others, such

Figure 4.4 Walking through a problem . . . financing course work.

CAUSES OF PROBLEM

Lost financial aid due to slipping grades

Part-time job doesn't bring in much money

STATE PROBLEM HERE:

I don't have enough money to cover tuition next semester

EFFECTS OF PROBLEM

Need to find money from a different source

Might be unable to continue school right now

Use boxes below to list possible solutions:

POTENTIAL POSITIVE EFFECTS

List for each solution:

Ability to stay on planned school schedule

Ability to stay in school

SOLUTION #1

Find new source of financial aid

POTENTIAL NEGATIVE EFFECTS

List for each solution:

Money might not be renewable like current grant

Time and effort spent to find and qualify for new aid

More money to pay for college

More on-the-job experience

SOLUTION #2

Find full-time, better-paying job

Less time for college

May have to take classes part-time, graduate later

More time to study

More ability to focus

SOLUTION #3

Take classes part-time next semester

Extends how long I'll be in college

Could make me ineligible for certain kinds of aid

Now choose the solution you think is best—and try it.

ACTUAL POSITIVE EFFECTS

List for chosen solution:

More money earned

More study time and ability to focus resulted in better grades

CHOSEN SOLUTION

For next semester, take classes part-time and work full-time

ACTUAL NEGATIVE EFFECTS

List for chosen solution:

Had to put off planned graduation date

Ineligible this semester for most aid, had to use my own money for tuition

FINAL EVALUATION: Was it a good or bad choice?

It was tough but it worked out well. Even though I had to pay for classes myself, the full-time job and fewer classes allowed me to do that. Then, with better focus, I was able to raise my GPA back up so that next semester I'll requalify for aid and can go back to being a full-time student.

Figure 4.5 Walking through a problem . . . relating to an instructor.

CAUSES OF PROBLEM

We have radically different views
and personality types
I don't feel listened to in class or
respected

STATE PROBLEM HERE:

I don't like my
instructor for a
particular course

EFFECTS OF PROBLEM

Dampened interest in the class
material
No motivation to work on assignments
Grades are suffering

Use boxes below to list possible solutions:

POTENTIAL POSITIVE EFFECTS

List for each solution:

Don't have to deal with that
instructor
Less stress

SOLUTION #1

Drop the course

POTENTIAL NEGATIVE EFFECTS

List for each solution:

Grade gets entered on my transcript
I'll have to take the course
eventually; it's required for
my major

Getting credit for the course
Feeling like I've honored a
commitment

SOLUTION #2

Put up with it until the
end of the semester

Stress every time I'm there
Lowered motivation
Probably not such a good final grade

A chance to express myself
Could get good advice
An opportunity to ask direct questions
of the instructor

SOLUTION #3

Schedule meetings with
advisor and instructor

Have to face instructor one-on-one
Might just make things worse

Now choose the solution you think is best—and try it.

ACTUAL POSITIVE EFFECTS

List for chosen solution:

Got some helpful advice from advisor
Talking in person with the
instructor actually promoted a
fairly honest discussion
I won't have to take the course again

CHOSEN SOLUTION

Schedule meetings with
both advisor and
instructor, and stick
with the course

ACTUAL NEGATIVE EFFECTS

List for chosen solution:

The discussion was difficult and
sometimes tense
I still don't know how much
learning I'll retain from this
course

FINAL EVALUATION: Was it a good or bad choice?

The solution has improved things. I'll finish the course, and even though the instructor and I aren't
the best of friends, we have a mutual understanding now. I feel more respected and more willing
to put my time into the course.

as what to major in or whether to quit your part-time job, require thoughtful evaluation, time, and perhaps the input of others you trust. The following is a list of steps for thinking critically through the more complex kind of decision.

1. *Identify a goal.* Why is this decision necessary? What result do you want from this decision, and what is its value? Considering the desired *effects* can help you formulate your goal.

2. *Establish needs.* *Recall* the needs of everyone involved in the decision. Consider all who will be affected.

3. *Name, investigate, and evaluate available options.* Brainstorm possible choices, and then look at the facts surrounding each. *Evaluate* the good and bad effects of each possibility. Weigh these effects in light of the needs you have established and judge which is the best course of action.

4. *Decide on a plan and take action.* Make a choice based on your evaluation, and act on it.

5. *Evaluate the result.* Was it useful? Not useful? Some of both? Weigh the positive and negative effects.

Look at this example to see one way of using the decision-making plan.

- *Step 1: Identify a goal.* A student currently attends a small private college. Her goal is to become a physical therapist. The school has a good program, but her father has changed jobs and the family can no longer pay the tuition and fees.

- *Step 2: Establish needs.* The student needs a school with a full physical therapy program; she and her parents need to cut costs; she needs to be able to transfer credits.

- *Step 3: Evaluate options.* Here are some possible decisions that the student might consider:

  a. *Continue at the current college.* **Positive effects:** No need to adjust to a new place or to new people; ability to continue course work as planned. **Negative effects:** Need to finance most of my tuition and costs on my own, such as through loans, grants, or work; may be difficult to find time to work as much as I would need to; might not qualify for aid.

  b. *Transfer to the state college.* **Positive effects:** Opportunity to reconnect with people there that I know from high school; cheaper tuition and room costs; ability to transfer credits. **Negative effects:** Need to earn some money or get financial aid; physical therapy program is small and not very strong.

  c. *Transfer to the community college.* **Positive effects:** Many of the courses I need to continue with the physical therapy curriculum are available; school is close so I could live at home and avoid paying housing costs; credits will transfer; tuition is reasonable. **Negative effects:** No personal contacts; less independence; no bachelor's degree offered.

- *Step 4: Decide.* In this case, the student might decide to go to the community college for two years and then transfer back to a four-year school to earn a bachelor's degree in physical therapy. Although she

Apply techniques in both your stronger and weaker intelligences to become a more versatile critical thinker.

INTELLIGENCE	SUGGESTED STRATEGIES	WHAT WORKS FOR YOU? WRITE NEW IDEAS HERE
Verbal–Linguistic	■ When a problem bothers you, write it out. Challenge yourself to come up with at least 10 possible solutions. ■ Discuss new ideas or problems with other people. Write down any useful ideas they come up with.	
Logical–Mathematical	■ Outline all possible outcomes to various possible actions. ■ Analyze each possible solution to a problem. What effects might occur? What is the best choice and why?	
Bodily–Kinesthetic	■ Pace while you brainstorm—have a tape recorder running and record your ideas as they come up. ■ Think about solutions to a problem while you are running or doing any other type of exercise.	
Visual–Spatial	■ Use a problem-solving flow chart like the one in Figure 4.4 and complete all the areas. ■ Brainstorm ideas about, and solutions to, a problem by drawing a think link about the problem.	
Interpersonal	■ When you are stuck on a problem, ask one of your friends to discuss it with you. Consider any new ideas or solutions the friend may offer. ■ Discuss new creative ideas with one or more people and analyze the feedback.	
Intrapersonal	■ Take time alone to think through a problem. Freewrite your thoughts about the problem in a journal. ■ Sit quietly and think about your ability to evaluate solutions to a problem. Write three ways you can improve.	
Musical	■ When you are stuck on a problem, shut down your brain for a while and listen to music you love. Come back to the problem later to see if new ideas have surfaced.	
Naturalistic	■ Take a long walk in nature to inspire creative ideas or to think of solutions to a problem. ■ Think about your favorite place in nature before concentrating on brainstorming about a problem.	

might lose some independence and contact with friends, the positive effects are money saved, opportunity to spend time on studies rather than working to earn tuition, and the availability of classes that match the physical therapy program requirements.

- *Step 5: Evaluate.* If the student decides to transfer, she may find that it can be hard being back at home, although her parents are adjusting to her independence and she is trying to respect their concerns. Fewer social distractions result in her getting more work done. The financial situation is favorable. All things considered, she evaluates that this decision is a good one.

Making important decisions can take time. Think through your decisions thoroughly, considering your own ideas as well as those of others you trust, but don't hesitate to act once you have your plan. You cannot benefit from your decision until you follow through on it.

How do you *reason?*

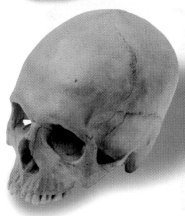

R*easoning* refers to using one's ability to connect idea to example and draw cause-and-effect conclusions. One aspect of reasoning that affects your ability to be a good critical thinker is determining the accuracy of information by distinguishing fact from opinion. Another important aspect—constructing and evaluating arguments—is addressed in Chapters 5 and 7 in the context of reading and writing.

Before you can distinguish fact from opinion, you must be able to define both. A *statement of fact,* according to the dictionary, is information presented as objectively real and verifiable—something that can be proven. A *statement of opinion* is defined as a belief, conclusion, or judgment and is inherently difficult, and sometimes impossible, to verify. Being able to distinguish fact from opinion is crucial to your ability to evaluate the credibility of what you read, hear, and experience.

Table 4.2 has some examples of factual statements versus statements of opinion; note that facts refer to the observable or measurable, while opinions usually involve cause-and-effect exploration. Use the blank lines to add your own examples.

Characteristics of Facts and Opinions

The following information will help you determine what is fact and what is opinion.[6]

Characteristics of fact are:

- *Statements that deal with actual people, places, objects, events.* If the existence of the elements involved can be verified through observation or record, chances are that the statement itself can also be proven true or false. "Jimmy Carter was a peanut farmer in Georgia before becoming president" is a fact, for example.

Table 4.2	How facts differ from opinions.	
TOPIC	**FACTUAL STATEMENT**	**STATEMENT OF OPINION**
Stock market	In 1999, the Dow Jones Industrial average rose above 10,000 for the first time.	The Dow Jones Industrial average will continue to grow throughout the first decade of the 21st century.
Weather	It's raining outside.	This is the worst rainstorm yet this year.
Cataloging systems	Computer databases have replaced card catalogs in most college libraries.	Computer databases are an improvement over card catalogs.

- *Statements that use concrete words or measurable statistics.* Any statement that uses concrete, measurable terms and avoids the abstract is likely to be a fact. Examples include "Thirty-six inches equal a yard" and "There are 2,512 full-time students enrolled this semester."

Characteristics of opinions include:

- *Statements that show evaluation.* Any statement of value, such as "Television is bad for children," indicates an opinion. Words such as *bad, good, pointless,* and *beneficial* indicate value judgments.

- *Statements that predict future events.* Nothing that will happen in the future can be definitively proven in the present. Most statements that discuss something that may happen in the future are opinions.

- *Statements that use abstract words.* Although "one gallon" can be defined, "love" has no specific definition. Abstract words—*strength, misery, success*—usually indicate an opinion.

- *Statements that use emotional words.* Emotions are by nature unverifiable. Chances are that statements using such words as *delightful, nasty, miserable,* or *wonderful* express an opinion.

- *Statements that use absolutes.* Absolute qualifiers, such as *all, none, never,* and *always,* point to an opinion. For example, "All students need to have a job while in school" is an opinion.

When you find yourself feeling that an opinion is fact, it may be because you agree strongly with the opinion. Don't discount your feelings; "not verifiable" is not the same as "inaccurate." Opinions are not necessarily wrong even if you cannot prove them. Also, when you think that an apparent statement of fact is an opinion, it may be because you don't trust the source.

ABSTRACT

Theoretical; disassociated from any specific instance.

QUALIFIER

A word, such as always, never, or often, that changes the meaning of another word or word group.

Investigating Truth and Accuracy

Once you label a statement as a fact or opinion, ask questions to explore its degree of truth. Because both stated facts and opinions can be true or false—for example, "There are 25 hours in a day" is a false factual statement—both require investigation through questioning. Critical-thinking experts Sylvan Barnet and Hugo Bedau state that when you test for the truth of a statement, you "determine whether what it asserts corresponds with reality; if it does, then it is true, and if it doesn't, then it is false."[7] In order to determine to what degree a statement "corresponds with reality," ask questions such as the following:

- What facts or examples provide evidence of truth?
- Is there another fact that disproves this statement or information or shows it to be an opinion?
- How reliable are the sources of information?
- What about this statement is similar to or different from other information I consider fact?
- Are these truly the causes and effects?

Distinguishing fact from opinion by asking important questions helps you to approach a variety of situations with an open mind. Supporting your opinions with indisputable facts increases your credibility; recognizing whether others support their opinions likewise helps you avoid responding in a reactionary, unsubstantiated way to issues that arise in school, work, or at home. The creative part of this process comes in the choice to be proactive—you consider what's possible instead of getting caught in your own tendencies to see the world a certain way, resting on certain assumptions.

How can you *open your mind* to new perspectives?

Perspective is complex and unique to each individual. You have your own way of looking at everything that you encounter. Perspective is the big-picture point of view that forms the basis for and guides your thoughts on ideas, activities, people, places, and so on. Consider the classic question: Do you generally see the glass as half full or half empty? Either view is an example of perspective.

A given perspective shapes various opinions and assumptions that in turn reflect the overall perspective of the thinker. For instance, your perspective on public education may lead you to specific opinions and assumptions about schools, teachers, and government involvement. Here is a set of examples to further explain:

PERSPECTIVE
A cluster of related assumptions and opinions that incorporate values, interests, and knowledge.

ASSUMPTION
An idea or statement accepted as true without examination or proof; a hardened opinion.

Perspective: Education is essential; everyone has the right to an education.

A related assumption: The amount of money school systems spend per student has a major impact on the quality of education.

A related opinion: State funding should attempt to equalize per-student spending so that all schools can deliver a quality education.

When your opinion clashes with someone else's, it often reflects a difference in perspective. If a friend has a negative opinion of your choosing to live with a significant other, for example, that friend might have a different perspective from yours on relationships, with accompanying different opinions and assumptions about how they should progress.

You probably know how difficult it can be when someone cannot understand your perspective on something. Perhaps an instructor thinks students should never miss class and can't understand an absence you had, or a parent can't understand why you would date someone of a different race. However, it is just as important for you to try to understand other perspectives as it is for others to try to understand yours. Seeing the world only from your point of view—and resisting any challenges to that perspective—can be inflexible, limiting, and frustrating to both you and others. Opening your mind to other perspectives both educates you and helps you to evaluate and refine your own views and behavior.

Evaluating Perspectives

Using an evaluation system based on the critical-thinking path (Figure 4.1) allows you to think more broadly about the world around you, introducing you to new ideas, improving your communication with others, and encouraging mutual respect.

Step 1: Take in New Information

The first step is to take in new perspectives and simply acknowledge that they exist without immediately judging, rejecting, or even accepting them. It's easy to feel so strongly about a topic—for example, whether capital punishment is morally defensible—that you don't even consider any other view. If someone offers an opposing view, hold back your opinions while you *listen*. Critical thinkers are able to allow for the existence of perspectives that differ from, and even completely negate, their own.

Step 2: Evaluate the Perspective

Asking questions helps you maintain flexibility and openness.

- What is similar and different about this perspective and mine? What personal experiences have led to our particular perspectives?
- What examples, evidence, or reasons could be used to support or justify this perspective? Do some reasons provide good support even if I don't agree with the reasons?
- What effects may come from this way of being, acting, or believing? Are the effects different on different people and in different situations?

Even if this perspective seems to have negative effects for me, how might it have positive effects for others and therefore have value?

- What can I learn from this different perspective? Is there anything I could adopt that would improve my life? Is there anything I wouldn't agree with but that I can still respect and learn from?

Step 3: Accept—and Perhaps Adopt

On the one hand, perhaps your evaluation leads you simply to recognize and appreciate the other perspective, even if you decide that it is not right for you. On the other hand, thinking through the new perspective may lead you to feel that you want to try it out or to adopt it as your own. You may feel that what you have learned has led you to a new way of seeing yourself, your life, or the world around you.

"We do not live to think, but, on the contrary, we think in order that we may succeed in surviving."

JOSÉ ORTEGA Y GASSET

Perspectives are made up of many different assumptions. Challenging assumptions is an important part of opening your mind to other perspectives. When you question the assumptions that you and others hold, you do the critical thinker's job of looking carefully at the validity of perspectives.

Identifying and Evaluating Assumptions

"A more expensive car is a better car." "Students get more work done in a library." These statements reveal assumptions—evaluations or generalizations influenced by values and based on observing *cause* and *effect*—that can often hide within seemingly truthful statements. An assumption can influence choices—you may assume that you should earn a certain degree or own a car. Many people don't question whether their assumptions make sense, nor do they challenge the assumptions of others.

Assumptions come from sources such as parents or relatives, television and other media, friends, and personal experiences. As much as you think such assumptions work for you, it's just as possible that they can close your mind to opportunities and even cause harm. Investigate each assumption as you would any statement of fact or opinion, questioning the truth of the supposed causes and effects.

The first step in uncovering the assumptions that underlie an opinion or perspective is to look at the cause-and-effect pattern, seeing whether the way reasons move to conclusions, or causes are connected to effects, is supported by evidence or involves a hidden assumption. Figure 4.6 has examples of questions you can ask to uncover and evaluate an assumption.

For example, here's how you might use these questions to investigate the following statement: "The most productive schedule involves getting

Figure 4.6   Questioning an assumption.

What is the source of this assumption? How reliable is the source—can it be counted on to have investigated this assumption?

What positive and negative effects has this assumption had on me or others?

What harm could be done by always taking this assumption as fact?

In what cases is this assumption valid or invalid? What examples prove or disprove it?

started early in the day." First of all, a cause-and-effect evaluation shows that this statement reveals the following assumption: "The morning is when people have the most energy and are most able to get things done." Here's how you might question the assumption:

- This assumption may be true for people who have good energy in the morning hours. Does it work for people who are at their best in the afternoon or evening hours?

- Society's basic standard of daytime classes and 8:00 A.M. to 5:00 P.M. working hours supports this assumption. Therefore, the assumption may work for people who have early jobs and classes. How does it work for people who work other shifts or who take evening classes?

- Were people who believe this assumption raised to start their days early, or do they just go along with what seems to be society's standard? Aren't there people who operate on a different schedule and yet enjoy successful, productive lives?

- What effect would taking this assumption as fact have on people who don't operate at their peak in the earlier hours? In situations that favor their particular characteristics—later classes and jobs, career areas that don't require early morning work—don't such people have as much potential to succeed as anyone else?

Be careful to question all assumptions, not just those that seem problematic from the start. Form your opinion after investigating the positive and negative effects of making the assumption.

The Value of Seeing Other Perspectives

Seeing beyond one's own perspective can be difficult. Why put in the effort? Here are some of the benefits of being able to see and consider other perspectives.

Improved communication. When you consider another person's perspective, you open the lines of communication. For example, if you want to add or drop a course and your advisor says it's impossible before listening to you, you might not feel much like explaining. But if your advisor asks to hear your underlying reasons, you may sense that your needs are respected and be ready to talk.

Mutual respect. When someone takes the time and energy to understand how you feel about something, you probably feel respected and, in return, offer respect to the person who made the effort. When people respect one another, relationships become stronger and more productive, whether they are personal, work-related, or educational.

Continued learning. Every time you open your mind to a different perspective, you can learn something new. There are worlds of knowledge and possibilities outside your experience. You may find different yet equally valid ways of getting an education, living as a family, or relating to others. Above all else, you may see that each person is entitled to his or her own perspective, no matter how foreign it may be to you.

By being able to recognize perspectives, the connection that you foster with others may mean the difference between success and failure in today's world. This becomes more significant as the Information Age introduces you to an increasing number of perspectives every day. This

"The best way to escape from a problem is to solve it."

ALAN SAPORTA

dynamic global environment requires that you broaden your perspectives, continually evaluate choices as objectively as possible, and push yourself to embrace new and innovative ideas. The more creative you are in terms of combining known elements to create new ideas or perspectives, the better your chances for success.

Why plan *strategically?*

f you've ever played a game of chess, participated in a martial arts match, or made a detailed plan of how to reach a particular goal, you have had experience with *strategy*. Strategy is the plan of action, the method or the "how," behind achieving any goal.

Strategic planning means looking at the next week, month, year, or 10 years and exploring the future positive and negative effects that current choices and actions may have. As a student, you have planned strategically by deciding that the effort of school is a legitimate price to pay for the skills and opportunities you will receive. Being strategic means using decision-making skills to choose how to accomplish tasks. It means asking questions. It sometimes means delaying immediate gratification for future gain.

Strategy and Critical Thinking

In situations that demand strategy, think critically by asking questions like these:

- If you aim for a certain goal, what actions may cause you to achieve that goal?
- What are the potential effects, positive or negative, of different actions or choices?
- What can you learn from previous experiences that may inspire similar or different actions?
- What could cause you to fail—what barriers stand in the way?
- What can you recall about what others have done in similar situations?
- Which set of effects are most helpful or desirable to you?

For any situation that would benefit from strategic planning, from getting ready for a study session to aiming for a career, the steps in this variation on the decision-making plan on page 127 will help you make choices that bring about the most positive effects. Throughout the process of achieving your goal, remember to be flexible. Because you never know what may happen to turn your plan upside down, the concept of flexibility is critical to landing on your feet. Chapter 12 has more strategies for being flexible.

1. *Establish a goal.* What do you want to achieve, and when? Why do you want to achieve it?

2. *Brainstorm possible plans.* What are some ways that you can get where you want to go? What steps toward your goal do you need to take today, 1 year, 5 years, 10 years, or 20 years from now?

3. *Anticipate as many potential effects of each plan as possible.* What positive and negative effects may occur, both soon and in the long term? What approach may best help you to overcome barriers and achieve your goal? Talk to people who are where you want to

PERSONAL TRIUMPH

*d*iscovering personal power can turn a life around. As mentors and activities helped Susie Ivy deal with her past and learn of her strength and creativity, she found ways to achieve that she never would have imagined.

People tell me I'm motivated and that I take initiative to make good things happen. It's funny because I see myself as a pretty laid-back person. But I do believe having someone who believes in you can make a difference. Everyone needs to be lifted up, at least once in a while.

I am the youngest of five children. My mother suffered from schizophrenia, and she was addicted to drugs. When my aunt called the Department of Child and Family Services and reported our situation, my brothers and sisters and I were placed in foster care. I was five years old.

We all were placed in the same home, where at times there were as many as 10 foster children living. Although we weren't physically abused, we didn't get the emotional support we needed. We didn't receive counseling, and no one ever explained how long we would be in foster care or what to expect. For years I fantasized that our mother would get her life together and bring us home. But that never happened.

When I was eight years old, we started attending a church youth group. I really enjoyed the activities and the youth leaders. I participated in the weekly meetings and went to summer camp. One of the youth leaders is still my mentor today. As I think back, I realize that this is when my positive childhood memories began to form.

During my teen years, many girls at my high school got pregnant and left school. Although I wasn't happy at home, I knew I didn't want that to be my fate. Instead, I joined the track and swim teams. I swam all four years and won most valuable player

Susie Ivy, Fashion Design major;
Dominican University, River Forest, Illinois

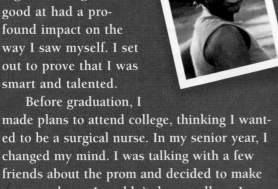

each year. Discovering something I was good at had a profound impact on the way I saw myself. I set out to prove that I was smart and talented.

Before graduation, I made plans to attend college, thinking I wanted to be a surgical nurse. In my senior year, I changed my mind. I was talking with a few friends about the prom and decided to make my own dress. I couldn't draw well, so I described the dress to my foster dad, and he drew it for me. I was so pleased with how the dress turned out! Right then and there I decided to major in fashion design, and I began applying to colleges that offered fashion design programs.

I love my major. I like exploring the creative process and pushing myself to do my best. Every year, my school sponsors a spring fashion show, and my clothes are modeled in front of an audience. Last year, I was selected from my school to go to New York City for a fashion tour, where I saw new designs and visited other colleges. These are the highlights of my college experience.

I've also discovered that competition is a motivating force in my life, especially when it comes to my designs. For example, a girl in one of my classes comes from a rich family. She can afford the nicest fabrics for her projects, and she doesn't have to work like I do to pay for school. But I remind myself that money can't buy talent. Everybody who is famous didn't start with a lot of money. When I think about where I've been, I'm happy about who I'm becoming.

Take a moment to consider . . .

- *What you consider to be the most motivating factor in your life.*
- *How you consider yourself creative, and what you are proud to have created.*

be—professionally or personally—and ask them what you should anticipate.

4. *Put your plan into action.* Act on the decision you have made.

5. *Evaluate continually.* Because a long-term goal lies in the future, the evaluation period could be long. Check regularly to see whether your strategies are having the effects you predicted. If you discover that events are not going the way you planned, for any reason, reevaluate and change your strategy.

The most important critical-thinking question for successful strategic planning begins with "how." How do you remember what you learn? How do you develop a productive idea at work? The process of strategic planning helps you find the best answer.

Benefits of Strategic Planning

Strategic planning has many positive effects, including the following:

Keeping up with technology. Technological developments have increased the pace of workplace change. Thinking strategically about job opportunities may lead you to a broader range of courses or a major and career in a growing career area, making it more likely that your skills will be in demand when you graduate.

Successful goal setting. Thinking strategically improves your ability to work through and achieve goals over time. For example, a student might have a goal of paying tuition; this student could plan a strategy of part-time jobs and cutting back on spending in order to achieve that goal. Strategy keeps you headed toward the target.

School and work success. A student who wants to do well in a course needs to plan study sessions. A lawyer needs to anticipate how to respond to points raised in court. Strategic planning creates a vision into the future that allows the planner to anticipate possibilities and to be prepared for them.

Strategic planning entails using critical thinking to develop a vision of your future.

Figure 4.7   The wheel of thinking.

Although you can't predict with certainty what will happen, you can ask questions about the potential effects of your actions. With what you learn, you can make plans that bring the best possible effects for you and others.

ϰϱινειν

The word *critical* is derived from the Greek word *krinein,* which means to separate in order to choose or select. To be a mindful, aware critical thinker, you need to be able to separate, evaluate, and select ideas, opinions, and facts.

Think of this concept as you apply critical thinking to your reading, writing, and interaction with others. Be aware of the information you absorb and how your mind works. Be selective in the thinking processes you use, and separate out and select the best solutions, decisions, perspectives, plans, arguments, and opinions. Critical thinking gives you the power to make sense of life by deliberately selecting how to respond to the information, people, and events that you encounter.

Building Skills

FOR COLLEGE, CAREER, AND LIFE SUCCESS

| Critical Thinking | *Applying Learning to Life* |

Make an Important Decision

First, write here a decision you need to make. Choose an important decision that needs to be made soon.

_____

_____

STEP 1: DECIDE ON A GOAL. Be specific: What goal, or desired effects, do you seek from this decision? For example, if your decision is a choice between two courses, effects you want might include credit toward a major and experience. Write down the desired effects here, prioritizing them from most important to least.

_____

_____

_____

_____

_____

STEP 2: ESTABLISH NEEDS. Who and what will be affected by your decision? If you are deciding how to finance your education and you have a family to support, for example, you must take into consideration their financial needs.

List here the people, things, or situations that may be affected by your decision and indicate how your decision will affect them.

_____

_____

_____

_____

STEP 3: NAME, INVESTIGATE, AND EVALUATE AVAILABLE OPTIONS. Look at any options you can imagine. Consider options even if they seem impossible or unlikely; you can evaluate them later. Some decisions only have two options (to move to a new apartment or not; to get a new roommate or not); others have a wider selection of choices.

List two possible options for your decision. Evaluate the potential good and bad effects of each.

Option 1 _____

Positive effects _____

Negative effects _____

Option 2 _____

Positive effects _____

Negative effects _____

Have you or someone else ever made a decision similar to the one you are about to make? If so, what can you learn from that decision that may help you?

_____

_____

_____

STEP 4: DECIDE ON A PLAN AND TAKE ACTION. Taking your entire analysis into account, decide what to do. Write your decision here.

_____

_____

_____

Next is perhaps the most important part of the process: Act on your decision.

STEP 5: EVALUATE THE RESULT. After you have acted on your decision, evaluate how everything turned out. Did you achieve the effects you wanted to achieve? What were the effects on you? On others? On the situation? To what extent were they positive, negative, or some of both?

List two effects here. Name each effect, circle whether it was positive or negative, and explain your evaluation.

Effect _____

Positive   *Negative*

Why? _____

Effect _____

Positive   *Negative*

Why? _____

_____

Final evaluation: Write one statement in reaction to the decision you made. Indicate whether you feel the decision was useful or not useful, and why. Indicate any adjustments that could have made the effects of your decision more positive.

_____

_____

_____

Brainstorming on the Idea Wheel

Your creative mind can solve problems when you least expect it. Many people report having sudden ideas while exercising, driving, showering, waking, or even dreaming. When you aren't directly thinking about a problem, the mind is often more free to roam through uncharted territory and bring back treasures.

To make the most of this "mind float," grab ideas right when they surface. If you don't, they roll back into your subconscious as if on a wheel. Because you never know how big the wheel is, you can't be sure when that particular idea will roll to the top again. That's why writers carry notebooks—they need to grab thoughts when they come to the top of the wheel.

Name a long-term goal for which you need to do some strategic planning. Brainstorm without a time limit. Be on the lookout for ideas, causes, effects, or related short-term goals coming to the top of your wheel. The minute it happens, write down your thought—in this book if it is available, or anywhere else you can write. Look at your ideas later and see how your creative mind may have pointed you toward some original and workable solutions. You may also want to keep a book by your bed to catch ideas that pop up before, during, or after sleep.

Goal: _____

Ideas: _____

_____

_____

_____

_____

_____

_____

GROUP PROBLEM SOLVING. As a class, brainstorm a list of problems in your lives. Write the problems on the board or on a large piece of paper attached to an easel. Include any problems you feel comfortable discussing with others. Such problems may involve academics, relationships, jobs, discrimination, parenting, housing, procrastination, and others. Divide into groups of two to four with each group choosing or being assigned one problem to work on. Use the empty problem-solving flowchart on the next page to fill in your work.

1. *Identify the problem.* As a group, state your problem specifically, without causes ("I'm not attending all of my classes" is better than "lack of motivation"). Then, explore and record the causes and effects that surround it. Remember to look for "hidden" causes (you may perceive that traffic makes you late to school, but getting up too late might be the hidden cause).

2. *Brainstorm possible solutions.* Determine the most likely causes of the problem; from those causes, derive possible solutions. Record all the ideas that group members offer. After 10 minutes or so, each group member should choose one possible solution to explore independently.

3. *Explore each solution.* In thinking independently through the assigned solution, each group member should (a) weigh the positive and negative effects, (b) consider similar problems, and (c) describe how the solution affects the causes of the problem. Evaluate your assigned solution. Is it a good one? Will it work?

4. *Choose your top solution(s).* Come together again as a group. Take turns sharing your observations and recommendations, and then take a vote: Which solution is the best? You may have a tie or may want to combine two different solutions. Either way is fine. Different solutions suit different people and situations. Although it's not always possible to reach agreement, try to find the solution that works for most of the group.

5. *Evaluate the solution you decide is best.* When you decide on your top solution or solutions, discuss what would happen if you went through with it. What do you predict would be the positive and negative effects of this solution? Would it turn out to be a truly good solution for everyone?

Figure 4.8 Walking through a problem . . . .

CAUSES OF PROBLEM	STATE PROBLEM HERE:	EFFECTS OF PROBLEM

Use boxes below to list possible solutions:

POTENTIAL POSITIVE EFFECTS	SOLUTION #1	POTENTIAL NEGATIVE EFFECTS
List for each solution:		*List for each solution:*

SOLUTION #2

SOLUTION #3

Now choose the solution you think is best—and try it.

ACTUAL POSITIVE EFFECTS	CHOSEN SOLUTION	ACTUAL NEGATIVE EFFECTS
List for chosen solution:		*List for chosen solution:*

FINAL EVALUATION: Was it a good or bad choice?

Writing | *Discovery Through Journaling*

To record your thoughts, use a separate journal or the lined page at the end of the chapter.

PERSPECTIVES. Write about a perspective that has a great deal of influence on your life. How did you develop this perspective—what are its sources? What effects, positive or negative, does it have on how you think and how you live? If it has some significant negative effects, do you want to change it? How do you plan to do so?

Career Portfolio | *Charting Your Course*

INVESTIGATE A CAREER. Choose one career that interests you. Use your critical-thinking processes to think through all aspects of this career strategically. Be an investigator. Find out as many facts as you can, and evaluate all opinions based on what you already know.

- What are the different kinds of jobs available in this career?
- What is the condition of the industry—growing, lagging, or holding steady?
- Does this career require you to live in a certain area of the country or world?
- Whom can you consult to find out more information about this career?
- What are the pros and cons (positive and negative effects) of working in this area?
- What types of people tend to succeed in this career, and what types tend not to do well?
- What are the opinions of those around you about this career?
- What preparation—in school or on the job—does this career require?

Then, write up your findings in a report. You may want to use each question as a separate heading. Keep your research in your portfolio with your other Career Portfolio work. Write below a brief conclusion about your prospects in this career area based on what you learned in your investigation.

_____

_____

_____

_____

If you have access to the CD-ROM Strategies for Success, *use the following questions to assess your thoughts and enhance your understanding of the chapter. The questions below represent only some of the activities provided on the CD for the chapter topics—try others if you have time.*

Click on the Creative Thinking bookmark. Use the following activities to expand your ability to think creatively:

1. Take the pre-assessment to determine your view of the role of creativity in your life.

2. Watch the video and think about the impact of creativity on your career. In the field provided, write about how you plan to use creative thinking on the job—or how you use it right now, if you currently have a job—and give specific examples.

3. Click on Activity Three: Journal Reflections. Scroll to the third question, which asks you to brainstorm a creative way to solve a school-related problem of yours, and type your answer.

4. Take the post-assessment to see how these activities have expanded your perspective on creativity.

Suggested Readings

Cameron, Julia with Mark Bryan. *The Artist's Way: A Spiritual Path to Higher Creativity.* New York: G.P. Putnam's Sons, 1995.

deBono, Edward. *Lateral Thinking: Creativity Step by Step.* New York: Perennial Library, 1990.

Noone, Donald J., Ph.D. *Creative Problem Solving.* New York: Barron's, 1998.

Sark. *Living Juicy: Daily Morsels for Your Creative Soul.* Berkeley, CA: Celestial Arts, 1994.

von Oech, Roger. *A Kick in the Seat of the Pants.* New York: Harper & Row Publishers, 1986.

von Oech, Roger. *A Whack on the Side of the Head.* New York: Warner Books, 1998.

Internet Resources

Roger von Oech's Creative Think Web site: www.creativethink.com

Endnotes

1. Roger von Oech, *A Kick in the Seat of the Pants.* New York: Harper & Row Publishers, 1986, pp. 5–21.

2. Frank T. Lyman, Jr., Ph.D., "Think-Pair-Share, Thinktrix, Thinklinks, and Weird Facts: An Interactive System for Cooperative Thinking." In *Enhancing Thinking Through Cooperative Learning,* Neil Davidson and Toni Worsham, eds. New York: Teachers College Press, 1992, pp. 169–181.

3. Dennis Coon, *Introduction to Psychology: Exploration and Application, 6th ed.* St. Paul: West Publishing Company, 1992, p. 295.

4. Roger von Oech, *A Whack on the Side of the Head.* New York: Warner Books, 1990, pp. 11–168.

5. Ibid.

6. Ben E. Johnson, *Stirring Up Thinking.* New York: Houghton Mifflin Company, 1998, pp. 268–270.

7. Sylvan Barnet and Hugo Bedau, *Critical Thinking, Reading, and Writing: A Brief Guide to Argument, 2nd ed.* Boston: Bedford Books of St. Martin's Press, 1996, p. 43.

JOURNAL

name   date

reading and studying

IN THIS CHAPTER

In this chapter you explore answers to the following questions:

- What will help you understand what you read? • **How can you set the stage for reading?** •
How can SQ3R help you own what you read? •
How can you respond critically to what you read? •
How and why should you study with others?

IT ISN'T JUST students with learning disabilities, like Darrin Estepp (see next page), who find college reading challenging. Your reading background—your past as a reader—may not necessarily prepare you for reading that often requires deep-level understanding. You may also experience an overload of assignments.

College reading and studying require a step-by-step approach aimed at the construction of meaning and knowledge. This chapter presents techniques that help you read and study efficiently, while still having time left over for other responsibilities and activities.

focusing on content

Darrin Estepp, Ohio State
University, Columbus, Ohio

Morgan Paar, Graduate Student,
Academy of Art College, San Francisco, California

How can I cope with learning disabilities?

One thing I learned in college was that there is more than one way to succeed . . .

In elementary school, I needed extra help with reading. By high school, I was having a hard time keeping up, and a test I took showed I had dyslexia. Study assistance helped, but I attended high school for an extra year to improve my record. Then, I enrolled in community college and worked part-time as a nursing home cook. I transferred to Ohio State after two years. Recently I was also diagnosed with attention deficit hyperactivity disorder (ADHD).

I learn best by hearing, seeing, and doing all at once. If I just hear something, it doesn't sink in very well. It seems no matter how hard I try, it's never enough. I keep hanging in there though. Eventually, I would like to help others in my career—I can see myself being on the lookout for the early signs of disabilities like mine. What suggestions do you have for how I can cope with my learning disabilities?

My reading-related disability was discovered in the fourth grade. I remember dreading to read out loud to my class; students would laugh. One thing I learned in college was that there is more than one way to succeed, even if I couldn't keep up with the reading. First, I attended every single class without exception. Second, if I got behind in my note taking (and I often did), I would borrow a friend's notes and rewrite mine, combining them with theirs. Third, I made friends with my teachers, and they would help me during their office hours.

One incident showed me that anything was possible. A friend worked for a newspaper and asked me to write a story. I laughed— I said I could barely spell my name, never mind write an article. He said, "Come on, computers have spell checkers." I labored through it; my friend loved the writing (though he did say that I had used some very creative grammar), and it appeared as a two-part story in the travel section. I have since had 17 articles published.

It never gets easy—but one route to success is to do something you love. I write travel stories because I love traveling and sharing stories. I am now a filmmaker, and I am studying film in graduate school so I can someday teach it. Darrin, you already know the skills you need to achieve your goals, though maybe they are deep in your subconscious mind. I was 27 years old before I knew what I really wanted to do. Just keep following your passions, never give up, figure out what you need to do to achieve your goals, and know that there is more than one path to your destination.

What will *help you understand* what you read?

More than anything else, reading is a process that requires you, the reader, to *make meaning* from written words. When you make meaning, you connect yourself to the concepts being communicated. Your prior knowledge or familiarity with a subject, culture and home environment, life experiences, and even personal interpretation of words and phrases affect your understanding. Because these factors are different for every person, your reading experiences are uniquely your own.

Reading *comprehension* refers to your ability to understand what you read. True comprehension goes beyond just knowing facts and figures—a student can parrot back a pile of economics statistics on a test, for example, without understanding what they mean. Only when you thoroughly comprehend the information you read can you make the most effective use of that information.

All reading strategies help you to achieve a greater understanding of what you read. Therefore, every section in this chapter will in some way help you maximize your comprehension. Following are some general comprehension boosters to keep in mind as you work through the chapter and as you tackle individual reading assignments.

Build knowledge through reading and studying. More than any other factor, what you already know before you read a passage influences your ability to understand and remember important ideas. Previous knowledge gives you a context for what you read.

CONTEXT

Written or spoken knowledge that can help to illuminate the meaning of a word or passage.

Think positively. Instead of telling yourself that you cannot understand, think positively. Tell yourself: *I can learn this material. I am a good reader.*

Think critically. Ask yourself questions. Do you understand the sentence, paragraph, or chapter you just read? Are ideas and supporting examples clear? Could you explain the material to someone else? Later in this chapter, you will learn strategies for responding critically to what you read.

Build vocabulary. Lifelong learners consider their vocabulary a work in progress. They never stop learning new words. The more you know, the more material you can understand without stopping to wonder what new words mean.

Look for order and meaning in seemingly chaotic reading materials. The information in this chapter on the SQ3R reading technique and on critical reading will help you discover patterns and achieve a depth of understanding. Finding order within chaos is an important skill, not just in the mastery of reading, but also in life. This skill gives you power by helping you "read" (think through) work dilemmas, personal problems, and educational situations.

How can you *set the stage* for reading?

On any given day during your college career, you may be faced with reading assignments like these:

- A textbook chapter on the history of South African apartheid (world history)
- An original research study on the relationship between sleep deprivation and the development of memory problems (psychology)
- Chapters 4–6 in John Steinbeck's classic novel *The Grapes of Wrath* (American literature)
- A technical manual on the design of computer antivirus programs (computer science—software design)

This material is rigorous by anyone's standards. To get through it—and master its contents—you need a systematic approach. The following strategies help you set the stage for reading success.

If you have a reading disability, if English is not your primary language, or if you have limited reading skills, you may need additional support (see "Quick Start to College" for more on learning disabilities and support services). Most colleges provide services for students through a reading center or tutoring program. Take the initiative to seek help if you need it. Many accomplished learners benefit from help in specific areas. Remember: The ability to succeed is often linked to the ability to ask for help.

Take an Active Approach to Difficult Texts

Because texts are often written to challenge the intellect, even well-written, useful texts may be difficult to read. Some textbook authors may not explain information in the friendliest manner for nonexperts. And, as every student knows, some textbooks are poorly written and organized.

Generally, the further you advance in your education, the more complex your required reading. You may encounter new concepts, words, and terms that seem like a foreign language. Assignments can also be difficult when the required reading is from *primary sources*—original documents rather than another writer's interpretation of these documents—or from academic journal articles and scientific studies that don't define basic terms or supply a wealth of examples. Primary sources include:

- historical documents
- works of literature (e.g., novels, poems, and plays)
- scientific studies, including lab reports and accounts of experiments
- journal articles

The following strategies may help you approach difficult material actively and positively:

Approach your reading assignments with an open mind. Be careful not to prejudge them as impossible or boring before you even start.

Know that some texts may require some extra work and concentration. Set a goal to make your way through the material and learn. Do whatever it takes.

Define concepts that your material does not explain. Consult resources—instructors, students, reference materials—for help.

To help with your make-meaning-of-textbooks mission, you may want to create your own mini-library at home. Collect reference materials that you use often, such as a dictionary, a thesaurus, a writer's style handbook, and maybe an atlas or computer manual (many of these are available as computer software or CD-ROMs). You may also benefit from owning reference materials in your particular areas of study. "If you find yourself going to the library to look up the same reference again and again, consider purchasing that book for your personal or office library," advises library expert Sherwood Harris.[1]

Choose the Right Setting

Finding a place and time that minimize distractions helps you achieve the focus and discipline that your reading requires. Here are some suggestions.

Select the right company (or lack thereof). If you prefer to read alone, establish a relatively interruption-proof place and time such as an out-of-the-way spot at the library or an after-class hour in an empty classroom. Even if you don't mind activity nearby, try to minimize distraction.

Select the right location. Many students study at a library desk. Others prefer an easy chair at the library or at home, or even the floor. Choose a spot that's comfortable but not so cushy that you fall asleep. Make sure that you have adequate lighting and aren't too hot or cold. You may also want to avoid the distraction of studying in a room where people are talking or a television is on.

"No barrier of the senses shuts me out from the sweet, gracious discourse of my book friends. They talk to me without embarrassment or awkwardness."

HELEN KELLER

Select the right time. Choose a time when you feel alert and focused. Try reading just before or after the class for which the reading is assigned, if you can. Eventually, you will associate preferred places and times with focused reading.

Deal with internal distractions. Although a noisy environment can get in the way of your work, so can internal distractions—for example, personal worries, anticipation of an event, or even hunger. Different strategies may help. You may want to take a break and tend to one of the issues that worries you. Physical exercise may relax and refocus you. For some people, studying while listening to music quiets a busy mind. For others, silence may do the trick. If you're hungry, take a snack break and come back to your work.

Students with families have an additional factor involved when deciding when, where, and how to read. Figure 5.1 explores some ways that parents or others caring for children may be able to maximize their study efforts. These techniques will also help after college if you choose to telecommute—work from home through an Internet-linked computer—while your children are still at home under your care.

Figure 5.1   **Managing children while studying.**

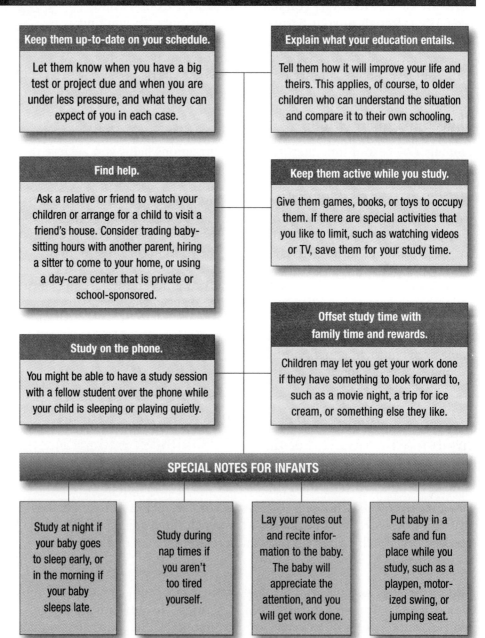

Keep them up-to-date on your schedule.

Let them know when you have a big test or project due and when you are under less pressure, and what they can expect of you in each case.

Explain what your education entails.

Tell them how it will improve your life and theirs. This applies, of course, to older children who can understand the situation and compare it to their own schooling.

Find help.

Ask a relative or friend to watch your children or arrange for a child to visit a friend's house. Consider trading baby-sitting hours with another parent, hiring a sitter to come to your home, or using a day-care center that is private or school-sponsored.

Keep them active while you study.

Give them games, books, or toys to occupy them. If there are special activities that you like to limit, such as watching videos or TV, save them for your study time.

Offset study time with family time and rewards.

Children may let you get your work done if they have something to look forward to, such as a movie night, a trip for ice cream, or something else they like.

Study on the phone.

You might be able to have a study session with a fellow student over the phone while your child is sleeping or playing quietly.

SPECIAL NOTES FOR INFANTS

Study at night if your baby goes to sleep early, or in the morning if your baby sleeps late.

Study during nap times if you aren't too tired yourself.

Lay your notes out and recite information to the baby. The baby will appreciate the attention, and you will get work done.

Put baby in a safe and fun place while you study, such as a playpen, motorized swing, or jumping seat.

Define Your Purpose for Reading

When you define your purpose, you ask yourself *why* you are reading a particular piece of material. One way to do this is by completing this sentence: "In reading this material, I intend to define/learn/answer/achieve . . ." With a clear purpose in mind, you can decide how much time and what kind of effort to expend on various reading assignments.

Achieving your reading purpose requires adapting to different types of reading materials. Being a flexible reader—adjusting your reading strategies and pace—helps you to adapt successfully.

Purpose Determines Reading Strategy

With purpose comes direction; with direction comes a strategy. Following are four reading purposes. You may have one or more for any "reading event."

Purpose 1: Read for understanding. In college, studying means reading to comprehend the material. The two main components of comprehension are *general ideas* and *specific facts or examples*. Facts and examples help to explain or support ideas, and ideas provide a framework that helps the reader to remember facts and examples.

- *General ideas.* Reading for a general idea is rapid reading that seeks an overview of the material. You search for general ideas by focusing on headings, subheadings, and summary statements.
- *Specific facts or examples.* At times, readers may focus on locating specific pieces of information—for example, the stages of intellectual development in children. Often, a reader may search for examples that support or explain general ideas—for example, the causes of economic recession.

Purpose 2: Read to evaluate critically. Critical evaluation involves understanding. It means approaching the material with an open mind, examining causes and effects, evaluating ideas, and asking questions that test the writer's argument and search for assumptions. Critical reading brings an understanding of the material that goes beyond basic information recall (see page 170 for more on critical reading).

Purpose 3: Read for practical application. A third purpose for reading is to gather usable information that you can apply toward a specific goal. When you read a computer manual or an instruction sheet for assembling a gas grill, your goal is to learn how to do something. Reading and action usually go hand in hand. Remembering the specifics requires a certain degree of general comprehension.

Purpose 4: Read for pleasure. Some materials you read for entertainment, such as *Sports Illustrated* magazine or the latest John Grisham courtroom thriller. Recreational reading may also go beyond materials that seem obviously designed to entertain. Whereas some people may read a Jane Austen novel for comprehension, as in a class assignment, others may read her books for pleasure.

Use selected reading techniques in Multiple Intelligence areas to strengthen your ability to read for meaning and retention.

INTELLIGENCE	SUGGESTED STRATEGIES	WHAT WORKS FOR YOU? WRITE NEW IDEAS HERE
Verbal–Linguistic	▪ Mark up your text with marginal notes while you read. ▪ When tackling a chapter, use every stage of SQ3R, taking advantage of each writing opportunity (writing Q stage questions, writing summaries, and so on).	
Logical–Mathematical	▪ Read material in sequence. ▪ Think about the logical connections between what you are reading and the world at large; consider similarities, differences, and cause-and-effect relationships.	
Bodily–Kinesthetic	▪ Take physical breaks during reading sessions—walk, stretch, exercise. ▪ Pace while reciting important ideas.	
Visual–Spatial	▪ As you read, take particular note of photos, tables, figures, and other visual aids. ▪ Make charts, diagrams, or think links illustrating difficult concepts you encounter in your reading.	
Interpersonal	▪ With a friend, have a joint reading session. One should read a section silently and then summarize aloud the important concepts for the other. Reverse the order of summarizer and listener for each section. ▪ Discuss reading material and clarify important concepts in a study group.	
Intrapersonal	▪ Read in a solitary setting and allow time for reflection. ▪ Think about how a particular reading assignment makes you feel, and evaluate your reaction by considering the material in light of what you already know.	
Musical	▪ Play music while you read. ▪ Recite important concepts in your reading to rhythms or write a song to depict those concepts.	
Naturalistic	▪ Read and study in a natural environment. ▪ Before reading indoors, imagine your favorite place in nature in order to create a relaxed frame of mind.	

Match Strategies to Different Areas of Study

Different subject matter presents different reading challenges. This is due in part to essential differences between the subjects (a calculus text and history of world religions text have very little in common), and in part to reader learning style and preferences (you are most likely more comfortable with some subjects than you are with others).

When you have a good idea of the kind of reading that is tough for you, you can choose the strategies that seem to help you the most. Although the information in this chapter will help with any academic subject, math and science often present unique challenges. You may benefit from using some of these specific techniques when reading math or science.

Interact with the material critically as you go. Math and science texts tend to move sequentially (later chapters build on concepts and information introduced in previous chapters) and are often problem-and-solution-based. Keep a pad of paper nearby and take notes of examples. Work steps out on your pad. Draw sketches to help visualize the material. Try not to move on until you understand the example and how it relates to the central ideas. Write down questions to ask your instructor or fellow students.

FORMULA

A general fact, rule, or principle usually expressed in mathematical symbols.

Note formulas. Evaluate the importance of formulas and recall whether the instructor emphasized them. Make sure you understand the principle behind the formula—why it works—rather than just memorizing the formula itself. Read the assigned material to prepare for any homework.

Use memory techniques. Science textbooks are often packed with vocabulary specific to that particular science (e.g., a chapter in a psychobiology course may give medical names for the parts of the brain). Put your memory skills to use when reading science texts—use mnemonic devices, test yourself using flash cards, and rehearse aloud or silently (see Chapter 6). Selective highlighting and writing summaries of your readings, in table format for example, also helps.

In this chapter's exercise set, you will see excerpts from textbooks treating three different subject areas. As you read them, notice the differences—and notice which seem easier or harder to you. This will give you some clues as to how you might approach longer reading assignments.

Build Reading Speed

Many students balance heavy academic loads with other important responsibilities. It's difficult to make time to study at all, let alone handle all of your reading assignments. If you can increase your reading speed, you will save valuable time and effort—as long as you don't sacrifice comprehension. Greater comprehension is the primary goal and actually promotes faster reading.

The average American adult reads between 150 and 350 words per minute, and faster readers can be capable of speeds up to 1,000 words per minute.[2] However, the human eye can only move so fast; reading speeds in excess of 350 words per minute involve "skimming" and "scanning" (see page 161). The following suggestions will help increase your reading speed:

- Try to read groups of words rather than single words.
- Avoid pointing your finger to guide your reading; use an index card to move quickly down the page.
- When reading narrow columns, focus your eyes in the middle of the column. With practice, you'll be able to read the entire column width as you read down the page.
- Avoid *vocalization*—speaking the words or moving your lips—when reading.

The key to building reading speed is practice and more practice, says reading expert Steve Moidel. To achieve your goal of reading between 500 and 1,000 words per minute, Moidel suggests that you start practicing at three times the rate you want to achieve, a rate that is much faster than you can comprehend.[3] For example, if your goal is 500 words per minute, speed up to 1,500 words per minute. Reading at such an accelerated rate pushes your eyes and mind to adjust to the faster pace. When you slow down to 500 words per minute—the pace at which you can read and comprehend—your reading rate will feel comfortable even though it is much faster than your original speed. You may even want to check into self-paced computer software that helps you improve reading speed.

Expand Your Vocabulary

As your reading materials at school and at work become more complex, how much you comprehend—and how readily you do it—depends on your vocabulary. A strong vocabulary increases reading speed and comprehension; when you understand the words in your reading material, you don't have to stop as often to think about what they mean.

The best way to build your vocabulary is to commit yourself to learning new and unfamiliar words as you encounter them. This involves certain steps.

Analyze Word Parts

Often, if you understand part of a word, you can figure out what the entire word means. This is true because many English words are made up of a combination of Greek and Latin prefixes, roots, and suffixes. *Prefixes* are word parts that are added to the beginning of a root. *Suffixes* are added to the end of the root. Table 5.1 contains just a few of the prefixes, roots, and suffixes you will encounter as you read. Knowing these verbal building blocks dramatically increases your vocabulary.

Figure 5.2 shows how one root can be the stem of many different words.

Using prefixes, roots, and suffixes, you can piece together the meaning of many new words you encounter. To use a simple example, the word *prologue* is made up of the prefix *pro* (before) and the root *logue* (to speak). Thus, *prologue* refers to words spoken or written before the main text.

ROOT

The central part or basis of a word, around which prefixes and suffixes can be added to produce different words.

Table 5.1   Common prefixes, roots, and suffixes.

Prefix	Primary Meaning	Example
a-, ab-	from	abstain, avert
con-, cor-, com-	with, together	convene, correlate, compare
il-	not	illegal, illegible
sub-, sup-	under	subordinate, suppose

Root	Primary Meaning	Example
-chron	time	synchronize
-ann	year	biannual
-sper	hope	desperate
-voc	speak, talk	convocation

Suffix	Primary Meaning	Example
-able	able	recyclable
-meter	measure	thermometer
-ness	state of	carelessness
-y	inclined to	sleepy

Figure 5.2   Building words from a single root.

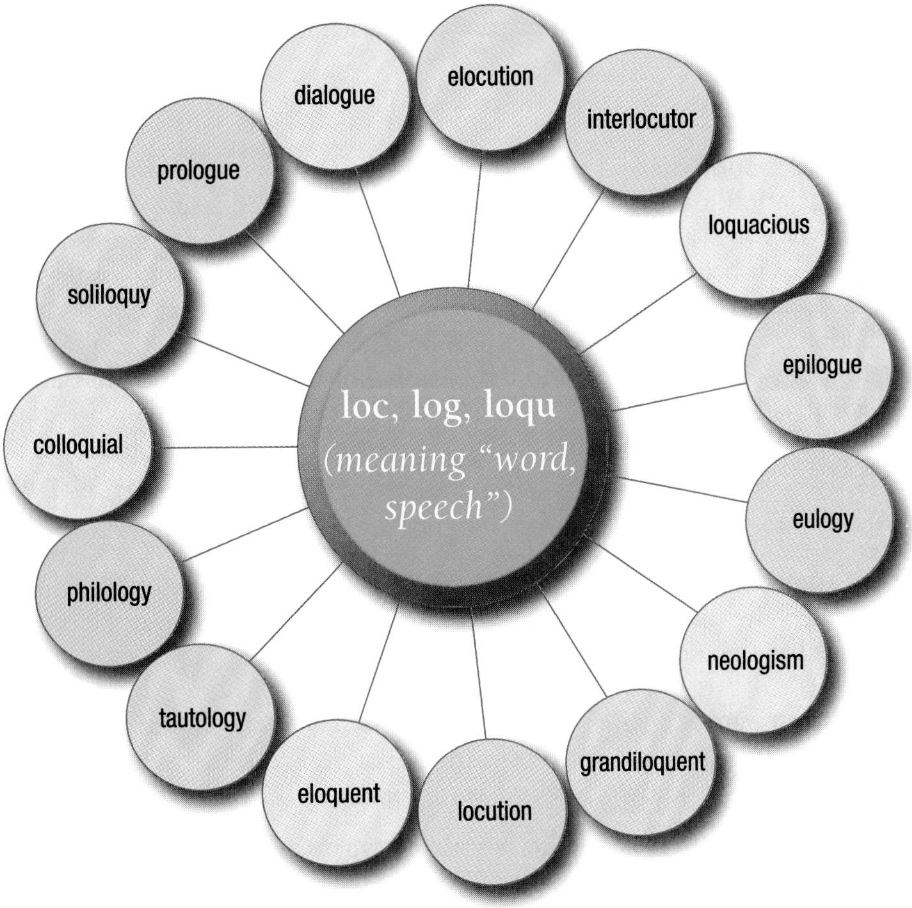

loc, log, loqu (meaning "word, speech")

dialogue, elocution, interlocutor, loquacious, epilogue, eulogy, neologism, grandiloquent, locution, eloquent, tautology, philology, colloquial, soliloquy, prologue

Use Words in Context

Most people learn words best when they read and use them in written or spoken language. Although a definition tells you what a word means, it may not include a context. Using a word in context after defining it helps to anchor the information so that you can remember it and continue to build on it. Here are some strategies for using context to solidify new vocabulary words.

Use new words in a sentence or two right away. Do this immediately after reading their definitions while everything is still fresh in your mind.

Reread the sentence where you originally saw the word. Go over it a few times to make sure that you understand how the word is used.

Use the word over the next few days whenever it may apply. Try it while talking with friends, writing letters or notes, or in your own thoughts.

Consider where you may have seen or heard the word before. When you learn a word, going back to sentences you previously didn't "get" may solidify your understanding. For example, most children learn the Pledge of Allegiance by rote without understanding what "allegiance" means. Later, when they learn the definition of "allegiance," the pledge provides a context that helps them better understand the word.

Seek knowledgeable advice. If after looking up a word you still have trouble with its meaning, ask an instructor or friend to help you figure it out.

Use a Dictionary

Standard dictionaries provide broad information such as word origin, pronunciation, part of speech, and multiple meanings. Using a dictionary whenever you read increases your comprehension. Buy a standard dictionary, keep it nearby, and consult it for help in understanding passages that contain unfamiliar words. Some textbooks also have a text-specific "dictionary" called a *glossary* that defines terms found in the text. Such definitions are often limited to the meaning of the term as used in that particular textbook.

You may not always have time to use the following suggestions, but when you can use them, they will help you make the most of your dictionary.

Read every meaning of a word, not just the first. Think critically about which meaning suits the context of the word in question, and choose the one that makes the most sense to you.

Substitute a word or phrase from the definition for the word. Use the definition you have chosen. Imagine, for example, that you read the following sentence and do not know the word *indoctrinated*:

The cult indoctrinated its members to reject society's values.

In the dictionary, you find several definitions, including *brainwashed* and *instructed*. You decide that the one closest to the correct meaning is brainwashed. With this term, the sentence reads as follows:

The cult brainwashed its members to reject society's values.

So far, this chapter has focused on reading as a deliberate, purposeful process of meaning construction. Recognizing obstacles and defining reading purposes lay the groundwork for effective studying—the process of mastering the concepts and skills contained in your texts.

How can SQ3R help you *own* what you read?

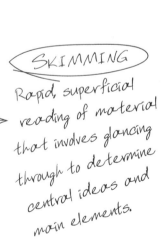

When you study, you take ownership of the material you read, meaning that you learn it well enough to apply it to what you do. For example, by the time students studying to be computer hardware technicians complete their course work, they should be able to analyze hardware problems that lead to malfunctions. On-the-job computer technicians use the same study technique to keep up with changing technology. Studying to understand and learn also gives you mastery over concepts. For example, a dental hygiene student learns the causes of gum disease, and a business student learns about marketing.

SQ3R is a technique that will help you grasp ideas quickly, remember more, and review effectively for tests. SQ3R stands for *Survey, Question, Read, Recite,* and *Review*—all steps in the studying process. Developed more than 55 years ago by Francis Robinson, the technique is still used today because it works.[4]

Moving through the stages of SQ3R requires that you know how to skim and scan. Skimming involves the rapid reading of chapter elements, including introductions, conclusions, and summaries; the first and last lines of paragraphs; boldfaced or italicized terms; and pictures, charts, and diagrams. The goal of skimming is a quick construction of the main ideas. In contrast, scanning involves the careful search for specific facts and examples. You might use scanning during the review phase of SQ3R when you need to locate particular information (such a formula in a chemistry text).

Approach SQ3R as a framework on which you build your house, not as a tower of stone. In other words, instead of following each step by rote, bring your personal learning styles and study preferences to the system. For example, you and another classmate may focus on elements in a different order when you survey, write different types of questions, or favor different sets of review strategies. Explore the strategies, evaluate what works, and then make the system your own.

SKIMMING
Rapid, superficial reading of material that involves glancing through to determine central ideas and main elements.

SCANNING
Reading material in an investigative way, searching for specific information.

Survey

Surveying refers to the process of previewing, or pre-reading, a book before you actually study it. Compare it to looking at a map before you drive somewhere—those few minutes taking a look at your surroundings and where you intend to go will save you a lot of time and trouble once you are on the road.

Most textbooks include devices that give students an overview of the whole text as well as of the contents of individual chapters. When you survey, pay attention to the following elements.

The front matter. Before you even get to page 1, most textbooks have a table of contents, a preface, and other materials. The table of contents gives you an overview with clues about coverage, topic order, and features. The preface, in particular, can point out the book's unique approach. For example, the preface for the American history text *Out of Many* states that it highlights "the experiences of diverse communities of Americans in the unfolding story of our country."[5] This tells you that cultural diversity is a central theme.

The chapter elements. Generally, each chapter has devices that help you make meaning out of the material. Among these are:

- The chapter title, which establishes the topic and perhaps author perspective
- The chapter introduction, outline, list of objectives, or list of key topics
- Within the chapter, headings, tables and figures, quotes, marginal notes, and photographs that help you perceive structure and important concepts
- Special chapter features, often presented in boxes set off from the main text, that point you to ideas connected to themes that run through the text
- Particular styles or arrangements of type (**boldface**, *italics*, <u>underline</u>, larger fonts, bullet points, boxed text) that call your attention to new words or important concepts

At the end of a chapter, a summary may help you tie concepts together. Review questions and exercises help you review and think critically about the material. Skimming these *before* reading the chapter gives you clues about what's important.

The back matter. Here some texts include a glossary. You may also find an *index* to help you locate individual topics and a *bibliography* that lists additional reading on particular topics covered in the text.

Figure 5.3 shows the many devices that books employ. Think about how many of these devices you already use, and which you can start using now to boost your comprehension.

Figure 5.3 Text and chapter previewing devices.

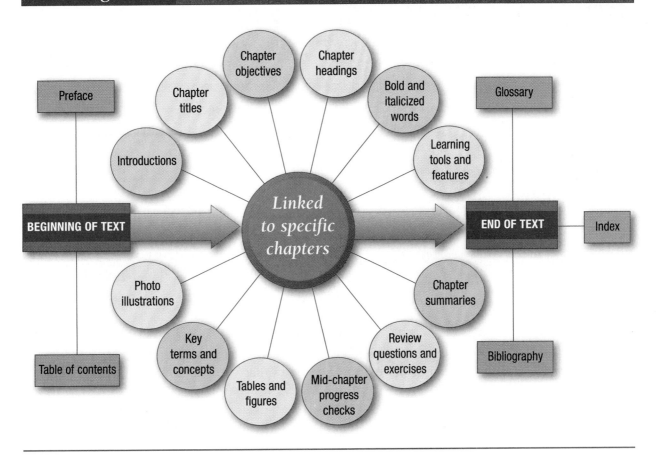

Question

Your next step is to examine the chapter headings and, on a separate piece of paper or in the margins, to write *questions* linked to them. If your reading material has no headings, develop questions as you read. These questions focus your attention and increase your interest, helping you build comprehension and relate new ideas to what you already know. You can take questions from the textbook or from your lecture notes, or come up with them on your own when you survey, based on what ideas you think are most important.

The table at the top of the next page shows how this works. The column on the left contains primary- and secondary-level headings from a section of *Out of Many*. The column on the right rephrases these headings in question form.

There is no "correct" set of questions. Given the same headings, you could create your own particular set of questions. The more useful kinds of questions engage the critical-thinking mind actions and processes discussed in Chapter 4.

The Meaning of Freedom	What did freedom mean for both slaves and citizens in the United States?
Moving About	Where did African Americans go after they were freed from slavery?
The African American Family	How did freedom change the structure of the African American family?
African American Churches and Schools	What effect did freedom have on the formation of African American churches and schools?
Land and Labor after Slavery	How was land farmed and maintained after slaves were freed?
The Origins of African American Politics	How did the end of slavery bring about the beginning of African American political life?

Read

Your questions give you a starting point for *reading,* the first R in SQ3R. Learning from textbooks requires that you read *actively.* Active reading means engaging with the material through questioning, writing, note taking, and other activities. As you can see in Figure 5.4, the activities of SQ3R promote active reading. Following are some specific strategies that will keep you active when you read.

Focus on your Q-stage questions. Read the material with the purpose of answering each question. As you come on ideas and examples that relate to your question, write them down or note them in the text.

Look for important concepts. As you read, record key words, phrases, and concepts in your notebook. Some students divide the notebook into two columns, writing questions on the left and answers on the right. This method is called the Cornell note-taking system (see Chapter 6).

Mark up your textbook. Being able to make notations will help you to make sense of the material; for this reason, owning your textbooks is an enormous advantage. You may want to write notes in the margins, circle key ideas, or highlight key points. Figure 5.5 shows how this is done on a marketing textbook section that introduces the concept of markets. Some people prefer to underline, although underlining adds more ink to the lines of text and may overwhelm your eyes. Bracketing an entire key passage is a good alternative to underlining.

Selective highlighting may help you pinpoint material to review before an exam, although excessive highlighting may actually interfere with comprehension. Here are some tips on how to strike a balance.

- Mark the text *after* you read the material once through. If you do it on the first reading, you may mark less important passages.

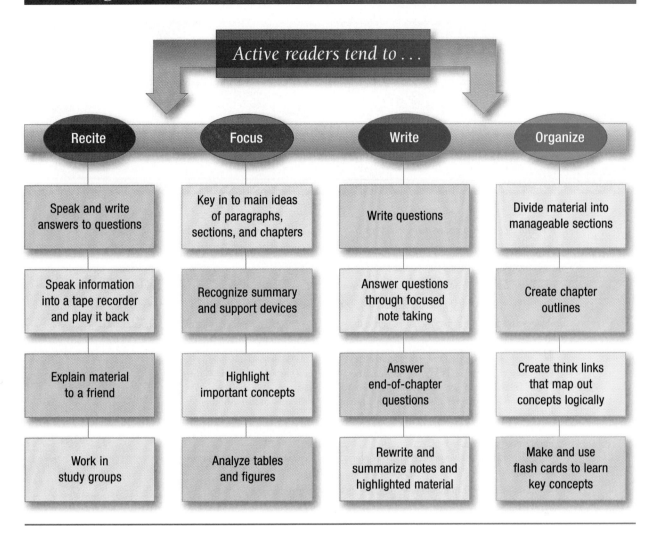

Figure 5.4   Use SQ3R to become an active reader.

Active readers tend to . . .

Recite	Focus	Write	Organize
Speak and write answers to questions	Key in to main ideas of paragraphs, sections, and chapters	Write questions	Divide material into manageable sections
Speak information into a tape recorder and play it back	Recognize summary and support devices	Answer questions through focused note taking	Create chapter outlines
Explain material to a friend	Highlight important concepts	Answer end-of-chapter questions	Create think links that map out concepts logically
Work in study groups	Analyze tables and figures	Rewrite and summarize notes and highlighted material	Make and use flash cards to learn key concepts

- Highlight key terms and concepts. Mark the examples that explain and support important ideas.
- Avoid overmarking. A phrase or two in any paragraph is usually enough. Set off long passages with brackets rather than marking every line.
- Don't mistake highlighting for learning. You will not learn what you highlight unless you interact with it through careful review—questioning, writing, and reciting.

Be sure to divide your reading into digestible segments, pacing yourself so that you understand as you go. If you find you are losing the thread of the ideas, you may want to try smaller segments or take a break and come back to it later. Try to avoid reading in mere sets of time—such as, "I'll read for 30 minutes and then quit"—or you may short-circuit your understanding by stopping in the middle of a key explanation.

Figure 5.5   Effective highlighting and marginal notes aid memory.

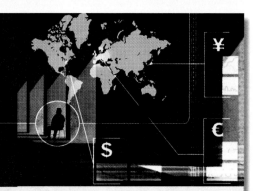

Markets

The term *market* has acquired many meanings over the years. In its original meaning, a market is a physical place where buyers and sellers gather to exchange goods and services. Medieval towns had market squares where sellers brought their goods and buyers shopped for goods. In today's cities, buying and selling occur in shopping areas rather than markets. To an economist, a market describes all the buyers and sellers who transact over some good or service. Thus, the soft-drink market consists of sellers such as Coca-Cola and PepsiCo, and of all the consumers who buy soft drinks. To a marketer, a market is the set of all actual and potential buyers of a product or service.

O rganizations that sell to consumer and business markets recognize that they cannot appeal to all buyers in those markets, or at least not to all buyers in the same way. Buyers are too numerous, too widely scattered, and too varied in their needs and buying practices. And different companies vary widely in their abilities to serve different segments of the market. Rather than trying to compete in an entire market, sometimes against superior competitors, each company must identify the parts of the market that it can serve best.

[margin note: Definition of a market]

[margin note: Companies can't appeal to everyone]

Sellers have not always practiced this philisophy. Their thinking has passed through three stages:

[margin note: One-size-fits-all approach]

- *Mass marketing.* In mass marketing, the seller mass produces, mass distributes, and mass promotes one product to all buyers. At one time, Coca-Cola produced only one drink for the whole market, hoping it would appeal to everyone. The argument for mass marketing is that it should lead to the lowest costs and prices and create the largest potential market.

[margin note: Offer variety to buyers]

- *Product-variety marketing.* Here, the seller produces two or more products that have different features, styles, quality, sizes, and so on. Later, Coca-Cola produced several soft drinks packaged in different sizes and containers that were designed to offer variety to buyers rather than to appeal to different market segments. The argument for product-variety marketing is that consumers have different tastes that change over time. Consumers seek variety and change.

[margin note: A tailored approach to specific market segments]

- *Target marketing.* Here, the seller identifies market segments, selects one or more of them, and develops products and marketing mixes tailored to each. For example, Coca-Cola now produces soft drinks for the sugared-cola segment (Coca-Cola Classic and Cherry Coke), the diet segment (Diet Coke and Tab), the no-caffeine segment (Caffeine-Free Coke), and the noncola segment (Minute Maid sodas).

[margin note: Current approach is usually TARGET MARKETING]

Today's companies are moving away from mass marketing and product-variety marketing toward target marketing. Target marketing can better help sellers find their marketing opportunities. Sellers can develop the right product for each target market and adjust their prices, distribution channels, and advertising to reach the target market efficiently. Instead of scattering their marketing efforts (the "shotgun" approach), they can focus on the buyers who have greater purchase interest (the "rifle" approach).

87

Finding the Main Idea

One crucial skill in textbook reading is finding the main, or central, idea of a piece of writing (e.g., a book, a chapter, an article, a paragraph). The *main idea* refers to the thoughts that are at the heart of the writing, the idea that creates its essential meaning. Comprehension depends on your ability to recognize main ideas and to link the author's other thoughts to them.

Where do you find the main idea? As an example, consider a paragraph. The main idea may be:

- In a *topic sentence* at the very beginning of the paragraph, stating the topic of the paragraph and what about that topic the author wants to communicate, and followed by sentences adding support.

- At the end of the paragraph, following supporting details that lead up to it.

- Buried in the middle of the paragraph, sandwiched between supporting details.

- In a compilation of ideas from various sentences, each of which contains a critical element. It is up to the reader to piece these elements together to create the essence of meaning.

- Never explicitly stated, but implied by the information presented in the paragraph.

How, then, do you decide just what the main idea is? Ophelia H. Hancock, a specialist in improving reading skills for college students, takes a three-step approach:[6]

1. *Search for the topic of the paragraph.* The topic of the paragraph is not the same thing as the main idea. Rather, it is the broad subject being discussed—for example, former President John F. Kennedy, hate crimes on campus, or the World Wide Web.

2. *Identify the aspect of the topic that is the paragraph's focus.* If the general topic is former President John F. Kennedy, the writer may choose to focus on any of literally thousands of aspects of that topic. Here are just a few: his health problems, his civil rights policies, key events in his early adult years, the people he chose as cabinet members, his effectiveness as a public speaker, his relationship with family.

3. *Find what the author wants you to know about the specific aspect being discussed, which is the main idea.* The main idea of a paragraph dealing with President Kennedy as a public speaker may be this:

President Kennedy was a gifted, charismatic speaker who used his humor, charm, and intelligence to make the presidency accessible to all Americans during regularly televised presidential news conferences.

You can use this three-step approach to find the main idea of the following paragraph:

Tone relates not so much to what you say as to how you say it. The tone of your writing has a major impact on what you are trying to communicate to your audience. Tone involves your choice of words interacting with your message. Have you ever reacted to someone's understanding of what you wrote with "That's not what I meant to say"? Your tone can be what has thrown your readers off track, although you can only be misunderstood if your writing is unclear or imprecise.[7]

Q: What is the topic of the paragraph?

A: The tone of your writing

Q: What aspect of tone is being discussed?

A: The meaning of tone and its impact on readers

Q: What main idea is being communicated about this aspect?

A: The tone of your writing has a major impact on what you are trying to communicate to your audience. In this paragraph, the second sentence completely states the main idea.

Recite

Once you finish reading a topic, stop and answer the questions you raised in the Q-stage of SQ3R. You may decide to *recite* each answer aloud, silently speak the answers to yourself, tell or teach the answers to another person, or write your ideas and answers in brief notes. Writing is often the most effective way to solidify what you have read because writing from memory checks your understanding.

"The best effect of any book is that it excites the reader to self-activity."

THOMAS CARLYLE

Keep your learning styles (Chapter 2) in mind when you explore different strategies. For example, an intrapersonal learner may prefer writing, while an interpersonal learner might want to recite answers aloud to a classmate. A logical–mathematical learner may benefit from organizing material into detailed outlines, while a musical learner might want to chant information aloud to a rhythm.

After you finish one section, read the next. Repeat the question–read–recite cycle until you complete the entire chapter. If you find yourself fumbling for thoughts, you may not yet "own" the ideas. Reread the section that's giving you trouble until you master its contents. Understanding each section as you go is crucial because the material in one section often forms a foundation for the next.

Review

Review soon after you finish a chapter. Reviewing, both immediately and periodically in the days and weeks after you read, is the step that solidifies your understanding. Chances are good that if you close the book after you read, much of your focused reading work will slip away from memory. Here are some techniques for reviewing—try many and use what works best for you.

- Skim and reread your notes. Then, try summarizing them from memory.

- Answer the text's end-of-chapter review, discussion, and application questions.

- Quiz yourself, using the questions you raised in the Q stage. If you can't answer one of your own or one of the text's questions, go back and scan the material for answers.

- Review and summarize in writing the material you have highlighted or bracketed.

- Create a chapter outline in standard outline form or think link form.

- Reread the preface, headings, tables, and summary.

- Recite important concepts to yourself, or record important information on a cassette tape and play it on your car's tape deck or your portable cassette player.

- Make flash cards that have an idea or word on one side and examples, a definition, or other related information on the other. Test yourself.

- Think critically: Break ideas down into examples, consider similar or different concepts, recall important terms, evaluate ideas, and explore causes and effects (see the next section for details).

- Discuss the concepts with a classmate or in a study group. Trying to teach study partners what you learned will pinpoint the material you know and what still needs work.

- Make think links that show how important concepts relate to one another.

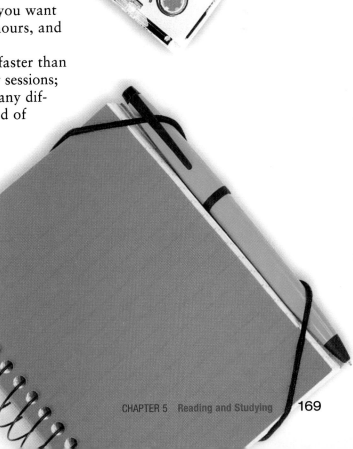

If you need help clarifying your reading material, ask your instructor. Pinpoint the material you want to discuss, schedule a meeting during office hours, and bring a list of questions.

Refreshing your knowledge is easier and faster than learning it the first time. Set up regular review sessions; for example, once a week. Reviewing in as many different ways as possible increases the likelihood of retention. Critical reading may be the most important of these ways.

How can you *respond critically* to what you read?

Textbook features often highlight important ideas and help you determine study questions. As you advance in your education, however, many reading assignments—especially primary sources—will not be so clearly marked. You need critical-reading skills to select important ideas, identify examples that support them, and ask questions about the text without the aid of any special features.

Critical reading enables you to develop a thorough understanding of reading material. A critical reader is able to discern the central idea of a piece of reading material, as well as identify what in that piece is true or accurate, such as when choosing material as a source for an essay. A critical reader can also compare one piece of material to another and evaluate which makes more sense, which proves its thesis more successfully, or which is more useful for the reader's purposes.

Engage your critical-thinking processes by using the following suggestions for critical reading.

Use SQ3R to "Taste" Reading Material

Sylvan Barnet and Hugo Bedau, authors of *Critical Thinking, Reading, and Writing: A Brief Guide to Argument,* suggest that the active reading of SQ3R helps you form an initial idea of what a piece of reading material is all about. Through surveying, skimming for ideas and examples, highlighting and writing comments and questions in the margins, and reviewing, you can develop a basic understanding of its central ideas and contents.[8]

Summarizing, part of the SQ3R review process, is one of the best ways to develop an understanding of a piece of reading material. To construct a summary, focus on the central ideas of the piece and the main examples that support them. A summary does not contain any of your own ideas or your evaluation of the material. It simply condenses the material, making it easier to focus on the structure and central ideas of the piece. At that point, you can begin asking questions, evaluating the piece, and introducing your own ideas. Using the mind actions described in Chapter 4 helps you.

SUMMARY

A concise restatement of the material, in your own words, that covers the main points.

Ask Questions Based on the Mind Actions

The essence of critical reading, as with critical thinking, is asking questions. Instead of simply accepting what you read, seek a more thorough understanding by questioning the material as you go along. Using the mind actions to formulate your questions helps you understand the material.

What parts of the material you focus on depends on your purpose for reading. For example, if you are writing a paper on the causes of World War II, you might look at how certain causes fit your thesis. If you are comparing two pieces of writing that contain opposing arguments, you may focus on picking out their central ideas and evaluating how well the writers use examples to support them.

You can question any of the following components of reading material:

- the central idea of the entire piece
- a particular idea or statement
- the examples that support an idea or statement
- the proof of a fact
- the definition of a concept

Following are some ways to critically question reading material. Apply them to any component you want to question by substituting the component for the words *it* and *this*.

Similarity:	What does this remind me of or how is it similar to something else I know?
Difference:	What different conclusions are possible? How is this different from my experience?
Cause and effect:	Why did this happen or what caused this? What are the effects or consequences of this? What effect does the author intend or what is the purpose of this material? What effects support a stated cause?
Example to idea:	How do I classify this or what is the best idea to fit this example? How do I summarize this or what are the key ideas? What is the thesis or central idea?
Idea to example:	What evidence supports this or what examples fit this idea?
Evaluation:	How do I evaluate this? Is it useful or well constructed? Does this example support my thesis or central idea? Is this information or point of view important to my work? If so, why?

Engage Critical-Thinking Processes

Certain thinking processes from Chapter 4, *reasoning* and *opening your mind to new perspectives,* can help to deepen your analysis and evaluation of what you read. Within these processes you ask questions that use the mind actions.

Reasoning

With what you know about how to reason, you can evaluate any statement in your reading material, identifying it as fact or opinion and challenging how it is supported. Evaluate statements using questions such as the following:

- Is this fact? Is the factual statement true? How does the writer know?
- Is this opinion? How could I test its validity?
- What else do I know that is similar to or different from this?
- What examples that I already know support or disprove this?

Your reasoning ability also helps you evaluate any argument you find in your reading material. In this case, *argument* refers to a persuasive case—a set of connected ideas supported by examples—that a writer makes to prove or disprove a point.

It's easy—and common—to accept or reject an argument outright, according to whether it fits with one's own opinions and views. If you ask questions about an argument, however, you can determine its validity and learn more from it. Furthermore, critical thinking helps you avoid accepting premises that are not supported by evidence.

Reasoning through an argument involves two kinds of evaluations:

- evaluating the quality of the evidence
- evaluating whether the evidence adequately supports the premise (whether the examples fit the idea)

Together, these evaluations help you see whether an argument works. If quality evidence (accurate input) combines with quality use of evidence (valid reasoning), you get a solid argument.

Evidence quality. Ask the following questions in order to see whether the evidence itself is accurate:

- What type of evidence is it—fact or opinion? Do the facts seem accurate?
- How is the evidence similar to, or different from, what I already believe to be true?
- Where is the evidence from? Are those sources reliable and free of bias?

PERSONAL TRIUMPH

*h*aving a particular drive to make something of yourself when deciding to attend college can make the experience that much more meaningful. Dani Day's determination led her through family strife and financial aid difficulties into a stimulating educational experience.

I was living in a subsidized apartment complex with an abusive husband and was pregnant with my third child. I decided I didn't want to put my kids through this anymore so I left him. I went through the pregnancy by myself and got my G.E.D. Even though I had few resources and low self-esteem, I had the will to survive.

In 1993, I became a home owner through Habitat for Humanity.* I put in 500 hours of manual labor, which Habitat calls "sweat equity." Getting my own home was the catalyst for change; it was the first step toward a new life for me and my family. My house was the first in the Denver area built entirely by women, so it brought a lot of publicity. I became a spokesperson for the organization and found I was comfortable in front of a camera speaking to groups of people.

The most significant decision I made was to attend college, but trying to come up with the money to pay for school became discouraging. Because I owned a house, I didn't qualify for financial assistance, and government agencies didn't want to pay for child care. Some financial aid representatives said they turned me down because I was "self-initiated." I rebelled at this, and my personal motto became "I'm going to school with or without any help."

Six months after moving in, I explored my desire to be in front of the camera by enrolling in a communications program. I also landed two internships, which helped me pay for college. I did on-camera pieces for public broadcasting networks, and I even tried stand-up comedy, but these jobs didn't pay the bills. Also, my schedule was crazy. I grew weary from the constant strain of trying to juggle my

Dani E. Day, Communication Studies;
Community College of Denver, Denver, Colorado

children's needs with work. I knew something had to change.

I found that opportunities for permanent jobs were in the technical fields, and I turned toward management for the normal work hours. Technical work wasn't my inclination, but I thought if nothing else it's a good opportunity to learn the other side of the business. To my surprise, I found that I had a knack for television engineering.

I'm still interested in being on television, maybe as a news anchor or as the host of a public television station. I won't let go of that desire, but right now I have three kids to feed and my oldest son has special needs. I need to make time for him and focus on being the most productive I can for my family.

I enjoy learning, and I try to apply what I need from each step and use that for my next step. Fear does not paralyze me; it actually motivates me to work harder. My children have seen the constant drive that it takes to succeed. Watching me is helping them embrace life's challenges. They want college, and they want to make something of their lives.

In every situation, I do the best I can to adapt. Negative situations will hold you back if you let them. One person insinuated that I would never be qualified to do more than minimum wage work. If I had believed that, I wouldn't be where I am today. It's not what other people believe about you that matters but what you believe about yourself.

*Habitat for Humanity International is a nonprofit organization that lends no-profit, no-interest mortgages to people in need. Since 1976, they have built more than 100,000 houses around the world.

Take a moment to consider . . .

- *How you think college will help you "make something of your life."*
- *A book you have read or a course you have taken that surprised you by showing you an interest you didn't know you had.*

Support quality. Ask these questions to determine whether you think the evidence successfully makes the argument:

- Do examples and ideas, and causes and effects, logically connect to one another?
- Do I believe this argument? How is the writer trying to persuade me?
- Are there enough pieces of evidence to adequately support the central idea?
- What different and perhaps opposing arguments seem just as valid?
- Has the argument evaluated all of the positive and negative effects involved? Are there any negative effects to the conclusion that haven't been considered?

Don't rule out the possibility that you may agree wholeheartedly with an argument. However, use critical thinking to make an informed decision rather than accepting the argument outright.

For example, imagine that you are reading an article whose main argument is, "The dissolving of the family unit is the main cause of society's ills." You might examine the facts and examples the writer uses to support this statement, looking carefully at the cause-and-effect structure of the argument. You might question the writer's sources. You might think of examples you know of that support the statement. You might find examples that disprove this argument, such as successful families that don't fit the traditional definition of family used by the writer. Finally, you might think your way through a couple of opposing arguments, thinking of the ideas and examples you would use to support those arguments.

Opening Your Mind to New Perspectives

This critical-thinking process helps you understand that many reading materials are written from a particular perspective. For example, if both a recording artist and a music censorship advocate were to write a piece about a controversial song created by that artist, their different perspectives would result in two very different pieces of writing.

To analyze perspective, ask questions like the following:

- What perspective is guiding this?

- Who wrote this and with what intent?
- How does the material's source affect its perspective?
- How is this perspective supported?
- What assumptions underlie this?
- What examples do not fit this assumption?

Think again about the example—the piece of writing claiming that "the dissolving of the family unit is the main cause of society's ills." Considering perspective, you might ask questions like these:

- How do I define the perspective of this piece? What are the central opinions that influence this material?
- Who wrote this and why? Is it designed to communicate statistics as objectively as possible, or does the author intend to promote a particular message?
- What is the source, and how does that affect the piece? (For example, a piece appearing in the *New York Times* may differ from one appearing in a magazine that promotes a particular way of living.)
- What examples and evidence does the author use to support the claim? Is the support valid? After reading it, do I feel comfortable with the perspective?
- What assumptions underlie this statement (e.g., assumptions about the definition of "family" or about what constitutes "society's ills")?
- Can I think of examples of families or success stories that do not fit these assumptions?

Seek Understanding

The fundamental purpose of all college reading is to understand the material. Think of your reading process as an archaeological dig. The first step is to excavate a site and uncover the artifacts, which corresponds to your initial survey and reading of the material. As important as the excavation is, the process is incomplete if you stop there. The second half of the process is to investigate each item, evaluate what they all mean, and derive new knowledge and ideas from what you discover. Critical reading allows you to complete that crucial second half of the process.

Critical reading takes time and focus. Give yourself a chance at success by finding a time, place, and purpose for reading. Learn from others by working in pairs or groups whenever you can.

Why and how should you *study with others?*

Much of what you know and will learn comes from your interaction with the outside world. Often this interaction takes place between you and one or more people. You listen to instructors and other students, you read materials that people have written, and you try out the behavior and ideas of those whom you most trust and respect. You often work in a *team*—a group of fellow students, coworkers, family members, or others who strive together to reach an objective.

Learning takes place the same way in your career and personal life. Today's workplace puts the emphasis on work done through team effort. Companies value the ideas, energy, and cooperation that result from a well-coordinated team.

Leaders and Participants

Study groups and other teams rely on both leaders and participants to accomplish goals. Becoming aware of the roles each plays will increase your effectiveness.[9] Keep in mind that participants sometimes perform leadership tasks and vice versa. In addition, some teams shift leadership frequently during a project.

Being an Effective Participant

Some people are most comfortable when participating in a group that someone else leads. However, even when they are not leading, participants are "part owners" of the team process with a responsibility for, and a stake in, the outcome. The following strategies will help you become more effective in this role.

- *Get involved.* Let people know your views on decisions.
- *Be organized.* The more focused your ideas, the more other group members will take them seriously.
- *Be willing to discuss.* Be open to the opinions of others, even if they differ from your own.
- *Keep your word.* Carry out whatever tasks you promise to do.
- *Play fairly.* Give everyone a chance to participate and always be respectful.

Being an Effective Leader

Some people prefer to initiate the action, make decisions, and control how things proceed. Leaders often have a "big-picture" perspective that allows them to envision how different aspects of a group project will come together. In any group, the following strategies help a leader succeed.

- *Define and limit projects.* The leader should define the group's purpose (e.g., brainstorming, decision making, or project collaboration) and limit tasks so that the effort remains focused.

- *Assign work and set a schedule.* A group functions best when everyone has a particular contribution to make and when deadlines are clear.

- *Set meeting and project agendas.* The leader should, with advice from other group members, establish and communicate goals and define how the work will proceed.

- *Focus progress.* It is the leader's job to keep everyone on target and headed in the right direction.

- *Set the tone.* If the leader is fair, respectful, encouraging, and hard working, group members are likely to follow the example.

- *Evaluate results.* The leader should determine whether the team is accomplishing its goals on schedule. If the team is not moving ahead, the leader should make changes.

Strategies for Study Group Success

Every study group is unique. The way a group operates may depend on the members' personalities, the subject you study, the location of the group, and the size of the group. No matter what your particular group's situation, though, certain general strategies will help.

Choose a leader for each meeting. Rotating the leadership, among members willing to lead, helps all members take ownership of the group. If a leader has to miss class for any reason, choose another leader for that meeting.

Set long-term and short-term goals. At your first meeting, determine what the group wants to accomplish over the semester. At the start of each meeting, have one person compile a list of questions to address.

Adjust to different personalities. Respect and communicate with members. The art of getting along will serve you well in the workplace, where you don't often choose your coworkers.

Share the workload. The most important factor is a willingness to work, not a particular level of knowledge.

Set a regular meeting schedule. Try every week, every two weeks, or whatever the group can manage.

Create study materials for one another. Give each group member the task of finding a piece of information to compile, photocopy, and review for the other group members.

Help each other learn. One of the best ways to solidify knowledge is to teach it. Have group members teach pieces of information; make up quizzes for each other; go through flash cards together.

Pool your note-taking resources. Compare notes with your group members and fill in any information you don't have. Try other note-taking styles: For example, if you generally use outlines, rewrite your notes in a think link. If you tend to map out ideas in a think link, try the Cornell System (see Chapter 6 for more on note taking).

Benefits of Working with Others

If you apply this information to your schoolwork, you will see that studying with a partner or in a group can enhance your learning in many ways. You benefit from shared knowledge, solidified knowledge, increased motivation, and increased teamwork ability.

"The wise person learns from everyone."

ETHICS OF THE FATHERS

Shared knowledge. Each student has a unique body of knowledge and individual strengths. Students can learn from one another. To have individual students pass on their knowledge to each other in a study group requires less time and energy than for each of those students to learn all of the material alone.

Solidified knowledge. When you discuss concepts or teach them to others, you reinforce what you know and strengthen your critical thinking. Part of the benefit comes from simply repeating information aloud and rewriting it on paper, and part comes from how you think through information in your mind before you pass it on to someone else.

Increased motivation. When you study by yourself, you are accountable to yourself alone. In a study group, however, others see your level of work and preparation, which may increase your motivation.

Increased teamwork ability. The more you understand the dynamics of working with a group and the more experience you have at it, the more you build your ability to work well with others. This is an invaluable skill for the workplace, and it contributes to your personal marketability.

читать

This word may look completely unfamiliar to you, but anyone who can read the Russian language and knows the alphabet will know that it means "read." People who read languages that use different kinds of characters, such as Russian, Japanese, or Greek, learn to process those characters as easily as you process the letters of your native alphabet. Your mind learns to process individually each letter or character you see. This ability enables you to move to the next level of understanding—making sense of those letters or characters when they are grouped to form words, phrases, and sentences.

Think of this concept when you read. Remember that your mind processes immeasurable amounts of information so that you can understand the concepts on the page. Give yourself the opportunity to succeed by reading often and by focusing on the elements that help you read to the best of your ability.

Building Skills

FOR COLLEGE, CAREER, AND LIFE SUCCESS

Critical Thinking *Applying Learning to Life*

Studying a Text Page

The following page is from the chapter "Groups and Organizations" in the sixth edition of John J. Macionis's *Sociology*.[10] Apply SQ3R as you read the excerpt. Using what you learned in this chapter about study techniques, complete the questions that follow the reading (some questions ask you to mark the page itself).

1. Identify the headings on the page and the relationship between them. Mark primary-level headings with a #1, secondary headings with a #2, and tertiary (third-level heads) with a #3. Which heading serves as an umbrella for the rest?

   _____

2. What do the headings tell you about the content of the page?

   _____

   _____

3. After reading the chapter headings, write two study questions.

   a. _____

   _____

   b. _____

   _____

4. Using a marker pen, highlight key phrases and sentences. Write short marginal notes to help you review the material at a later point.

5. After reading this page, list three key concepts that you need to study.

   a. _____

   b. _____

   c. _____

SOCIAL GROUPS

Virtually everyone moves through life with a sense of belonging; this is the experience of group life. A **social group** refers to *two or more people who identify and interact with one another.* Human beings continually come together to form couples, families, circles of friends, neighborhoods, churches, businesses, clubs, and numerous large organizations. Whatever the form, groups encompass people with shared experiences, loyalties, and interests. In short, while maintaining their individuality, the members of social groups also think of themselves as a special "we."

Groups, Categories, and Crowds

People often use the term "group" imprecisely. We now distinguish the group from the similar concepts of category and crowd.

Category. A *category* refers to people who have some status in common. Women, single fathers, military recruits, homeowners, and Roman Catholics are all examples of categories.

Why are categories not considered groups? Simply because, while the individuals involved are aware that they are not the only ones to hold that particular status, the vast majority are strangers to one another.

Crowd. A *crowd* refers to a temporary cluster of individuals who may or may not interact at all. Students sitting in a lecture hall do engage one another and share some common identity as college classmates; thus, such a crowd might be called a loosely formed group. By contrast, riders hurtling along on a subway train or bathers enjoying a summer day at the beach pay little attention to one another and amount to an anonymous aggregate of people. In general, then, crowds are too transitory and impersonal to qualify as social groups.

The right circumstances, however, could turn a crowd into a group. People riding in a subway train that crashes under the city streets generally become keenly aware of their common plight and begin to help one another. Sometimes such extraordinary experiences become the basis for lasting relationships.

Primary and Secondary Groups

Acquaintances commonly greet one another with a smile and the simple phrase, "Hi! How are you?" The response is usually a well scripted, "Just fine, thanks, how about you?" This answer, of course, is often more formal than truthful. In most cases, providing a detailed account of how you are *really* doing would prompt the other person to beat a hasty and awkward exit.

Sociologists classify social groups by measuring them against two ideal types based on members' genuine level of personal concern. This variation is the key to distinguishing *primary* from *secondary* groups.

According to Charles Horton Cooley (1864–1929), a **primary group** is a *small social group whose members share personal and enduring relationships.* Bound together by primary relationships, individuals in primary groups typically spend a great deal of time together, engage in a wide range of common activities, and feel that they know one another well. Although not without periodic conflict, members of primary groups display sincere concern for each other's welfare. The family is every society's most important primary group.

Cooley characterized these personal and tightly integrated groups as *primary* because they are among the first groups we experience in life. In addition, the family and early play groups also hold primary importance in the socialization process, shaping attitudes, behavior, and social identity.

SOCIOLOGY

145

Source: Sociology 6/E by Macionis, © 1997. Reprinted by permission of Pearson Education, Inc., Upper Saddle River, NJ.

Building Your Vocabulary

Read the excerpt from the sixth edition of *Management* by Stephen P. Robbins and Mary Coulter.[11] Find three words that are new—or, if not new, unclear—to you and write them below. Look them up in the dictionary and write the definition next to the word. Finally, include the word in a sentence you write. If there are no unfamiliar words in this page, choose three words from any reading assignment you have this week.

1. _____

_____

_____

_____

Sentence: _____

_____

2. _____

_____

_____

Sentence: _____

_____

3. _____

_____

_____

_____

Sentence: _____

_____

Focusing on Your Purpose for Reading

Use SQ3R to read the excerpt on air pollution taken from the seventh edition of *Health Promotion Strategies through the Life Span* by Ruth Beckmann Murray and Judith Proctor Zentner.[12] When you have finished, answer the questions that follow.

1. *Reading for critical evaluation.* Evaluate the material by answering these questions:

Management Roles

In the late 1960s, Mintzberg did a detailed study of five top managers at work. What he discovered challenged several long-held notions about the manager's job. For instance, in contrast to the predominant views at the time that managers were reflective thinkers who carefully and systematically processed information before making decisions, Mintzberg found that his managers engaged in a large number of varied, unpatterned, and short-duration activities. There was little time for reflective thinking because the managers encountered constant interruptions. Half of these managers' activities lasted less than nine minutes each. In addition to these insights on what managers did, Mintzberg provided a categorization scheme for defining what managers do based on actual managers on the job.

Mintzberg concluded that managers perform 10 different but highly interrelated roles. The term **management roles** refers to specific categories of managerial behavior. (Think of the different roles you play and the different behaviors you're expected to exhibit and the different work you're expected to do in these roles: a student, a sibling, an employee, a volunteer, and so forth.) As shown in Table 1-2, Mintzberg's 10 managerial roles can be grouped as those primarily concerned with interpersonal relationships, the transfer of information, and decision making.

INTERPERSONAL ROLES. All managers are required to perform duties that involve people (subordinates and persons outside the organization) and other duties that are ceremonial and symbolic in nature. These are **interpersonal roles.** When a college president hands out diplomas at commencement or a factory supervisor gives a group of high school students a plant tour, he or she is acting in a *figurehead* role. All managers have a role as a *leader.* This role includes hiring, training, motivating, and disciplining employees. The third role within the interpersonal grouping is the *liaison* role. Mintzberg described this activity as contacting external sources who provide the manager with information. These sources are individuals or groups outside the manager's unit and may be inside or outside the organization. The sales manager who obtains information from the human resources manager in his or her same company has an internal liaison relationship. When that sales manager confers with other sales executives at a marketing trade association meeting, he or she has an outside liaison relationship.

INFORMATIONAL ROLES. All managers, to some degree, have **informational roles:** receiving, collecting, and disseminating information. Typically, if they're getting this information from outside their own organization, they do so by reading magazines and talking with others to learn of changes in the public's tastes, what competitors may be planning, and the like. Mintzberg called this the *monitor* role. Managers also act as conduits of information to organizational members. This is the *disseminator* role. When they represent the organization to outsiders, managers also perform a *spokesperson* role.

DECISIONAL ROLES. Finally, Mintzberg identified four **decisional roles,** which revolve around making choices. As *entrepreneurs,* managers initiate and oversee new projects that will improve their organization's performance. As *disturbance handlers,* managers take corrective action in response to unforeseen problems. As *resource allocators,* managers are responsible for allocating human, physical, and monetary resources. Last, managers perform as *negotiators* when they discuss and bargain with other groups to gain advantages for their own units.

Source: Management 6/E by Robbins/Coulter, © 1999. Reprinted by permission of Pearson Education, Inc., Upper Saddle River, NJ.

a. Were the ideas clearly supported by examples? If you feel one or more were not, give an example.

_____

_____

b. Do you feel the authors made any assumptions? If so, name one or more.

_____

_____

c. Do you disagree with any part of the material? If so, which part, and why?

_____

_____

2. _Reading for practical application._ Imagine you have to give a presentation on this material the next time the class meets. On a separate sheet of paper, create an outline or think link that maps out the key elements you would discuss.

3. _Reading for comprehension._ Answer the following questions to determine the level of your comprehension:

a. Name the five most common air pollutants and give one example of each.

_____

_____

_____

_____

b. What is the PSI and who developed it?

_____

_____

c. At what point should persons with respiratory ailments reduce outdoor activity?

_____

_____

d. What practices are contributing to the depletion of the ozone layer?

_____

_____

_____

Air Pollution

You will care for patients in acute, chronic, and community care settings who have diseases caused by air pollution. It is critical to prevent these diseases by reducing all forms of pollution described in this section.

PROBLEMS OF AIR POLLUTION

Air pollution is not a new problem; people have known for centuries that air can carry poisons. Miners would take canaries with them into the mines—a dead bird meant the presence of lethal gas. Natural processes, such as forest and prairie fires, volcanic eruptions, and wind erosion, have long contaminated the air. A dramatic example of natural air pollution in the United States was caused by the 1980 eruption of Mount St. Helens in the state of Washington. Gases and dust from the volcano were spewed into the atmosphere, and local communities were covered with volcanic ash. Human activities, such as burning of fossil fuels, surface mining of coal, incineration of solid wastes, and manufacturing process-

es, are recognized as sources of pollution. The current problem of toxic air pollution came sharply into focus in late 1984 when more than 2500 people died and as many as 100,000 were left with permanent disabilities as a result of a gas leak from a Union Carbide Corporation fertilizer plant in Bhopal, India.

Air pollution and water pollution act interchangeably; together they present a world problem. All people on the earth share the oceans and the air. Significant local pollution of either can greatly affect distant areas, especially if the oceans cannot, by the processes of precipitation, oxidation, and absorption, cleanse the atmosphere before harmful effects occur. Given enough time, the oceans can cleanse the atmosphere; but if the amount of pollution exceeds the ocean's capacity to neutralize the waste, harmful materials are dispersed into the atmosphere, and we realize the effects by breathing contaminated air.

SOURCES OF AIR POLLUTION

The five most common pollutants found in the air are **carbon monoxide** (typical source: car exhaust), **sulfur oxides** (typical source: industrial coal and oil burning), **nitrogen oxides** (typical source: burning fossil fuels such as gasoline and coal), **suspended particles** (typical source: deteriorating asbestos), and **hydrocarbons** (typical source: chemical vapors). The sources of these air pollutants vary, and the effects on humans differ according to length and degree of exposure to the pollutant. Air pollution is most harmful to the very young, the very old, and persons with respiratory and cardiac disease.

A major cause of air contamination is imperfect or incomplete combustion. **Perfect or complete combustion** exists only in chemistry books and is the *result of hydrogen and carbon uniting completely with oxygen, thereby relinquishing heat, water vapor, light, and carbon dioxide to the air.* **Imperfect or incomplete combustion** refers to the *additional liberation of carbon monoxide, sulfur oxides, nitrogen oxides, and hydrocarbons into the air.*

The EPA has developed the **Pollutant Standards Index (PSI)** as a *means of reporting daily air pollution concentrations.* The PSI converts the pollutant concentrations measured in a community's air to a number on a scale of 0 to 500. Intervals of the PSI scale are related to the potential health effects of the daily measured concentrations of the five major pollutants previously described. The intervals and terms used to describe the air quality levels are as follows: 0 to 50—good; above 50—moderate; above 100—unhealthful; 201 to 300—first stage alert, very unhealthful; 301 to 400—second stage alert, hazardous; 401 to 500—third stage alert, significant harm. When the pollution index is greater than 100, individuals with existing heart or respiratory ailments should reduce physical exertion and outdoor activity.

Four additional air pollution problems should be mentioned: (1) depletion of the upper atmosphere ozone layer; (2) increasing levels of atmospheric carbon dioxide; (3) acid rain; and (4) radioactive substances. As noted, a thin layer of ozone surrounds the earth and blocks much of the sun's ultraviolet radiation from reaching the earth's surface. The ozone layer is in danger of being depleted by the continued use of fluorocarbons (freon) and chlorofluoromethanes that release chlorine into the stratosphere to combine with ozone. The continued use of fluorocarbon-propelled aerosol products and supersonic transport planes adds to that danger.

Large sport utility vehicles, with their low gas mileage, are exacerbating global warming because of the tonnage of carbon dioxide produced. For information about the tons of carbon dioxide produced by cars of all sizes and makes, visit www.toowarm.org. The pollution-free automotive vehicle is a fantasy at this point because of consumer indifference.

The Environment   **144**

Source: *Health Promotion Strategies Through the Life Span* 7/E by Murray/Zentner, © 2001. Reprinted by permission of Pearson Education, Inc., Upper Saddle River, NJ.

e. Mark the following statements as true (T) or false (F).

_____ Air pollution has been a problem only since the invention of the automobile.

_____ Given enough time, the oceans have the capacity to cleanse the air of pollutants.

_____ Large sport utility vehicles produce a larger tonnage of carbon dioxide because of their low gas mileage.

_____ Acid rain and nuclear energy are two additional air pollution problems.

Teamwork *Combining Forces*

READING AND GROUP DISCUSSION. Divide into small groups of three or four. Take a few minutes to preview an article or other short section of reading material assigned to you for this class (other than your textbook). Then, as a group, write down the questions that came up during the preview. Each person should select one question to focus on while reading (no two people should have the same question). Group members should then read the material on their own, using critical-thinking skills to explore their particular questions as they read, and finally, they should write down answers to their questions.

When you answer your question, focus on finding ideas that help to answer the question and examples that support them. Consider other information you know, relevant to your question, that may be similar to or different from the material in the passage. If your questions look for causes or effects, scan for them in the passage. Be sure to make notes as you read.

When you have finished reading critically, gather as a group. Each person should take a turn presenting the question, the response or answer that was derived through critical reading, and any other ideas that came up while reading. The group then has an opportunity to present any other ideas to add to the discussion. Continue until all group members have had a chance to present what they worked on.

Writing *Discovery Through Journaling*

To record your thoughts, use a separate journal or the lined page at the end of the chapter.

READING CHALLENGES. What is your most difficult college reading challenge? A challenge might be a particular kind of reading material, a reading situation, or the achievement of a reading goal. Considering the tools that this chapter presents, make a plan that addresses this challenge. What techniques might be able to help, and how will you test them? What positive effects do you anticipate they may have?

Career Portfolio | *Charting Your Course*

READING SKILLS ON THE JOB. The society you live and work in revolves around the written word. Although the growth of computer technology may seem to have made technical knowledge more important than reading, the focus on word processing and computer handling of documents has actually increased the need for literate employees. As a 1996 Condition of Education report states, "In recent years, literacy has been viewed as one of the fundamental tools necessary for successful economic performance in industrialized societies. Literacy is no longer defined merely as a basic threshold of reading ability, but rather as the ability to understand and use printed information in daily activities, at home, at work, and in the community."[13]

On a separate sheet of paper, do the following: For each of the skill areas listed, indicate all of the ways you know of in which you use that skill on the job or know you will need to use it in your future career. Then, also for each skill, rate your ability on a scale from 1 to 10, with 10 being highest. Finally, on the same sheet of paper, circle the two skills that you think will be most important for your career.

- Ability to define your reading purpose
- Reading speed
- Reading comprehension
- Vocabulary building
- Identification and use of text-surveying devices
- Evaluating reading material with others
- Ability to understand and use visual aids

For the two skill areas in which you rated yourself lowest, think about how you can improve your abilities. Make a problem-solving plan for each (use a flowchart like the one on page 143).

Assess Yourself | *Student Success Strategies*

If you have access to the CD-ROM Strategies for Success, *use the following questions to assess your thoughts and enhance your understanding of the chapter. The questions below represent only some of the activities provided on the CD for the chapter topics—try others if you have time.*

Click on the **Reading Effectively** bookmark. Use the following activities to further boost your reading powers:

1. Take the pre-assessment to clarify your perspective on reading.
2. Click on **Activity One: Surveying Skills.** Read the passage, type in what you believe are the most important key words and phrases, and then compare them to the ideal list.

3. Click on **Activity Two: Surveying Technical Material.** Complete the exercise to assess your competence with technical material and to see what improvements you may have made based on your experience with Activity One.

4. Click on **Activity Three: Journal Reflections.** Scroll to the second question, which asks you to compare the reading strategies you use for classes with varying levels of difficulty. Type your answer in the field provided.

Suggested Readings

Armstrong, William H. and M. Willard Lampe II. *Barron's Pocket Guide to Study Tips: How to Study Effectively and Get Better Grades.* New York: Barron's Educational Series, 1990.

Chesla, Elizabeth. *Reading Comprehension Success: In 20 Minutes a Day, 2nd ed.* Garden Grove, CA: Learning Express, 1998.

Frank, Steven. *The Everything Study Book.* Holbrook, MA: Adams Media, 1996.

Luckie, William R., Wood Smethurst, and Sarah Beth Huntley. *Study Power Workbook: Exercises in Study Skills to Improve Your Learning and Your Grades.* Cambridge, MA: Brookline Books, 1999.

Silver, Theodore. *The Princeton Review Study Smart: Hands-on, Nuts and Bolts Techniques for Earning Higher Grades.* New York: Villard Books, 1996.

Internet Resources

SQ3R Method: www.u.arizona.edu/ic/wrightr/other/sq3r.html

Study Web: www.studyweb.com

Prentice Hall Student Success Supersite—Study Skills: www.prenhall.com/success/StudySkl/index.html

Endnotes

1. Sherwood Harris, *The New York Public Library Book of How and Where to Look It Up.* Englewood Cliffs, NJ: Prentice Hall, 1991, p. 13.

2. Steve Moidel, *Speed Reading.* Hauppauge, NY: Barron's Educational Series, 1994, p. 18.

3. Ibid.

4. Francis P. Robinson, *Effective Behavior.* New York: Harper & Row, 1941.

5. John Mack Faragher, et al., *Out of Many, 3rd ed.* Upper Saddle River, NJ: Prentice Hall, p. xxxvii.

6. Ophelia H. Hancock, *Reading Skills for College Students, 5th ed.* Upper Saddle River, NJ: Prentice Hall, 2001, pp. 54–59.

7. Excerpted from Lynn Quitman Troyka, *Simon & Schuster Handbook for Writers, 5th ed.* Upper Saddle River, NJ: Prentice Hall, 1999, p. 12.

8. Sylvan Barnet and Hugo Bedau, *Critical Thinking, Reading, and Writing: A Brief Guide to Argument, 2nd ed.* Boston, MA: Bedford Books of St. Martin's Press, 1996, pp. 15–21.

9. Louis E. Boone, David L. Kurtz, and Judy R. Block, *Contemporary Business Communication.* Englewood Cliffs, NJ: Prentice Hall, 1994, pp. 489–499.

10. John J. Macionis, *Sociology, 6th ed.* Upper Saddle River, NJ: Prentice Hall, 1997, p. 174.

11. Stephen P. Robbins and Mary Coulter, *Management, 6th ed.* Upper Saddle River, NJ: Prentice Hall, 1999, pp. 13–15.

12. Ruth Beckmann Murray and Judith Proctor Zentner, *Health Promotion Strategies through the Life Span.* Upper Saddle River, NJ: Prentice Hall, 2001, pp. 74–78.

13. U.S. Department of Education, National Center for Education Statistics, *The Condition of Education 1996,* NCES 96–304, by Thomas M. Smith. Washington, DC: U.S. Government Printing Office, 1996, p. 84.

JOURNAL

name

date

visit: www.prenhall.com/carter NY Times link for this chapter

Listening, note taking, and memory

In this chapter you explore answers to the following questions: • How can you become a better listener? • How can you make the most of note taking? • Which note-taking system should you use? • How can you write faster when taking notes? • How does memory work? • How can you improve your memory?

IN THIS CHAPTER

COLLEGE exposes you daily to facts, opinions, and ideas—and, as Litzka Stark is discovering (see next page), your job as a student is to find a way to retain what you learn. This chapter shows you how to do just that through listening (taking in information), note taking (recording what's important), and memory skills (remembering information). Compare your skills to using a camera: You start by locating an image through the viewfinder, then you carefully focus the lens (listening), record the image on film (note taking), and produce a print (remembering). The chapter also shows you how better retention leads to the ability to apply your new knowledge to new situations.

taking in, recording, and retaining information

Litzka Stark, Sarah Lawrence College, Bronxville, New York

Carlos Vela Shimano, ITESM Campus, Queretaro, Mexico

How can I improve my memory?

I learned to link random ideas together in a chain.

I learn best when I study themes, understand concepts, and try to integrate the material into my life. At my college, most of our exams are essay. I haven't had to expend much effort memorizing facts. When I do, though, I use the standard mnemonic devices and write the information on index cards.

The greatest difficulty I have with memorization is being able to retain what I've learned. In a very short time, the information is gone unless it's somehow reinforced. My question is, how do I retain the material or formulas I'm asked to remember and not forget all of it down the road? I know that in particular subjects I just can't accomplish learning without memorization.

When I was in junior high, I took an alternative class that taught memorization skills. I learned to link random ideas together in a chain. That way, I could visualize numerous concepts that were not necessarily related.

Today, in my classes, I create mind maps during lectures. I draw a circle in the middle of the page representing the main theme. Then, I link smaller circles off to one side or the other with related themes. Each one of those has circles of material or ideas relating to it. This really helps me keep the information visually organized. I think for me that is probably the best way to remember things.

I also have another method that helps me to remember dates, phone numbers, combination numbers, and PIN numbers. I link the number with something else in my life. For instance, I play on a soccer team. My PIN number for one of my accounts is the number of my jersey, plus the numbers of my two friends' jerseys who also play on the team. Because I love sports, I link numbers I need to remember with the shirts of famous athletes. My locker combination number has the same numbers as the ones Michael Jordan and Magic Johnson wear.

Finally, if you learn to build ideas from the simplest to the most complex—really understanding the reasons behind the concept and where and why the concepts were developed in the first place—it will truly help you retain more of what you study.

How can you become a
better listener?

T he act of hearing isn't quite the same as the act of listening. While *hearing* refers to sensing spoken messages from their source, *listening* involves a complex process of communication. Successful listening occurs when the speaker's intended message reaches the listener. In school and at home, poor listening may cause communication breakdowns and mistakes. Skilled listening, however, promotes progress and success. Listening is a teachable—and learnable—skill.

Ralph G. Nichols, a pioneer in listening research, studied 200 students at the University of Minnesota over a nine-month period. His findings demonstrate that effective listening depends as much on a positive attitude as on specific skills.[1] Just as understanding the mind actions involved in critical thinking helps you work out problems, understanding the listening process helps you become a better listener.

LISTENING

A process that involves sensing, interpreting, evaluating, and reacting to spoken messages.

Know the Stages of Listening

Listening is made up of four stages that build on one another: sensing, interpreting, evaluating, and reacting. These stages take the message from the speaker to the listener and back to the speaker (see Figure 6.1).

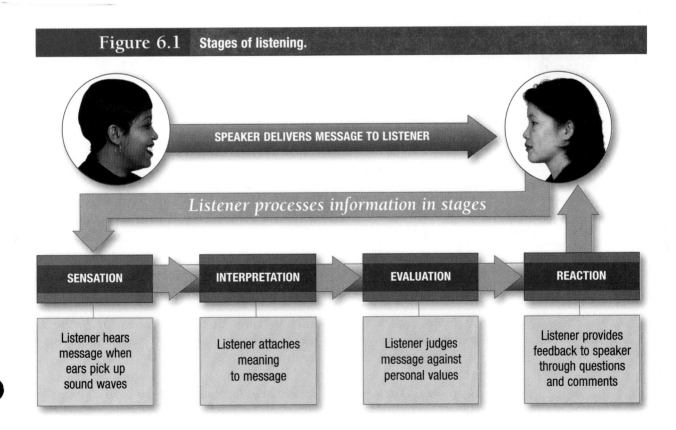

Figure 6.1   Stages of listening.

SPEAKER DELIVERS MESSAGE TO LISTENER

Listener processes information in stages

SENSATION	INTERPRETATION	EVALUATION	REACTION
Listener hears message when ears pick up sound waves	Listener attaches meaning to message	Listener judges message against personal values	Listener provides feedback to speaker through questions and comments

- During the *sensation* stage (also known as hearing), your ears pick up sound waves and transmit them to the brain. For example, you are sitting in class and hear your instructor say, "The only opportunity to make up last week's test is Tuesday at 5:00 P.M."

- In the *interpretation* stage, listeners attach meaning to a message. This involves understanding what is being said and relating it to what you already know. For example, you relate this message to your knowledge of the test, whether you need to make it up, and what you are doing on Tuesday at 5:00 P.M.

- In the *evaluation* stage of listening, you decide what you think or how you feel about the message—whether, for example, you like it or agree with it. This involves considering the message as it relates to your needs and values. In this example, if you do need to make up the test but have to work Tuesday at 5 P.M., you may evaluate the message as less than satisfactory.

- The final stage of listening involves a *reaction* to the message in the form of direct feedback. Your reaction, in this example, may be to ask the instructor for an alternative to the scheduled makeup test time.

Improving your listening skills involves two primary actions: managing listening challenges and becoming an active listener. Although becoming a better listener will help in every class, it is especially important in subjects that are challenging for you.

Manage Listening Challenges

Communication barriers can interfere with listening at every stage. In fact, classic studies have shown that immediately after listening, students are likely to recall only half of what was said. This is partly due to particular listening challenges such as divided attention and distractions, the tendency to shut out the message, the inclination to rush to judgment, and partial hearing loss or learning disabilities.[2]

To help create a positive listening environment in both your mind and your surroundings, explore how to manage these challenges.

Divided Attention and Distractions

Imagine you are talking with a coworker in the company cafeteria when you hear your name mentioned across the room. You strain to hear what someone might be saying about you and, in the process, hear neither your friend nor the person across the room very well. This situation illustrates the consequences of divided attention. Although you are capable of listening to more than one message at the same time, you may not completely hear or understand any of them.

Internal and external distractions often divide your attention. *Internal distractions* include anything from hunger to headache to personal worries. Something the speaker says may also trigger a recollection that causes your mind to drift. In contrast, *external distractions* include noises (e.g., whispering or sirens) and excessive heat or cold. It can be hard to listen in an overheated room in which you are falling asleep.

Your goal is to reduce distractions so that you can focus on what you're hearing. Sitting near the front where you can clearly see and hear helps you to listen. To avoid distracting activity, you may want to sit away from people who might chat or make noise. Dress comfortably, paying attention to the temperature of the classroom, and try not to go to class hungry or thirsty. Work to concentrate on class when you're in class and worry about personal problems later.

Shutting Out the Message

Instead of paying attention to everything the speaker says, many students fall into the trap of focusing on specific points and shutting out the rest of the message. If you perceive that a subject is too difficult or uninteresting, you may tune out. Shutting out the message makes listening harder from that point on because the information you miss may be the foundation for future class discussions.

> "No one cares to speak to an unwilling listener. An arrow never lodges in a stone; often it recoils upon the sender of it."

ST. JEROME

Creating a positive listening environment includes accepting responsibility for listening. Although the instructor is responsible for communicating information to you, he or she cannot force you to listen. You are responsible for taking in that information. Instructors often cover material from outside the textbook during class and then test on that material. If you work to take in the whole message in class, you can read over your notes later and think critically about what is most important.

The Rush to Judgment

People tend to stop listening when they hear something they don't like. If you rush to judge what you've heard, making a quick uncritical assumption about it, your focus turns to your personal reaction rather than the content of the message. Judgments also involve reactions to the speakers themselves. If you do not like your instructors or if you have preconceived notions about their ideas or background, you may assume that their words have little value.

Work to recognize and control your judgments by listening first without jumping to conclusions. Ask critical-thinking questions about assumptions (see page 136). Stay aware of what you tend to judge so that you can avoid rejecting messages that clash with your opinions. Consider education as a continuing search for evidence, regardless of whether that evidence supports or negates your perspective.

Partial Hearing Loss and Learning Disabilities

Good listening techniques don't solve every listening problem. If you have some level of hearing loss, seek out special services that can help you listen in class. For example, you may be able to tape record the lecture and play it back at a louder-than-normal volume after class, have special tutoring, or arrange for a classmate to take notes for you. In addition, you may be able to arrange to meet with your instructor outside of class to clarify your notes.

Other disabilities, such as attention deficit disorder (ADD) or a problem with processing spoken language, can make it hard to focus on and understand oral messages. If you have one of these disabilities, don't blame yourself for your difficulty. Visit your school's counseling or student health center, or talk with your advisor or instructors about getting the help you need to meet your challenges.

Become an Active Listener

On the surface, listening seems like a passive activity; you sit back and listen as someone else speaks. Effective listening, however, is really an active process that involves setting a purpose for listening, paying attention to verbal signposts, and asking questions.

VERBAL SIGNPOSTS

Spoken words or phrases that call your attention to the information that follows.

Set purposes for listening. Active listening is possible only if you know (and care) why you are listening. In any situation, establish what you want to achieve through listening, such as greater understanding of the material or better note taking. Having a purpose gives you a goal that motivates you to listen.

Pay attention to verbal signposts. You can identify important facts and ideas and predict test questions by paying attention to the speaker's specific choice of words. Verbal signposts often involve transition words and phrases that help organize information, connect ideas, and indicate what is and is not important. Let phrases like those in Table 6.1 direct your attention to the material that follows them.

Ask questions. Successful listening is closely linked to asking questions. A willingness to ask questions shows a desire to learn and is the mark of a critical thinker. Asking questions has two benefits. First of all, it helps

Table 6.1	Verbal signposts point out important information.

Signals Pointing to Key Concepts	Signals of Support
There are two reasons for this . . .	For example, . . .
A critical point in the process involves . . .	Specifically, . . .
Most importantly, . . .	For instance, . . .
The result is . . .	Similarly, . . .
Signals Pointing to Differences	**Signals that Summarize**
On the contrary, . . .	Finally, . . .
On the other hand, . . .	Recapping this idea, . . .
In contrast, . . .	In conclusion, . . .
However, . . .	As a result, . . .

you to deepen your understanding of what you hear. This happens when you ask either informational or clarifying questions. *Informational* questions, such as any questions beginning with "Can you explain . . ." seek information that you haven't yet heard or acquired. *Clarifying* questions ask if your understanding of something you just heard is correct, such as "So some learning disabilities can be improved with treatment?" Second, of all, questions help to solidify your memory of what you are hearing. As you think of the question, raise your hand, speak, and listen to the answer, brain activity and physical activity combine to reinforce the information you are taking in.

Listening in order to acquire knowledge is only the first step. Once you hone your listening skills, you need to make a record of what you've heard by taking effective notes.

How can you *make the most* of note taking?

Notes help you learn when you are in class, doing research, or studying. Because it is virtually impossible to take notes on everything you hear or read, the act of note taking encourages you to decide what is worth remembering, and involves you in the learning process in many important ways:

- Your notes provide material that helps you study and prepare for tests.
- When you take notes, you listen better and become more involved in class.
- Notes help you think critically and organize ideas.
- The information you learn in class may not appear in any text; you will have no way to study it without writing it down.
- If it is difficult for you to process information while in class, having notes to read can help you process and learn the information.
- Note taking is a skill that you will use on the job, in community activities, and in your personal life.

Good note taking demands good listening. The listening skills you just explored are what allow you to hear what you will be evaluating and writing down. Listening and note taking depend on one another.

Recording Information in Class

Your notes have two purposes: First, they should reflect what you heard in class, and second, they should be a resource for studying, writing, or comparing with your text material. If lectures include material that is not in your text or if your instructor talks about specific test questions, your class notes become even more important as a study tool.

Preparing to Take Class Notes

Taking good class notes depends on good preparation.

Preview your reading material. Survey the text (or any other assigned reading material) to become familiar with the topic and any new concepts that it introduces. Visual familiarity helps note taking during lectures.

Gather your supplies. Use separate pieces of 8.5 × 11 inch paper for each class. If you use a three-ring binder, punch holes in handouts and insert them immediately following your notes for that day. Make sure your pencils are sharp and your pens aren't about to run out.

Location, location, location. Find a comfortable seat where you can easily see and hear—sitting near the front, where you minimize distraction and maximize access to the lecture or discussion, might be your best bet. Be ready to write as soon as the instructor begins speaking.

Choose the best note-taking system. Select a system that is most appropriate for the situation. Later in the chapter, you will learn about different note-taking systems. Take the following factors into account when choosing one to use in any class:

- *The instructor's style* (you'll be able to determine this style after a few classes). Whereas one instructor may deliver organized lectures at a normal speaking rate, another may jump from topic to topic or talk very quickly.
- *The course material.* After experimenting for a few class meetings, you may decide that an informal outline works best for your philosophy course, but that a think link works for your sociology course.
- *Your learning style.* Choose strategies that make the most of your strong points and help boost weaker areas. A visual–spatial learner might prefer think links or the Cornell system (see page 206), for example, while a Thinker type might stick to outlines; an interpersonal learner might use the Cornell system and fill in the cue column in a study group setting (see Chapter 2 for a complete discussion of learning styles).

Gather support. For each class, set up a support system with two students. That way, when you are absent, you can get the notes you missed from one or the other.

What to Do During Class

Because no one has time to write down everything he or she hears, the following strategies will help you choose and record what you feel is important in a format that you can read and understand later. This is not

Note taking is a critical learning tool. The tips below will help you retain information for both the short and long term.

INTELLIGENCE	SUGGESTED STRATEGIES	WHAT WORKS FOR YOU? WRITE NEW IDEAS HERE
Verbal–Linguistic	■ Rewrite important ideas and concepts in class notes from memory. ■ Write summaries of your notes in your own words.	
Logical–Mathematical	■ Organize the main points of a lecture or reading using outline form. ■ Make charts and diagrams to clarify ideas and examples.	
Bodily–Kinesthetic	■ Make note taking as physical as possible—use large pieces of paper and different colored pens. ■ When in class, choose a comfortable spot where you have room to spread out your materials and shift body position when you need to.	
Visual–Spatial	■ Take notes using colored markers. ■ Rewrite lecture notes in think link format, focusing on the most important and difficult points from the lecture.	
Interpersonal	■ Whenever possible, schedule a study group right after a lecture to discuss class notes. ■ Review class notes with a study buddy. See what you wrote that he or she missed and vice versa.	
Intrapersonal	■ Schedule some quiet time as soon as possible after a lecture to reread and think about your notes. If no class is meeting in the same room after yours and you have free time, stay in the room and review there.	
Musical	■ Play music while you read your notes. ■ Write a song that incorporates material from one class period's notes or one particular topic. Use the refrain to emphasize the most important concepts.	
Naturalistic	■ Read or rewrite your notes outside. ■ Review notes while listening to a nature CD—running water, rain, forest sounds.	

a list of "musts." Rather, it is a list of ideas to try as you work to find the note-taking strategies that work best for you. Experiment until you feel that you have found a successful combination.

Remember that the first step in note taking is to listen actively; you can't write down something that you don't hear. Use the listening strategies you read earlier in the chapter to make sure you are prepared to take in the information that comes your way.

- Date and identify each page. When you take several pages of notes during a lecture, add an identifying letter or number to the date on each page; for example, 11/27 A, 11/27 B, or 11/27—1 of 3, 11/27—2 of 3. This helps you keep track of the order of your pages. Add the specific topic of the lecture at the top of the page. For example: 11/27—U.S. Immigration Policy After World War II.

- If your instructor jumps from topic to topic during class, try starting a new page for each new topic.

- Ask yourself critical-thinking questions: Do I need this information? Is the information important or just a digression? Is the information fact or opinion? If it is opinion, is it worth remembering? (Chapter 4 discusses how to distinguish between fact and opinion.)

- Record whatever an instructor emphasizes—key terms, definitions, ideas, and examples (see Figure 6.2 for specifics on how an instructor might call attention to particular information).

- Continue to take notes during class discussions and question-and-answer periods. What your fellow students ask about may help you as well.

Figure 6.2 How to pick up on instructors' cues.

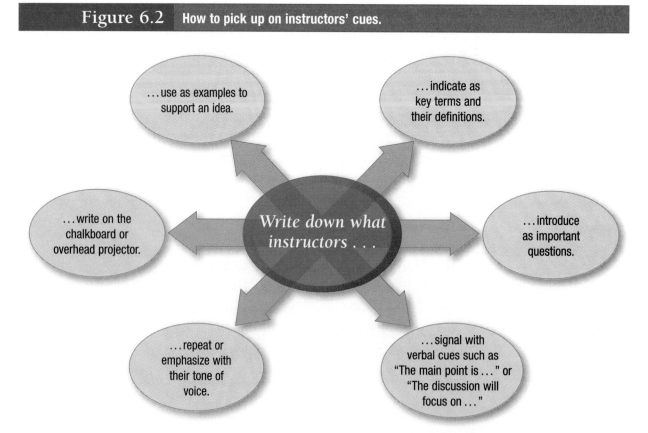

- Leave one or more blank spaces between points. This white space helps you review your notes because information appears in self-contained sections.
- Draw pictures and diagrams that help illustrate ideas.
- Indicate material that is especially important with a star, with underlining, with a highlighting marker, or by writing words in capital letters.
- If you don't understand something, leave space and place a question mark in the margin. Then, take advantage of your resources—ask the instructor to explain it after class, discuss it with a classmate, or consult your textbook—and fill in the blank when the idea is clear.
- Take notes until the instructor stops speaking. If you stop writing a few minutes before the class is over, you might miss critical information.
- Make your notes as legible and organized as possible—you can't learn from notes that you can't read or understand. But don't be too fussy; you can always rewrite and improve your notes.
- Consider that your notes are part, but not all, of what you need to learn. Using your text to add to your notes after class makes a superior, "deeper and wider" set of information to study.

Reviewing and Revising Your Notes

Even the most comprehensive notes in the world won't do you any good unless you review them. The crucial act of reviewing helps you solidify the information in your memory so that you can recall it and use it. It also helps you link new information to information you already know, which is a key step in building new ideas. The review and revision stage of note taking should include time for planning, critical thinking, adding information from other sources, summarizing, and working with a study group.

Plan a Review Schedule

When you review your notes affects how much you are likely to remember. Reviewing right after the lecture but not again until the test, reviewing here and there without a plan, or cramming it all into one crazy night does not allow you to make the most of your abilities. Do yourself a favor by planning your time strategically.

Review within a day of the lecture. Reviewing while the material is still fresh in your mind helps you to remember it. You don't have to sit down for two hours and focus on every word. Just set some time aside to reread your notes, if you can, and perhaps write questions and comments on them. If you know you have an hour between classes, for example, that is an ideal time to work in a quick review.

Review regularly. Try to schedule times during the week for reviewing notes from that week's class meetings. For example, if you know you always have from 2 P.M. to 5 P.M. free every Tuesday and Thursday afternoon, you can plan to review notes from two courses on Tuesday and from two others on Thursday. Having a routine helps ensure that you look at material regularly.

Review with an eye toward tests. When you have a test coming up, step up your efforts. Schedule longer review sessions, call a study group meeting, and review more frequently. Shorter sessions of intense review work interspersed with breaks may be more effective than long hours of continuous studying. Some students find that recopying their notes before an exam or at an earlier stage helps cement key concepts in memory.

Read and Rework Using Critical Thinking

The critical-thinking mind actions help you make the most of your notes.

- *Recall.* Read your notes to learn information, clarify points, write out abbreviations, and fill in missing details.

- *Similarity.* Consider what similar facts or ideas the information brings to mind. Write them in the margins or white space on the page if they are helpful to you.

- *Difference.* Consider how the information differs from what you already know. Is there a discrepancy you should examine? If something seems way off base, could you have written it down inaccurately?

- *Cause and effect.* Look at how ideas, facts, and statements relate to one another. See if any of them have cause-and-effect relationships. You might even want to use another color pen to draw a line linking related ideas or facts on the page.

- *Example to idea.* Think about what new ideas you can form from the information in your notes. If any come to mind, write them in your notes or on a separate page. If particular information seems to fit together more specifically than your notes initially indicate, you may want to add headings and subheadings, and insert clarifying phrases or sentences.

- *Idea to example.* Think carefully about the ideas in your notes. What do they mean? Do examples in your notes support or negate them? If you have no examples in your notes as written, add them as you review.

- *Evaluation.* Use evaluation skills to select and underline or highlight the most important ideas and information. Think about why they are important and work to understand them as completely as possible.

Revise Using Other Sources

Revising and adding to your notes using material from your texts, other required course readings, and the Internet is one of the best ways to build your understanding and link new information to information you already know. Try using the following critical-thinking actions when you add to your notes:

- Brainstorm and write down examples from other sources that illustrate central ideas in your notes.

- Pay attention to similarities between your text materials and class notes (ideas that appear in both are probably important to remember).

- Think of facts or ideas from the reading that can support and clarify ideas from your notes.

- Consider what in your class notes differs from your reading, and why.

- Write down any new ideas that come up when reviewing your notes.

- Look at cause-and-effect relationships between material from your notes and reading material. Note how ideas, facts, and examples relate to one another.

Summarize

Writing a summary of your notes is another important review technique. Summarizing involves critically evaluating which ideas and examples are most important and then rewriting the material in a shortened form, focusing on those important ideas and examples.

You may prefer to summarize as you review, with the notes in front of you. If you are using the Cornell system (see page 206), you summarize in the space saved at the bottom of the page. Other ideas include summarizing on a separate page that you insert in your loose-leaf binder or summarizing on the back of the previous page (this is possible if you only take notes on one side of the paper).

Another helpful review technique is to summarize your notes from memory after you review them. This gives you an idea of how well you have retained the information. You may even want to summarize as you read, then summarize from memory, and compare the two summaries.

Work with Study Groups

When you work with a study group, you have the opportunity to review both your personal notes and those of other members of the class. This can be an enormous help if, for example, you lost concentration during part of a lecture and your notes don't make much sense. You and another student may even have notes that contradict each other or have radically different information. When this happens, try to reconstruct what the instructor said and, if necessary, bring in a third group member to clear up the confusion. See Chapter 5 for more on effective studying in groups.

You can take notes in many ways. Different note-taking systems suit different people and situations. Explore each system and choose what works for you.

Which *note-taking system* should you use?

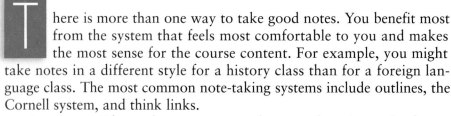

There is more than one way to take good notes. You benefit most from the system that feels most comfortable to you and makes the most sense for the course content. For example, you might take notes in a different style for a history class than for a foreign language class. The most common note-taking systems include outlines, the Cornell system, and think links.

As you consider each system, remember your learning styles from Chapter 2. In each class, choose a system that takes both your learning styles and the class material into account. For example, a visual learner may take notes in think link style most of the time, but may find that only the Cornell style works well for a particular chemistry course. Experiment to discover what works best in any situation.

Taking Notes in Outline Form

When a reading assignment or lecture seems well organized, you may choose to take notes in outline form. When you use an outline, you construct a line-by-line representation, with certain phrases set off by varying indentations, showing how ideas relate to one another and are supported by facts and examples.

Formal outlines indicate ideas and examples using Roman numerals, capital and lowercase letters, and numbers. When you are pressed for time, such as during class, you can use an informal system of consistent indenting and dashes instead. Formal outlines also require at least two headings on the same level—that is, if you have a IIA you must also have a IIB. Figure 6.3 shows an outline on civil rights legislation.

Guided Notes

From time to time, an instructor may give you a guide, usually in the form of an outline, to help you take notes in the class. This outline may be on a page that you receive at the beginning of the class, on the board, on an overhead projector, or even posted on-line prior to the class.

Although guided notes help you follow the lecture and organize your thoughts, they do not replace your own notes. Because they are more of a basic outline of topics than a comprehensive coverage of information, they require that you fill in what they do not cover in detail. If your mind wanders because you think that the guided notes are all you need, you may miss important information.

When you receive guided notes on paper, write directly on the paper if there is room. If not, use a separate sheet and copy the outline categories that the guided notes suggest. If the guided notes are on the board or overhead, copy them, leaving plenty of space in between for your own notes.

Figure 6.3 Sample formal outline.

CIVIL RIGHTS LEGISLATION: 1860–1968

I.   Post-Civil War Era
   A.   Fourteenth Amendment, 1868: equal protection of the law for all citizens
   B.   Fifteenth Amendment, 1870: constitutional rights of citizens regardless of race, color, or previous servitude

II.   Civil Rights Movement of the 1960s
   A.   National Association for the Advancement of Colored People (NAACP)
      1.   Established in 1910 by W.E.B. DuBois and others
      2.   Legal Defense and Education fund fought school segregation
   B.   Martin Luther King Jr., champion of nonviolent civil rights action
      1.   Led bus boycott: 1955–1956
      2.   Marched on Washington, D.C.: 1963
      3.   Awarded NOBEL PEACE PRIZE: 1964
      4.   Led voter registration drive in Selma, Alabama: 1965
   C.   Civil Rights Act of 1964: prohibited discrimination in voting, education, employment, and public facilities
   D.   Voting Rights Act of 1965: gave the government power to enforce desegregation
   E.   Civil Rights Act of 1968: prohibited discrimination in the sale or rental of housing

Using the Cornell Note-Taking System

The Cornell note-taking system, also known as the T-note system, was developed more than 45 years ago by Walter Pauk at Cornell University.[3] The system is successful because it is simple—and because it works. It consists of three sections on ordinary notepaper:

- Section 1, the largest section, is on the right. Record your notes here in informal outline form.

- Section 2, to the left of your notes, is the *cue column*. Leave it blank while you read or listen; then fill it in later as you review. You might fill it with comments that highlight main ideas, clarify meaning, suggest examples, or link ideas and examples. You can even draw diagrams.

- Section 3, at the bottom of the page, is the *summary area*. Here you use a sentence or two to summarize the notes on the page. When you review, use this section to reinforce concepts and provide an overview.

When you use the Cornell system, create the note-taking structure before class begins. Picture an upside-down letter T and use Figure 6.4 as your guide.

- Start with a sheet of standard loose-leaf paper. Label it with the date and title of the lecture.

- To create the cue column, draw a vertical line about 2.5 inches from the left side of the paper. End the line about 2 inches from the bottom of the sheet.

- To create the summary area, start at the point where the vertical line ends (about 2 inches from the bottom of the page) and draw a horizontal line that spans the entire paper.

Figure 6.4 shows how a student used the Cornell system to take notes in an introductory business course.

Creating a Think Link

A *think link,* also known as a mind map, is a visual form of note taking. When you draw a think link, you diagram ideas by using shapes and lines that link ideas and supporting details and examples. The visual design makes the connections easy to see, and the use of shapes and pictures extends the material beyond just words. Many learners respond well to the power of visualization. You can use think links to brainstorm ideas for paper topics as well.

One way to create a think link is to start by writing your topic in the middle of a sheet of paper and putting a circle around it. Next, draw a line from the circled topic and write the name of one major idea at the end of the line. Circle that idea also. Then, jot down specific facts related to the idea, linking them to the idea with lines. Continue the process, connecting thoughts to one another by using circles, lines, and words. Figure 6.5 shows a think link on a sociology concept called social stratification.

VISUALIZATION

The interpretation of verbal ideas through the use of mental visual images.

Figure 6.4   Sample Cornell system notes.

October 3, 200X, p. 1

UNDERSTANDING EMPLOYEE MOTIVATION

Why do some workers have a better attitude toward their work than others?	Purpose of motivational theories — To explain role of human relations in motivating employee performance — Theories translate into how managers actually treat workers

Some managers view workers as lazy; others view them as motivated and productive.	2 specific theories
	— Human resources model, developed by Douglas McGregor, shows that managers have radically different beliefs about motivation.
	    — Theory X holds that people are naturally irresponsible and uncooperative
	    — Theory Y holds that people are naturally responsible and self-motivated

Maslow's Hierarchy
 	
self-actualization needs (challenging job)
esteem needs (job title)
social needs (friends at work)
security needs (health plan)
physiological needs (pay)
	— Maslow's Hierarchy of Needs says that people have needs in 5 different areas, which they attempt to satisfy in their work.
	    — Physiological need: need for survival, including food and shelter
	    — Security need: need for stability and protection
	    — Social need: need for friendship and companionship
	    — Esteem need: need for status and recognition
	    — Self-actualization need: need for self-fulfillment
	Needs at lower levels must be met before a person tries to satisfy needs at higher levels.
	—Developed by psychologist Abraham Maslow

Two motivational theories try to explain worker motivation. The human resources model includes Theory X and Theory Y. Maslow's Hierarchy of Needs suggests that people have needs in 5 different areas: physiological, security, social, esteem, and self-actualization.

Figure 6.5   **Sample think link.**

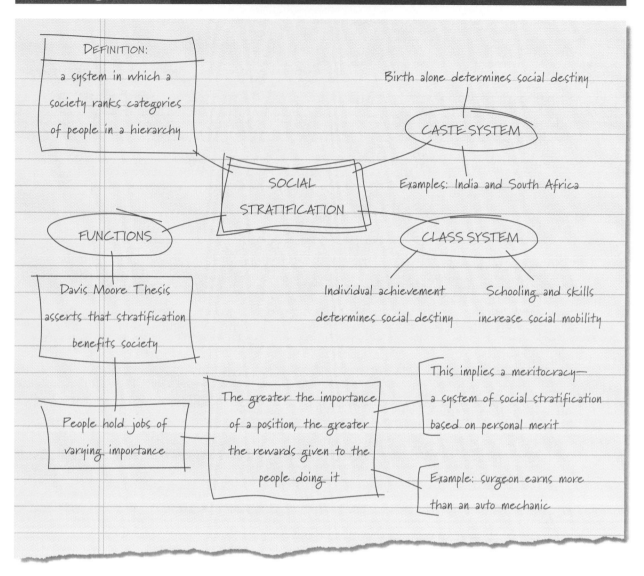

DEFINITION:
a system in which a society ranks categories of people in a hierarchy

SOCIAL STRATIFICATION

Birth alone determines social destiny

CASTE SYSTEM

Examples: India and South Africa

FUNCTIONS

CLASS SYSTEM

Davis Moore Thesis asserts that stratification benefits society

Individual achievement determines social destiny

Schooling and skills increase social mobility

People hold jobs of varying importance

The greater the importance of a position, the greater the rewards given to the people doing it

This implies a meritocracy—a system of social stratification based on personal merit

Example: surgeon earns more than an auto mechanic

This is only one of many think link styles; other examples include stair steps (showing connecting ideas that build to a conclusion) and a tree shape (roots as causes and branches as effects). Look back to Figure 5.4 on page 165 for a type of think link sometimes referred to as a "jellyfish." You can design any think link that makes sense to you.

A think link may be tough to construct in class, especially if your instructor talks quickly. In this case, use another note-taking system during class. Then, make a think link as you review your notes.

Using Other Visual Note-Taking Strategies

Several other note-taking strategies help you organize your information and are especially useful to visual learners. These strategies may be too involved to complete quickly during class, so you may want to use them when taking notes on a text chapter or when rewriting your notes for review.

Time lines. A time line can help you organize information—such as dates of French Revolution events or eras of different psychology practices—into chronological order. Draw a vertical or horizontal line on the page and connect each item to the line, in order, noting the dates.

Tables. There are tables throughout this text that show information through vertical or horizontal columns. Use tables to arrange information according to particular categories.

Hierarchy charts. These charts can help you understand information in terms of how each piece fits into the hierarchy. A hierarchy chart could show levels of government, for example, or levels of the scientific classification of animals and plants. One version of a hierarchy is called a *matrix*—a table that has categories listed across the top and left side. Each box inside shows information that relates to the categories above and beside it. Table 10.4 on page 362 is an example of a matrix.

HIERARCHY

A graded or ranked series.

Once you choose a note-taking system, your success depends on how well you use it. Personal shorthand will help you make the most of whatever system you choose.

How can you *write faster* when taking notes?

SHORTHAND

A system of rapid handwriting that employs symbols, abbreviations, and shortened words to represent words, phrases, and letters.

When taking notes, many students feel that they can't keep up with the instructor. Using some personal shorthand (not standard secretarial shorthand) can help you push your pen faster. Shorthand is writing that shortens words or replaces them with symbols. Because you are the only intended reader, you can misspell and abbreviate words in ways that only you understand.

The only danger with shorthand is that you might forget what your writing means. To avoid this problem, review your shorthand notes while your abbreviations and symbols are fresh in your mind. If there is any confusion, spell out words as you review.

Here are some suggestions that will help you master this important skill:

1. Use the following standard abbreviations in place of complete words:

w/	with	cf	compare, in comparison to
w/o	without	ff	following
→	means; resulting in	Q	question
←	as a result of	p.	page
↑	increasing	*	most importantly
↓	decreasing	<	less than

∴	therefore	>	more than
∵ or b/c	because	=	equals
≈	approximately	%	percent
+ or &	and	△	change
−	minus; negative	2	to; two; too
NO. or #	number	vs	versus; against
i.e.	that is,	e.g.	for example
etc.	and so forth	c/o	care of
ng	no good	lb	pound

2. Shorten words by removing vowels from the middle of words:

prps   =   purpose

Crvtte   =   Corvette (as on a vanity license plate for a car)

3. Substitute word beginnings for entire words:

assoc   =   associate; association

info   =   information

4. Form plurals by adding s:

prblms   =   problems

prntrs   =   printers

5. Make up your own symbols and use them consistently:

b/4   =   before

2thake   =   toothache

6. Use key phrases instead of complete sentences ("German—nouns capped" instead of "In German, all nouns are capitalized.")

Finally, throughout your note taking, remember that the primary goal is for you to generate materials that help you learn and remember information. No matter how sensible any note-taking strategy, abbreviation, or system might be, it won't do you any good if it doesn't help you reach that goal. Keep a close eye on what works for you and stick to it.

If you find that your notes aren't comprehensive, legible, or focused enough, think critically about how you might improve them. Can't read your notes? You might have been too sleepy, or you might have a handwriting issue. Confusing gaps in the information? You might be distracted in class, have an instructor who skips around, or have a lack of understanding of the course material. Put your problem-solving skills to work and brainstorm solutions from the variety of strategies in this chapter. With a little time and effort, your notes will truly become a helpful learning tool in school and beyond.

Once you have figured out how to effectively record what you hear, your next task is to remember it so that you can use it. The following information about memory will help you remember what you learn so that you can put it to use.

How does *memory* work?

Your memory enables you to use the knowledge you take in. Human memory works like a computer. Both have essentially the same purpose: to encode, store, and retrieve information.

- During the *encoding* stage, information is changed into usable form. On a computer, this occurs when keyboard entries are transformed into electronic symbols and stored on a disk. In the brain, sensory information becomes impulses that the central nervous system reads and codes. You are encoding, for example, when you study a list of chemistry formulas.

"The true art of memory is the art of attention."

SAMUEL JOHNSON

- During the *storage* stage, information is held in memory (the mind's version of a computer hard drive) for later use. In this example, after you complete your studying of the formulas, your mind stores them until you need to use them.

- During the *retrieval* stage, memories are recovered from storage by recall, just as a saved computer program is called up by name and used again. In this example, your mind retrieves the chemistry formulas when you have to take a test or solve a problem.

Memories are stored in three different storage banks. The first, called *sensory memory,* is an exact copy of what you see and hear and lasts for a second or less. Certain information is then selected from sensory memory and moves into *short-term memory,* a temporary information storehouse that lasts no more than 10 to 20 seconds. You are consciously aware of material in your short-term memory. Whereas unimportant information is quickly dumped, important information is transferred to *long-term memory*—the mind's more permanent information storehouse.

Having information in long-term memory does not necessarily mean that you will be able to recall it when needed. Particular techniques can help you improve your recall.

How can you *improve* your memory?

ost forgetting occurs within minutes after memorization. In a classic study conducted in 1885, researcher Herman Ebbinghaus memorized a list of meaningless three-letter words such as CEF and LAZ. Within one hour, he measured that he had forgotten more than 50 percent of what he learned. After two days, he knew less than 30 percent. Although his recall remained fairly stable after that, the experiment showed how fragile memory can be—even when you take the time and energy to memorize information.[4]

People with superior memories may have an inborn talent for remembering. More often, though, they have mastered techniques for improving recall. Remember that techniques aren't a cure-all for memory difficulties. If you have a learning disability, the following strategies may help but may not be enough. Seek specific assistance if you consistently have trouble remembering.

Use Specific Strategies

As a student, your job is to understand, learn, and remember information—everything from general concepts to specific details. The following suggestions will help improve your recall.

Have purpose and intention. Why can you remember the lyrics to dozens of popular songs, but not the functions of the pancreas? Perhaps this is because you want to remember the lyrics, you connect them to a visual image, or you have an emotional tie to them. To achieve the same results at school or on the job, make sure you have a purpose for what you are trying to remember. When you know why it is important, you are able to strengthen your intention to remember it.

Understand what you memorize. Information that has meaning is easier to recall than gibberish. This basic principle applies to everything you study—from biology and astronomy to history and English literature. If something you need to memorize makes no sense, consult textbooks, fellow students, or an instructor for an explanation. Use organizational tools, such as outlines (see page 204) or think links (see page 206), to make logical connections between different pieces of information.

Recite, rehearse, and write. When you *recite* material, you repeat it aloud to remember it. Reciting helps you retrieve information as you learn it and is a crucial step in studying (see Chapter 5). *Rehearsing* is similar to reciting but is done silently. It is the process of repeating, summarizing, and associating information with other information. *Writing* is rehearsing on paper. The physical nature of the acts of speaking and writing help to solidify the information in your memory.

Study during short but frequent sessions. Research shows that you can improve your chances of remembering material if you learn it more than once. Study in short sessions followed by brief rest periods, rather than studying continually with little or no rest. Even though studying for an hour straight may feel productive, you'll probably remember more from three 20-minute sessions. Try studying between classes or during other breaks in your schedule.

Separate material into manageable sections. When material is short and easy to understand, studying it from start to finish may work. With longer material, however, you may benefit from dividing it into logical sections, mastering each section, putting all the sections together, and then testing your memory of all the material.

Use a tape recorder selectively. If permitted in class, you can record lectures. Unless you have a learning disability that makes note taking difficult, take notes just as you would if the tape recorder were not there. Later, you can listen to the tapes to clarify your notes and help you remember important ideas. You can also make your own study tapes: Use your tape recorder to record study questions, leaving 10 to 15 seconds between questions so that you can answer out loud. Record the correct answer after the pause for quick feedback.

Use Visual Aids

Any kind of visual representation of study material can help you remember. Try converting material into a think link or outline. Use any visual that helps you recall it and link it to other information. If you have handouts of visuals that coordinate with class topics, have them ready as you study. Pay close attention to figures and tables in your texts; they help to remind you of important information.

Flash cards (easily made from index cards) are a great visual memory tool. They give you short, repetitive review sessions that provide immediate feedback. Use the front of each card to write a word, idea, or phrase you want to remember. Use the back side for a definition, explanation, and other key facts. Figure 6.6 shows two flash cards for studying psychology.

| Figure 6.6 | Sample flash cards. |

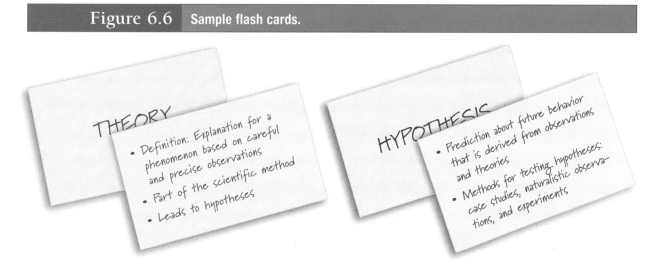

THEORY
- Definition: Explanation for a phenomenon based on careful and precise observations
- Part of the scientific method
- Leads to hypotheses

HYPOTHESIS
- Prediction about future behavior that is derived from observations and theories
- Methods for testing hypotheses: case studies, naturalistic observations, and experiments

Here are some additional suggestions for making the most of your flash cards:

- Carry the cards with you and review them frequently.
- Shuffle the cards and learn the information in various orders.
- Test yourself in both directions (e.g., first look at the terms and provide the definitions or explanations; then turn the cards over and reverse the process).

Use Critical Thinking

Your knowledge of the critical-thinking mind actions can help you remember information. Many of the mind actions use the principle of *association*—considering new information in relation to information you already know. The more you can associate a piece of new information with your current knowledge, the more likely you are to remember it.

Imagine that you have to remember information about a specific historical event—for example, the signing of the Treaty of Versailles, the agreement that ended World War I. You might put the mind actions to work in the following ways:

R *Recall* everything that you know about the topic.

 Think about how this event is *similar* to other events in history, either recent events or events from long ago.

 Consider what is *different* and unique about this treaty in comparison to other treaties.

 Explore the *causes* that led up to this event, and look at the event's *effects*.

 From the general *idea* of treaties that ended wars, explore other *examples* of such treaties.

 Think about *examples* of what happened during the treaty signing, and from those examples come up with *ideas* about the tone of the event.

 Looking at the facts of the event, *evaluate* how successful you think the treaty was.

PERSONAL TRIUMPH

*e*ven the most painful memory can be an inspiration for learning and change. Nathalie Piraino's experience as a refugee from Rwanda has led her to achieve educational goals and to strive to create a lasting memorial for those she left behind.

I grew up in Rwanda with my family. Although we had nothing materially, my papa passed on many important values to me. One of the most enduring is that he believed in higher education. When I was a child, we were forced to leave our home as a result of ethnic strife and were displaced into the south of the country. We lived in a refugee camp for two years with very little to eat.

As poor as we were, my father always made sure we had enough coffee beans or other products to sell in order to have the cash to purchase notebooks. We had to do many chores before and after school, but he always had oil for our lanterns so we could study at night. He would walk many kilometers on mountainous paths to attend school meetings. His participation boosted my self-esteem.

In 1993, I left my country and began taking classes shortly after I arrived in the United States. College was a dream come true for me. But my happiness was short lived.

In 1994, Rwanda erupted into a volcano of violence. When I began receiving the news, I cried a river of tears. My family had been massacred. The men who killed my mother worked on our farm. I remember that she would serve them food before us. She said, "If it weren't for the workers, we wouldn't be able to eat." She respected all people. I dropped classes because I couldn't focus. At night, I couldn't sleep because of recurring nightmares. I frantically called

Nathalie Piraino, English student;
Essex Community College, Baltimore, Maryland

organizations, doing everything I could, to try and save a life in my beloved country. Then, in 1995, my husband and I went to Rwanda. Even though I knew it would be incredibly painful, I also knew I needed closure. I couldn't believe what I saw. I couldn't recognize where my home used to be. I saw skeletons of children, some still with their shoes on. No one can ever describe the horror that went on there.

Last year, I experienced a major episode of depression, and once again, I had to audit my college courses. With the help of medicine and therapy, I'm feeling better now. I don't think you ever completely recover from traumas like these, but there are healthy things you can do to cope.

I have three goals in my life. The first is to adopt my niece, now 16 and living in an orphanage in Rwanda, who survived the massacre by hiding in a swamp for 36 days with her brother and eating leaves. She desperately needs love and therapy. The second is to help raise money to erect a monument for my people. My husband and I visited the Holocaust museum. I want to help erect such a memorial for my people in an effort to honor their lives. My third goal is to complete my degree in writing so that I can write a book about this tragedy. I owe it to myself and to my family to get an education. This is something my father wanted for his children. Faith is a survival tool my father gave me. By faith, I will fulfill his dream and mine.

Take a moment to consider . . .

- *How much you value your education, and what sacrifice you may have made for the sake of that education.*

- *How you feel your being educated will benefit others in your life.*

You don't have to use every mind action in every memory situation. Choose the ones that help you most. The more information and ideas you can associate with the new item you're trying to remember, the more successful at remembering it you will be.

Critical thinking also helps you perform the crucial task of separating main points from less important details. When you select and focus on the most important information, you don't waste time memorizing items you don't really need to know. As you read your texts, ask questions about what is most crucial to remember; then highlight only the most important information and write notes in the margins about central ideas. When you review your lecture notes, highlight or rewrite the most important information to remember.

Use Mnemonic Devices

Mnemonic devices (pronounced neh-MAHN-ick) work by connecting information you are trying to learn with simpler information or information that is familiar. Instead of learning new facts by rote (repetitive practice), associations give you a hook on which to hang and retrieve these facts. Mnemonic devices make information familiar and meaningful through unusual, unforgettable mental associations and visual pictures.

Here's an example of the power of mnemonics. Suppose you want to remember the names of the first six presidents of the United States. The first letters of their last names—Washington, Adams, Jefferson, Madison, Monroe, and Adams—together are W A J M M A. To remember them, you might add an E after the J and create a short nonsense word: *wajemma.*

Visual images, idea chains, acronyms, and songs and rhymes are the more widely used kinds of mnemonic devices. Apply them to your own memory challenges.

Create Visual Images and Associations

Visual images are often easier to remember than images that rely on words alone. The best mental images often involve bright colors, three dimensions, action scenes, inanimate objects with human traits, ridiculousness, and humor.

Turning information into mental pictures helps improve memory, especially for visual learners. To remember that the Spanish artist Picasso painted *The Three Women,* you might imagine the women in a circle dancing to a Spanish song with a pig and a donkey (pig-asso). Don't reject outlandish images—as long as they help you.

Use an Idea Chain to Remember Items in a List

An idea chain is a memory strategy that involves forming exaggerated mental images of a large group of items. The first image is connected to the second image, which is connected to the third image, and so on. Imagine, for example, that you want to remember the seven mind actions that appear in the critical-thinking discussion in Chapter 4: *recall, similarity, difference, cause and effect, example to idea, idea to example,* and *evaluation.* You can use the visual icons to form an idea chain that goes like this:

> The letter R (recall) rolls down a hill and bumps into two similar intersecting circles (similarity), which start rolling and bump into two different intersecting circles (difference). Everything rolls past a sign with two circling arrows on it telling them to keep rolling (cause and effect), and then bump into an "EX" at the bottom of the hill, which turns on a light bulb (example to idea). That light bulb shines on another "EX" (idea to example). The two "EX"s are sitting on either side of a set of scales (evaluation).

Create Acronyms

Another helpful association method involves the use of the **acronym.** In history, you can remember the "big three" Allies during World War II—Britain, America, and Russia—with the acronym BAR. The word (or words) spelled don't necessarily have to be real words; for example, see Figure 6.7 for a "name" acronym that often helps students remember the colors of the spectrum.

Other acronyms take the form of an entire sentence in which the first letter of each word in each sentence stands for the first letter of the memorized term. This is also called a *list order acronym.* For example, when

| Figure 6.7 | Spectrum acronym. |

red
orange
yellow
green
blue
indigo
violet

R O Y G. B I V

science students want to remember the list of planets in order of their distance from the sun (Mercury, Venus, Earth, Mars, Jupiter, Saturn, Uranus, Neptune, and Pluto), they may learn the sentence:

My very elegant mother just served us nine pickles.

Use Songs or Rhymes

Some of the most classic mnemonic devices are rhyming poems that tend to stick in your mind effectively. One you may have heard is the rule about the order of "i" and "e" in spelling:

I before E, except after C, or when sounded like "A" as in "neighbor" and "weigh."

Four exceptions if you please: either, neither, seizure, seize.

"Memory is the stepping-stone to thinking, because without remembering facts, you cannot think, conceptualize, reason, make decisions, create, or contribute."

HARRY LORAYNE

Make up your own poems or songs, linking tunes or rhymes that are familiar to you with information you want to remember. Thinking back to the "wajemma" example, imagine that you want to remember the presidents' first names as well. You might set those first names—George, John, Thomas, James, James, and John—to the tune of "Happy Birthday." Or, to extend the history theme, you might use the first musical phrase of the National Anthem.

Improving your memory requires energy, time, and work. In school, it also helps to master SQ3R, the textbook study technique that was introduced in Chapter 5. By going through the steps in SQ3R and using the specific memory techniques described in this chapter, you will be able to learn more in less time—and remember what you learn long after exams are over.

In Sanskrit, the classical written language of India and other Hindu countries, these characters read as *sem ma yeng chik,* mean "do not be distracted." This advice can refer to the focus of the work you are currently doing, the concentration required to critically think and talk through a problem, or the mental discipline of meditation, among other things.

Think of this concept as you strive to improve your listening, note taking, and memory techniques. Focus on the task, the person, or the idea at hand. Try not to be distracted by other thoughts, other people's notions of what you should be doing, or any negative messages. Be present in the moment to take in and retain what is happening around you. Do not be distracted.

Building Skills
FOR COLLEGE, CAREER, AND LIFE SUCCESS

Critical Thinking *Applying Learning to Life*

Optimum Listening Conditions

Think of a recent situation (this semester or last semester) in which you were able to understand and retain most of what you heard in the classroom.

Describe the environment (course title, type of classroom setting, etc.):

_____

_____

Describe the instructor's style (lecture, group discussion, Q & A, etc.):

_____

_____

Describe your level of preparation for the class:

_____

_____

Describe your attitude toward the course:

_____

_____

Describe any barriers to listening that you had to overcome in this situation:

_____

_____

Now describe a classroom situation you recently experienced where you feel you didn't retain information well.

Describe the environment (course title, type of classroom setting, etc.):

_____

_____

Describe the instructor's style (lecture, group discussion, Q & A, etc.):

_____

_____

Describe your level of preparation for the class:

_____

_____

Describe your attitude toward the course:

_____

_____

Describe any barriers to listening that were present in this situation:

_____

_____

Examine the two situations. Based on your descriptions, name three conditions that seem crucial for you to listen effectively and retain information.

_____

_____

_____

Describe one way in which you could have improved your listening and retention in the more difficult situation.

_____

_____

Class vs. Reading

Pick a class for which you have a regular textbook. Choose a set of class notes on a subject that is also covered in that textbook. Read the textbook section that corresponds to the subject of your class notes, taking notes as you go. Compare your reading notes to the notes you took in class.

1. Did you use a different system with the textbook, or the same as in class? Why?

_____

_____

2. Which notes can you understand better? Why do you think that's true?

_____

_____

3. What did you learn from your reading notes that you want to bring to your class note-taking strategy?

_____

_____

_____

Create a Mnemonic Device

Look back at the memory principles examined in this chapter. Using what you learned about mnemonic devices, create a mnemonic that allows you to remember these memory principles quickly. You can create a mental picture or an acronym. If you are using a mental picture, describe it here and attach a drawing if you like; if you are using an acronym, write it and then indicate what each letter stands for.

_____

_____

_____

_____

_____

_____

Teamwork   *Combining Forces*

STUDY GROUP NOTES EVALUATION. Choose one particular meeting of this class when people were likely to take notes—or, if students in your class happen to share other classes together, try using a set of notes from another class. Join with two or three other classmates, all of whom were in class that day, and make a temporary study group. Make enough photocopies of your notes to give one copy to each of the other group members.

First, look over the sets of notes on your own. Think about:

- readability of handwriting
- information covered
- note-taking systems used
- clarity of the ideas and examples

Then, gather together and talk through the four topics, one by one. Approach the notes as though you were in a study group session.

- Can you read each other's handwriting? If not, the information won't be of much use to you.
- Did you cover the same information? If someone missed a topic, someone else can help them fill in the blanks.
- Did you use the same or different note-taking systems? You might gather insight from the way someone else structures their notes.
- Could you understand what the notes were saying? If you are confused about something in your own notes, someone else might have a helpful perspective. If you don't understand someone else's notes, together you can figure out which information is confusing or missing.

Finally, write one change you plan to make in your note taking based on your study group session.

Writing | *Discovery Through Journaling*

To record your thoughts, use a separate journal or the lined page at the end of the chapter.

REMEMBERING. Think about your memory. What do you tend to remember, and memorize, well? What just doesn't stick in your head? Write about your toughest memory challenge. Discuss any strategies from this chapter that you think will help you improve, and plan how you will implement them.

Career Portfolio | *Charting Your Course*

MATCHING CAREER TO CURRICULUM. Your success in most career areas depends in part on your academic preparation. Some careers, such as medicine, require very specific curriculum choices (e.g., you have to take a number of biology and chemistry courses to be considered for medical school). Some careers require certain courses that teach basic competencies; for example, to be an accountant, you have to take accounting and bookkeeping. Other career areas, such as many business careers, don't have specific requirements, but employers often look for certain curriculum choices that indicate the mastery of particular skills.

Put your listening and note-taking skills to work as you investigate your options. Choose two of the career areas in which you are interested. For each, interview two people to find out about both required curriculum and beneficial, but not required, courses. Choose one person from your academic setting (e.g., an instructor in a related subject area, a student further along that career track, an academic advisor) and one from the working world (e.g., a person working in that career, a career planning and placement office counselor). Interview each in a setting where you can listen well and take effective notes.

When you have completed your interviews, create two lists—one for each career area—of recommended courses. Write each career at the top of its list. To set off the courses that are absolutely required from those that are simply recommended, mark them with a star.

Assess Yourself | *Student Success Strategies*

If you have access to the CD-ROM Strategies for Success, use the following questions to assess your thoughts and enhance your understanding of the chapter. The questions below represent only some of the activities provided on the CD for the chapter topics—try others if you have time.

Click on the Note Taking bookmark. Use the following activities to enhance your ability to take good notes:

1. Take the pre-assessment to identify your current understanding of how to take notes successfully.

2. Watch the video and consider how specific note-taking actions involving writing can heighten your learning and retention. In the space provided, answer the question regarding active and passive learning.

3. Click on Activity One: The Cornell System of Note Taking. Read the passage; then, in the T-note fields provided, take notes on the passage using the Cornell system.

4. Take the post-assessment to further evaluate your note-taking knowledge.

Suggested Readings

DePorter, Bobbi and Mike Hernacki. *Quantum Notes: Whole-Brain Approaches to Note Taking.* Chicago, IL: Learning Forum, 2000.

Dunkel, Patricia A., Frank Pialorsi, and Joane Kozyrez. *Advanced Listening Comprehension: Developing Aural & Note-Taking Skills.* Boston, MA: Heinle & Heinle, 1996.

Robbins, Harvey A. *How to Speak and Listen Effectively.* New York: AMACOM, 1992.

Higbee, Kenneth L. *Your Memory: How It Works and How to Improve It.* Marlowe & Co., 2001.

Lebauer, R. Susan. *Learn to Listen, Listen to Learn: Academic Listening and Note Taking.* Upper Saddle River, NJ: Prentice Hall, 2000.

Levin, Leonard. *Easy Script Express: Unique Speed Writing Methods to Take Fast Notes and Dictation.* Chicago, IL: Legend Publishing, 2000.

Lorayne, Harry. *Super Memory—Super Student: How to Raise Your Grades in 30 Days.* Boston, MA: Little, Brown & Company, 1990.

Lorayne, Harry. *The Memory Book: The Classic Guide to Improving Your Memory at Work, at School, and at Play.* New York: Ballantine Books, 1996.

Roberts, Billy. *Educate Your Memory: Improvement Techniques for Students of All Ages.* London: Allison & Busby, 2000.

Roberts, Billy. *Working Memory: Improving Your Memory for the Workplace.* London Bridge Trade, 1999.

Internet Resources

ForgetKnot: A Source for Mnemonic Devices: http://members.tripod.com/~ForgetKnot/

Prentice Hall Student Success Supersite—Study Skills: www.prenhall.com/success/StudySkl/index.html

Endnotes

1. Ralph G. Nichols, "Do We Know How to Listen? Practical Helps in a Modern Age," *Speech Teacher* (March 1961), pp. 118–124.

2. Ibid.

3. Walter Pauk, *How to Study in College,* 5th ed. Boston, MA: Houghton Mifflin Company, 1993, pp. 110–114.

4. Herman Ebbinghaus, *Memory: A Contribution to Experimental Psychology,* trans. H. A. Ruger and C. E. Bussenius. New York: New York Teacher's College, Columbia University, 1885.

JOURNAL

name   date

IN THIS CHAPTER

In this chapter you explore answers to the following questions: • How can you make the most of your library? • How can you do research on the Internet? • What are the elements of effective writing? • What is the writing process? • How can you deliver an effective oral presentation?

researching and writing

RESEARCH AND WRITING are powerful tools, and Beverly Andre (see next page) wants to know how to make the most of them. Research enables you to gather and learn information from sources all over the world. Writing enables you to communicate information and perspectives to others. Whether you write an essay in English class or a report at work, words allow you to transform your thoughts into a form that others can read.

This chapter helps you achieve two goals: To improve your skill in finding information at your college library and on the Internet, and to use words to communicate your thoughts and research findings. You also learn how good writing is linked to clear thinking and effective research. In class or at work, knowing how to find information and writing well are essential to learning and success.

gathering and communicating ideas

Beverly Andre, Triton College—
Continuing Education Program,
River Grove, Illinois

Raymond Montolvo, Jr., Writers Program,
University of Southern California, Los Angeles, California

*How can I become a
more confident writer?*

*The first step is to read. Reading helps you
learn to organize your thoughts . . .*

The best thing I ever wrote was in the sixth grade. My teacher let us pick a topic, and I chose to write about riding horses because I loved it and knew a lot about it. In high school, writing was okay because my teacher was helpful. College papers, on the other hand, have been a real challenge. I don't think my topic ideas are very original, and I feel that my vocabulary is not that advanced. If a professor assigns a topic I know nothing about, I usually don't have as much interest as with something familiar.

One of the reasons I don't like to write is because I don't like researching. Knowing how to begin gets confusing because there's so much to choose from. Once I do pull the information together, I can't seem to expand on an idea without being redundant. I also go off on all sorts of tangents. The bottom line is that I find it difficult to put my thoughts to paper. How can I become a better writer?

No matter what your writing goal, in most cases the person you are writing for, your instructor, wants you to improve. Keeping this in mind may help you concentrate on trying to improve your skills instead of worrying about getting a good grade.

I suggest a two-pronged approach to better writing. The first step is to read. Read novels, the newspaper, and nonfiction articles. Reading helps you learn to organize your thoughts, and it increases your vocabulary. If you want to focus on a specific area of study, read publications in that area. Create file folders for pieces of writing that you like. For example, make a copy of a business letter that you think is well written, and refer to it when you need to write similar correspondence.

Second, bridge the gap between what you should know and what an instructor can tell you. Ask your instructor what he or she thinks you need to work on. Focus your energy on understanding the assignment and strengthening technical skills such as sentence structure and grammar. Another tip is to read what you've written, sentence by sentence, and think about how you could say it better.

If you don't know where to begin your research, start with what feels comfortable. If you are at ease with computers, use the Internet. If you prefer libraries, start by asking the reference librarian for assistance. The main point with research is to jump right in. Once you read something that relates to your topic, it will refer you to something else.

Finally, don't get frustrated by setbacks. Writing is a process that you learn as you would an exercise. Set goals you can attain. Finishing something builds confidence.

How can you *make the most* of your *library?*

A library is a home for information; consider it the "brain" of your college. Your job is to find what you need as quickly and efficiently as you can.

Start with a Road Map

Most college libraries are bigger than high school and community libraries, so you may feel lost on your first few visits. Make your life easier by learning how your library is organized.

Circulation desk. All publications are checked out at the circulation desk, which is usually near the library entrance.

Reference area. Here you'll find reference books, including encyclopedias, directories, dictionaries, almanacs, and atlases. You'll also find librarians and other library employees who can direct you to information. Computer terminals, containing the library's catalog of holdings, as well as on-line bibliographic and full-text databases, are usually part of the reference area.

Book area. Books—and, in many libraries, magazines and journals in bound or boxed volumes—are stored in the *stacks.* A library with "open stacks" allows you to search for materials on your own. In a "closed-stack" system, a staff member retrieves materials for you.

Periodicals area. Here you'll find recent issues of popular and scholarly magazines, journals, and newspapers. Most college libraries collect **periodicals** ranging from *Time* to the *New England Journal of Medicine.* Because unbound periodicals are generally not circulated, you may find photocopy machines nearby where you can copy pages.

> **PERIODICALS**
> Magazines, journals, and newspapers that are published on a regular basis throughout the year.

Audio/visual materials areas. Many libraries have special areas for video, art and photography, and recorded music collections.

Computer areas. Computer terminals, linked to databases and the Internet, may be scattered throughout the building or set off in particular areas. You may be able to access these databases and the Internet from computer labs and writing centers. Many college dorm rooms are also wired for computer access, enabling students to connect via their personal computers.

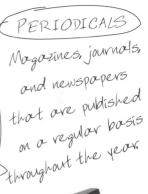

Microform areas. Most libraries have microform reading areas. Microforms are materials printed in reduced size on film, either *microfilm* (a reel of film) or *microfiche* (a sheet or card of film), that is viewed through special machines. Many microform reading machines can print hard copies of images.

To learn about your college library, take a tour or training session. Almost all college libraries offer orientation sessions on how to locate books, periodicals, and databases and use the Internet. If your school has more than one library, explore each one you intend to use.

Learn How to Conduct an Information Search

The most successful and timesaving library research involves following a specific *search strategy*—a step-by-step method for finding information that takes you from general to specific sources. Starting with general sources usually works best because they provide an overview of your research topic and can lead you to more specific information and sources. For example, an encyclopedia article on the archaeological discovery of the Dead Sea Scrolls—manuscripts written between 250 B.C. and A.D. 68 that trace the roots of Judaism and Christianity—may mention that one of the most important books on the subject is *Understanding the Dead Sea Scrolls,* edited by Hershel Shanks (New York: Random House, 1992). This book, in turn, leads you to 13 experts who wrote specialized text chapters.

Narrowing your topic is critical to research success because broad topics yield too much data. Here, instead of using "Dead Sea Scrolls" in your search, consider narrowing your topic. For example:

- How the Dead Sea Scrolls were discovered by Bedouin shepherds in 1947
- The historical origins of the scrolls
- The process archaeologists used to reconstruct scroll fragments

Conducting a Keyword Search

To narrow your topic, conduct a *keyword search* of the library database—a method for locating sources through the use of topic-related words and phrases. For example, instead of searching through the broad category *Art,* use a keyword search to focus on *French Art* or, more specifically, *nineteenth century French Art.*

Keyword searches use natural language, rather than specialized classification vocabulary. Table 7.1 includes tips that will help you use the keyword system. The last three entries describe how to use "or," "and," and "not" to narrow searches with what is called Boolean logic.

As you search, keep in mind that:

- double quotes around a word or phrase will locate the exact term you entered ("financial aid").
- using upper or lower case does not affect the search (*Scholarships* will find *scholarships*).
- singular terms will find the plural (*scholarship* will find *scholarships*).

Table 7.1	How to perform an effective keyword search.		
If you are searching for . . .	**Do this**		**Example**
A word	Type the word normally		Aid
A phrase	Type the phrase in its normal word order (use regular word spacing) or surround the phrase with double quotation marks		financial aid or "financial aid"
Two or more keywords without regard to word order	Type the words in any order, surrounding the words with quotation marks (use *and* to separate the words)		"financial aid" and "scholarships"
Topic A or topic B	Type the words in any order, surrounding the words with quotation marks (use *or* to separate the words)		"financial aid" or "scholarships"
Topic A but not topic B	Type topic A first within quotation marks, and then topic B within quotation marks (use *not* to separate the words)		"financial aid" not "scholarships"

Conducting Research Using a Search Strategy

Knowing where to look during each phase of your search helps you find information quickly and efficiently. A successful search strategy often starts with general references and moves to more specific references (see Figure 7.1). Your search may also involve electronic sources from the Internet.

Use General Reference Works

Begin your research with *general reference works*. These works cover many different topics in a broad, nondetailed way. General reference guides are often available on-line or on CD-ROM.

Among the works that fall into the general reference category are these:

- Encyclopedias such as the multivolume *Encyclopedia Americana* and the single-volume *New Columbia Encyclopedia*
- Almanacs such as the *World Almanac and Book of Facts*
- Yearbooks such as the *McGraw-Hill Yearbook of Science and Technology* and the *Statistical Abstract of the United States*
- Dictionaries such as *Webster's New World College Dictionary*

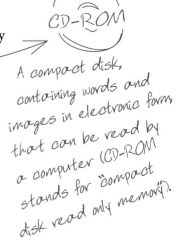

CD-ROM

A compact disk, containing words and images in electronic form that can be read by a computer (CD-ROM stands for "compact disk read only memory").

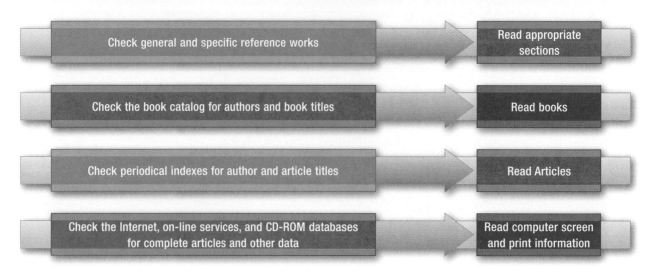

Figure 7.1 Library search strategy.

- Biographical reference works such as the *New York Times Biographical Service, Webster's Biographical Dictionary,* and various editions of *Who's Who*
- Bibliographies such as *Books in Print* (especially the *Subject Guide to Books in Print*)

Scan these sources for an overview of your topic. Bibliographies at the end of encyclopedia articles may also lead to important sources.

Search Specialized Reference Works

Turn next to *specialized reference works* for more specific facts. Specialized reference works include encyclopedias and dictionaries that focus on a narrow field. Although the entries in these volumes are short summaries, they focus on critical ideas and on the keywords you need to conduct additional research. Bibliographies that accompany the articles point to the works of recognized experts. Examples of specialized reference works, organized by subject, include the following:

- history *(Encyclopedia of American History)*
- science and technology *(Encyclopedia of Biological Sciences)*
- social sciences *(Dictionary of Education)*
- current affairs *(Social Issues Resources Series [SIRS])*

Browse Through Books on Your Subject

Use the computerized *library catalog* to find books and other materials on your topic. The catalog tells you which publications the library owns and where they can be found and is searchable by author, title, and subject. For example, a library that owns *The Artist's Way: A Spiritual Path to Higher Creativity* by Julia Cameron may list the book in the author catalog under Cameron, Julia (last name first); in the title catalog under

Artist's Way (articles such as *the, a,* and *an* are dropped from the beginnings of titles and subjects); and in the subject catalog under "Creative Ability—problems, exercises, etc.," "Self-actualization—psychology," and "Creation—literary, artistic, etc."

Each catalog listing refers to the library's classification system, which tells you exactly where the publication can be found. The Dewey Decimal and Library of Congress systems are among the most common classification systems. Getting to know your library's system will help save time and trouble.

Use Periodical Indexes to Search for Periodicals

Periodicals are a valuable source of current information and include journals, magazines, and newspapers. *Journals* are written for readers with specialized knowledge. Whereas *Newsweek* magazine may run a general-interest article on AIDS research, the *Journal of the American Medical Association* may print the original scientific study for an audience of doctors and scientists. Many libraries display periodicals that are up to a year or two old and convert older copies to microfilm or microfiche. Many full-text articles are also available on computer databases.

Periodical indexes lead you to specific articles. The *Reader's Guide to Periodical Literature,* available in print and on CD-ROM, indexes general information sources including articles in hundreds of general-interest publications. Look in the *Infotrac* family of databases (available on-line or on CD-ROM) for other periodical indexes such as *Health Reference Center* and *General Business File.* Another periodical database family—*Ebsco Host*—catalogs general and health-related periodicals.

Indexing information is listed in the *Standard Periodical Directory, Ulrich's International Periodicals Directory,* and *Magazines for Libraries.* Each database also lists the magazines and periodicals it indexes. Because there is no all-inclusive index for technical, medical, and scholarly journal articles, you'll have to search indexes that specialize in narrow subject areas. Such indexes also include *abstracts* (article summaries). Among the available indexes are *ERIC (Educational Resources Information Center),* the *Humanities Index, Index Medicus,* and *Psychological Abstracts.* You'll also find separate newspaper indexes in print, in microform, on CD-ROM, or on-line.

Almost no library owns all of the publications listed in these and other specialized indexes. However, journals that are not part of your library's collection or that are not available in full-text form on-line may be available through an interlibrary loan, which requests materials from other libraries. The librarian will help you arrange the loan.

Ask the Librarian

Librarians can assist you in solving research problems. They can help you locate unfamiliar or hard-to-find sources, navigate catalogs and databases, and uncover research shortcuts. Say, for example, you are researching a gun-control bill that is currently before Congress, and you want to contact groups on both sides of the issue. The librarian may lead you to the

Encyclopedia of Associations, which lists the National Rifle Association, a pro-gun organization, and Handgun Control Inc., a gun-control group. By contacting these groups or visiting their Web sites, you will get information on current legislation.

Librarians are not the only helpful people in the library. For simplicity's sake, this book uses the term *librarian* to refer to both librarians and other staff members who are trained to help. Here are some tips that will help you get the advice you are seeking from the librarian.

Be prepared and be specific. Instead of asking for information on the American presidency, focus on the topic you expect to write about in your American history paper—for example, how President Franklin D. Roosevelt's physical disability may have affected his leadership during World War II.

Ask for help when you can't find a specific source. For example, when a specific book is not on the shelf, the librarian may direct you to another source that works as well.

Ask for help with computer and other equipment. Librarians are experts in using the library's computers and other equipment, so turn to them if you encounter a technical problem you can't solve.

The library is one of your college's most valuable resources, so take advantage of it. Your library research and critical-thinking skills give you the ability to collect information, weigh alternatives, and make decisions. These skills last a lifetime and may serve you well if you choose one of the many careers that require research ability. The library is not your only research resource, however. The Internet is becoming a primary research tool for both school and work.

How can you do *research* on the *Internet?*

The *Internet* is a computer network that links organizations and people around the world. A miracle of technology, it can connect you to billions of information sources instantaneously. According to a recent survey, students spend an average of 8.1 hours on-line a week, with research being the primary on-line activity for almost half of these students.[1]

Because of its widespread reach, the Internet is an essential research tool—if used wisely. This section helps you make the most of the time you spend on-line now and in the future. As the Internet becomes more important, it opens up a world of opportunities: For example, it may be the medium through which you continue your studies via on-line courses, do your work at a home-based office, purchase products and services, find medical information, book airlines and hotels, investigate potential employers, file your taxes, make investments, and more.

Internet research depends on your critical judgment. Bob Kieft, library director at Haverford College in Pennsylvania, says that students must be able to "think critically and independently about the sources they use, be curious and imaginative about the projects they are working on, be open to the topic in ways that lead them to ask good questions, and bring their analytical powers to bear. . . . What students know about technology is less important than how they think about their work."[2]

The Basics

With a basic knowledge of the Internet, you can access facts and figures, read articles and reports, purchase products, download files, send messages electronically via e-mail, and even "talk" to people in real time. Following is some basic information.

Access. Users access the Internet through Internet Service Providers (ISPs). Some ISPs are commercial, such as America Online or Earthlink. Others are linked to companies, colleges, and other organizations. When you sign up with an ISP, you choose a *screen name,* which is your on-line address.

Information locations. Most information is displayed on *Web sites,* cyberspace locations developed by companies, government agencies, organizations, and individuals. Together, these sites make up the *World Wide Web.* By visiting particular Web sites, you can research topics, as well as buy and sell products. Other locations where information resides include *newsgroups* (collections of messages from people interested in a particular topic), *FTP sites* (File Transfer Protocol sites enable users to download files), *gophers,* and other non-Web sites that provide access to databases or library holdings.

Finding locations. The string of text and numbers that identifies an Internet site is called a *URL* (Universal Resource Locator). Look at the Internet Resources at the end of this chapter, or any other, for some examples of URLs. You can type in a URL to access a specific site. Many Web sites include *hyperlinks*—URLs that are underlined and highlighted in color— that take you directly to another location when you click on them.

Now that you have some basic knowledge, explore how to search for information.

Search Directories and Search Engines

You need a *search directory* or *search engine* to find and select Web sites and other information locations. Following are some details about these essential search tools.

Search Directories

Search directories are large collections of Web sites sorted by category, much as Yellow Pages directories organize business telephone numbers. Information is accessible through keyword searches. When searching, start with a search directory first because the results may be more manageable than with a search engine. Some of the most popular and effective search directories include Yahoo! (www.yahoo.com) and Excite (www.excite.com).

"Seeing research as a quest for an answer makes clear that you cannot know whether you have found something unless you know what it is you are looking for."

LYNN QUITMAN TROYKA

Each search directory has particular features. Some have different search options (simple search, advanced search); some are known for having strong lists of sites for particular topics; some have links that connect you to lists of sites that fall under particular categories. The search directory's Web site helps you learn how to best use the directory.

Search Engines

Slightly different from search directories, search engines search for keywords through the entire Internet—newsgroups, Web sites, and other resources—instead of just Web sites. This gives you wider access but may yield an enormous list of hits unless you know how to limit your search effectively. Some useful search engines include: AltaVista (www.altavista.com), HotBot (www.hotbot.com), Lycos (www.lycos.com), GoTo (www.goto.com), and Ask Jeeves (www.askjeeves.com). As with search directories, each search engine includes helpful search tools and guides.

Search Strategy

Start with this basic search strategy when researching on-line:

1. *Think carefully about what you want to locate.* University of Michigan Professor Eliot Soloway recommends phrasing your search in the form of a question—for example, *What vaccines are given to children before age 5?* Then, he advises identifying the important words in the question (*vaccines, children, before age 5*) as well as other related words (*chicken pox, tetanus, polio, shot, pediatrics,* and so on). This gives you a collection of terms to use in different combinations as you search.[3]

2. *Use a search directory to isolate sites under your desired topic or category.* Save the sites that look useful. (Most browsers have a "bookmark" feature for sites you want to find again.)

3. *Explore these sites to get a general idea of what's out there.* If the directory takes you where you need to go, you're in luck. More often in academic research, you need to dig deeper. Notice useful keywords and information locations in the search directory.

4. *Move on to a search engine to narrow your search.* Use your keywords in a variety of ways to uncover as many possibilities as you can.

   - Vary their order if you are using more than one (e.g., search under *education, college, statistics* and *statistics, education, college*).

   - Use *Boolean operators*—the words "and," "not," and "or"—in ways that limit your search (see Table 7.1 for techniques for using keywords for library searches).

5. *Evaluate the list of links that appear.* If there are too many, narrow your search by using more keywords or more specific keywords (*Broadway* could become *Broadway* AND *"fall season"* AND *2002*). If there are too few, broaden your search by using fewer or different keywords.

6. *When you think you are done, start over.* Choose another search directory or search engine and perform your search again. Why do this? Because different systems access different sites.

Non-Web Resources

The Web is not your only source of information. Newsgroups and Gopher can also help you achieve your research goals.

Newsgroups

Usenet, the system of *newsgroups,* is a series of "bulletin boards" where users can post messages. Other users can then read posts and respond to them. Posts are grouped in "threads" (a series of posts that follow, and are in response to, a particular topic). Newsgroups focus on specific topics—from silent film stars to modern architecture to text fonts.

You may want to post a question and start a new thread or look at the titles of existing threads to see if your question has already been answered. The more specific your question, the greater the likelihood you will get a useable answer. Looking through threads may ultimately reward you with information. However, the process takes time and patience.

Choose your newsgroups carefully when researching. Many newsgroups are more recreational than information-focused. For example, if you are looking for information on plants, *sci.bio.botany* will probably be more of a pertinent scientific resource ("Second European Symposium on Aerobiology" reads one thread) than *rec.gardens.edible* (with threads like "couple of green tomatoes"). Every newsgroup has an FAQ (Frequently Asked Questions) list that you should read before you post.

Gopher Searches

There are thousands of *Gopher* servers, or sites, mostly located on campuses or at government agencies (the name comes from the mascot of the University of Minnesota, where the Gopher system was developed). These servers contain data and archived writings available for search and retrieval. The data is arranged much like in a library, with keywords that refer to sections, divided repeatedly into subsections, eventually arriving at the smallest segments of information.

Among the tools that help you navigate Gopher sites is Veronica, which matches keywords to long Gopher entries. Veronica does for Gopher searches what a search engine does for Web searches. It helps sort through vast amounts of information. You can access Veronica through your ISP. Look for "Gopher Worldwide" to find a list of the servers, organized by continent, country, and organization.

Use Critical Thinking to Evaluate Every Source

If all information were equal, you could trust the accuracy of every source you find at the library and on the Internet. Because that isn't the case, critical-thinking skills are needed to evaluate sources. Here are some critical-thinking questions to ask about every source:

- *Is the author a recognized expert?* A journalist who writes his or her first article on child development may not have the same credibility as a psychologist who has authored three child-development texts.

- *Does the author write from a particular perspective?* An article evaluating liberal democratic policies written by a Republican conservative almost certainly has a bias.

- *Is the source recent enough for your purposes?* Whereas a history published in 1990 on the U.S. Civil War will probably be accurate in the year 2002, a 1990 analysis of current computer technology will be hopelessly out of date.

- *Are the author's sources reliable?* Where did the author get the information? Check the bibliography and footnotes for source quality. Find out whether they are reputable, established publications. If the work is based on *primary evidence,* the author's original work or direct observation, analyze whether the proof is solid enough to support the conclusions. If it is based on *secondary evidence,* an analysis of the works of others, are the conclusions supported by evidence?

Evaluate Internet Sources

It is up to you to evaluate the truth and usefulness of the information you find on the Internet. Because the Internet is largely an uncensored platform for free-flowing information, you must decide which sources have value and which should be ignored. It takes time and experience to develop the instincts you need to make these evaluations, so talk to your instructor if you have questions about specific sources.

If you are informed about the potential pitfalls of Internet research and do your best to avoid them, through critical thinking, you will get the most from your time and effort. Use the following strategies to investigate the value of each source.[4]

Be prepared for Internet-specific problems. The nature of the Internet causes particular problems for researchers, including changing information (new information arrives daily; old information may not be removed or updated) and technology problems (Web sites may move, be deleted, or have

technical problems that deny access). It is smart to budget extra time to handle problems and to investigate whether information is current.

Evaluate the source. Note the Web site name and the organization that creates and maintains the site. Is the organization reputable? Is it known as an authority on the topic you are researching? If you are not sure of the source, the URL usually gives you a clue. For example, URLs ending in .edu originate at an educational institution, and .gov sites originate at government agencies.

Evaluate the material. Can you tell if the material is valid and accurate? Evaluate it the way you would any other material you read. See if sources are noted and if you trust them. Is the source a published document (e.g., newspaper article, professional journal article) or is it simply one person's views? Can you verify the data by comparing it to other material? Pay attention, also, to writing quality. Texts with grammatical and spelling errors, poor organization, or factual mistakes are likely to be unreliable.

Take advantage of the wealth of material the Internet offers—but be picky. Always remember that your research is only as strong as your critical thinking. If you work hard to ensure that your research is solid and comprehensive, the products of your efforts will speak for themselves.

Perhaps your best bet is to combine library and Internet resources. Remember that the library is laid out in an established system and may be more navigable than the tangle of Internet sites. Plus, library employees can help you in person. You might want to seek out library materials to help you verify the authenticity of what you discover on the Internet.

Learn to Be Media Literate

Your skill in evaluating library and Internet resources will help you critically evaluate all media—including movies, television, and TV and print advertising—rather than accepting messages right away as fact. Critical thinking helps you become *media literate* (able to "read" or analyze media you encounter) in the following ways:[5]

MEDIA

The agencies of mass communication —television, film and journalism (magazines and newspapers).

- You will better understand that messages are often constructed so that viewers feel certain emotions, develop particular opinions, or buy specific products. Words, background music, colors, images, and other factors are carefully chosen to produce a desired effect.
- You will look for the underlying values and views of the people who created the message and evaluate how they affect the message.
- You will be better able to determine whether something is being sold and to look for the effects these commercial interests have on how the message is conveyed.

Becoming media literate helps raise your awareness of the need to analyze all information sources you encounter in college, in your career, and in your personal life.

Whether you are zapping electronic mail across the globe or using a pencil and pad to write a research paper, the success of your communication depends on your ability to write. In the next section, you explore ways to improve your writing.

What are the elements of *effective writing?*

Over the years to come you may write papers, essays, answers to essay test questions, job application letters, résumés, business proposals and reports, e-mails to coworkers, and letters to customers and suppliers. Good writing skills help you achieve the goals you set with each writing task.

Good writing depends on and reflects clear thinking and is influenced greatly by reading. Exposing yourself to the works of other writers introduces you to new concepts and perspectives as it helps you discover different ways to express ideas.

Every writing situation is unique, depending on your purpose, topic, and  audience. Your goal is to understand each element before you begin.

AUDIENCE

The reader or readers of any piece of written material.

Writing Purpose

Writing without a clear purpose is like driving without a destination. You'll get somewhere, but chances are it won't be the right place. Therefore, when you write, always decide what you want to accomplish before you start. The two most common writing purposes are to inform and to persuade.

Informative writing presents and explains ideas in an unbiased way. A research paper on how hospitals process blood donations informs readers without trying to mold opinions. Most newspaper articles, except on the opinion and editorial pages, are examples of informative writing.

Persuasive writing attempts to convince readers to adopt a point of view. For example, as the health editor of a magazine, you write a column to persuade readers to give blood. Examples of persuasive writing include newspaper editorials, business proposals, and books with a point of view.

Knowing Your Audience

In almost every case, a writer creates written material so that others can read it. The writer and audience are partners in this process. Knowing who your audience is helps you communicate successfully.

Key Questions About Your Audience

In school, your primary audience is your instructors. For many assignments, instructors want you to assume that they are *typical readers* who know little about your topic and need full explanations. In contrast, *informed readers* know your subject and require less information. Ask yourself some or all of the following questions to help you define how much information your readers need:

- What are my readers' roles? Are they instructors, students, employers, customers?
- How much do they know about my topic? Are they experts or beginners?
- Are they interested, or do I have to convince them to read my material?
- Can I expect readers to have open or closed minds about my topic?

Use your answers as a guide to help you shape what you write. Remember, communication is successful only when readers understand your message as you intended it. Effective and successful writing involves following the steps in the writing process.

What is the writing *process?*

The writing process for research papers gives you the opportunity to state and rework your thoughts until you have expressed yourself clearly. The four main parts of the process are planning, drafting, revising, and editing. Critical thinking plays an important role throughout.

Planning

Planning gives you a chance to think about what to write and how to write it. Planning involves brainstorming for topic ideas, using prewriting strategies to define and narrow your topic, conducting research, writing a thesis statement, and writing a working outline. Although these steps are listed in sequence, in real life they overlap one another as you plan your document.

Open Your Mind Through Brainstorming

Whether your instructor assigns a specific topic (the unfolding relationships between mothers and daughters in Amy Tan's novel, *The Joy Luck Club*), a partially defined topic (novelist Amy Tan), or a general category within which you make your own choice (Asian-American authors), you should brainstorm to develop topic ideas. Brainstorming is a creative technique that involves generating ideas about a subject without making judgments (see pages 121–122).

First, let your mind wander. Write down anything on the assigned subject that comes to mind, in no particular order. Then, organize that list into an outline or think link that helps you see the possibilities more clearly. To make the outline or think link, separate the items you've listed into general ideas or categories and sub-ideas or examples. Then, associate the sub-ideas or examples with the ideas they support or fit. Figure 7.2 shows a portion of an outline that student Michael B. Jackson constructed from his brainstorming list. The assignment is a five-paragraph essay on a life-changing event. Here Michael chose to brainstorm the topic of "boot camp" as he organized his ideas into categories.

PREWRITING STRATEGIES

Techniques for generating ideas about a topic and finding out how much you already know before you start your research and writing.

Figure 7.2   Part of a brainstorming outline.

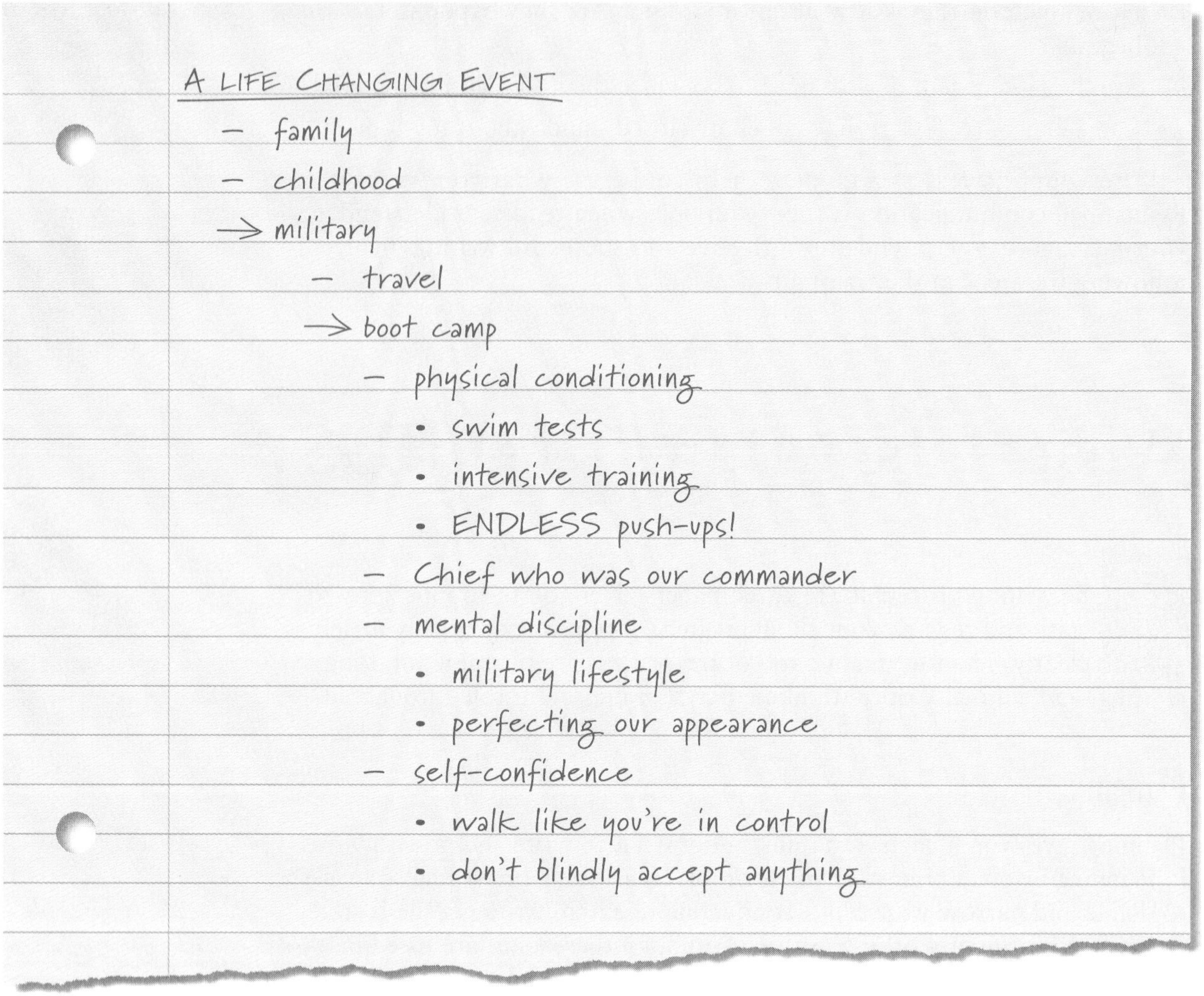

A LIFE CHANGING EVENT
— family
— childhood
→ military
　　— travel
　　→ boot camp
　　　　— physical conditioning
　　　　　• swim tests
　　　　　• intensive training
　　　　　• ENDLESS push-ups!
　　　　— Chief who was our commander
　　　　— mental discipline
　　　　　• military lifestyle
　　　　　• perfecting our appearance
　　　— self-confidence
　　　　　• walk like you're in control
　　　　　• don't blindly accept anything

Narrow Your Topic Through Prewriting Strategies

Next, narrow your topic, focusing on the specific sub-ideas and examples from your brainstorming session. Explore one or more of these with prewriting strategies such as brainstorming, freewriting, and asking journalists' questions.[6] Prewriting strategies help you decide which of your possible topics you would most like to pursue.

Brainstorming. The same process you used to generate ideas also helps you narrow your topic. Write down your thoughts about the possibility you have chosen, and then organize them into categories, noticing any patterns that appear. See if any of the sub-ideas or examples might make good topics.

Freewriting. When you freewrite, you write whatever comes to mind without censoring ideas or worrying about grammar, spelling, punctuation, or organization. Freewriting helps you think creatively and gives you an opportunity to begin integrating the information you know. Freewrite on the sub-ideas or examples you created to see if you want to pursue them. Here is a sample of freewriting:

Boot camp for the Coast Guard really changed my life. First of all, I really got in shape. We had to get up every morning at 5 A.M., eat breakfast, and go right into training. We had to do endless military-style push-ups, but we later found out that these have a purpose, to prepare us to hit the deck in the event of enemy fire. We had a lot of aquatic tests, once we were awakened at 3 A.M. to do one in full uniform! Boot camp also helped me to feel confident about myself and be disciplined. Chief Marzloff was the main person who made that happen. He was tough but there was always a reason. He got angry when I used to nod my head whenever he would speak to me, he said that made it seem like I was blindly accepting whatever he said, which was a weakness. From him I have learned to keep an eye on my body's movements when I communicate. I learned a lot more from him too.

Asking journalists' questions. When journalists start working on a story, they ask themselves: Who? What? Where? When? Why? and How? You can use these *journalists' questions* to focus your thinking. Ask these questions about any sub-idea or example to discover what you may want to discuss.

Who?   Who was at boot camp? Who influenced me the most?

What?   What about boot camp changed my life? What did we do?

When?   When in my life did I go to boot camp and for how long?

Where? Where was camp located? Where did we spend our day-to-day time?

Why?   Why did I decide to go there? Why was it such an important experience?

How?   How did we train in the camp? How were we treated? How did we achieve success?

As you prewrite, keep an eye on paper length, due date, and other requirements (such as topic area or purpose). These requirements influence your choice of a final topic. For example, if you have a month to write an informative 20-page paper on a learning disability, you might discuss the symptoms, effects, and treatment of attention deficit disorder. If you have a week to write a five-page persuasive essay, you might write about how elementary school students with ADD need special training.

Prewriting helps you develop a topic broad enough to give you something with which to work but narrow enough to be manageable. Prewriting also helps you see what you know and what you don't know. If your assignment requires more than you already know, you may need to do research.

Conduct Research

In some cases, prewriting strategies may generate all the ideas and information you need. In other writing situations, research is needed to find outside sources. Try doing your research in stages. In the first stage, look for a basic overview that can lead to a thesis statement. In the second stage, go into more depth, tracking down information that helps you fill in gaps and complete your thoughts.

As you research, create source notes and content notes on index cards. These help you organize your work, keep track of your sources, and avoid **plagiarism.**

PLAGIARISM

The act of using someone else's exact words, figures, unique approach or specific reasoning without giving appropriate credit.

- *Source notes* are the preliminary notes you take as you review research. They include vital bibliographic information, as well as a short summary and critical evaluation of the work. Each source note should include the author's full name; the title of the work; the edition, if any; the publisher, year, and city of publication; issue and/or volume number when applicable (such as for a magazine); and the page numbers you consulted. Figure 7.3 shows an example of how you can write source notes on index cards.

- *Content notes* provide an in-depth look at the source, taken during a thorough reading. They are longer and more detailed than source notes. Use them to record the information you need to write your draft.

Figure 7.3	Sample source note.

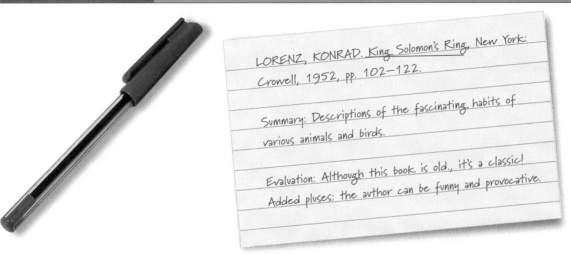

LORENZ, KONRAD. *King Solomon's Ring.* New York: Crowell, 1952, pp. 102–122.

Summary: Descriptions of the fascinating habits of various animals and birds.

Evaluation: Although this book is old., it's a classic! Added pluses: the author can be funny and provocative.

Write a Thesis Statement

Your work has prepared you to write a thesis statement, the central message you want to communicate to readers. The thesis statement states your subject and point of view, reflects your writing purpose and audience, and acts as the organizing principle of your paper. Here is an example from Michael's paper:

Topic:	Coast Guard boot camp
Purpose:	To inform
Audience:	Instructor who probably knows little about the topic
Thesis statement:	Chief Marzloff, our Basic Training Company Commander at the U.S. Coast Guard Basic Training Facility, shaped my life through physical conditioning, developing self-confidence, and instilling strong mental discipline.

A thesis statement is just as important in a short document, such as a letter, as it is in a long paper. For example, when you write a job application letter, a clear thesis statement helps you tell the recruiter why you should be hired.

Write a Working Outline

The final step in the preparation process is writing a working outline. Use this outline as a loose guide instead of a final structure. As you draft your paper, your ideas and structure may change. Only by allowing changes to occur do you get closer to what you really want to say. Some students prefer a formal outline structure, while others like to use a think link.

Create a Checklist

Use the checklist in Table 7.2 to make sure your preparation is complete. Under Date Due, create your own writing schedule, giving each task an intended completion date. Work backward from the date the assignment is due and estimate how long it will take to complete each step. Refer to Chapter 3 for time-management skills that will help you schedule your writing process.

You'll probably move back and forth among the tasks on the schedule. You might find yourself doing two and even three things on the same day. Stick to the schedule as best you can, while balancing the other demands of your life, and check off your accomplishments as you complete them.

DATE DUE	TASK	IS IT COMPLETE?
	Brainstorm	
	Define and narrow	
	Use prewriting strategies	
	Conduct research if necessary	
	Write thesis statement	
	Write working outline	
	Complete research	

Table 7.2 Preparation checklist.

Drafting

A *first draft* involves putting ideas down on paper for the first time—but not the last. You may write many versions of the assignment until you are satisfied. Each version moves you closer to saying exactly what you want in the way you want to say it.

The process of writing a first draft includes freewriting, crafting an introduction, organizing the ideas in the body of the paper, formulating a conclusion, citing sources, and soliciting feedback. When you think of drafting, it might help to imagine that you are creating a kind of "writing sandwich." The bottom slice of bread is the introduction, the top slice is the conclusion, and the sandwich stuffing is made of central ideas and supporting examples (see Figure 7.4).

Freewriting Your Draft

Take everything that you have developed in the planning stages and freewrite a rough draft. For now, don't consciously think about your introduction, conclusion, or the structure within the paper's body. Simply focus on getting your ideas out onto paper. When you have the beginnings of a paper, you can start to shape it into something with a more definite form. First, work on how you want to begin.

Writing an Introduction

The introduction tells readers what the rest of the paper contains, and includes a thesis statement. On the next page, for example, is a draft of an introduction for Michael's paper about the Coast Guard. The thesis statement is underlined at the end of the paragraph.

Figure 7.4   The "writing sandwich."

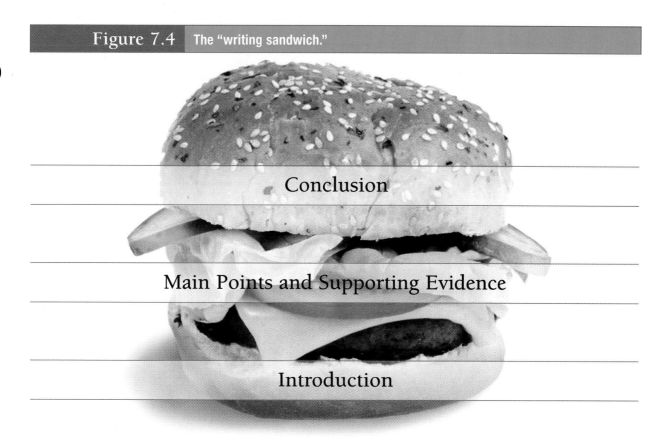

Chief Marzloff took on the task of shaping the lives and careers of the youngest, newest members of the U.S. Coast Guard. During my eight weeks in training, he was my father, my instructor, my leader, and my worst enemy. He took his job very seriously and demanded that we do the same. The Chief was instrumental in conditioning our bodies, developing our self-confidence, and instilling mental discipline within us.

When you write an introduction, use one or more *hooks* to catch the reader's attention and encourage him or her to want to read further. Useful hooks include relevant anecdotes, quotations, dramatic statistics, or questions that encourage thinking. Always link your strategy to your thesis statement. After you craft an introduction that establishes the purpose of your paper, make sure the body fulfills that purpose.

Creating the Body of a Paper

The body of the paper contains your central ideas and supporting evidence. *Evidence*—proof that informs or persuades—consists of the facts, statistics, examples, and expert opinions.

Look at the array of ideas and evidence in your draft in its current state. Think about how you might group evidence with the particular ideas it supports. Then, try to find a structure that helps you organize your ideas and evidence into a clear pattern. Here are some strategies to consider:

- *Arrange ideas by time.* Describe events in order or in reverse order.
- *Arrange ideas according to importance.* Start with the idea that carries the most weight and move to less important ideas. Or move from the least important to the most important idea.
- *Arrange ideas by problem and solution.* Start with a specific problem and then discuss solutions.

You might want to use "chain-link support"—a set of reasons that build on one another. Be sure to consider arguments that oppose yours, and consider presenting evidence that counteracts such arguments.

Writing the Conclusion

Your conclusion is a statement or paragraph that summarizes the information that is in the body of your paper and critically evaluates what is important about it. Try one of the following strategies:

- Summarize main points (if material is longer than three pages)
- Relate a story, statistic, quotation, or question that makes the reader think
- Call the reader to action
- Look to the future

Try not to introduce new facts or restate what has already been proven ("I have shown that violent cartoons are linked to violence in children"). Let your ideas in the body of the paper speak for themselves. Readers should feel that they have reached a natural point of completion.

"Omit needless words. . . . This requires not that the writer make all his sentences short, or that he avoid all detail and treat his subjects only in outline, but that every word tell."

WILLIAM STRUNK, JR.[7]

Crediting Authors and Sources

When you write a research paper, you often incorporate ideas from other sources into your work. These ideas are the writer's *intellectual property.* Using another writer's words, content, unique approach, or illustrations without crediting the author is called *plagiarism* and is illegal and unethical. It is just as serious as any other theft and may have unfavorable

Figure 7.5   Avoid plagiarism by learning how to paraphrase.

QUOTATION

"The most common assumption that is made by persons who are communicating with one another is . . . that the other perceives, judges, thinks, and reasons the way he does. Identical twins communicate with ease. Persons from the same culture but with a different education, age, background, and experience often find communication difficult. American managers communicating with managers from other cultures experience greater difficulties in communication than with managers from their own culture."*

UNACCEPTABLE PARAPHRASE (The underlined words are taken directly from the quoted source.)

When we communicate, we assume that the person to whom we are speaking perceives, judges, thinks, and reasons the way we do. This is not always the case. Although identical twins communicate with ease, persons from the same culture but with a different education, age, background, and experience often encounter communication problems. Communication problems are common among American managers as they attempt to communicate with managers from other cultures. They experience greater communication problems than when they communicate with managers from their own culture.

ACCEPTABLE PARAPHRASE

Many people fall into the trap of believing that everyone sees the world exactly as they do and that all people communicate according to the same assumptions. This belief is difficult to support even within our own culture as African-Americans, Hispanic-Americans, Asian-Americans, and others often attempt unsuccessfully to find common ground. When intercultural differences are thrown into the mix, such as when American managers working abroad attempt to communicate with managers from other cultures, clear communication becomes even harder.

*Source of quotation: Lynn Quitman Troyka, *Simon & Schuster Handbook for Writers* (Upper Saddle River, NJ: Prentice Hall, 1996).

consequences. Most colleges have stiff penalties for plagiarism, as well as for any other cheating offense (see Quick Start to College).

To avoid plagiarism, learn the difference between a quotation and a paraphrase. A *quotation* repeats a source's exact words, which are set off from the rest of the text by quotation marks. A *paraphrase* is a restatement of the quotation in your own words. A restatement requires that you completely rewrite the idea, not just remove or replace a few words. A paraphrase may not be acceptable if it is too close to the original. Figure 7.5 demonstrates these differences.

Plagiarism often begins accidentally during research. You may forget to include quotation marks around a quotation, or you may intend to cite or paraphrase a source but never do. To avoid forgetting, write detailed source and content notes as you research. Try writing something like *Quotation from original; rewrite later* next to quoted material you copy into your notes, and add all bibliographic information you will need (title, author, source, page number, etc.), so you don't spend hours trying to locate it later.

Even an acceptable paraphrase requires a citation to the source of the ideas within it. Take care to credit any source that you quote, paraphrase, or use as evidence. To credit a source, write a footnote or endnote that describes it. Use the format preferred by your instructor. Writing handbooks, such as the *Simon & Schuster Handbook for Writers* by Lynn Quitman Troyka, explain the two standard documentation styles from the American Psychological Association (APA) and the Modern Language Association (MLA). A good writing handbook tells you how to cite various types of sources in the body of a paper and compile a list of works cited at the end of your paper.

Students who choose to plagiarize are placing their academic careers at risk because of instructors' increasing use of anti-plagiarism computer software. These programs find strings of words that are identical to those in a database and alert the instructor to suspicious patterns. When a physics professor at the University of Virginia suspected that his students were copying term papers, he ran their papers through a program that looked for similarities of six or more consecutive words. He found 122 cases of abuse. These students are facing possible expulsion.[8]

Continue Your Checklist

Create a checklist for your first draft (see Table 7.3). The elements of a first draft do not have to be written in order. In fact, many writers prefer to write the introduction after the body of the paper, so the introduction reflects the paper's content and tone. Whatever order you choose, make sure your schedule allows you to get everything done—with enough time left over for revisions.

Table 7.3	First draft checklist.	
DATE DUE	**TASK**	**IS IT COMPLETE?**
	Freewrite a draft	
	Plan and write the introduction	
	Organize the body of the paper	
	Include research evidence in the body	
	Plan and write the conclusion	
	Check for plagiarism and rewrite passages to avoid it	
	Credit sources	
	Solicit feedback	

The techniques below allow you to access your power as a writer by uncovering valuable research sources and clearly communicating what you really want to say.

INTELLIGENCE	SUGGESTED STRATEGIES	WHAT WORKS FOR YOU? WRITE NEW IDEAS HERE
Verbal–Linguistic	■ Read many resources and take comprehensive notes on them. Summarize the main points from your resources. ■ Interview someone about the topic and take notes.	
Logical–Mathematical	■ Take notes on 3x5 cards and organize them according to topics and subtopics. ■ Create a detailed, sequential outline of your writing project, making sure that your argument is logical if your assignment requires persuasive writing.	
Bodily–Kinesthetic	■ Pay a visit to numerous sites that hold resources you need or that are related to your topic—businesses, libraries, etc. ■ After brainstorming ideas for an assignment, take a break involving physical activity. During the break, think about your top three ideas and see what insight occurs to you.	
Visual–Spatial	■ Create full-color charts as you read each resource or interview someone. ■ Use think link format or another visual organizer to map out your main topic, subtopics, and related ideas and examples. Use different colors for different subtopics.	
Interpersonal	■ Discuss material with a fellow student as you gather it. ■ Pair up with a classmate and become each other's peer editors. Read each other's first drafts and next-to-final drafts, offering constructive feedback.	
Intrapersonal	■ Take time to mull over any assigned paper topic. Think about what emotions it raises in you, and why. Let your inner instincts guide you as you begin to write. ■ Schedule as much research time as possible.	
Musical	■ Play your favorite relaxing music while you brainstorm topics for a writing assignment.	
Naturalistic	■ Pick a research topic that relates to nature. ■ Build confidence by envisioning your writing process as a successful climb to the top of a mountain.	

Figure 7.6 **Sample first draft with revision comments.**

military recruits undergo

Of the changes that ~~happened to us,~~ the physical transformation is the ~~biggest. When~~ *most evident*

Too much   *Maybe—* *upon my January arrival at the training facility,*

~~we arrived at the training facility, it was January, cold and cloudy. At the time,~~ I was a

little thin, but I had been working out and thought that I could physically do anything.

Oh boy, was I wrong! The Chief said to us right away: "Get down, maggots!" Upon this *← his trademark phrase*

were   *endless*

command, we ~~all~~ to drop to the ground and do military-style push-ups. Water survival tac-

← unnecessary

tics were also part of the training ~~that we had to complete.~~ Occasionally, my dreams of

home were interrupted at 3 a.m. when we had a surprise aquatic test. Although we ~~didn't~~

resented   *mention how chief was involved*

~~feel too happy about~~ this sub-human treatment at the time, we learned to appreciate how

the conditioning was turning our bodies into fine-tuned machines. *say more about this (swimming in uniform incident?)*

Revising

When you revise, you critically evaluate the word choice, paragraph structure, and style of your first draft. Be thorough as you add, delete, replace, and reorganize words, sentences, and paragraphs. You may want to print your draft and correct the hard copy before you make changes on the computer. Some classes include a peer review process in which students read one another's work and offer suggestions. Having a different perspective on your writing is extremely valuable. Figure 7.6 shows a paragraph from Michael's first draft, with revision comments added.

The elements of revision include being a critical writer, evaluating paragraph structure, and checking for clarity and conciseness.

Being a Critical Writer

Critical thinking helps you move beyond restating what you learned from other sources to creating your own perspective. One key to critical writing is asking the question "So what?" For example, if you were writing a piece on nutrition, you might discuss a variety of good eating habits. Asking "So what?" could lead into a discussion of *why* these habits are helpful.

If your paper contains arguments, use critical thinking to make sure they are well constructed and convincing. Using what you know from the discussion in Chapter 4, think through your arguments and provide solid support with facts and examples.

Use the mind actions to guide your revision. Ask yourself questions that can help you evaluate ideas, develop original insights, and be complete and clear. Here are some examples of questions you may ask:

- Are these examples clearly connected to the idea?
- Am I aware of similar concepts or facts that can act as support?
- What else can I recall that can help to support this idea?
- In evaluating a situation, have I clearly indicated causes and effects?
- What new idea comes to mind when I think about these facts?
- How do I evaluate any effect, fact, or situation?
- Are there different arguments that I should address here?

Finally, critical thinking can help you evaluate the content and form of your paper. As you start your revision, ask yourself these questions:

- Will my audience understand my thesis and how I've supported it?
- Does the introduction prepare the reader and capture attention?
- Is the body of the paper organized effectively?
- Is each idea fully developed, explained, and supported by examples?
- Are my ideas connected to one another through logical transitions?
- Do I have a clear, concise, simple writing style?
- Does the paper fulfill the requirements of the assignment?
- Does the conclusion provide a natural ending to the paper?

Evaluating Paragraph Structure

Make sure that each paragraph has a *topic sentence* that states the paragraph's main idea (a topic sentence does for a paragraph what a thesis statement does for an entire paper). The rest of the paragraph should support the idea with evidence. Most topic sentences are at the start of the paragraph, although sometimes topic sentences appear elsewhere. The topic sentence in the following paragraph is underlined:

Chief Marzloff played an integral role in the development of our self-confidence. He taught us that anything less than direct eye contact was disrespectful to both him and ourselves. He encouraged us to be confident about our own beliefs and to think about what was said to us before we decided whether to accept it. Furthermore, the Chief reinforced self-confidence through his own example. He walked with his chin up and chest out, like the proud parent of a newborn baby. He always gave the appearance that he had something to do and that he was in complete control.

Examine how paragraphs flow into one another by evaluating your transitions, which connect ideas. Transitions take the form of connecting sentences, phrases, and words. Among the words and phrases that are helpful are *also,* *in addition,* and *next.* Similarly, *finally, as a result,* and *in conclusion* tell readers that a summary is on its way.

Checking for Clarity and Conciseness

Aim to say what you want to say clearly and concisely. Try to eliminate extra words and phrases. Rewrite wordy phrases in a more straightforward, conversational way. For example, write "if" instead of "in the event that," or "now" instead of "at this point in time."

"See revision as 'envisioning again.' If there are areas in your work where there is a blur or vagueness, you can simply see the picture again and add the details that will bring your work closer to your mind's picture."

NATALIE GOLDBERG

Editing

Editing involves correcting technical mistakes in spelling, grammar, and punctuation, as well as checking style consistency for such elements as abbreviations and capitalizations. Editing comes last, after you are satisfied with your ideas, organization, and writing style. If you use a computer, start with the grammar check and spell check to find mistakes, realizing that you still need to check your work. Although a spell checker won't pick up the mistake in the sentence, "They are not hear on Tuesdays," someone who is reading for sense will.

PERSONAL TRIUMPH

*y*ou can't always judge a person by past academic performance. Kevin Leman was near the bottom of his high school class and dropped out of college twice. Later, with the help of inspiring people in his life, he graduated and became a nationally known writer and psychologist.

Kevin Leman was the most disinterested screwball of a student you ever met. "My high school guidance counselor told me he couldn't get me admitted to reform school, much less college," Leman admits. Growing up in western New York, he was the youngest of three siblings. His sister was the captain of the cheerleading squad; his brother was the high-school football hero. And young Kevin was, as he describes himself, "the best at being the worst." "My mother was in high school more than I was," he recalls. "I was never there. I'd cut school. She always went to those meetings they had, you know, and she'd come home with the standard story—'If only Kevin would apply himself . . .'"

Herein lay the problem: Leman really didn't know how to apply himself. He graduated near the bottom of his class with SAT scores to match. "They were in the zero percentile—which is pretty hard to do, just by the mathematics alone," he said. And he still remembers one of his college rejection letters that read, "Most regrettably, Kevin's record does not support admission, which our studies show could lead to his failure, and we must decline his application." Although he made it into another school, they threw him out a year later. Leman seemed destined for academic failure and found a job as a janitor at the local hospital.

It was here that destiny took an unexpected turn. At the hospital, he met Sande Buchheit, a nurse's assistant, who would later become his wife. Sande believed in Leman and introduced him to other people who had vision for their lives. He began to believe that there was some purpose to life and his motivation blossomed. Next, he decided to enroll at the University of Arizona.

This story has been rewritten with permission from Dan Huff, whose original article,

Kevin Leman, Counselor and Public Speaker; Tucson, Arizona

"I was walking on campus," he recalls, "not really knowing where I was, and I found this guy named Robert Leonard, a professor. He sat down with me and went way beyond what you'd expect. He got the catalog out and spent two hours with me, showing me exactly what I needed to do."

To his astonishment, Leman made the dean's list that first semester. In that moment, Leman discovered one of the beauties of life: Every day offers a chance to make a new start. He decided he wanted to be a psychologist based, in part, on his earlier run-in with his high school guidance counselor who told him reform school was too high to shoot for. "I remember thinking, 'He's a counselor?'" Ironically, Leman dedicated his first book to this man.

Leman credits much of his success to the power of mentoring. When speaking about one of his professors from the U of A, Leman says, "He was a guy who changed my life. He taught me how to work with people, and he taught me that I could turn kids' behavior around, in some cases in a matter of days. I'm very grateful to him."

Kevin Leman is living proof that anyone can be a success. Today, he has a private practice as a psychologist and counselor and is a nationally known authority on family issues, having written 21 popular psychology books that have sold in the millions. He has also been a featured guest on shows like *The Today Show* and *Oprah.* "Looking back on my UA experience," he says, "I felt like I belonged. I had people there who cared about me, and that made all the difference."

Take a moment to consider . . .

- *When you've experienced a "turning point" in your life.*
- *What you might write about if you were to write books that helped and informed others.*

"The Living Proof," first appeared in *Arizona Alumnus,* Spring 2001.

Look also for *sexist language,* which characterizes people according to gender. Sexist language often involves the male pronouns *he, him,* or *his.* For example, "An executive often spends hours a day going through his electronic mail" implies that executives are always men. A simple change to a plural subject eliminates the problem: "Executives often spend hours each day going through their electronic mail." Try to be sensitive to words that slight women. *Mail carrier* is preferable to *mailman, student* to *coed.*

Proofreading is the last editing stage and happens after your paper is in its final form. Proofreading means reading every word and sentence for accuracy. Look for technical mistakes, run-on sentences, and sentence fragments. Look for incorrect word usage and unclear references.

A Final Checklist

You are now ready to complete your revising and editing checklist. All the tasks listed in Table 7.4 should be done before you submit your paper. Figure 7.7 shows the final version of Michael's paper.

Your final paper reflects your hard work. Ideally, you have a piece of work that shows your writing ability and that communicates interesting and important ideas. Because of how closely writing and speaking skills are related, solid writing skills also help you craft a speech or oral presentation.

Figure 7.7 **Sample final version of paper.**

Michael B. Jackson   March 19, 2002

BOYS TO MEN

His stature was one of confidence, often misinterpreted by others as cockiness. His small frame was lean and agile, yet stiff and upright, as though every move were a calculated formula. For the longest eight weeks of my life, he was my father, my instructor, my leader, and my worst enemy. His name is Chief Marzloff, and he had the task of shaping the lives and careers of the youngest, newest members of the U.S. Coast Guard. As our Basic Training Company Commander, he took his job very seriously and demanded that we do the same. Within a limited time span, he conditioned our bodies, developed our self-confidence, and instilled within us a strong mental discipline.

Of the changes that recruits in military basic training undergo, the physical transformation is the most immediately evident. On my January arrival at the training facility, I was a little thin, but I had been working out and thought that I could physically do anything. Oh boy, was I wrong! The Chief wasted no time in introducing me to one of his trademark phrases: "Get down, maggots!" Upon this command, we were all to drop to the ground and produce endless counts of military-style push-ups. Later, we found out that exercise prepared us for hitting the deck in the event of enemy fire. Water survival tactics were also part of the training. Occasionally, my dreams of home were interrupted at about 3 A.M. when our company was selected for a surprise aquatic test. I recall one such test that required us to swim laps around the perimeter of a pool while in full uniform. I felt like a salmon swimming upstream, fueled only by natural instinct. Although we resented this subhuman treatment at the time, we learned to appreciate how the strict guidance of the Chief was turning our bodies into fine-tuned machines.

Beyond physical ability, Chief Marzloff also played an integral role in the development of our self-confidence. He would often declare in his raspy voice, "Look me in the eyes when you speak to me! Show me that you believe what you're saying!" He taught us that anything less was an expression of disrespect. Furthermore, he appeared to attack a personal habit of my own. It seemed that whenever he would speak to me individually, I would nervously nod my head in response. I was trying to demonstrate that I understood, but to him, I was blindly accepting anything that he said. He would roar, "That is a sign of weakness!" Needless to say, I am now conscious of all bodily motions when communicating with others. The Chief also reinforced self-confidence through his own example. He walked with his square chin up and chest out, like the proud parent of a newborn baby. He always gave the appearance that he had something to do, and that he was in complete control. Collectively, the methods that the Chief used were all successful in developing our self-confidence.

Perhaps the Chief's greatest contribution was the mental discipline that he instilled in his recruits. He taught us that physical ability and self-confidence were nothing without the mental discipline required to obtain any worthwhile goal. For us, this discipline began with adapting to the military lifestyle. Our day began promptly at 0500 hours, early enough to awaken the oversleeping roosters. By 0515 hours, we had to have showered, shaved, and perfectly donned our uniforms. At that point, we were marched to the galley for chow, where we learned to take only what is necessary, rather than indulging. Before each meal, the Chief would warn, "Get what you want, but you will eat all that you get!" After he made good on his threat a few times, we all got the point. Throughout our stay, the Chief repeatedly stressed the significance of self-discipline. He would calmly utter, "Give a little now, get a lot later." I guess that meant different things to all of us. For me, it was a simple phrase that would later become my personal philosophy on life. The Chief went to great lengths to ensure that everyone under his direction possessed the mental discipline required to be successful in boot camp or in any of life's challenges.

Chief Marzloff was a remarkable role model and a positive influence on many lives. I never saw him smile, but it was evident that he genuinely cared a great deal about his job and all the lives that he touched. This man single-handedly conditioned our bodies, developed our self-confidence, and instilled a strong mental discipline that remains in me to this day. I have not seen the Chief since March 28, 1992, graduation day. Over the years, however, I have incorporated many of his ideals into my life. Above all, he taught us the true meaning of the U.S. Coast Guard slogan, "Semper Peratus" (Always Ready).

Table 7.4 Revising and editing checklist.

DATE DUE	TASK	IS IT COMPLETE?
	Check the body of the paper for clear thinking and adequate support of ideas	
	Finalize introduction and conclusion	
	Check word spelling, usage, and grammar	
	Check paragraph structure	
	Make sure language is familiar and concise	
	Check punctuation and capitalization	
	Check transitions	
	Eliminate sexist language	
	Get feedback from peers and/or instructor	

How can you deliver an *effective* oral presentation?

In school, you may be asked to deliver a speech, take an oral exam, or present a team project. When you ask a question or make a comment in class, you are using public speaking skills. On the job, you will need these skills to deliver presentations to clients, run meetings, and give speeches.

The public speaking skills that you learn for *formal* presentations help you make a favorable impression in *informal* settings, such as when you meet with an instructor, summarize a reading for your study group, or have a planning session at work. When you are articulate, others take notice.

Prepare as for a Writing Assignment

Speaking in front of others involves preparation, strategy, and confidence. Planning a speech is similar to planning a piece of writing; you must know your topic and audience and think about presentation strategy, organization, and word choice. Specifically, you should:

- *Think through what you want to say and why.* What is your purpose—to make or refute an argument, present information, entertain? Have a goal for your speech.

- *Plan.* Take time to think about who your listeners are and how they are likely to respond. Then, get organized. Brainstorm your topic—narrow it with prewriting strategies, determine your thesis, write an outline, and do research.

- *Draft your thoughts.* Draft your speech. Illustrate ideas with examples, and show how examples lead to ideas. As in writing, have a clear beginning and end. Start with an attention-getter and conclude with a wrap-up that summarizes your thoughts and leaves your audience with something to remember.

- *Integrate visual aids.* Think about building your speech around visual aids including charts, maps, slides and photographs, and props. Learn software programs to create presentation graphics.

Practice Your Performance

The element of performance distinguishes speaking from writing. Here are tips to keep in mind:

- *Know the parameters.* How long do you have? Where are you speaking? Be aware of the setting—where your audience will be and available props (e.g., a podium, table, a blackboard).

- *Use index cards or notes.* Reduce your final draft to "trigger" words or phrases that remind you of what you want to say and refer to the cards and to your visual aids during your speech.

- *Pay attention to the physical.* Your body position, voice, and clothing contribute to the impression you make. Your goal is to look and sound good and to appear relaxed. Try to make eye contact with your audience, and walk around if you are comfortable presenting in that way.

- *Practice ahead of time.* Do a test run with friends or alone. If possible, practice in the room where you will speak. Audiotape or videotape your practice sessions and evaluate your performance.

- *Be yourself.* When you speak, you express your personality through your words and presence. Don't be afraid to add your own style to the presentation. Take deep breaths. Smile. Know that you can speak well and that your audience wants to see you succeed. Finally, envision your own success.

suà

Suà is a Shoshone Indian word, derived from the Uto-Aztecna language, meaning "think." By focusing on *suà*, you are able to evaluate research sources as the basis for your positions and communicate your conclusions effectively in your writing and speaking. Through the power of thought, you can choose sources that support your thesis and express your insights.

Building Skills

FOR COLLEGE, CAREER, AND LIFE SUCCESS

Critical Thinking   *Applying Learning to Life*

Audience Analysis

As a reporter for your college newspaper, you have been assigned the job of writing a story about some part of campus life. You submit the following suggestions to your editor-in-chief:

- The campus parking lot squeeze: Too many cars and too few spaces.
- Drinking on campus: Is the problem getting better or worse?
- Diversity: How students accept differences and live and work together.

Your editor-in-chief asks you the following questions about reader response (consider that your different "audiences" include students, faculty and administrators, and community members):

1. Which subject would likely appeal to all audiences at your school and why?

   _____

   _____

   _____

2. How would you adjust your writing according to how much readers know about the subject?

   _____

   _____

   _____

3. For each topic, name the audience (or audiences) that you think would be most interested. If you think one audience would be equally interested in more than one topic, you can name an audience more than once.

   Campus parking lot _____

   Drinking on campus _____

   Student diversity _____

4. How can you make a specific article interesting to a general audience?

_____

_____

_____

Prewriting

Choose a topic you are interested in and know something about—for example, college sports or handling stress. Narrow your topic; then, use the following prewriting strategies to discover what you already know about the topic and what you would need to learn if you had to write an essay about the subject for one of your classes (if necessary, continue this prewriting exercise on a separate sheet of paper):

BRAINSTORM YOUR IDEAS.

_____

_____

_____

_____

_____

_____

_____

_____

FREEWRITE.

_____

_____

_____

_____

_____

_____

_____

ASK JOURNALISTS' QUESTIONS.

_____

_____

_____

_____

_____

_____

Writing a Thesis Statement

Write two thesis statements for each of the following topics. The first statement should inform the reader, and the second should persuade. In each case, use the thesis statement to narrow the topic.

1. The rising cost of a college education
   a. Thesis with an informative purpose:

   _____

   _____

   b. Thesis with a persuasive purpose:

   _____

   _____

2. Handling test anxiety
   a. Thesis with an informative purpose:

   _____

   _____

   b. Thesis with a persuasive purpose:

   _____

   _____

Teamwork *Combining Forces*

TEAM RESEARCH. Join with three other classmates and decide on two relatively narrow research topics that interest all of you and that you can investigate by spending no more than an hour in the library. The first topic should be current and in the news—for example, tire and rollover problems in sport utility vehicles (SUVs), body piercing, or the changing U.S. family. The second topic should be more academic and historical—for example, the polio epidemic in the 1950s, the Irish potato famine, or South African apartheid.

Working alone, team members should use the college library and the Internet to research both topics. Set a research time limit of no more than one hour per topic. The goal should be to collect a list of sources for later investigation. When everyone is through, the group should come together to discuss the research process. Among the questions group members should ask each other are:

- How did you "attack" and organize your research for each topic?
- What research tools did you use to investigate each topic?
- How did the nature of your research differ from topic to topic? Why do you think this was the case?
- Discuss how your use of library and Internet research differed from topic to topic.

- What research techniques yielded the best results? What techniques led to dead ends?

Next, compare the specific results of everyone's research. Analyze each source for what it is likely to yield in the form of useful information. Finally, come together as a group and discuss what you learned that might improve your approach to library and Internet research.

Writing | *Discovery Through Journaling*

To record your thoughts, use a separate journal or the lined page at the end of the chapter.

LEARNING FROM OTHER WRITERS. Identify a piece of powerful writing that you have recently read. (It could be a work of literature, a biography, a magazine or newspaper article, or even a section from one of your college texts.) Describe, in detail, why it was powerful. Did it make you feel something, think something, or take action? Why? What can you learn about writing from this piece that you can apply to your own writing?

Career Portfolio | *Charting Your Course*

WRITING SAMPLE: A JOB INTERVIEW LETTER. To secure a job interview, you may have to write a letter describing your background and explaining your value to the company. To include in your portfolio, write a one-page, three-paragraph cover letter to a prospective employer. (The letter will accompany your résumé.) Be creative—you may use fictitious names, but select a career and industry that interest you. Use the format shown in the sample letter on page 261.

- *Introductory paragraph:* Start with an attention getter—a statement that convinces the employer to read on. For example, name a person the employer knows who told you to write, or refer to something positive about the company that you read in the paper. Identify the position for which you are applying, and tell the employer that you are interested in working for the company.

- *Middle paragraph:* Sell your value. Try to convince the employer that hiring you will help the company in some way. Center your "sales effort" on your experience in school and the workplace. If possible, tie your qualifications to the needs of the company. Refer indirectly to your enclosed résumé.

- *Final paragraph:* Close with a call to action. Ask the employer to call you, or tell the employer to expect your call to arrange an interview.

Figure 7.8 Sample job interview letter.

First name Last name
1234 Your Street
City, ST 12345

November 1, 2002

Ms. Prospective Employer
Prospective Company
5432 Their Street
City, ST 54321

Dear Ms. Employer:

On the advice of Mr. X, career center advisor at Y College, I am writing to inquire about the position of production assistant at KKKK Radio. I read the description of the job and your company on the career center's employment-opportunity bulletin board, and I would like to apply for the position.

I am a senior at Y College and will graduate this spring with a degree in communications. Since my junior year when I declared my major, I have wanted to pursue a career in radio. For the last year I have worked as a production intern at KCOL Radio, the college's station, and have occasionally filled in as a disc jockey on the evening news show. I enjoy being on the air, but my primary interest is production and programming. My enclosed résumé will tell you more about my background and experience.

I would be pleased to talk with you in person about the position. You can reach me anytime at 555/555-5555 or by e-mail at xxxx@xx.com. Thank you for your consideration, and I look forward to meeting you.

Sincerely,

Sign Your Name Here

First name Last name

Enclosure(s) *(use this notation if you have included a résumé or other item with your letter)*

Exchange your first draft with a classmate. Read each other's letter and make notes in the margins that try to improve the letter's impact and persuasiveness, as well as its writing style, grammar, punctuation, and spelling. Discuss each letter and make whatever corrections are necessary to produce a well-written, persuasive letter. Create a final draft for your portfolio.

Assess Yourself *Student Success Strategies*

If you have access to the CD-ROM Strategies for Success, use the following questions to assess your thoughts and enhance your understanding of the chapter. The questions below represent only some of the activities provided on the CD for the chapter topics—try others if you have time.

Click on the Research bookmark. Use the following activities to expand your ability to research effectively:

1. Take the pre-assessment to clarify your view of, and approach to, researching.

2. Watch the video and think about when in your research you should use the Internet, the library, or both. In the field provided, indicate some basic guidelines for each of these sources of information.

3. Click on Activity Two: Narrow Your Topic. Hone your skills by answering the questions in the fields provided for each of four given topics.

4. Click on Activity Three: Journal Reflections. Scroll to the third question, which asks you to talk about your experiences in the library and how students can combat being overwhelmed by the library. Type your answer in the field provided.

Suggested Readings

Becker, Howard S. *Tricks of the Trade: How to Think About Your Research While You're Doing It*. Chicago, IL: University of Chicago Press, 1998.

Booth, Wayne C., Gregory G. Columb, and Joseph M. Williams. *The Craft of Research*. Chicago, IL: University of Chicago Press, 1995.

Cameron, Julia. *The Right to Write: An Invitation Into the Writing Life*. New York: Putnam, 1999.

Gibaldi, Joseph and Phyllis Franklin. *MLA Handbook for Writers of Research Papers, 5th ed*. New York: Modern Language Association of America, 1999.

LaRocque, Paula. *Championship Writing: 50 Ways to Improve Your Writing*. Oak Park, IL: Marion Street Press, 2000.

Markman, Peter T. and Roberta H. Markman. *10 Steps in Writing the Research Paper, 5th ed*. New York: Barron's Educational Series, 1994.

Strunk, William, Jr. and E. B. White. *The Elements of Style, 4th ed*. Upper Saddle River, NJ: Prentice Hall, 2000.

Troyka, Lynn Quitman. *Simon & Schuster Handbook for Writers, 5th ed*. Upper Saddle River, NJ: Prentice Hall, 1999.

Walsch, Bill. *Lapsing into a Comma: A Curmudgeon's Guide to the Many Things That Can Go Wrong in Print—and How to Avoid Them*. New York: Contemporary Books, 2000.

Williams, Joseph M. *Style: Toward Clarity and Grace*. Chicago, IL: University of Chicago Press, 1995.

Internet Resources

Prentice Hall Student Success SuperSite (study skills section has valuable information on writing and research): **www.prenhall.com/success**

National Writing Centers Association (a collection of writing labs and writing centers on the Web): **http://iwca.syr.edu**

Online Writing Lab—Purdue University: **http://owl.english.purdue.edu**

Endnotes

1. Lisa Guernsey, "For the New College B.M.O.C., 'M' Is for 'Machine,'" *The New York Times*, August 10, 2000, p. G7.
2. Joyce Kasman Valenza, "Skills That College Freshmen Need," *The Philadelphia Inquirer*, April 26, 2001, p. NA.
3. Lori Leibovich, "Choosing Quick Hits Over the Card Catalog," *The New York Times*, August 10, 2000, p. 1.
4. Floyd H. Johnson (May 1996), "The Internet and Research: Proceed With Caution" (on-line). Available at www.lanl.gov/SFC/96/posters.html#johnson (August 2000).
5. 1998, Center for Media Literacy.
6. Analysis based on Lynn Quitman Troyka, *Simon & Schuster Handbook for Writers*. Upper Saddle River, NJ: Prentice Hall, 1996, pp. 22–23.
7. *The Elements of Style*, Strunk and White, © 2000. Reprinted by permission of Pearson Education, Inc.
8. Diana Jean Schemo, "U. of Virginia Hit by Scandal over Cheating," *The New York Times*, May 10, 2001, p. A1.

JOURNAL

name   date

visit: www.prenhall.com/carter NY Times link for this chapter

In this chapter you explore answers to the following
questions: • How can preparation improve test performance? •
How can you work through test anxiety? • What general strategies can
help you succeed on tests? • How can you master different types of test
questions? • How can you learn from test mistakes?

IN THIS CHAPTER

*T*est taking

ANALYZE

FOR A RUNNER, a race is the equivalent of a test because it measures ability at a given moment. Doing well in a race requires training similar to the studying you do for exams. The best runners—and test takers—understand that they train not just for the race or test, but to achieve a level of competence that will stay with them. Knowing that you will continue to use the skills on which you are being tested gives you the perspective that *owning* these skills is more important than achieving a perfect score.

Tests provoke anxiety for Peter Changsak (see next page) and for many students. To find the positive side of exams, see them as preparation for life. When you get a job or even work on your budget, you'll apply what you know and put your skills into action—exactly what you do when you take a test. As you will see in this chapter, test taking is about preparation, persistence, and strategy. It's also about conquering fears, paying attention to details, and learning from mistakes.

showing what you know

Peter Changsak, Sheldon-Jackson College, Sitka, Alaska

Tim Nordberg, Executive Director, Chicago Youth Project

How can I combat test anxiety?

Study to learn . . . Good test scores reflect your passion to know what you have studied

I am a Yu'pik Eskimo from a village on the Yukon River. Before attending college, I worked for six years as a clerk at the Native Corporation, a gas station and general store. When the manager passed away, the business offered to make me a manager. Even though I knew how to do much of the work, I didn't feel I was ready, so I decided to go to school for more training.

College life is different from what I am accustomed to. The hardest part has been taking tests. I study hard, but then when I get in class and the test begins, my mind goes blank. When I read, I understand what I'm reading, but as soon as I close the book, I can't remember what I just read. My favorite class is biology lab—probably because we can walk around.

I love mechanics and construction. When I worked at the Native Corporation, we built a new building. I felt like I was a success at work, but I don't feel successful as a student. Sometimes I feel like quitting, but I also think it can help me have more choices if I stick with it. I'm learning how to be a serious student, but it isn't easy. Can you give suggestions about how I can get over my test anxiety?

In many ways my experience in college was similar to yours. I was raised in a car industry town and was the first person in my family to go to college. My first year was hard—I discovered that I read at an eighth grade level. I hated studying and taking tests. During the spring, the college began a building project. I wanted to be outside doing manual work, too. I constantly felt a battle going on within me.

Two factors gave me the endurance to go on: One was seeing my old high school buddies, who seemed stuck in the past, and the second factor was my desire to fulfill my goals. I decided that if I fail, it won't be because I haven't given it my best; I'm not going to fail because I refuse to try.

That summer I took a reading class. School was still not easy that fall, but I was not studying as much out of fear or duty; rather, I was studying to do my best. Classes began to take on a different meaning. I was beginning to learn because I enjoyed the challenge. I took tests to see how well I knew the subject. Today, I still love sports and carpentry, but I also love to learn.

Don't fear failure. Just try to do your best. Concentrate on the task at hand. Study to learn, not to take a test. Good test scores reflect your passion to know what you have studied rather than how good you are at test taking. You are being challenged to survive in new ways, and you are not alone. Ask the student services office to help you through this adjustment process. Ask your advisor if there is a class that teaches study and test-taking tips.

Also, try to remember why you came to college in the first place—to better equip yourself. As you prepare for classes and tests, remind yourself what this experience will do for you someday when it is all behind you. Growing in any area of life isn't always fun and may not seem within reach. But if we give up, we may miss out on a part of us that, in time, would have brought greater rewards.

How can preparation *improve* test performance?

like a runner who prepares for a marathon by exercising, eating right, taking practice runs, and getting enough sleep, you can take steps to master your exams. The primary step, occupying much of your preparation time, is to listen when material is presented, read carefully, and study until you know the material that will be on the test (Chapter 5 examines the art of effective studying). In this sense, staying on top of your class meetings, readings, and assignments over the course of the semester is one of the best ways to prepare for tests. Other important steps are the preparation strategies that follow.

Identify Test Type and Material Covered

Before you begin studying, find out as much as you can about the type of test you will be taking and what it will cover. Try to identify:

- *What topics the test will cover* (Will it cover everything since the semester began or will it be limited to a narrow topic?)
- *The type of questions on the test*—objective (multiple choice, true–false, sentence completion), subjective (essay), or a combination.
- *What material you will be tested on* (Will the test cover only what you learned in class and in the text or will it also cover outside readings?)

Your instructors may answer these questions for you. Even though they may not reveal specific test questions, they might let you know the question format or information covered. Some instructors may even drop hints about possible test questions, either directly ("I might ask a question on this subject on your next exam") or more subtly ("One of my favorite theories is . . .").

Here are a few other strategies for predicting what may be on a test.

Use SQ3R to identify what's important. Often, the questions you write and ask yourself when you read assigned materials may be part of the test. Textbook study questions are also good candidates.

Talk to people who already took the course. Try to find out how difficult the instructor's tests are, whether they focus primarily on assigned readings or on class notes, what materials are usually covered, and what types of questions are asked. Also ask about instructors' preferences. If you learn that the instructor pays close attention to specific facts, for example, use flash cards to drill yourself on major and minor details. If he or she emphasizes a global overview, focus on conceptualization and example-to-idea thinking (see discussion in Chapter 4).

Examine old tests, if they are available. You may find them in class, on-line, or on reserve in the library. Old tests help to answer the following questions:

- Does the instructor focus on examples and details, general ideas and themes, or a combination?
- Can you do well through straight memorization or should you take a critical-thinking approach?
- Are the questions straightforward or confusing and sometimes tricky?
- Do the tests require that you integrate facts from different areas in order to draw conclusions?

"A little knowledge that acts is worth infinitely more than much knowledge that is idle."

KAHLIL GIBRAN

If you can't get copies of old tests and your instructor doesn't give too many details, use clues from the class to predict test questions. After taking the first exam in the course, you will have more information about what to expect.

Create a Study Plan and Schedule

Once you have identified as much as you can about what will be covered on the test, choose your study materials. Go through your notes, texts, related primary sources, and handouts, and then set aside materials you don't need.

Then, use your time-management skills to prepare a schedule. Consider all of the relevant factors—your study materials, the number of days until the test, and the time you can study each day. If you establish your schedule ahead of time and write it in a date book, you are more likely to follow it.

Schedules vary widely according to the situation. For example, if you have three days before the test and no other obligations during that time, you might set two 2-hour study sessions during each day. On the other hand, if you have two weeks before a test, classes during the day, and work three nights a week, you might spread out your study sessions over the nights you have off during those two weeks.

A checklist, like the one in Figure 8.1, helps you get organized and stay on track as you prepare. Use a checklist to assign specific tasks to particular study times and sessions. That way, not only do you know when you have time to study, but you also have defined goals for each study session.

Prepare Through Careful Review

By thoroughly reviewing your materials, you will have the best shot at remembering their contents. Use the following strategies when you study.

Figure 8.1   **Pretest checklist.**

Course: _____   Instructor: _____

Date, time, and place of test: _____

Type of test *(e.g., is it a midterm or a minor quiz?):* _____

What the instructor has told you about the test, including the types of test questions, the length of the test, and how much the test counts toward your final grade:

_____

_____

Topics to be covered on the test in order of importance:

1. _____

2. _____

3. _____

4. _____

5. _____

Study schedule, including materials you plan to study *(e.g., texts and class notes)* and dates you plan to complete each:

MATERIAL   DATE OF COMPLETION

1. _____   _____

2. _____   _____

3. _____   _____

4. _____   _____

5. _____   _____

Materials you are expected to bring to the test *(e.g., your textbook, a sourcebook, a calculator):*

_____

_____

Special study arrangements *(e.g., plan study group meetings, ask the instructor for special help, get outside tutoring):*

_____

_____

_____

Life-management issues *(e.g., rearrange work hours):*

_____

_____

_____

Source: Adapted from Ron Fry, *"Ace" Any Test,* 3rd ed. (Franklin Lakes, NJ: Career Press, 1996), 123–124.

Use SQ3R. The reading method you studied in Chapter 5 provides an excellent structure for reviewing your reading materials.

- *Surveying* gives you an overview of topics.
- *Questioning* helps you focus on important ideas and determine what the material is trying to communicate.
- *Reading* (or, in this case, rereading) reminds you of the ideas and supporting information.
- *Reciting* helps to anchor the concepts in your head.
- *Review* tasks, such as quizzing yourself on the Q-stage questions, summarizing sections you have highlighted, making flash cards for important concepts, and constructing a chapter outline, help you solidify your learning so that you are able to use it at test time and beyond.

Review your notes. Recall the section in Chapter 6 for making your notes a valuable after-class reference. Use the following techniques to effectively review notes:

- *Time your reviews carefully.* Review notes for the first time within a day of the lecture, if you can, and then review again closer to the test day.
- *Mark up your notes.* Reread them, filling in missing information, clarifying points, writing out abbreviations, and highlighting key ideas.
- *Organize your notes.* Consider adding headings and subheadings to your notes to clarify the structure of the information. Rewrite them using a different organizing structure—for example, an outline if you originally used a think link.
- *Summarize your notes.* Evaluate which ideas and examples are most crucial, and then rewrite your notes in shortened form, focusing on those ideas and examples. Summarize your notes in writing or with a summary think link. Try summarizing from memory as a self-test.

Think critically. Using the techniques from Chapter 4, approach test preparation as a critical thinker, working to understand the material rather than just repeat facts. As you study, try to analyze causes and effects, look at issues from different perspectives, and connect concepts that, on the surface, appear unrelated. This work will increase your understanding and probably result in a higher exam grade. Critical thinking is especially important for essay tests that ask you to develop and support a thesis.

Take a Pretest

Use questions from your textbook to create your own pretest. Most textbooks include end-of-chapter questions. If your course doesn't have an assigned text, develop questions from your notes and assigned outside readings. Choose questions that are likely to be covered on the test, then answer them under testlike conditions—in quiet, with no books or notes to help you (unless your exam is open book), and with a clock telling you when to quit.

If the topic or format of a test challenges your stronger or weaker intelligences, these tips will help you make the most of your time and abilities.

INTELLIGENCE	SUGGESTED STRATEGIES	WHAT WORKS FOR YOU? WRITE NEW IDEAS HERE
Verbal–Linguistic	■ Think of and write out questions your instructor may ask on a test. Answer the questions and then try rewriting them in a different format (essay, true–false, and so on). ■ Underline important words in review questions or practice questions.	
Logical–Mathematical	■ Make diagrams of review or practice questions. ■ Outline the key steps involved in topics on which you may be tested.	
Bodily–Kinesthetic	■ Use your voice to review out loud. Recite concepts, terms and definitions, important lists, dates, and so on. ■ Create a sculpture, model, or skit to depict a tough concept that will be on your test.	
Visual–Spatial	■ Create a think link to map out an important topic and its connections to other topics in the material. Study it and redraw it from memory a day before the test. ■ Make drawings related to possible test topics.	
Interpersonal	■ Develop a study group and encourage each other. ■ In your group, come up with as many possible test questions as you can. Ask each other these questions in an oral exam-type format.	
Intrapersonal	■ Brainstorm test questions. Then, come back to them after a break or even a day's time. On your own, take the sample "test" you developed. ■ Make time to review in a solitary setting.	
Musical	■ Play music while you read if it does not distract you. ■ Study concepts by reciting them to rhythms you create or to music.	
Naturalistic	■ Bring your text, lecture notes, and other pertinent information to an outdoor spot that inspires you and helps you to feel confident, and review your material there.	

Prepare Physically

Most tests ask you to work efficiently under time pressure. If your body is tired or under stress, your performance may suffer. If you can, avoid staying up all night. Get some sleep so that you can wake up rested and alert. Remember that adequate sleep can help cement memories by reducing interference from new memories (see Chapter 6).

Eating right is also important. Sugar-laden snacks bring up your energy, only to send you crashing down much too soon. Also, too much caffeine can add to your tension and make it difficult to focus. Eating nothing leaves you drained, but too much food can make you sleepy. The best advice is to eat a light, well-balanced meal before a test. When time is short, grab a quick-energy snack such as a banana, orange juice, or a granola bar.

Make the Most of Last-Minute Studying

Cramming—studying intensively, and often round the clock, right before an exam—often results in information going into your head and popping right back out shortly after the exam is over. Because study conditions aren't always ideal, nearly every student crams during college, especially when a busy schedule leaves only a few hours to prepare. Use these hints to make the most of your study time:

- *Go through your flash cards,* if you have them, one last time.
- *Focus on crucial concepts;* don't worry about the rest. Resist reviewing notes or texts page by page.
- *Create a last-minute study sheet.* On a single sheet of paper, write down key facts, definitions, formulas, and so on. Try to keep the material short and simple. If you prefer visual notes, use think links to map out ideas and supporting examples.
- *Arrive early.* Study the sheet or your flash cards until you are asked to clear your desk.
- *While it is still fresh, record any helpful information on scrap paper.* Do this before looking at the test. Review this information as needed during the test.

After your exam, evaluate the effects cramming had on your learning. Even if you passed, you might remember very little. This low level of retention won't do you much good in the real world where you have to make use of information instead of just recalling it for a test. Think about how you can plan strategically to start earlier and improve the situation next time.

Whether you have to cram or not, you may experience anxiety on test day. Following are some ideas for how to handle test anxiety when it strikes.

How can you work through *test anxiety?*

A certain amount of stress can be a good thing. Your body is alert, and your energy motivates you to do your best (for more on stress and stress management, see Chapter 10). Some students, however, experience incapacitating stress levels before and during exams, especially midterms or finals.

Test anxiety can cause physical symptoms, such as sweating, nausea, dizziness, headaches, and fatigue, as well as psychological symptoms such as the inability to concentrate and feeling overwhelmed. You can minimize your anxiety by working on your preparation and attitude.

TEST ANXIETY
A bad case of nerves that can make it hard to think or to remember.

Preparation

Preparation is the basic defense against anxiety. The more confident you feel about the material, the better you will perform on test day. In this sense, consider all the preparation and study information in this chapter as test anxiety assistance. Also, finding out what to expect on the exam will help you feel more in control. Seek out information about what material will be covered, the question format, the length of the exam, and the points assigned to each question.

Creating a detailed study plan builds knowledge as it combats anxiety. Divide the plan into small tasks. As you finish each, you will increase your sense of accomplishment, confidence, and control. Instead of worrying about the test, take active steps that will help you succeed.

Attitude

Although good preparation is a confidence builder, maintaining a positive *attitude* is equally important. Here are some key ways to maintain an attitude that will help you succeed.

See the test as an opportunity to learn. A test is an opportunity to show what you have learned. All too often, students view tests as contests. If you pass, or "win" a contest, you might feel no need to retain what you've learned. If you fail, or "lose" the contest, you might feel no need to try again. However, if you see the test as a signpost along the way to a greater goal, mastering the material will be more important than "winning."

Understand that tests measure performance, not personal value. Your grade does not reflect your ability to succeed. Whether you get an A or an F, you are still the same person.

Appreciate your instructor's purpose. Instructors don't intend to make you miserable. They test you to give you an opportunity to grow and demonstrate what you have accomplished. They test you so that, in rising to the challenge, you become better prepared for challenges outside of school. Don't hesitate to engage your instructors in your quest to learn and succeed. Visit them during office hours; send them e-mail questions to clarify material and issues before tests.

Seek study partners who challenge you. Your anxiety may get worse if you study with someone who is also anxious. Find someone who can inspire you to do your best. For more on how to study effectively with others in study groups, see Chapter 5.

Set yourself up for success. Expect progress and success—not failure. Take responsibility for creating success through your work and attitude. Know that, ultimately, you are responsible for the outcome.

Practice relaxation. When you feel test anxiety mounting, breathe deeply, close your eyes, and visualize positive mental images such as getting a good grade and finishing with time to spare. Do whatever you have to do to ease muscle tension—stretch your neck, tighten and then release your muscles.

These strategies will help in most test anxiety situations. However, many students have issues surrounding math tests that require special attention.

Coping with Math Anxiety

QUANTITATIVE

Of, relating to, or involving the measurement of amount or number.

Math anxiety is the uncomfortable feeling associated with **quantitative** thinking. Math anxiety is often based on common misconceptions about math, such as the notion that people are born with or without an ability to think quantitatively, or the idea that real quantitative thinkers solve problems in their heads. Some students feel that they can't do math at all, and as a result may give up without asking for help. Use the questionnaire in Figure 8.2 to get an idea of your math anxiety level.

The best way to overcome test-time anxiety is to practice quantitative thinking and thereby increase your confidence. Keeping up with your homework, attending class, preparing well for tests, and doing extra problems will help you feel confident by increasing your familiarity with the material. Figure 8.3 shows additional ways to reduce math anxiety.

Test Anxiety and the Returning Student

If you're returning to school after years away, you may wonder if you can compete with younger students or if your mind is still able to learn. To counteract these feelings of inadequacy, focus on the useful skills you have learned in life. For example, managing work and a family requires strong time-management, planning, and communication skills that can help you plan your study time, juggle school responsibilities, and interact with students and instructors.

In addition, life experiences give you contexts through which you can understand ideas. For example, your relationship experiences may help you understand social psychology concepts and managing your finances may help you understand accounting. If you permit yourself to

| Figure 8.2 | Explore your math anxiety. |

Rate each of the following statements on a scale of 1 (Strongly Disagree) to 5 (Strongly Agree).

① ② ③ ④ ⑤   1. I don't like math classes and haven't since high school.

① ② ③ ④ ⑤   2. I do okay at the beginning of a math class, but I always feel it will get to the point where it is impossible to understand.

① ② ③ ④ ⑤   3. I don't seem to concentrate in math classes. I try, but I get nervous and distracted and think about other things.

① ② ③ ④ ⑤   4. I don't like asking questions in math class. I'm afraid that the teacher or the other students will think I'm stupid.

① ② ③ ④ ⑤   5. I stress out when I'm called on in math class. I seem to forget even the easiest answers.

① ② ③ ④ ⑤   6. Math exams scare me far more than any of my other exams.

① ② ③ ④ ⑤   7. I can't wait to finish my math requirement so that I'll never have to do any math again.

SCORING KEY: 28–35   You suffer from full-blown math anxiety.

              21–27   You are coping, but you're not happy about mathematics.

              14–20   You're doing okay.

               7–13   So, what's the big deal about math? You have very little problem with anxiety.

Source: Freedman, Ellen (March 1997). *Test Your Math Anxiety* [on-line]. Available at http://fc.whyy.org/CCC/algl/anxtest.htm (March 1998).

| Figure 8.3 | Ten ways to reduce math anxiety and do well on tests. |

1. Overcome your negative self-image about math.

2. Ask questions of your teachers and your friends, and seek outside assistance.

3. Math is a foreign language—practice it often.

4. Don't study mathematics by trying to memorize information and formulas.

5. READ your math textbook.

6. Study math according to your personal learning style.

7. Get help the same day you don't understand something.

8. Be relaxed and comfortable while studying math.

9. "TALK" mathematics. Discuss it with people in your class. Form a study group.

10. Develop a sense of responsibility for your own successes and failures.

Source: Freedman, Ellen (March 1997). *Ten Ways to Reduce Math Anxiety* [on-line]. Available at http://fc.whyy.org/CCC/algl/reduce.htm (March 1998).

feel positive about the knowledge and skills you have acquired, you may improve your ability to achieve your goals.

Parents who have to juggle child-care with study time can find the challenge especially difficult before a test. Here are some suggestions that might help:

- *Tell your children why the test is important.* Discuss the situation in concrete terms. For example, doing well in school might mean a high-paying job after graduation, which, in turn, can mean more money for family vacations, summer camps, and less stress over paying bills.
- *Explain the time frame.* Tell them your study schedule and when the test will occur. Plan a reward after your test—going for ice cream, seeing a movie, or having a picnic.
- *Plan activities.* Stock up on games, books, and videos.
- *Find help.* Ask a relative or friend to watch the children during study time, or arrange for your child to visit a friend. Consider trading baby-sitting hours with another parent, hiring a baby-sitter who will come to your home, or enrolling your child in daycare.

"Fear is nature's warning sign to get busy."

HENRY C. LINK

When you have prepared by using the strategies that work for you, you are ready to take your exam. Now, you can focus on methods to help you succeed when the test begins.

What general strategies can help you *succeed* on tests?

E ven though every test is different, there are general strategies that will help you handle almost all tests, including short-answer and essay exams.

Write Down Key Facts

Before you even look at the test, write down key information—including formulas, rules, and definitions—that you studied recently. Use the back of the question sheet or a piece of scrap paper for your notes (be sure your instructor knows that this paper didn't come into the test room already filled in). Recording this information at the start makes forgetting less likely.

Begin with an Overview of the Exam

Although exam time is precious, spend a few minutes at the start of the test getting a sense of the kinds of questions you'll be answering, what type of thinking they require, the number of questions in each section, and their point values. Use this information to schedule your time. For example, if a two-hour test is divided into two sections of equal point value—an essay section with 4 questions and a short-answer section with 60 questions—you can spend an hour on the essays (15 minutes per question) and an hour on the short-answer section (1 minute per question). As you calculate, think about the level of difficulty of each section. If you think you can handle the short-answer questions in less than an hour and that you'll need more time for the essays, rebudget your time.

Read Test Directions

Reading test directions carefully can save you trouble. For example, although a history test of 100 true-or-false questions and one essay may look straightforward, the directions may tell you to answer 80 of the 100 questions or that the essay is an optional bonus. If the directions indicate that you are penalized for incorrect answers—meaning that you lose points instead of simply not gaining points—avoid guessing unless you're fairly certain. These questions may do damage, for example, if you earn two points for every correct answer and lose one point for every incorrect answer.

When you read directions, you may learn that some questions or sections are weighted more heavily than others. For example, the short-answer questions may be worth 30 points, whereas the essays are worth 70. In this case, it's smart to spend more time on the essays than on the short answers. To stay aware of the specifics of the directions, circle or underline key words and numbers.

Work from Easy to Hard

Begin with the questions that seem easiest to you. You can answer these questions quickly, leaving more time for questions that require greater effort. If you like to work through questions in order, mark difficult questions as you reach them and return to them after you answer the questions you know. Answering easier questions first also boosts your confidence.

Watch the Clock

Keep track of how much time is left and how you are progressing. You may want to plan your time on a piece of scrap paper, especially if you have one or more essays to write. Wear a watch or bring a small clock with you to the test room. A wall clock may be broken, or there may be no clock at all.

Some students are so concerned about time that they rush through the test and have time left over. Instead of leaving early, spend the remaining time refining and checking your work. You may correct inadvertent errors, change answers, or add more information to an essay.

279

Master the Art of Intelligent Guessing

When you are unsure of an answer on a short-answer test, you can leave it blank or you can guess. As long as you are not penalized for incorrect answers, guessing helps you. "Intelligent guessing," writes Steven Frank, an authority on student studying and test taking, "means taking advantage of what you do know in order to try to figure out what you don't. If you guess intelligently, you have a decent shot at getting the answer right."[1]

First, eliminate all the answers you know—or believe—are wrong. Try to narrow your choices to two possible answers; then choose the one you think is more likely to be correct. Strategies for guessing the correct answer on a multiple-choice test are discussed later in the chapter.

When you check your work at the end of the test, ask yourself whether you would make the same guesses again. Chances are that you will leave your answers alone, but you may notice something that makes you change your mind—a qualifier that affects meaning, a remembered fact that enables you to answer the question without guessing, or a miscalculation in a math problem.

Follow Directions on Machine-Scored Tests

Machine-scored tests require that you use a special pencil to fill in a small box on a computerized answer sheet. When the computer scans the sheet, it can tell whether you answered the questions correctly.

Taking these tests requires special care. Use the right pencil (usually a number 2) and mark your answer in the correct space, filling the space completely. Periodically, check the answer number against the question number to make sure they match. If you mark the answer to question 4 in the space for question 5, not only do you get question 4 wrong, but your responses for all subsequent questions are off by a line. To avoid this problem, put a small dot next to any number you skip and plan to return to later.

Neatness counts on these tests because the computer can misread stray pencil marks or partially erased answers. If you mark two answers to a question and only partially erase one, the computer will read both responses and charge you with a wrong answer.

Use Critical Thinking to Avoid Errors

Critical thinking can help you work through each question thoroughly and avoid errors. Following are some critical-thinking strategies to use during a test.

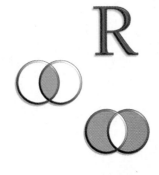

Recall facts, procedures, rules, and formulas. Base your answers on the information you recall. Think carefully to make sure your recall is accurate.

Think about similarities. If you don't know how to attack a question or problem, consider similar questions or problems that you have worked on in class or while studying.

Note differences. Especially with objective questions, items that seem different from the material you studied may lead to answers you can eliminate.

Think through causes and effects. For a numerical problem, think about how you plan to solve it and see if the answer—the effect of your plan—makes sense. For an essay question that asks you to analyze a condition or situation, consider both what caused it and what effects it has.

Find the best idea to match the example(s) given. For a numerical problem, decide what formula (idea) best applies to the example or examples (the data of the problem). For an essay question, decide what idea applies to, or links, the examples given.

Support ideas with examples. When you present an idea in an answer to an essay question, be sure to back it up with supporting examples.

Evaluate each test question. In your initial approach to a question, decide what kinds of thinking will best help you solve it. For example, essay questions often require cause-and-effect and idea-to-example thinking, whereas objective questions often benefit from thinking about similarities and differences.

Use Special Techniques for Math Tests

In addition to these general test-taking strategies, here are several techniques that can help you achieve better results on math exams:

- *Read through the exam first.* When you first get an exam, read through every problem quickly. Make notes on how you might attempt to solve the problem if something occurs to you immediately.

- *Analyze problems carefully.* Categorize problems according to type. Take the "givens" into account, and write down any formulas, theorems, or definitions that apply before you begin. Focus on what you want to find or prove, and take the time you need to be precise.

- *Estimate before you begin to come up with a "ballpark" solution.* Work the problem and check the solution against your estimate. The two answers should be close. If they're not, recheck your calculations. You may have made a simple calculation error.

- *Break the calculation into the smallest possible pieces.* Go step-by-step and don't move on to the next step until you are clear about what you've done so far.

- *Recall how you solved similar problems.* Past experience can give you valuable clues to how a particular problem should be handled.

- *Draw a picture to help you see the problem.* This can be a diagram, a chart, a probability tree, a geometric figure, or any other visual image that relates to the problem.

- *Be neat.* When it comes to numbers, mistaken identity can mean the difference between a right and a wrong answer. A 4 that looks like a 9 will be marked wrong.

- *Use the opposite operation to check your work.* Work backward from your answer to see if you are right. Use subtraction to check your addition; use division to check multiplication.

- *Look back at the question to be sure you did everything that was asked.* Did you answer every part of the question? Did you show all required work?

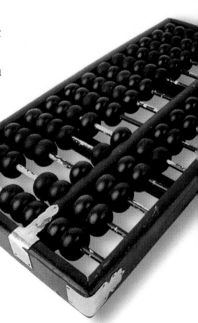

Maintain Academic Integrity

When you take a test honestly, following all the rules of the test, you strengthen the principle of trust between students and instructors, which is at the heart of academic integrity (see Chapter 1). You also receive an accurate reading on your performance, from which you can determine what you know and what you still have to learn. Finally, you reinforce the habit of honesty.

Cheating as a strategy to pass a test or get a better grade robs you of the opportunity to learn the material on which you are being tested, which, ultimately, is your loss. It also makes fair play between students impossible. When one student studies hard for an exam and another cheats and both get the same high grade, the efforts of the hard-working student are diminished. It is important to realize that cheating jeopardizes your future at college if you are caught. You may be seriously reprimanded—or even expelled—if you violate your school's code of academic integrity.

Now that you have explored these general strategies, you can use what you've learned to address specific types of test questions.

How can you *master* different types of *test questions?*

OBJECTIVE QUESTIONS

Short-answer questions that test your ability to recall, compare, and contrast information and to choose the right answer from a limited number of choices.

SUBJECTIVE QUESTIONS

Essay questions that require you to express your answer in terms of your own personal knowledge and perspective.

Every type of test question has a different way of finding out how much you know about a subject. Answering different types of questions is part science and part art. The strategy changes according to whether the question is objective or subjective.

For objective questions, you choose or write a short answer you believe is correct, often making a selection from a limited number of choices. Multiple-choice, fill-in-the-blank, matching, and true-or-false questions fall into this category. Subjective questions demand the same information recall as objective questions, but they also require you to plan, organize, draft, and refine a written response. They may also require more extensive critical thinking and evaluation. All essay questions are subjective. Although some guidelines will help you choose the right answers to both types of questions, part of the skill is learning to "feel" your way to an answer that works.

Multiple-Choice Questions

Multiple-choice questions are the most popular type of question on standardized tests. The following strategies can help you answer them.

Carefully read the directions. Directions can be tricky. For example, whereas most test items ask for a single correct answer, some give you the option of marking several choices that are correct. For some tests, you might be required to answer only a certain number of questions.

Read each question thoroughly. Then, look at the choices and try to answer the question. This strategy reduces the possibility that the choices will confuse you.

Underline key words and phrases. If the question is complicated, try to break it down into small sections that are easy to understand.

Pay attention to words that could throw you off. For example, it is easy to overlook negatives in a question ("Which of the following is not . . .").

If you don't know the answer, eliminate those answers you know or suspect are wrong. Your goal is to leave yourself with two possible answers, which would give you a 50–50 chance of making the right choice. The following questions will help you eliminate choices:

- *Is the choice accurate on its own terms?* If there's an error in the choice—for example, a term that is incorrectly defined—the answer is wrong.
- *Is the choice relevant?* An answer may be accurate, but it may not relate to the essence of the question.
- *Are there any qualifiers?* Absolute qualifiers, like *always, never, all, none,* or *every,* often signal an exception that makes a choice incorrect. For example, the statement "Normal children always begin talking before the age of two" is untrue (most normal children begin talking before age two, but some start later). Analysis has shown that choices containing conservative qualifiers (e.g., *often, most, rarely,* or *may sometimes be*) are often correct.
- *Do the choices give clues?* Does a puzzling word remind you of a word you know? If you don't know a word, does any part of the word—its prefix, suffix, or root—seem familiar? (See Chapter 5 for information on the meanings of common prefixes, suffixes, and roots.)

Make an educated guess by following helpful patterns. The ideal is to know the material so well that you don't have to guess, but that isn't always possible. Test-taking experts have found patterns in multiple-choice questions that may help you. Here is their advice:

- Consider the possibility that a choice that is *more general* than the others is the right answer.
- Consider the possibility that a choice that is *longer* than the others is the right answer.
- Look for a choice that has a middle value in a range (the range can be from small to large or from old to recent). It is likely to be the right answer.
- Look for two choices that have similar meanings. One of these answers is probably correct.
- Look for answers that agree grammatically with the question. For example, a fill-in-the-blank question that has an *a* or *an* before the blank gives you a clue to the correct answer.

Make sure you read every word of every answer. Instructors have been known to include answers that are almost right, except for a single word. Focus especially on qualifying words such as *always, never, tend to, most, often,* and *frequently.*

When questions are keyed to a reading passage, read the questions first. This will help you focus on the information you need to answer the questions.

Here are some examples of the kinds of multiple-choice questions you might encounter in an Introduction to Psychology course[2] (the correct answer follows each question):

1. Arnold is at the company party and has had too much to drink. He releases all of his pent-up aggression by yelling at his boss, who promptly fires him. Arnold normally would not have yelled at his boss, but after drinking heavily he yelled because
   A. parties are places where employees are supposed to be able to "loosen up"
   B. alcohol is a stimulant
   C. alcohol makes people less concerned with the negative consequences of their behavior
   D. alcohol inhibits brain centers that control the perception of loudness

(The correct answer is C)

2. Which of the following has not been shown to be a probable cause of or influence on the development of alcoholism in our society?
   A. intelligence   C. personality
   B. culture   D. genetic vulnerability

(The correct answer is A)

3. Geraldine is a heavy coffee drinker who has become addicted to caffeine. If she completely ceases her intake of caffeine over the next few days, she is likely to experience each of the following EXCEPT
   A. depression   C. insomnia
   B. lethargy   D. headaches

(The correct answer is C)

True-or-False Questions

True-or-false questions test your knowledge of facts and concepts. Read them carefully to evaluate what they truly say. If you're stumped, guess (unless you're penalized for wrong answers).

Look for qualifiers in true-or-false questions—such as *all, only,* and *always* (the absolutes that often make a statement false) and *generally, often, usually,* and *sometimes* (the conservatives that often make a statement true)—that can turn a statement that would otherwise be true into one that is false or vice versa. For example, "The grammar rule 'I before E except after C' is always true" is false, whereas "The grammar rule 'I before E except after C' is usually true" is true. The qualifier makes the difference.

Here are some examples of the kinds of true-or-false questions you might encounter in an Introduction to Psychology course (the correct answer follows each question).

Are the following questions true or false?

1. Alcohol use is clearly related to increases in hostility, aggression, violence, and abusive behavior. (True)

2. Marijuana is harmless. (False)

3. Simply expecting a drug to produce an effect is often enough to produce the effect. (True)

4. Alcohol is a stimulant. (False)

Matching Questions

Matching questions ask you to match the terms in one list with the terms in another list, according to the directions. For example, the directions may tell you to match a communicable disease with the pathogen that usually causes it. The following strategies will help you handle these questions.

Make sure you understand the directions. The directions tell you whether each answer can be used once or more than once.

Work from the column with the longest entries. This saves time because you are looking at each long phrase only once as you scan the column with the shorter phrases for the match.

Start with the matches you know. On your first run-through, mark these matches immediately with a penciled line, waiting to finalize your choices after you've completed all the items. Keep in mind that if you can use an answer only once, you may have to change answers if you reconsider any of your original choices.

Finally, tackle the matches you're not sure of. On your next run-through, focus on the more difficult matches. Look for clues and relationships you might not have thought of at first. Think back to class lectures, notes, and study sessions and try to visualize the correct response.

Consider the possibility that one of your sure-thing answers is wrong. If one or more phrases seem to have no correct answer, look back at your easy matches to be sure that you did not jump too quickly. See if another phrase can be used instead, thus freeing up an answer for use in another match.

Fill-in-the-Blank Questions

Fill-in-the-blank questions, also known as sentence completion questions, ask you to supply one or more words or phrases with missing information that completes the sentence. These strategies will help you make the right choices.

Be logical. Insert your answer; then reread the sentence from beginning to end to be sure it is factually and grammatically correct and makes sense.

Note the length and number of the blanks. Use these as important clues, but not as absolute guideposts. If two blanks appear right after one another, the instructor is probably looking for a two-word answer. If a blank is longer than usual, the correct response may require additional space. However, if you are certain of an answer that doesn't fit the blanks, trust your knowledge and instincts.

Pay attention to how blanks are separated. If there is more than one blank in a sentence and the blanks are widely separated, treat each one separately. Answering each as if it were a separate sentence-completion question increases the likelihood that you will get at least one answer correct. Here is an example:

> When Toni Morrison was awarded the _____ Prize for Literature, she was a professor at _____ University.
>
> (Answer: Morrison received the Nobel Prize and is a professor at Princeton University.)

In this case, and in many other cases, your knowledge of one answer has little impact on your knowledge of the other answer.

Think out of the box. If you can think of more than one correct answer, put them both down. Your instructor may be impressed by your assertiveness and creativity.

Make a guess. If you are uncertain of an answer, make an educated guess. Use qualifiers like *may, sometimes,* and *often* to increase the chance that your answer is at least partially correct. Have faith that after hours of studying, the correct answer is somewhere in your subconscious mind and that your guess is not completely random.

Essay Questions

An essay question allows you to express your knowledge and views more extensively than a short-answer question. With the freedom to express your views, though, comes the chal-

PERSONAL TRIUMPH

*e*veryone has to face tests in life. From the difficulty of those tests can come important lessons and incredible drive. Rusmir Music has come from war-torn Bosnia to a stellar academic performance in his adopted country and an ability to proudly assert his differences.

Talk about square pegs: This year's No. 2 graduate at Holy Cross, a Roman Catholic college in Worcester, Massachusetts, is an openly gay Muslim from Bosnia.

Rusmir Music, 23, is a chemistry major who sings racy Madonna lyrics at every opportunity. He wears T-shirts with slogans rare on this J. Crew campus. He sprinkles glitter on his face, and often spikes his hair (which he used to bleach blond) into horns.

"That's why I think I'm here—I like to shock people, push their limits," Mr. Music said. "I can't say it was easy, but it was worth it. I am who I am today because I had to fight."

Born in Brcko, Bosnia, Mr. Music left home for Croatia in 1992, shortly before the bridge to his village was bombed. He lived with his mother and twin younger siblings in Nasice for four years, the only Muslim refugees in a Catholic town, biking five miles to a job checking coats at a nightclub. English lessons began in fifth grade, but Mr. Music got fluent watching soap operas like "Santa Barbara" and "Beverly Hills, 90210."

At 17, he joined a program that sent Bosnian students to live with American families, arriving in San Francisco on Super Bowl Sunday. He soon won a scholarship to Holy Cross—his host brother's alma mater—and people he met through the private United States high school where he spent three semesters added $30,000 to cover room, board and books.

Helen Whall, a professor of English, met Mr. Music when he signed up for her freshman seminar, "Shakespeare the Loyal Rebel." She

Source: Jodi Wilgoren, "Holy Cross: Fighting for the Right to Live on the Edge," *New York*

Rusmir Music, Graduate of Holy Cross College, Worcester, Massachusetts

said that course's title summed up the essence of her best student. His favorite Shakespearean character, she said, is Touchstone, the fool from "As You Like It."

While amassing a grade-point average of 3.93 and getting elected to Phi Beta Kappa in his junior year, Mr. Music served as a resident adviser, worked on plays and helped found Mecca, the Muslim Endeavor to Create Cultural Awareness—as well as the Association of Bisexuals, Gays and Lesbians, known as ABiGaLe.

The buttoned-down community offered few dating opportunities, but plenty of chances to shock his many friends and comfort those on the fringe. "I do talk a lot about sex," he admitted. "I don't necessarily get a lot of sex— I don't get any sex, really—but it's something I think people should be comfortable talking about."

Next year he will pursue a master's degree at New York University, creating an interdisciplinary program focusing on race, gender and sexuality.

Mr. Music's mother canceled plans to attend his graduation Friday, fearful of losing her job in Tusla, so he was on his own, as he has been, really, for years.

"Wherever a voice needed to be heard, where normally you might expect students to be shy and pull back, you could count on Rusmir being there," Professor Whall said. "He's made it O.K. for square pegs to make round holes accommodate them."

Take a moment to consider . . .

- *In what way you feel like you don't quite fit in—like you're a "square peg in a round hole."*
- *How you have handled an event in your life that has tested your ability to adapt.*

Here are examples of fill-in-the-blank questions you might encounter in an Introduction to Astronomy course[3] (correct answers follow questions):

1. A _____ is a collection of hundreds of billions of stars. (galaxy)

2. Rotation is the term used to describe the motion of a body around some _____. (axis)

3. The solar day is measured relative to the sun; the sidereal day is measured relative to the _____. (stars)

4. On December 21, known as the _____ _____, the sun is at its _____ _____. (winter solstice; southernmost point)

lenge to exhibit knowledge and demonstrate your ability to organize and express that knowledge clearly.

Strategies for Answering Essay Questions

The following steps will help improve your responses to essay questions. Many of these guidelines reflect methods for approaching any writing assignment. That is, you undertake an abbreviated version of the writing process as you plan, draft, revise, and edit your response (see Chapter 7). The primary differences here are that you are writing under time pressure and that you are working from memory.

1. *Start by reading the questions.* Decide which to tackle (if there's a choice). Then, focus on what each question is asking and the mind actions you need to use. Read the directions carefully and do everything that you are asked to do. Some essay questions may contain more than one part. Knowing what you have to accomplish, budget your time accordingly. For example, if you have 1 hour to answer 3 questions, you might budget 20 minutes for each question and break that down into stages (3 minutes for planning, 15 minutes for drafting, 2 minutes for revising and editing).

2. *Watch for action verbs.* Certain verbs can help you figure out how to think. Figure 8.4

Figure 8.4   Common action verbs on essay tests.

Analyze—Break into parts and discuss each part separately.	**Explain**—Make the meaning of something clear, often by making analogies or giving examples.
Compare—Explain similarities and differences.	**Illustrate**—Supply examples.
Contrast—Distinguish between items being compared by focusing on differences.	**Interpret**—Explain your personal view of facts and ideas and how they relate to one another.
Criticize—Evaluate the positive and negative effects of what is being discussed.	**Outline**—Organize and present the main examples of an idea or sub-ideas.
Define—State the essential quality or meaning. Give the common idea.	**Prove**—Use evidence and argument to show that something is true, usually by showing cause and effect or giving examples that fit the idea to be proven.
Describe—Visualize and give information that paints a complete picture.	**Review**—Provide an overview of ideas and establish their merits and features.
Discuss—Examine in a complete and detailed way, usually by connecting ideas to examples.	**State**—Explain clearly, simply, and concisely, being sure that each word gives the image you want.
Enumerate/List/Identify—Recall and specify items in the form of a list.	**Summarize**—Give the important ideas in brief.
Evaluate—Give your opinion about the value or worth of something, usually by weighing positive and negative effects, and justify your conclusion.	**Trace**—Present a history of the way something developed, often by showing cause and effect.

explains some words commonly used in essay questions. Underline these words as you read the question, clarify what they mean, and use them to guide your writing.

3. *Plan your essay.* Brainstorm ideas and examples. Create an informal outline or think link to map your ideas and indicate the examples you plan to cite in support. (See Chapter 7 for a discussion of these organizational devices.)

4. *Draft your essay.* Start with a thesis statement that states clearly what your essay will say. Then, devote one or more paragraphs to the main points in your outline. Back up the general statement that starts each paragraph with evidence in the form of examples, statistics, and so on. Use simple, clear language, and look back at your outline to make sure you cover everything. Wrap it up with a short, pointed conclusion. Unlike the drafting stage of the writing process, you probably won't have time for further drafts. Therefore, try to be as complete and organized as possible as you write.

5. *Revise your essay.* Make sure you have answered the question completely and have included all of your points. Look for ideas you left out, ideas you didn't support with examples, paragraphs with faulty structure, and confusing sentences. Make cuts or changes or add sentences in the

margins, indicating with an arrow where they fit. Try to be as neat as possible when making last-minute changes.

6. *Edit your essay.* Check for mistakes in grammar, spelling, punctuation, and usage. No matter your topic, being technically correct in your writing makes your work more impressive.

Neatness is a crucial factor in essay writing. If your instructor can't read your ideas, it doesn't matter how good they are. You might consider printing and skipping every other line if you know your handwriting is a problem. Avoid writing on both sides of the paper if it makes your work hard to read. If your handwriting is dismal, ask if it is possible to take the test on a laptop computer.

Here are some examples of essay questions you might encounter in an Interpersonal Communication course. In each case, notice the action verbs from Figure 8.4.

1. Summarize the role of the self-concept as a key to interpersonal relationships and communication.

2. Explain how internal and external noise affects the ability to listen effectively.

3. Describe three ways that body language affects interpersonal communication.

(Figure 8.5 shows an essay that responds effectively to question 3.)

How can you *learn from* test *mistakes?*

T he purpose of a test is to see how much you know, not merely to achieve a grade. Making mistakes, or even failing a test, is human. Rather than ignoring mistakes, examine them and learn from them as you learn from mistakes on the job and in relationships. Working through your mistakes helps you avoid repeating them on another test. The following strategies will help.

Try to identify patterns in your mistakes. Look for the following:

- *Careless errors.* In your rush to complete the exam, did you misread the question or directions, blacken the wrong box on the answer sheet, inadvertently skip a question, write illegibly?

Figure 8.5   **Response to an essay question.**

QUESTION: Describe three ways that body language affects interpersonal communication.

Body language plays an important role in interpersonal communication and helps shape the impression you make, especially when you meet someone for the first time. Two of the most important functions of body language are to contradict and reinforce verbal statements. When body language contradicts verbal language, the message conveyed by the body is dominant. For example, if a friend tells you that she is feeling "fine," but her posture is slumped, her eye contact minimal, and her facial expression troubled, you have every reason to wonder whether she is telling the truth. If the same friend tells you that she is feeling fine and is smiling, walking with a bounce in her step, and has direct eye contact, her body language is accurately reflecting and reinforcing her words.

The nonverbal cues that make up body language also have the power to add shades of meaning. Consider this statement: "This is the best idea I've heard all day." If you were to say this three different ways—in a loud voice while standing up; quietly while sitting with arms and legs crossed and looking away; and while maintaining eye contact and taking the receiver's hand—you might send three different messages.

Finally, the impact of nonverbal cues can be greatest when you meet someone for the first time. Although first impressions emerge from a combination of nonverbal cues, tone of voice, and choice of words, nonverbal elements (cues and tone) usually come across first and strongest. When you meet someone, you tend to make assumptions based on nonverbal behavior such as posture, eye contact, gestures, and speed and style of movement.

In summary, nonverbal communication plays a crucial role in interpersonal relationships. It has the power to send an accurate message that may belie the speaker's words, offer shades of meaning, and set the tone of a first meeting.

- *Conceptual or factual errors.* Did you misunderstand a concept or never learn it? Did you fail to master certain facts? Did you skip part of the text or miss classes in which ideas were covered?

If you have time, rework the questions you got wrong. Based on instructor feedback, try to rewrite an essay, recalculate a math problem from the original question, or redo questions following a reading selection. If you see patterns of careless errors, promise yourself that you'll be more careful in the future and that you'll save time to double-check your work. If you pick up conceptual and factual errors, rededicate yourself to better preparation.

After reviewing your mistakes, fill in your knowledge gaps. If you made mistakes on questions because you didn't know or understand them, develop a plan to comprehensively learn the material. Solidifying your knowledge can help you on future exams and in life situations that involve the subject you're studying. You might even consider asking to retake the exam. The score might not count, but you may find that focusing on learning, rather than on grades, can improve your knowledge.

"The secret of a leader lies in the tests he has faced over the whole course of his life and the habit of action he develops in meeting those tests."

GAIL SHEEHY

Talk to your instructors. You can learn a lot from consulting an instructor about specific mistakes you made or about subjective essays on which you were marked down. Respectfully ask the instructor for an explanation of grades or comments. In the case of a subjective test where the answers are often not clearly right or wrong, ask for specifics about what you could have done to earn a better grade. Take advantage of this opportunity to find out solid details about how you can do better next time.

If you fail a test, don't throw it away. Keep it as a reminder that many students have been in your shoes and that you have room to improve if you supply the will to succeed.

sine qua non

Although Latin is no longer spoken and is considered a "dead" language, it plays an important role in modern English because many English words and phrases have Latin roots. The Latin phrase *sine qua non* (pronounced sihn-ay kwa nahn) means, literally, "without which not." In other words, a *sine qua non* is "an absolutely indispensable or essential thing."

Think of mastery as the *sine qua non* of test taking. When you have worked hard to learn, review, and retain information, you are well prepared for tests, no matter what form they take. Focus on knowledge to transform test taking from an intimidating challenge into an opportunity to demonstrate your mastery.

Building Skills

FOR COLLEGE, CAREER, AND LIFE SUCCESS

Critical Thinking *Applying Learning to Life*

Test Analysis

When you get back your next test, take a detailed look at your performance.

1. Write what you think of your test performance and grade. Were you pleased or disappointed? Briefly explain why.

_____

_____

_____

2. Next, list the test preparation activities that helped you on the exam and the activities you wish you had done—and intend to do—for the next exam.

   Actions I took that had positive effects:

_____

_____

_____

   Actions I did not take this time, but intend to take next time:

_____

_____

_____

3. Finally, list any action or situation you don't intend to repeat when studying for the next test.

_____

_____

_____

Learning from Your Mistakes

For this exercise, use an exam on which you made one or more mistakes or scored lower than you had hoped to. Thinking specifically about what happened will help you to avoid the same mistakes next time.

First, look at the potential problems listed here. Circle the ones that you feel were a factor in this exam. Fill in the empty spaces with any key problems not listed.

Incomplete preparation	Weak understanding of concepts	Test anxiety
Fatigue	Poor guessing techniques	
Feeling rushed during the test	Confusion about directions	

Using the problem(s) you circled as a guide, explain in more detail why you made mistakes, if it was an objective exam, or why you didn't score well, if it was an essay exam. Be specific about the factors involved in this particular situation.

_____

_____

_____

Now be strategic about the future. What will you do differently the next time you face a similar test?

_____

_____

_____

Teamwork *Combining Forces*

TESTING STUDY GROUP. Form a study group with two or three other students. When your instructor announces the next exam, ask each study group member to record everything he or she does to prepare for the exam, including:

- learning what to expect on the test (topics and material that will be covered, types of questions that will be asked)
- examining old tests
- creating and following a study schedule and checklist
- using SQ3R to review material
- taking a pretest
- getting a good night's sleep before the exam

- doing last-minute cramming
- mastering general test-taking strategies
- mastering test-taking strategies for specific types of test questions (multiple-choice, true/false, matching, fill-in-the-blank, essay)

After the exam, come together to compare preparation regimes. What important differences can you identify in the routines followed by group members? How do you suspect that different routines affected test performance and outcome? On a separate piece of paper, for your own reference, write down what you learned from the test preparation habits of your study mates that may help you as you prepare for upcoming exams.

Writing | *Discovery Through Journaling*

To record your thoughts, use a separate journal or the lined page at the end of the chapter.

TEST ANXIETY. Do you experience test anxiety? Describe how tests generally make you feel (you might include an example of a specific test situation and what happened). Identify your specific test-taking fears, and write out your plan to overcome fears and self-defeating behaviors.

Career Portfolio | *Charting Your Course*

ON-THE-JOB TESTING. Depending on what careers you are considering, you may encounter one or more tests. Some are for entry into the field (e.g., medical boards); some test your proficiency on particular equipment (e.g., a proficiency test on Microsoft Word); and some move you to the next level of employment (e.g., a technical certification test to become a certified actuary). Choose one career you are thinking about and investigate what tests are involved as you advance through different stages of the field. Be sure to look for tests in any of the areas described above. On a separate piece of paper, write down everything you find out about each test involved. For example:

- what it tests you on
- when, in the course of pursuing this career, you would need to take the test
- what preparation is necessary for the test (including course work)
- whether the test needs to be retaken at any time (e.g., airline pilots usually need to be recertified every few years)

Finally, see if you can review any of the tests you will face if you pursue this career. For example, if your career choice requires proficiency on a specific computer program, your college's career or computer center may have the test available.

Assess Yourself *Student Success Strategies*

If you have access to the CD-ROM Strategies for Success, use the following questions to assess your thoughts and enhance your understanding of the chapter. The questions below represent only some of the activities provided on the CD for the chapter topics—try others if you have time.

Click on the Test Taking bookmark. Use the following activities to broaden your knowledge of what it takes to succeed on tests:

1. Take the pre-assessment to clarify your perspective on test taking.

2. Watch the video and think about your own habits. Do you cram? What effects has it had on your learning? In the field provided, write a response to the questions on the video page.

3. Click on Activity Two: Practice Your Test Taking Skills. Print and read the article carefully, using the SQ3R method. Then take the test that follows and submit your results to see how you did.

4. Take the post-assessment to see how these activities have improved your knowledge of test taking.

Suggested Readings

Browning, William G., Ph.D. *Cliffs Memory Power for Exams.* Lincoln, NE: Cliffs Notes Inc., 1990.

Frank, Steven. *Test Taking Secrets: Study Better, Test Smarter, and Get Great Grades.* Holbrook, MA: Adams Media Corporation, 1998.

Fry, Ron. *"Ace" Any Test, 3rd ed.* Franklin Lakes, NJ: Career Press, 1996.

Hamilton, Dawn. *Passing Exams: A Guide for Maximum Success and Minimum Stress.* Herndon, VA: Cassell Academic, 1999.

Kesselman, Judy and Franklynn Peterson. *Test Taking Strategies.* New York: NTC/Contemporary Publishing, 1981.

Luckie, William R. and Wood Smethurst. *Study Power: Study Skills to Improve Your Learning and Your Grades.* Cambridge, MA: Brookline Books, 1997.

Internet Resources

Prentice Hall Student Success Supersite (testing tips in study skills section): www.prenhall.com/success

Florida State University (list of sites offering information on test taking skills): http://osi.fsu.edu/hot/testtaking/skills.htm

NetStudyAids.com—(study aids, skills, guides, and techniques): www.netstudyaids.com/

University of Minnesota Duluth (study strategies home page): www.d.umn.edu/student/loon/acad/strat/

Endnotes

1. Steven Frank, *The Everything Study Book.* Holbrook, MA: Adams Media Corporation, 1996, p. 208.

2. Many of the examples of objective questions used in this chapter are from Gary W. Pigrem, Test Item File for Charles G. Morris, *Understanding Psychology, 3rd ed.* Upper Saddle River, NJ: Prentice Hall, 1996.

3. Questions from Eric Chaisson and Steve McMillan, *Astronomy Today, 2nd ed.* Upper Saddle River, NJ: Prentice Hall, 1996, p. 27.

JOURNAL

name   date

visit: www.prenhall.com/carter NY Times link for this chapter

Part II
DEVELOPING YOUR LEARNING SKILLS

Becoming a Better Test Taker

MULTIPLE CHOICE. Circle or highlight the answer that seems to fit best.

1. The activity that lies at the heart of critical thinking is
   A. solving problems.
   B. taking in information.
   C. reasoning.
   D. asking questions.

2. *Primary sources* are defined as
   A. periodicals.
   B. original documents.
   C. expert opinions of experimental results.
   D. resource materials.

3. When in class, you should choose a note-taking system that
   A. suits the instructor's style, the course material, and your learning style.
   B. you've used in other classes successfully.
   C. matches what you use when you study outside of class.
   D. is recommended by your instructor.

4. *Association* means
   A. considering how information is updated.
   B. finding the differences between two sets of information.
   C. considering new information on its own terms.
   D. considering new information in relation to information you already know.

5. A library search strategy takes you from
   A. specific reference works to general reference works.
   B. general reference works to specific reference works.
   C. encyclopedias to almanacs.
   D. encyclopedias to the Internet.

6. When answering an essay question on a test
   A. spend most of your time on the introduction because the grader sees it first.
   B. skip the planning steps if your time runs short.
   C. use the four steps of the writing process but take less time for each step.
   D. write your essay and then rewrite it on another sheet or booklet.

FILL-IN-THE-BLANK. Complete the following sentences with the appropriate word(s) or phrase(s) that best reflect what you learned in the chapter. Choose from the items that follow each sentence.

1. The three parts of the path of critical thinking are
   _____, _____ , and _____.
   (recall/idea to example/example to idea, taking in information/asking questions about information/using information, taking in information/using information/communicating information)

2. A broad range of interests and a willingness to take risks are two common characteristics of _____. (creativity, critical thinking, cause and effect)

3. When you begin to read new material, what you already know gives you _____ that helps you understand and remember new ideas. (ideas, context, headers)

4. In the Cornell note-taking system, Section 2 is called the _____ and is used for filling in comments and diagrams as you review. (cue column, summary area, main body)

5. A _____ is a memory technique that works by connecting information you are trying to learn with simpler or familiar information. (mnemonic device, acronym, idea chain)

6. _____ encourages you to put your _____ ideas on paper and is an important part of the _____ process. (Freewriting/uncensored/planning, Editing/polished/planning, Researching/censored/editing)

ESSAY QUESTIONS. The following essay questions will help you organize and communicate your ideas in writing, just as you must do on an essay test. Before you begin answering a question, spend a few minutes planning (brainstorm possible approaches, write a thesis statement, jot down main thoughts in outline or think link form). To prepare yourself for actual test conditions, limit writing time to no more than 30 minutes per question.

1. Describe the steps of the reading strategy SQ3R. What is involved in each step? How does each step contribute to your understanding of your reading material?

2. Write an essay that supports or rejects all or part of the following statement: *"The tests you take in college not only help ensure that you acquire important skills and knowledge, but also help prepare you for the day-to-day learning demands that are associated with twenty-first century careers."* If possible, support your position with references to career areas that interest you.

PERSONAL TRIUMPH

Albert Einstein, theoretical physicist

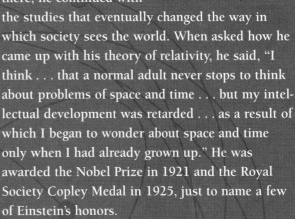

*e*ven the most successful and brilliant people in the world have had to face difficulties in their life and education. Far from being an ideal student, Albert Einstein battled dyslexia and fought against a tide of disinterested instructors. His eventual success is an inspiration to all students.

Renowned as one of the top philosophers and thinkers of all time, Albert Einstein significantly changed how people view nature and society. His ideas, and his courage to pursue them, inspired others to follow their own dreams. With all his fame and success, it is easy to assume that Einstein's problems were minimal. To the contrary, he had many personal obstacles to overcome and fears to face.

Born on March 14, 1879 in Ulm, Germany, Albert Einstein was not what you would call a typical child. There was nothing about his first years that indicated his genius mind. In fact, as a toddler, Einstein was extremely late to speak, causing his parents to wonder if he was mentally retarded. By age nine, he was still not fluent in his native language and did not feel at ease in common conversation. To make things even more difficult, he suffered from a form of dyslexia. He often experienced the frustration and the anger of feeling different from the rest of society.

Einstein was looked down on by many of his educators. One went so far as to say that "it doesn't matter (what profession he chooses); he'll never make a success of anything." He was determined to prove them wrong. When instructors at his school labeled him as "dumb" or "incapable," he learned to question authority instead of internalizing the criticism. Because he found no supportive atmosphere at school, he became motivated to teach himself mathematics and physics. Eventually, in 1900, he graduated as a math and physics teacher.

While working a job in a patent office from 1902 through 1909, Einstein worked on and received his doctorate from the Univer- sity of Zurich in 1905 for his thesis *On a New Determination of Molecular Dimensions.* From there, he continued with the studies that eventually changed the way in which society sees the world. When asked how he came up with his theory of relativity, he said, "I think . . . that a normal adult never stops to think about problems of space and time . . . but my intellectual development was retarded . . . as a result of which I began to wonder about space and time only when I had already grown up." He was awarded the Nobel Prize in 1921 and the Royal Society Copley Medal in 1925, just to name a few of Einstein's honors.

Despite the negative attitudes surrounding him as an adolescent and as a young adult, Albert Einstein was able to persevere and use his differences to his benefit. He didn't allow other people's judgments to define his sense of self-worth and intelligence. Instead, he learned to rely on his mind and his way of learning and became an independent thinker. It was this creative and different way of thinking that allowed him to change the face of scientific and mathematical thought.

Take a moment to consider . . .

- *How you've dealt with negative feedback from instructors or other authority figures.*
- *What about your childhood has had the most profound effect on how you learn.*

Sources: www.groups.dcs.st-andrews.ac.uk/~history/Mathematicians/Einstein.html; Clark, Ronald W., *Einstein: The Life and Times* (New York: Avon Books, 1965).

READING. Choose two chapters from a textbook you are currently using for one of your classes. Read one chapter in your normal fashion. Then, go to **www.prenhall.com/success** and click on the Reading link in the Study Skills section. Explore each of the steps outlined there—the parts in a "well-planned reading episode." Before you read the second chapter, survey it (the first of the steps) and answer the following questions on a separate sheet of paper.

1. How many pages is the chapter? How long do you think it will take you to read?
2. How is the chapter organized?
3. What note-taking system will work best for this chapter?
4. What questions do you want to be able to answer when you finish the chapter? Write down 3–5 questions that you think are important.

Next, read the chapter, keeping the steps in mind. Finally, answer the following questions after you have finished reading.

1. Describe your usual method for reading. How does this new strategy compare?
2. Which steps in the Reading link helped you the most?
3. Answer the questions you raised while surveying the chapter.
4. Click on the word "Article" and read Mary Bixby's article about reading. Write down what you consider your biggest "problem on the page" and "problem off the page" and describe some ideas you have to solve these problems.
5. Using a search engine, locate and list three sites that have helpful information on reading. For each site, write down one helpful hint that you would like to try when reading your texts.

Creating Success

IN THIS CHAPTER

In this chapter you explore answers to the following questions: • Why is it important to embrace diversity? • **How can critical thinking help you explore diversity?** • How can minority students make the most of college? • **How can you communicate effectively?** • How do you make the most of personal relationships? • **How can you handle conflict?**

relating to others

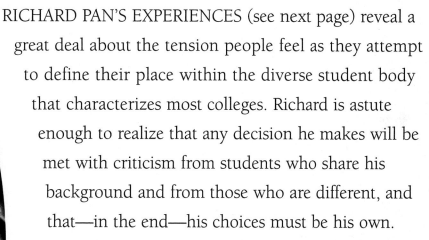

RICHARD PAN'S EXPERIENCES (see next page) reveal a great deal about the tension people feel as they attempt to define their place within the diverse student body that characterizes most colleges. Richard is astute enough to realize that any decision he makes will be met with criticism from students who share his background and from those who are different, and that—in the end—his choices must be his own.

In this chapter, you explore how having a strong network of relationships can help you grow as a person and progress toward your goals. You see how your ability to open your mind can positively affect the way in which you perceive and relate to others. Special attention is paid to the choices minority students, like Richard, face. You also explore communication problems and strategies, techniques for enhancing personal relationships, and methods for handling different forms and levels of conflict.

communicating in a diverse world

Richard Pan, Columbia University, New York, New York

Jo Anne Roe, Spanish Instructor, Oak Park-River Forest High School, Oak Park, Illinois

How can I deal with diversity?

. . . follow the Golden Rule: treat other people the way you want them to treat you.

I was born in Taiwan and came to the United States when I was 12. At my high school in California, everyone mingled well. When I started college, however, I noticed a difference. The Asian kids hung out only with other Asians, and the Caucasians did the same. I'm used to hanging out with all sorts of people, but now I feel this tension, as if Asians are thinking, "Why is he bothering with them?"

During a summer work program, I roomed with a Chinese-American who advised me to avoid being friends with people from different ethnic groups. Although I don't feel comfortable with his advice, I do think you get judged by all sides when you try to be friends with everybody. Sometimes I feel like I'm having an identity crisis. I ask myself, "Which side am I on?" Do you have any ideas about how I could do better managing this problem?

It is wonderful that you have developed the ability to mingle with and enjoy the company of people from diverse backgrounds. This is a skill that many people do not possess; it is a skill that will be immensely valuable for your personal and professional future. Your comfort in a multicultural setting reflects self-assurance, maturity, and a clearly defined sense of identity.

The problem that you face—prejudice—does not originate within you, rather, it is being imposed upon you. To accuse one specific group of having a monopoly on this practice would be a denial of the truth. Misunderstanding of, apprehension toward, and nonacceptance of others who are different are facets of an elemental and, sadly, universal flaw in the human psyche. And because it is so painful, it is natural for people to guard themselves against its damage. I imagine that the other Asian-Americans are advising you out of sincere concern for you not to be hurt by people with whom they have had negative encounters in the past. The bottom line is that you are not at fault!

The best advice that I can offer to you is to follow the "Golden Rule": Treat other people the way you want them to treat you. In following the wisdom of this refrain, you neither compromise your own outlook on life nor give in to the fears and insecurities of other people, and you maintain human dignity in general. Continue as you are and be patient. Eventually, you will begin to see gradual and positive changes in the actions of your friends, directly due to the impact you will have made on them through your positive, accepting attitude.

Why is it important to *embrace diversity?*

W hether you grew up in a small town, a suburb, or a large city, inevitably you will encounter people who are nothing like anyone you've ever met. They may be of a different race or mix of races, have different religious beliefs, or express their sexuality in nontraditional ways. With society becoming more diverse, the likelihood of these encounters is increasing. As Figure 9.1 shows, the population of the United States not only grew by nearly 27.5 million between 1990 and 2000, it also became more of a "gorgeous mosaic"— a metaphor first coined by David Dinkins, New York City's first African-American mayor, to describe the city's diversity.

According to the 2000 census, one in four Americans is a minority group member, compared with one in five in 1980. And, for the first time, with the census allowing people to choose from an array of racial identities—white, black, Asian, American Indian, Alaska native, Pacific Islander and Hawaiian native, or "some other race"—Americans now describe themselves in terms of 63 different racial categories, compared with only five in 1990.[1]

The Diversity Within You

To think about the concept of diversity, look first within yourself. You are a complex jumble of internal and external characteristics that makes you markedly different than everyone else. Just as no two snowflakes are alike, no two people are alike— even identical twins.

> *Your example:* Take a minute to write down the characteristics that best describe you (e.g., Cuban-American, blonde, laid-back, only child, 24 years old, interested in rap music, training to be an exercise physiologist, fraternity member, good sense of humor).

_____

_____

_____

_____

Everything about you—your gender, race, ethnicity, sexual orientation, age, unique personality, talents, and skills—adds up to who you are. Accepting your strengths and weaknesses, your background and group identity is a sign of psychological health. You have every reason to feel proud and to make no

Figure 9.1

Minorities are changing the face of the United States.

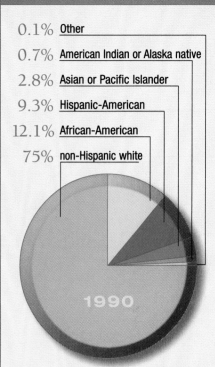

0.1%	Other
0.7%	American Indian or Alaska native
2.8%	Asian or Pacific Islander
9.3%	Hispanic-American
12.1%	African-American
75%	non-Hispanic white

1990

Total population 253,979,140

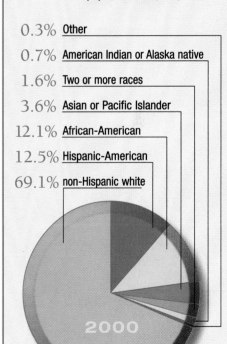

0.3%	Other
0.7%	American Indian or Alaska native
1.6%	Two or more races
3.6%	Asian or Pacific Islander
12.1%	African-American
12.5%	Hispanic-American
69.1%	non-Hispanic white

2000

Total population 281,421,906

Source: U.S. Census Bureau. Data from 2000 Census of the Population.

Figure 9.2

How the student body is expected to change by 2015.

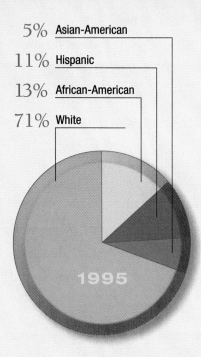

5% Asian-American
11% Hispanic
13% African-American
71% White

1995

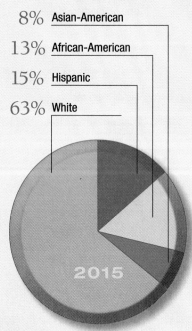

8% Asian-American
13% African-American
15% Hispanic
63% White

2015

(Percentages do not equal 100 because of rounding)

Source: Data from Educational Testing Service. Adapted from Jodi Wilgoren, "Swell of Minority Students Is Predicted at Colleges," *The New York Times*, May 24, 2000, A16.

apologies for your choices, as long as they do not intentionally hurt anyone.

Diversity on Campus

College campuses reflect society, so diversity on campus is on the upswing. Most students will notice different races and ethnicities around them at school, and projections are for greater population shifts to come. As Figure 9.2 shows, while white students made up 71 percent of the student population in 1995, their percentage is expected to drop to 63 percent in 2015. During the same 20-year period, Hispanic-American and Asian-American students will grow more numerous, while African-American enrollment will hold steady at about 13 percent. Some areas show even more dramatic trends. By 2015, whites will be a *minority* on campuses in California, the District of Columbia, Hawaii, and New Mexico.[2]

Minorities are becoming more visible because of their sheer numbers. Enrollment on campuses nationwide is expected to jump from 14.3 million in 1997 to 19 million in 2015, with African American, Hispanic-American, and Asian-American students responsible for 80 percent of the growth.

How will increasing diversity affect your life at school? Almost certainly, you will meet people like the following:

- Classmates and instructors who are bi- or multiracial or come from families with more than one religious tradition.
- Classmates and instructors who speak English as a second language and who may be immigrants.
- Classmates who are older than "traditional" 18- to 22-year-old students.
- Classmates and instructors who are in wheelchairs and those with other disabilities.
- Classmates who adopt different lifestyles—often expressed in the way they dress, their interests, and leisure activities.

In addition, you may see posters on campus for diverse clubs, such as those for African-Americans, Asian-Americans, Hispanic-Americans, gays and lesbians, and religious organizations including those for Christians, Jews, and Muslims. Your school may also have campus-wide ethnic, racial, and gay and lesbian pride celebrations.

Your example: Describe a person you've met recently who is a member of a group or groups with which you have little experience. Did you react to that person primarily as an individual or as a group member?

Every time you meet someone new, you have a *choice* about how to relate—or whether to relate at all. No one can force you to interact or to adopt a particular attitude because it is "right." Considering two important responsibilities may help you analyze your options:

Your responsibility to yourself is to carefully consider your feelings. Observe your reactions to others. Then, use critical thinking to make decisions that are fair to others and right for you.

Your responsibility to others lies in treating people with tolerance and respect. You won't like everyone, but acknowledging that others have a right to their opinions builds understanding. Being open-minded rather than closed-minded about others is necessary for relationships to thrive.

"Minds are like parachutes. They only function when they are open."

SIR JAMES DEWAR

Table 9.1 demonstrates the dramatic difference between an open-minded and a closed-minded approach to diversity.

Accepting others depends on being able to answer the following question with a firm yes: *Do I always give people a chance no matter who they are?* Prejudice, stereotyping, and discrimination often get in the way of fairness to others. Your problem-solving skills will help you overcome these barriers.

Table 9.1	The value of an open-minded approach to diversity.		
YOUR ROLE	**SITUATION**	**CLOSED-MINDED APPROACH**	**OPEN-MINDED APPROACH**
Fellow student	For an assignment, you are paired with a student old enough to be your mother.	You assume the student will be closed off to the modern world. You think she might preach to you about how to do the assignment.	You get to know the student as an individual. You stay open to what you can learn from her experiences and knowledge.
Friend	You are invited to dinner at a friend's house. When he introduces you to his partner, you realize that he is gay.	You are turned off by the idea of two men in a relationship. You make an excuse to leave early. You avoid your friend after that evening.	You have dinner with the two men and make an effort to get to know more about what their lives are like and who they are individually and as a couple.
Employee	Your new boss is of a different racial and cultural background than you.	You assume that you and your new boss don't have much in common and you think he will be distant and uninterested in you.	You rein in your assumptions, knowing they are based on stereotypes, and approach your new boss with an open mind.

How can critical thinking help you *explore diversity?*

Negative responses to diversity are based on prejudice and stereotypic thinking, which, in turn, can lead to discrimination and hate. As you read, think about what you can do to prevent some of the worst parts of human nature from taking hold within yourself and others.

Understand Prejudice, Discrimination, and Hate

PREJUDICE

A preconceived judgment or opinion, formed without just grounds or sufficient knowledge.

Prejudice occurs when people *prejudge* others, usually on the basis of external characteristics such as gender, race, sexual orientation, and religion. Particular prejudices are so pervasive that they have their own names: *racism* (prejudice based on race), *sexism* (prejudice based on sex), and *ageism* (prejudice based on age) are just a few. Here are some reasons why people judge others before they know anything about them:

- *Family and culture.* Children learn attitudes, including intolerance and hate, from their parents, peers, and community. They may also learn to feel superior to others.

- *Fear of differences.* When people who grew up in the midst of prejudice encounter others from different backgrounds, those differences are too unsettling.

- *Insecurity and jealousy.* When things go wrong, it is easier to blame others than to take responsibility. Similarly, when you are filled with self-doubt and insecurity, it is easier to devalue others than to look at your personal flaws.

- *Experience.* One bad experience with a person of a particular race or religion may lead you to condemn all people with the same background, even though your condemnation is illogical. Prejudice may also stem from having no experience with members of a minority group. Some people find it easy to think the worst in the absence of information.

STEREOTYPE

A standardized mental picture that represents an over-simplified opinion or uncritical judgment.

Prejudice Is Based on Stereotypes

A **stereotype** is an assumption made about the characteristics of a person or group of people. It is an idea that is accepted and generalized without proof or critical thinking. Although stereotypes can be "positive" or "negative," as the examples in Table 9.2 show, even "positive" stereotypes aren't always harmless or true. Stereotypes are the foundation for prejudiced thinking.

Table 9.2	Positive and negative stereotypes involve generalizations that may not be true.
POSITIVE STEREOTYPE	**NEGATIVE STEREOTYPE**
All women are nurturing.	Women are too emotional for business.
African-Americans are the best athletes.	African-Americans do poorly in school.
Hispanic-Americans are very family oriented.	Hispanic-Americans have too many kids.
White people are successful in business.	White people are cold and power hungry.
Gay people are artistic.	Gay people sleep around.
Because people with disabilities have been through so much, they are sensitive to the suffering of others.	People with disabilities can't hold jobs.
Older people have wisdom.	Older people can't learn new skills.
Asian-Americans are good in math and science.	Asian-Americans are poor leaders.

What are some reasons for stereotypes?

- *A desire for patterns and logic.* People often try to make sense of the world by using the labels, categories, and generalizations that stereotypes provide.
- *The media.* The more people see stereotypical images—the airhead beautiful blonde, the jolly fat man—the easier it is to believe that stereotypes are universal.
- *Laziness.* Labeling a group according to a characteristic they seem to have in common takes less energy than exploring unique qualities within individual group members.
- *A need to justify your actions.* Labeling people allows you to justify acts of discrimination. If you think women are poor in math, you won't ask any to join your math study group.

Your example: Describe a stereotype that you have witnessed in others or seen in the media that influences the way people treat each other.

_____

_____

_____

Stereotypes communicate the message that you don't respect others enough to discover who they really are. Although stereotyping a stranger is "easy," it comes at a high interpersonal cost. You never experience the personality, character, talents, sense of humor, or intelligence of others if you immediately plug them into stereotypical categories.

Prejudice Causes Discrimination

Prejudice—and the stereotypes it is based on—can lead to discrimination. *Discrimination* is made up of concrete actions that deny people equal employment, educational, and housing opportunities, and treat people as second-class citizens. As Sheryl McCarthy, an African-American columnist for *New York Newsday,* a daily newspaper, explains, "Nothing is quite so basic and clear as having a cab go right past your furiously waving body and pick up the white person next to you."[3]

If you are the victim of discrimination, it is important to know that federal law is on your side: You cannot be denied basic opportunities and rights because of your race, creed, color, age, gender, national or ethnic origin, religion, marital status, potential or actual pregnancy, or potential or actual illness or disability (unless the illness or disability prevents you from performing required tasks and unless accommodations are not possible).

Unfortunately, the law is often broken with the result that many people suffer the impact of discrimination. Some people don't report violations, fearing reprisals. Others aren't aware that discrimination has occurred or that there are laws to protect them from its consequences.

The many faces of prejudice and discrimination are showing up on college campuses. Students may not want to work with students of other races. Members of campus clubs may reject prospective members because of their religion. Outsiders may harass students attending gay and lesbian alliance meetings. Students may find that instructors judge their abilities and attitudes according to their gender, weight, or body piercings. Actions like these block mutual understanding and respect and can derail you from the pursuit of knowledge, which is at the heart of education.

Your example: Have you personally witnessed discriminatory acts at your school or been a victim of discrimination? If so, briefly describe what happened.

_____

_____

_____

Hate Crimes: The Awful Consequences of Prejudice

When prejudice turns violent and ugly, it often manifests itself in hate crimes directed at racial, ethnic, and religious minorities and homosexuals:

> HATE CRIME
> A crime motivated by a hatred of a specific characteristic thought to be possessed by the victim.

- In Wyoming in 1998, Matthew Shepard, a gay college student, was kidnapped and tied to a fence where his captors beat and abandoned him. He died of his injuries.

- In 1999, Eric Harris and Dylan Klebold opened fire in Columbine High School in Littleton, Colorado, killing 12 students and one teacher and wounding others. Their writings revealed their desire to harm minorities, athletes, and others different from them.

- In 1999, Buford O. Furrow entered the North Valley Jewish Community Center near Los Angeles, California, and shot three preschool children and two adults because they were Jewish. He then shot and killed a Filipino-American letter carrier.

The increase in hate crimes in recent years—particularly the substantial rise of these crimes on college campuses—is alarming. According to the latest statistics compiled by the U.S. Department of Education, campus hate crimes increased from 1,312 in 1997 to 2,067 in 1999, with more than 90 percent of the offenses involving assaults.[4]

The increase is linked, in part, to the Internet, which has given a "safe haven" to groups that espouse hate. The Internet gives hate-filled individuals a platform to express their racism, anti-Semitism, homophobia (hatred of gays), misogyny (hatred of women), and other prejudices. Some sites even promote prejudices to children through games and other interactive formats.

Your experience: Are you familiar with Internet sites that preach hate? Why do you think people visit these sites?

_____

_____

_____

Be Part of the Solution

As you know from Chapter 4, the best and most lasting solutions come when you address the causes rather than the effects of behavior. Therefore, the best way to fight discrimination and hate crimes is to work to eliminate prejudice.

Start with Yourself

If you can gradually broaden your horizons, you will benefit immensely—and so will the world. *Think critically about any prejudices you have.* Ask yourself: Am I prejudiced against any group or groups? How did I develop this prejudice? How does it affect me and others? How can I change the way I think?

Dr. Martin Luther King, Jr. believed in the power of critical thinking to change ingrained attitudes. He said:

> The tough-minded person always examines the facts before he reaches conclusions: in short, he postjudges. The tender-minded person reaches conclusions before he has examined the first fact; in short, he prejudges and is prejudiced. . . . There is little hope for us until we become tough minded enough to break loose from the shackles of prejudice, half-truths, and down-right ignorance.[5]

As you think critically, realize that the opinions of family, friends, and the media may sometimes lead you to adopt attitudes that you haven't thought through. Think about the attitudes you *want* to hold and make choices that are right for you and fair to others.

Try to avoid judgments based on external characteristics. If you meet a woman in a wheelchair, try not to define her only in terms of her disability. Rather, make the effort to learn who she really is. She may be an accounting major, a daughter, and a mother. She may love baseball, politics, and science fiction novels. These characteristics—not her wheelchair—describe who she is.

Cultivate relationships with people of different cultures, races, perspectives, and ages. Through personal experience and reading, find out how other people live and think, and see what you can learn from them. Then, take concrete actions: Choose a study partner from a different ethnic or racial background. Go to synagogue with a Jewish friend; go to a mosque with a Muslim friend. If you are uncomfortable doing this, start by respecting people who are different from you and allowing them to live peacefully and privately.

Explore who you are. Learn about your personal ethnic and cultural heritage by talking with family and reading. Then, share your knowledge with others.

Learn from history. Read about the atrocities of slavery, the Holocaust, and the "ethnic cleansing" in Kosovo. Cherish your freedom and seek continual improvement at home and in the world.

Be sensitive to the needs of others. Ask yourself what you would feel and do if you were in another person's shoes.

Help others in need. Newspaper columnist Sheryl McCarthy wrote about an African-American who, in the midst of the 1992 Los Angeles riots, saw an Asian-American man being beaten and helped him to safety: "When asked why he risked grievous harm to save an Asian man he didn't even know, the African-American man said, 'Because if I'm not there to help someone else, when the mob comes for me, will there be someone there to save me?'"[6] Continue the cycle of kindness.

Take personal responsibility. Avoid blaming problems on people who are different from you.

Recognize that people everywhere have the same basic needs. Everyone loves, thinks, hurts, hopes, fears, and plans. Strive to find out what is special about others instead of how they fit your preconceived idea of who they are. People are united through their essential humanity.

Encountering Others Who Are Prejudiced

What should you do when someone you know makes prejudiced remarks or takes actions that discriminate against you or others? It can be hard to stand up to someone and risk a confrontation, even though right—and the law—are on your side. You may choose to say nothing, make a small comment, or get help. If you approach an authority, start with the person who can most directly affect the situation—an instructor or supervisor. At each decision stage, weigh all of the positive and negative effects that are possible as a result of your action and evaluate whether the action is wise for you and others.

It is everyone's responsibility to sound the alarm on hate crimes. Let the authorities know if you suspect that a crime is about to occur. Join campus protests. Express your opinion by writing letters to the editor of your school newspaper and attend lectures sponsored by the Anti-Defamation League and other organizations that encourage acceptance and tolerance.

How can minority students *make the most* of college?

Who fits into the category of "minority student" at your school? The term *minority* includes students of color; students who are not part of the majority Christian religions; and gay, lesbian, and bisexual students. However, even for members of these groups, there is no universal "minority" experience. Each person's experiences are filtered through the lens of his or her background.

Most colleges have special organizations and support services that center on minority groups. Among these are specialized student associations, cultural centers, arts groups with a minority focus, residence halls for minority students, minority fraternities and sororities, and political-action groups. Your level of involvement with these groups depends on whether you are comfortable within a community of students who share your background or whether you want to extend your social connections.

Define Your Experience

When you start school and know no one, it's natural to gravitate to people with whom you share common ground. You may choose to live with a roommate from the same background, sit next to other minority students in class, and attend minority-related social events and parties. However, if you define your *entire* college experience by these ties, you may be making a choice that limits your understanding of others, thereby limiting your opportunities for growth.

Many minority students adopt a balanced approach, involving themselves in activities with members of their group, as well as with the college mainstream. For example, a student may be a member of the African-American Students Association and also join clubs for all students such as the campus newspaper or an athletic team. Such students believe that both worlds have much to offer.

To make choices as a minority student on campus, ask yourself these questions:

- Do I want to limit, as much as possible, my social interactions to people who share my background? How much time do I want to spend pursuing minority-related activities? Do I want to focus my studies on a minority-related field, such as African-American studies?
- Do I want to minimize my ties with my minority group and be "just another student"? Will I care if other minority students criticize my choices?
- Do I want to achieve a balance in which I spend part of my time among people who share my background and part with students from other groups?

You may feel pressured to make certain choices based on what your peers do—but if these decisions go against your gut feelings, they are almost always a mistake. Your choice should be right for you, especially because it will determine your college experiences. Plus, the attitudes and habits you develop now may have implications for the rest of your life—in your choice of friends, where you decide to live, your work, and even your family. Think long and hard about the path you take, and always follow your head and heart.

Understand Stereotype Vulnerability

Some minority students deal with the adjustment to college by distancing themselves from the qualities they think others associate with their group. In this phenomenon, called *stereotype vulnerability,* students avoid facing a problem because they think that admitting it perpetuates a group stereotype.[7] For example, an immigrant to the United States may resist tutoring in English for fear of seeming like just another foreigner. Such avoidance cuts people off from assistance and communication that could connect them with others and improve their lives.

In another side of stereotype vulnerability, people refuse help because they believe that these offerings are motivated by pity: "She considers me disadvantaged because I'm from Taiwan"; "He feels sorry for me because of my learning disability." These defensive responses are based on assumptions about what the other person is thinking. Frequently, the person who offers help has the honest desire to aid another human being.

If you see stereotype vulnerability in yourself, you may be trying to deny who you are in an attempt to fit into the larger culture. This inevitably brings trouble because the task you have set out to accomplish is impossible. Instead, if you need help, approach someone who can give it and allow that person to get to know you. The helper will see you not as a representative of a group but as an individual.

"I have a dream that one day on the red hills of Georgia the sons of former slaves and the sons of former slave owners will be able to sit down together at the table of brotherhood."

MARTIN LUTHER KING, JR.

The concept of diversity examined so far in this chapter has focused on the need to accept and embrace the multiculturalism that defines the United States and students' experiences in college. However, some forms of diversity are more subtle, including differences in the way people communicate. While one person may be direct and disorganized, another may be analytic and organized, and a third may hardly say a word. Just as there is diversity in skin color and ethnicity, there is also diversity in the way people communicate.

Accepting diversity includes accepting differences in communication style and working to understand them. This is especially important because successful relationships depend on effective communication. If you strive to express yourself clearly and interpret what others say in the way they intend, you can connect with people in all aspects of your life.

How can you *communicate* effectively?

lear spoken communication promotes success at school, at work, and in your personal relationships. Clarity comes from understanding communication styles, learning to give and receive criticism, becoming knowledgeable about body language, and developing techniques to solve specific communication problems.

Adjusting to Communication Styles

When you speak, your goal is for listeners to receive the message as you intended. Problems arise when one person has trouble "translating" a message that comes from someone with a different style of communication.

Your knowledge of the Personality Spectrum (see Chapter 2) will help you understand different styles of communication. Particular communication styles tend to accompany dominance in particular dimensions. Recognizing specific styles in yourself and others will help you communicate more effectively.

Identifying Your Styles

Following are some communication styles that tend to be associated with the four dimensions in the Personality Spectrum. No one style is better than another. Successful communication depends on understanding your personal style and becoming attuned to the styles of others.

Thinker-dominant communicators focus on facts and logic. As speakers, they tend to rely on logic to communicate ideas and prefer quantitative concepts to those that are conceptual or emotional. As listeners, they often do best with logical messages. They may also need time to process what they have heard before responding. Written messages—on paper or via e-mail—are often useful because writing can allow for time to put ideas together logically.

Organizer-dominant communicators focus on structure and completeness. As speakers, they tend to deliver well-thought-out, structured messages that fit into an organized plan. As listeners, they often appreciate a well-organized message that has tasks defined in clear, concrete terms. As with Thinkers, a written format is often an effective form of communication to or from an Organizer.

Giver-dominant communicators focus on concern for others. As speakers, they tend to cultivate harmony and work toward closeness in their relationships. As listeners, they often appreciate messages that emphasize personal connection and address the emotional side of the issue. Whether speaking or listening, they often favor direct, in-person interaction over written messages.

Adventurer-dominant communicators focus on the present. As speakers, they tend to convey a message as soon as the idea arises and then move on to the next activity. As listeners, they appreciate up-front, short, direct messages that don't get sidetracked. Like Givers, they tend to communicate and listen more effectively in person.

Use this information not as a label but as a jumping-off point for your self-exploration. Just as people tend to demonstrate characteristics from more than one Personality Spectrum dimension, communicators may demonstrate different styles. Think about the communication styles associated with your dominant Personality Spectrum dimensions. Consider, too, how you tend to communicate and how others generally respond to you. Are you convinced only in the face of logical arguments? Are you attuned most to feelings? Use what you discover to get a better idea of what works best for you.

Speakers Adjust to Listeners

Listeners may interpret messages in ways you never intended. Think about how you can address this problem as you read the following example involving a Giver-dominant instructor and a Thinker-dominant student (the listener):

> Instructor: "Your essay didn't communicate any sense of your personal voice."
>
> Student: "What do you mean? I spent hours writing it. I thought it was on the mark."

- *Without adjustment:* The instructor ignores the student's need for detail and continues to generalize. Comments like, "You need to elaborate. Try writing from the heart. You're not considering your audience," will probably confuse and discourage the student.

- *With adjustment:* Greater logic and detail will help. For example, the instructor might say: "You've supported your central idea clearly, but you didn't move beyond the facts into your interpretation of what they mean. Your essay reads like a research paper. The language doesn't sound like it is coming directly from you."

Listeners Adjust to Speakers

As a listener, you can improve understanding by being aware of stylistic differences and translating the message into one that makes sense to you. The following example of an Adventurer-dominant employee speaking to an Organizer-dominant supervisor shows how adjusting can pay off.

> Employee: "I'm upset about the e-mail you sent me. You never talked to me and just let the problem build into a crisis. I don't feel I've had a chance to defend myself."

- *Without adjustment:* If the supervisor is annoyed by the employee's insistence on direct personal contact, he or she may become defensive: "I told you clearly what needs to be done, and my language wasn't a problem. I don't know what else there is to discuss."

- *With adjustment:* In an effort to improve communication, the supervisor responds by encouraging the in-person, real-time exchange that is best for the employee. "Let's meet after lunch so you can explain to me how we can improve the situation."

Using techniques corresponding to your stronger intelligences boosts your communication skills both as a speaker and as a listener.

INTELLIGENCE	SUGGESTED STRATEGIES	WHAT WORKS FOR YOU? WRITE NEW IDEAS HERE
Verbal–Linguistic	■ Find opportunities to express your thoughts and feelings to others—either in writing or in person. ■ Remind yourself that you have two ears and only one mouth. Listening is more important than talking.	
Logical–Mathematical	■ Allow yourself time to think through solutions before discussing them—try writing out a logical argument on paper and then rehearsing it orally. ■ Accept the fact that others may have communication styles that vary from yours and that may not seem logical.	
Bodily–Kinesthetic	■ Have an important talk while walking or performing a task that does not involve concentration. ■ Work out physically to burn off excess energy before having an important discussion.	
Visual–Spatial	■ Make a drawing or diagram of points you want to communicate during an important discussion. ■ If your communication is in a formal classroom or work setting, use visual aids to explain your main points.	
Interpersonal	■ Observe how you communicate with friends. If you tend to dominate the conversation, brainstorm ideas about how to communicate more effectively. ■ Remember to balance speaking with listening.	
Intrapersonal	■ When you have a difficult encounter, take time alone to evaluate what happened and to decide how you can communicate more effectively next time. ■ Remember that, in order for others to understand clearly, you may need to communicate more than you expect to.	
Musical	■ Play soft music during an important discussion if it helps you, making sure it isn't distracting to the others involved.	
Naturalistic	■ Communicate outdoors if that is agreeable to all parties. ■ If you have a difficult exchange, imagine how you might have responded differently had it taken place outdoors.	

Although adjusting to communication styles helps you speak and listen more effectively, you also need to understand the nature of criticism and learn to handle criticism as a speaker and listener.

Constructive and Nonconstructive Criticism

Criticism can be either constructive or nonconstructive. *Constructive criticism* involves goodwill suggestions for improvement, promoting the hope that things will be better. In contrast, *nonconstructive criticism* focuses on what went wrong, doesn't offer alternatives or help, and is often delivered negatively, creating bad feelings and defensiveness.

Consider a case in which someone has continually been late to study group sessions. The group leader can comment in either of these ways:

- *Constructive.* The group leader talks privately with the student: "I've noticed that you've been late a lot. Because our success depends on what each of us contributes, we are all depending on your contribution. Is there a problem that is keeping you from being on time? Can we help?"

- *Nonconstructive.* The leader watches the student arrive late and says, in front of everyone, "Nice to see you could make it. If you can't start getting here on time, we might look for someone else who can."

Which comment would encourage you to change your behavior? When offered constructively and carefully, criticism can help bring about important changes.

While at school, your instructors will constructively criticize your class work, papers, and exams. On the job, constructive criticism comes primarily from supervisors and coworkers. No matter the source, positive comments can help you grow as a person. Be open to what you hear, and always remember that most people want to help you succeed.

Offering Constructive Criticism

When offering constructive criticism, use the following strategies to be effective:

- *Criticize the behavior rather than the person.* Avoid personal attacks—they inevitably result in defensive behavior. In addition, make sure that a behavior is within a person's power to change. Chronic lateness can be changed if the person has poor time-management skills; it can't be changed if a physical disability slows the person down.

- *Define specifically the behavior that bothers you.* Focus on the facts. Substantiate with specific examples and avoid emotions. Avoid dragging in other complaints. People can hear criticisms better if they are discussed one at a time.

- *Suggest new approaches.* Talk about different ways of handling the situation. Help the person see options he or she may have never considered.

- *Use a positive approach and hopeful language.* Express the conviction that changes will occur and that the person can turn the situation around.

CONSTRUCTIVE
Promoting improvement or development.

- *Stay calm and be brief.* Avoid threats, ultimatums, or accusations. Use "I" messages that help the person see how his or her actions are affecting you.
- *Offer help in changing the behavior.* Do what you can to make the person feel supported.

Receiving Criticism

When you find yourself on criticism's receiving end, use the following techniques:

- *Use critical thinking to analyze the comments.* Listen carefully, and then carefully evaluate what you heard. Does it come from a desire to help or from jealousy or frustration? Try to let nonconstructive comments go without responding.
- *If the feedback is constructive, ask for suggestions on how to change your behavior.* Ask, "How would you like me to handle this in the future?"
- *Summarize the criticism and your response to it.* Make sure everyone understands the situation in the same way.
- *Plan a specific strategy.* Decide how to change and take concrete steps to make it happen.

Criticism, as well as other thoughts and feelings, may be communicated through nonverbal communication. You will become a more effective communicator if you understand what body language may be saying.

The Role of Body Language

Considered by many to be the most "honest" form of communication because of its capacity to express people's real feelings, body language often reveals a great deal though gestures, eye movements, facial expressions, body positioning and posture, touching behaviors, vocal tone, and use of personal space. Although reading body language is far from an exact science, understanding its basics will help you use it to your advantage as you speak and listen.

Figure 9.3 shows examples of body language that are associated with specific meanings in our culture. Keep in mind that culture influences how body language is interpreted. For example, in the United States, looking away from someone may be a sign of anger or distress; in Japan, the same behavior is usually a sign of respect.

How Body Language Works

Here are some important principles of body language.

Nonverbal communication strongly influences first impressions. First impressions emerge from a combination of verbal and nonverbal cues. Nonverbal elements, including tone of voice, posture, eye contact, and speed and style of movement, usually come across first and strongest.

Figure 9.3 Body language provides possible communication clues.

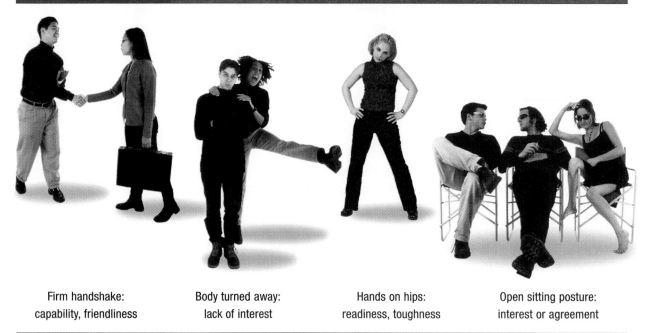

| Firm handshake: | Body turned away: | Hands on hips: | Open sitting posture: |
| capability, friendliness | lack of interest | readiness, toughness | interest or agreement |

Body language can reinforce or contradict verbal statements. When you greet a friend with a smile and a strong handshake, your body language reinforces your words of welcome. When, on the other hand, your body language contradicts your words, your body generally tells the real story. For example, if right before finals a friend asks how you feel, a response of "fine" is confusing if your arms are folded tightly across your chest and your eyes are averted. These cues communicate tension, not well-being.

Nonverbal cues shade meaning. The statement, *"This is the best idea I've heard all day,"* can mean different things depending on vocal tone. Said sarcastically, the words may mean that the speaker considers the idea a joke. In contrast, the same words said while sitting with your arms and legs crossed and looking away may communicate that you dislike the idea, but are unwilling to say so. Finally, if you maintain eye contact and take the receiver's hand while speaking, you may be communicating that the idea is close to your heart.

Nonverbal cues may reveal a lie. Signs that a lie is being told include behaviors that end as soon as the lie ends (the speaker stops fidgeting, averting her glance, or licking her lips), unusual vocal qualities (changes in vocal tone and sentence structure), and jabbering (an unconscious attempt to hide a lie in a load of information).

Using Body Language to Your Advantage

The following strategies will help you maximize your awareness of body language so that you can use it—as a speaker and a listener—to your advantage.

Become aware. Pay attention to what other people are really saying through their nonverbal cues and to what you communicate through your own cues.

Match your words with your body language. Try to monitor your personal body language when you deliver important messages. For example, if you really want to communicate satisfaction to an instructor, look the instructor in the eye and speak enthusiastically.

Note cultural differences. Cultural factors influence how nonverbal cues are interpreted. For example, in Arab cultures, causal acquaintances stand close together when speaking, while in the United States, the same distance is reserved for intimate conversation. Similarly, in the United States, people get right down to business in meetings, while in Asian cultures, business is preceded by personal conversation that builds trust and relationships.[8] With any cross-cultural conversation, you can discover what seems appropriate by paying attention to what the other person does on a consistent basis.

No matter how much you know about verbal and nonverbal communication, you will still encounter communication problems. Here are strategies for solving some common ones.

Solving Communication Problems

Although every communication situation is different, many communication problems have common threads that are easy to identify. As you study the problems described next, think about whether you are "guilty" of any of them. If you are, try applying these strategic fixes.

ASSERTIVE

Able to declare and affirm one's own opinions while respecting the rights of others to do the same.

Problem: Being too passive or aggressive in the way you communicate.
Solution: Take the middle ground. Be assertive.

No matter what your dominant learning styles, you tend to express yourself in one of three ways—through *aggressive, passive,* and *assertive communication.* The assertive style will help you communicate in the clearest, most productive way. Assertive communicators are likely to get their message across without attacking others or sacrificing their own needs, while still giving listeners the opportunity to speak.

In contrast, aggressive communicators focus primarily on their own needs. They can become angry and impatient when those needs are not immediately satisfied. Passive communicators deny themselves power by focusing almost exclusively on the needs of others, often experiencing unexpressed frustration and tension in the process.

Table 9.3 compares the characteristics of these communicators. Assertive behavior strikes a balance between aggression and passivity.

To become more assertive, aggressive communicators should take time before speaking, use "I" statements that accept personal responsibility, listen to others, and avoid giving orders. Similarly, passive

Table 9.3   Assertiveness fosters clear communication.

AGGRESSIVE	PASSIVE	ASSERTIVE
Loud, heated arguing	Concealing one's own feelings	Expressing feelings without being nasty or overbearing
Physically violent encounters	Denying one's own anger	Acknowledging emotions but staying open to discussion
Blaming, name-calling, and verbal insults	Feeling that one has no right to express anger	Expressing oneself and giving others the chance to express themselves equally
Walking out of arguments before they are resolved	Avoiding arguments	Using "I" statements to defuse arguments
Being demanding: "Do this"	Being noncommittal: "You don't have to do this unless you really want to . . ."	Asking and giving reasons: "I would appreciate it if you would do this, and here's why . . ."

communicators who want to become more assertive might try to acknowledge anger or hurt, express opinions, exercise their right to make requests, and know that their ideas and feelings are important.

Problem: Attacking the receiver.
Solution: Send "I" messages.

When a conflict arises, often the first instinct is to pinpoint what someone else did wrong. Unfortunately, accusations put others on the defensive as they shut down communication.

"I" messages help you communicate your needs rather than attacking someone else. Creating these messages involves nothing more than some simple rephrasing: "You didn't lock the door!" becomes "I felt uneasy when I came to work and the door was unlocked." Similarly, "You never called last night" becomes "I was worried about you when I didn't hear from you last night."

"Do not use a hatchet to remove a fly from your friend's forehead."

CHINESE PROVERB

"I" statements soften the conflict by highlighting the effects that the other person's actions have on you, rather than focusing on the person or the actions themselves. When you focus on your own responses and needs, your receiver may feel freer to respond, perhaps offering help and even acknowledging mistakes.

Problem: Choosing bad times to communicate.
Solution: Be sensitive to the cues in your environment.

When you have something to say, choose a time when you can express yourself clearly. Spoken too soon, ideas can come out sounding nothing like you intended. Left simmering too long, your feelings can spill over into other issues. Rehearsing mentally or talking your thoughts through with a friend can help you choose the most effective strategy, words, and tone.

Good timing also requires sensitivity to your listener. Even a perfectly worded message won't get through to someone who isn't ready to receive it. If you try to talk to your instructor when she is rushing out the door, she won't pay attention to what you are saying. If a classmate calls to discuss a project while you are cramming for an exam, his point will be lost. Pay attention to mood as well. If a friend had an exhausting week, it's smart to wait before asking a favor.

The way you communicate has a major impact on your relationships with friends and family. Successful relationships are built on self-knowledge, good communication, and hard work.

How do you make the most of *personal* relationships?

Personal relationships with friends, classmates, spouses and partners, and parents can be sources of great satisfaction and inner peace. Relationships have the power to motivate you to do your best in school, on the job, and in life.

When things go wrong with relationships, however, nothing in your world may seem right. You may be unable to eat, sleep, or concentrate. Because of this, relationship strategies can be viewed as all-around survival strategies that add to your mental health. Sigmund Freud, the father of modern psychiatry, defined mental health as the ability to love and to work.

Use Positive Relationship Strategies

Here are some strategies for improving your personal relationships.

Make personal relationships a high priority. Life is meant to be shared. In some marriage ceremonies, the bride and groom share a cup of wine, symbolizing that the sweetness of life is doubled by tasting it together and the bitterness is cut in half when shared by two.

Invest time. You devote time to education, work, and sports. Relationships benefit from the same investment. In addition, spending time with people you like can relieve stress.

Spend time with people you respect and admire. Life is too short to hang out with people who bring you down or encourage you to do things that go against your values. Develop relationships with people whose choices you admire and who inspire you to fulfill your potential.

If you want a friend, be a friend. If you treat others with the kind of loyalty and support that you appreciate yourself, you are likely to receive the same in return.

Work through tensions. Negative feelings can fester when left unspoken. Instead of facing a problem, you may become angry about something else or irritable in general. Get to the root of a problem by discussing it, compromising, forgiving, and moving on.

Take risks. It can be frightening to reveal your deepest dreams and frustrations, to devote yourself to a friend, or to fall in love. However, if you open yourself up, you stand to gain the incredible benefits of companionship, which for most people outweigh the risks.

Don't force yourself into a pattern that doesn't suit you. Some students date exclusively and commit early. Some students prefer to socialize in groups. Some students date casually. Be honest with yourself—and others—about what you want in a relationship, and don't let peer pressure change your mind.

Keep personal problems in their place. Try to separate your problems from your schoolwork. Mixing the two may hurt your performance, while doing nothing to solve your problem.

If a relationship fails, find ways to cope. When an important relationship becomes strained or breaks up, use coping strategies to help you move on. Some people need time alone; others need to be with friends and family. Some seek counseling. Some throw their energy into school or exercise. Some cry. Whatever you do, believe that in time you will emerge from the experience stronger.

PERSONAL TRIUMPH

*m*aking a connection with others can be difficult, especially if you start out feeling exceptionally different. Gustavo Minaya spoke no English when he came to a completely unfamiliar United States as a child. Through learning and getting involved in activities, he has found his niche.

I am native of Peru. When I was six years old, my mother told me that we were going to America for a better life. My father was already living in the United States, so my mother went to the embassy to apply for a visa, but our visa was denied. In desperation, she decided to hire "coyotes." These are people who know secret routes to the United States. Their job was to help us cross the border.

Our journey began at night with cold train rides. At different points, we stopped to eat or to get on a different train. Along the way, other families joined us. At the Mexico–Texas border, the "coyotes" instructed us to walk under a highway. Once we were out again in the open, everyone began running for the U.S. border. Helicopters were circling overhead with their search lights on, and people were shouting. It was pandemonium.

Exhausted, we made it across the border and onto a van, where people were stacked on top of each other. At another border check, my mother and I were arrested and taken into custody by immigration officers who took our fingerprints. They arranged to have us transported to an emergency shelter run by the American Red Cross. Meanwhile, my Dad completed the paperwork for legal immigration, and we joined him a few months later.

Of course, I didn't know English. When I started school in the second grade, I looked different than the other kids, and I sounded different because of my accent. Some of the kids picked on me. I cried a lot back then. The next year, I took English as a Second Language (ESL) classes. Gradually, I learned English and began to feel like I fit in.

Gustavo Minaya, Freshman, Business Administration;
Essex Community College, Baltimore, Maryland

When I look back over my experiences, I believe the one thing that has helped me adjust to the changes is friendliness. I like to make people laugh, and I go into things with a positive attitude. Being friendly with other students, and people in general, has helped me gain a sense of belonging.

My main advice to international students who want to make the most of their education is to participate in campus activities. You can join a club or work on campus, maybe at the school store or library. This way you meet new people, and you'll learn English faster. You can't fit in if you isolate yourself.

Participation is also important for developing leadership skills. I look at clubs and other campus activities as opportunities to enhance my education. For example, I joined the International Student Association (ISA) and am now the president. During the meetings, I give my ideas and show my support by volunteering for projects. I've discovered that one of my strengths is bringing people together for a good cause.

I'm very proud of my parents for how hard they worked to make a better life for me and my brothers and sisters. In my native country of Peru, you can work as hard as you want, but it gets you nowhere. Some of the smartest people there are taxicab drivers because they can't find jobs doing anything else. Here, if you are willing to work, you can have a profession and achieve what you want. I plan to achieve as much as I can.

Take a moment to consider . . .

- *What important opportunity you feel that living in this country offers you, whether you are an immigrant or native-born.*

- *How you plan to "gain a sense of belonging" at your school.*

Choose Communities That Enhance Your Life

Personal relationships often take place in the context of communities, or groups, that include people who share your interests—for example, martial arts groups, bridge clubs, sororities, fraternities, athletic teams, political groups, etc. It is common to have ties to several communities, often with one holding your greatest interest.

Try to affiliate with communities that are involved in life-affirming activities. You will surround yourself with people who are responsible and character-rich and who may be your friends and professional colleagues for the rest of your life. You may find among them your future husband, wife, or partner; best friend; the person who helps you land your first job; your doctor, accountant, real estate agent, and so on. So much of what you accomplish in life is linked to your network of personal contacts, so start now to make positive connections.

If you find yourself drawn toward communities that are negative and even harmful, such as groups that haze pledges or gangs, stop and think before you get in too deep. Be aware of cliques that bring out negative qualities including aggression, hate, and superiority. Use critical thinking to analyze why you are drawn to these groups. In many people, fears and insecurities spur these relationships. Look into yourself to understand the attraction and to resist the temptation to join. If you are already involved and want out, believe in yourself and be determined. Never consider yourself a "victim."

The biggest threat to personal relationships is conflict, which can result in anger and even violence. With effort, you can manage conflict successfully—and stay away from those who cannot.

How can you handle *conflict?*

onflicts, both large and small, arise when there is a clash of ideas or interests. You may have small conflicts with a housemate over a door left unlocked or a sink filled with dirty dishes. You may have major conflicts with your partner about finances or with an instructor about a failing grade. Conflict, as unpleasant as it can be, is a natural element in the dynamic of getting along with others. No relationship is conflict free.

Conflict Resolution Strategies

When handled poorly, conflicts create anger and frustration. All too often, people deal with these negative feelings through avoidance (a passive tactic that shuts down communication) or escalation (an aggressive tactic that often leads to fighting). Avoidance doesn't make the problem go away—in fact, it often makes things worse—and a shouting match destroys the opportunity to problem solve.

Conflict resolution strategies use calm communication and critical thinking to avoid extreme reactions. Think through the conflicts in your relationships by using what you know about problem solving (see Chapter 4):

1. *Identify and analyze the problem.* Determine the severity of the problem by looking at its effects on everyone involved. Then, find and analyze its causes.

2. *Brainstorm possible solutions.* Consider as many angles as you can, without judgment. Try to apply what you did in similar situations.

3. *Explore each solution.* Evaluate each solution, including its possible benefits and risks. Look at options from the perspective of others as you try to determine which would cause the least stress. Make sure everyone has a chance to express an opinion.

4. *Choose, carry out, and evaluate the solution you decide is best.* Translate the solution into actions, and then evaluate what happens. Decide whether you made the best choice, and make mid-course corrections, if necessary.

Your efforts to resolve conflict will work only if you begin with good will and motivation. Also needed is a determination to focus on the problem rather than on placing blame. All people get angry at times—at people, events, and themselves. However, excessive anger—out-of-control, loud, irrational, and sometimes physical—has the power to contaminate relationships, stifle communication, and turn friends and family away.

Managing Anger

People who continually respond to disappointments and frustrations by shouting, cursing, or even physically lashing out find that emotions get in the way of personal happiness and school success. It is hard to concentrate on American history when you are raging over being cut off in traffic. It is hard to focus during a study group if you can't let go of your anger with a group member who forgot a book.

For years, psychologists believed that venting your anger—letting it all hang out—would help you deal with your feelings even if you hurt others in the process. They now realize that instead of helping, bouts of uncontrolled rage intensify your aggression as you increasingly lose control. Angry outbursts do nothing to resolve problems and may actually make things worse.

What can you do when you feel yourself losing control or when anger turns into rage that you just can't drop? First, remember that it doesn't help to explode. Then, try one of these anger-management techniques until you calm down.

Relax. Calm down by breathing deeply while slowly repeating a calming word or phrase, such as "Take it easy" or "It's just not worth it" or "Relax."

Try to change the way you process what is happening. Instead of reacting to the frustration of being closed out of a course by cursing and yelling, change the way you think. Say to yourself, "I'm frustrated and upset, but it's not the end of the world. I'll talk to my advisor about taking the course next semester. And besides, getting angry is not going to get me a seat in the class."

Change your environment. Take a walk, go to the gym, see a movie. Take a break from what's upsetting you. Try to build break time into your daily schedule. You'll decompress from the pressures of school and be better able to handle problems without blowing up.

Change your language. Language can inflame anger, so turn your language down a notch. Instead of barking orders to your lab partner, such as "Hand me the flask right now or my experiment will be ruined," calmly say, "My experiment is at a crucial point. Thanks for handing me the flask as soon as you can." The person to whom you are talking is more likely to do what you ask if you stay in control.

Think before you speak. When angry, most people tend to say the first thing that comes to mind, even if it's mean. Inevitably, this escalates the hard feelings and the intensity of the argument. Instead, count to 10—slowly—if necessary, until you are in control.

Try not to be defensive. No one likes to be criticized, and it's natural to respond by fighting back. It's also self-defeating. Instead, try to hear the message that's behind the criticism. Ask questions to make sure you understand the other person's point. If you focus on the problem—and if the other person works with you—anger will take a back seat.

Do your best to solve a problem, but remember that not all problems can be solved. Analyze a challenging situation, make a plan, resolve to do your best, and begin. If you fall short, you will know you did all you could and be less likely to turn your frustration into anger.

Get help if you can't keep your anger in check. If you try these techniques and still find yourself lashing out, you may need the help of a counselor. Many schools have licensed mental health professionals available to students, but it's up to you to set up an appointment (see Quick Start to College).

Anger directed primarily at women sometimes takes the form of sexual harassment. When this anger turns violent, it involves partners in destructive relationships. Anger also fuels rape, including date rape.

Sexual Harassment

The facts. Sexual harassment covers a wide range of behavior, divided into the following types:

• *Quid pro quo harassment* refers to a request for some kind of sexual favor or activity in exchange for something else. It is a kind of bribe or threat. ("If you don't do X for me, I will fail you/fire you/make your life miserable.")

• *Hostile environment harassment* indicates any situation where sexually charged remarks, behavior, or displayed items cause discomfort. Harassment of this type ranges from lewd conversation or jokes to the display of pornography.

Both men and women can be victims of sexual harassment, although the most common targets are women. Sexist attitudes can create an environment in which men feel they have the right to make statements that degrade women. Even though physical violence is not involved, the fear and mental trauma associated with harassment are harmful.

How to cope. If you feel degraded by anything that goes on at school or work, address the person who you believe is harassing you. If you are uncomfortable doing that, speak to an authority. Try to avoid assumptions—perhaps the person is unaware that the behavior is offensive. On the other hand, the person may know exactly what is going on and even enjoy your discomfort. Either way, you are entitled to ask the person to stop.

Violence in Relationships

The facts. Violent relationships among students are increasing. Here are some chilling statistics from the Corporate Alliance to End Partner Violence, a Bloomington, Illinois-based advocacy group.[9]

• One in five college students has experienced and reported at least one violent incident while dating, from being slapped to more serious violence.

• In three out of four violent relationships, problems surface after the couple has dated for a while.

• In six out of ten cases, drinking and drugs are associated with the violence.

Women in their teens and twenties, who make up the majority of women in college, are more likely to be victims of domestic violence than older women. There are a number of reasons for this, says law professor and domestic violence expert Sally Goldfarb. First, many college students accept traditional sex roles that place the woman in a subservient position. Second, when trouble occurs, students are likely to turn to friends, rather than professional counselors or the law. Third, peer pressure makes them uneasy about leaving the relationship; they would rather be abused than alone. And finally, because of their inexperience in dating, they may believe that violent relationships are "normal."[10]

How to cope. Start by recognizing the warning signs of impending violence including possessive, jealous, and controlling behavior; unpredictable mood swings; personality changes associated with alcohol and drugs; and outbursts of anger. If you see a sign, think about ending the relationship.

If you are being abused, your safety and sanity depend on seeking help. Call a shelter or abuse hotline and talk to someone who understands. Seek counseling at your school or at a community center. If you need medical attention, go to a clinic or hospital emergency room. If you believe that your life is in danger, get out. Then, get a restraining order that requires your abuser to stay away from you.

Rape and Date Rape

The facts. Any intercourse or anal or oral penetration by a person against another person's will is defined as rape. Rape is primarily a controlling, violent act of rage, not a sexual act.

Rape, especially acquaintance rape or date rape, is a problem on many campuses. Any sexual activity during a date that is against one partner's will constitutes date rape, including situations where one partner is too drunk or drugged to give consent. Currently appearing on campuses is a drug called Rohypnol, known as Roofies, that is sometimes used by date rapists to sedate their victims and is difficult to detect in a drink.

Campus Advocates for Rape Education (C.A.R.E.), an organization at Wheaton College, describes the collateral damage caused by date rape. "One's trust in a friend, date, or acquaintance is violated. As a result, a victim's fear, self-blame, guilt, and shame are magnified because the assailant is known."[11]

How to cope. Beware of questionable situations or drinks when on a date with someone you don't know well or who you suspect is unstable or angry. If you are raped, get medical attention immediately. Don't shower or change clothes; doing so destroys evidence. Next, talk to a close friend or counselor. Consider reporting the incident to the police or to campus officials, if it occurred on campus. Finally, consider pressing charges, especially if you can identify your assailant. Whether or not you take legal action, continue to get help through counseling, a rape survivor group, or a hotline.

DATE RAPE

Sexual assault perpetrated by the victim's escort during an arranged social encounter.

kente

The African word *kente* means "that which will not tear under any condition." *Kente* cloth is worn by men and women in African countries such as Ghana, Ivory Coast, and Togo. There are many brightly colored patterns of *kente,* each beautiful, unique, and special.

Think of how this concept applies to people. Like the cloth, all people are unique, with brilliant and subdued aspects. Despite mistreatment or misunderstanding by others, you need to remain strong so that you don't tear, allowing the weaker fibers of your character to show through. The *kente* of your character can help you endure, stand up against injustice, and fight peacefully, but relentlessly, for the rights of all people.

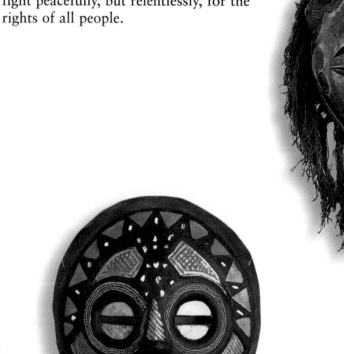

Building Skills
FOR COLLEGE, CAREER, AND LIFE SUCCESS

Critical Thinking *Applying Learning to Life*

Diversity Discovery

Express your own personal diversity. Describe yourself in response to the following questions:

How would you identify yourself? Write words or short phrases that describe you.

_____

_____

_____

Name one or more facts about yourself that would not be obvious to someone who just met you.

_____

_____

_____

Name two values or beliefs that govern how you live, what you pursue, or with whom you associate.

_____

_____

_____

Describe a particular choice you have made that tells something about who you are.

_____

_____

_____

Now, join with a partner in your class. Choose someone you don't know well. Your goal is to communicate what you have written to your partner and for your partner to communicate to you in the same way. Talk to each other for 10 minutes, and take notes on what the other person says. At the end of that period, join together as a class. Each person will describe his or her partner to the class.

Name something you learned about your partner that intrigued and even surprised you.

_____

_____

_____

What did you learn that went against any assumptions you may have made about that person?

_____

_____

_____

On your own time, reflect on how this exercise may have altered your perspective on yourself and others.

Handling Criticism Positively

Bring to mind one of two circumstances—either a time when someone offered criticism to you or you offered criticism to someone else. Write the *topic* of the criticism here. (For example, if you offered criticism to someone regarding how she treated a friend, you could write "behavior toward a friend" as the topic.)

_____

_____

_____

Now, whether the criticism was yours or not, put yourself in the shoes of the person offering the criticism. In the space below, write what you consider to be a constructive way of offering this criticism.

_____

_____

_____

Finally, compare your constructive criticism to what actually happened. Are they similar? If what you have written is an improvement, describe how, and discuss what you would have liked to have seen happen in the actual situation.

_____

_____

_____

Your Communication Style

Look back at the communication styles on pages 315–316. Write the two styles that fit you best.

1. _____

2. _____

Of these two styles, which one has more positive effects on your ability to communicate? What are those effects?

_____

_____

Which style has more negative effects?

_____

_____

Read the following sentences and circle the ones that sound like something you would say to a peer. Then go through the sentences again, marking each as either passive (use a P), aggressive (use an AG), or assertive (use an AS). Note what your circled sentences say about your tendencies.

_____ 1. Get me the keys.

_____ 2. Would you mind if I stepped out just for a second?

_____ 3. Don't slam the door.

_____ 4. I'd appreciate it if you would have this done by two o'clock. The client is coming at three.

_____ 5. I think maybe it needs a little work just at the end, but I'm not sure.

_____ 6. Please take this back to the library.

_____ 7. You will have a good time if you join us.

_____ 8. Your loss.

_____ 9. If you think so, I'll try it.

_____ 10. Let me know what you want me to do.

_____ 11. Turn it this way and see what happens.

_____ 12. We'll try both our ideas and see what works best.

_____ 13. I want it on my desk by the end of the day.

_____ 14. Just do what I told you.

_____ 15. If this isn't how you wanted it to look, I can change it. Just tell me and I'll do it.

- Aggressive communicators would be likely to use sentences 1, 3, 8, 13, and 14.
- Passive communicators would probably opt for sentences 2, 5, 9, 10, and 15.
- Assertive communicators would probably choose sentences 4, 6, 7, 11, and 12.

From which category did you choose the most sentences?

If you scored as an assertive communicator, you are on the right track. If you scored in the aggressive or passive categories, analyze your style. What are the effects? Give an example in your own life of the effects of your style.

Turn back to pages 321–322 to review suggestions for aggressive or passive communicators. What can you do to improve your skills?

Teamwork *Combining Forces*

PROBLEM SOLVING CLOSE TO HOME. Divide into small groups of two to five students. Assign one group member to take notes. Discuss the following questions, one by one:

1. What are the three largest problems my school faces with regard to how people get along with and accept others?
2. What could my school do to deal with these three problems?
3. What can each individual student do to deal with these three problems? (Talk about what you specifically feel that you can do.)

When all groups have finished, gather as a class and hear each group's responses. Observe the variety of problems and solutions. Notice whether more than one group came up with one or more of the same problems. If there is time, one person in the class, together with your instructor, could gather these responses into an organized document that you can give to administrators at your school.

Writing *Discovery Through Journaling*

To record your thoughts, use a separate journal or the lined page at the end of the chapter.

NEW PERSPECTIVE.[12] Imagine that you must change either your gender or your racial/ethnic group. Which would you change and why? What do you anticipate would be the positive and negative effects of the change—in your social life, in your family life, on the job, and at school?

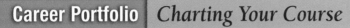

Career Portfolio | *Charting Your Course*

COMPILING A RÉSUMÉ. What you have accomplished in various work and school situations will be important for you to emphasize as you strive to land a job that is right for you. Whether on the job, in school, in the community, or at home, your roles help you gain knowledge and experience.

Use two pieces of paper. On one, list your education and skills information. On the other, list job experience. For each job, record job title, the dates of employment, and the tasks that this job entailed (if the job had no particular title, come up with one yourself). Be as detailed as possible—it's best to write down everything you remember. When you compile your résumé, you can make this material more concise. Keep this list current by adding experiences and accomplishments as you go along.

Using the information you have gathered and Figure 9.4 as your guide, draft a résumé for yourself. Remember that there are many ways to construct a résumé; consult other resources, such as those listed in the bibliography, for different styles. You may want to reformat your résumé according to a style that your career counselor or instructor recommends, that best suits the career area you plan to enter, or that you like best.

Keep your résumé draft on hand—and on a computer disk. When you need to submit a résumé with a job application, update the draft and print it out on high-quality paper.

Here are some general tips for writing a résumé:

- Always put your name and contact information at the top. Make it stand out.

- State an objective if it is appropriate—if your focus is specific or you are designing this résumé for a particular interview or career area.

- List your post-secondary education, starting from the latest and working backward. This may include summer school, night school, seminars, and accreditations.

- List jobs in reverse chronological order (most recent job first). Include all types of work experience (full-time, part-time, volunteer, internship, and so on).

- When you describe your work experience, use action verbs and focus on what you have accomplished, rather than on the description of assigned tasks.

- Have references listed on a separate sheet. You may want to put "References upon request" at the bottom of your résumé.

- Use formatting (larger font sizes, different fonts, italics, bolding, and so on) and indents selectively to help the important information stand out.

- Get several people to look at your résumé before you send it out. Other readers will have ideas that you haven't thought of and may pick up errors that you have missed.

Figure 9.4   **Sample résumé.**

Désirée Williams

237 Custer Street, San Francisco, CA 92017 • 650/555-5252 (w) or 415/555-7865 (h) • fax: 707/555-2735 • e-mail: desiree@zzz.com

EDUCATION

1999 to present   San Francisco State University, San Francisco, CA

Pursuing a B.A. in the Spanish BCLAD (Bilingual, Cross-Cultural Language Acquisition Development) Education and Multiple Subject Credential Program. Expected graduation: June, 2003

PROFESSIONAL EMPLOYMENT

10/00 to present   **Research Assistant, Knowledge Media Lab**

Developing ways for teachers to exhibit their inquiry into their practice of teaching in an online, collaborative, multimedia environment.

5/99 to present   **Webmaster/Web Designer**

Worked in various capacities at QuakeNet, an Internet Service Provider and Web Commerce Specialist in San Mateo, CA. Designed several sites for the University of California, Berkeley, Graduate School of Education, as well as private clients such as A Body of Work and Yoga Forever.

9/99 to 6/00   **Literacy Coordinator**

Coordinated, advised, and created literacy curriculum for an America Reads literacy project at Prescott School in West Oakland. Worked with non-reader 4th graders on writing and publishing, incorporating digital photography, Internet resources, and graphic design.

8/99   **Bilingual Educational Consultant**

Consulted for Children's Television Workshop, field-testing bilingual materials. With a research team, designed bilingual educational materials for an ecotourism project run by an indigenous rain forest community in Ecuador.

1/99 to 6/99   **Technology Consultant**

Worked with 24 Hours in Cyberspace, an on-line worldwide photojournalism event. Coordinated participation of schools, translated documents, and facilitated public relations.

SKILLS

Languages: Fluent in Spanish.
Proficient in Italian and Shona (majority language of Zimbabwe).

Computer: Programming ability in HTML, Javascript, Pascal, and Lisp. Multimedia design expertise in Adobe Photoshop, Netobjects Fusion, Adobe Premiere, Macromedia Flash, and many other visual design programs.

Personal: Perform professionally in Mary Schmary, a women's a cappella quartet. Have climbed Mt. Kilimanjaro.

Assess Yourself *Student Success Strategies*

If you have access to the CD-ROM Strategies for Success, *use the following questions to assess your thoughts and enhance your understanding of the chapter. The questions below represent only some of the activities provided on the CD for the chapter topics—try others if you have time.*

Click on the Relating to Others bookmark. Use the following activities to further develop your perspective on the people with whom you interact from day to day:

1. Take the pre-assessment to get an idea of your perspective on friendships and relationships.

2. Watch the video and consider the importance of self-knowledge and openness to your relationships. In the field provided, reflect on your perception of yourself since you made the transition to college.

3. Click on Activity One: Explore Your Cultural Background. Answer the questions in the activity to learn more about how your culture may influence how you communicate with others.

4. Take the post-assessment to reinforce what you have learned about relating to others.

Suggested Readings

Stephen D. Bertholf. *What Every College Age Woman Should Know About Relationships.* Wichita, KS: Abbey House Books, 1999.

Blank, Rennee and Sandra Slipp. *Voices of Diversity: Real People Talk About Problems and Solutions in a Workplace Where Everyone Is Not Alike.* New York: American Management Association, 1994.

Dublin, Thomas, ed. *Becoming American, Becoming Ethnic: College Students Explore Their Roots.* Philadelphia, PA: Temple University Press, 1996.

Feagin, Joe R., Hernan Vera and Nikitah O. Imani. *The Agony of Education: Black Students at White Colleges and Universities.* New York: Routledge, 1996.

Gonzales, Juan L., Jr. *The Lives of Ethnic Americans, 2nd ed.* Dubuque, IA: Kendall/Hunt, 1994.

Hockenberry, John. *Moving Violations.* New York: Hyperion, 1996.

Levey, Marc, Michael Blanco and W. Terrell Jones. *How to Succeed on a Majority Campus: A Guide for Minority Students.* Belmont, CA: Wadsworth Publishing Co., 1997.

Qubein, Nido R. *How to Be a Great Communicator: In Person, on Paper, and at the Podium.* New York: John Wiley, 1996.

Schuman, David and Dick W. Olufs. *Diversity on Campus.* Boston, MA: Allyn & Bacon, 1994.

Suskind, Ron. *A Hope in the Unseen: An American Odyssey from the Inner City to the Ivy League.* New York: Broadway Books, 1998.

Takaki, Ronald. *A Different Mirror: A History of Multicultural America.* Boston, MA: Little, Brown, 1994.

Tannen, Deborah. *You Just Don't Understand: Women and Men in Conversation.* New York: Ballantine Books, 1991.

Terkel, Studs. *Race: How Blacks and Whites Think and Feel About the American Obsession.* New York: Free Press, 1995.

Trotter, Tamera and Joycelyn Allen. *Talking Justice: 602 Ways to Build and Promote Racial Harmony.* Saratoga, FL: R & E Publishers, 1993.

Internet Resources

Prentice Hall Student Success Supersite (see success stories from students from a diversity of backgrounds): www.prenhall.com/success

Asian-American Resources: www.ai.mit.edu/people/irie/aar/

Britannica Guide to Black History: http://blackhistory.eb.com

Latino USA: www.latinousa.org

Latino Website Pathfinder: www.sscnet.ucla.edu.csrc/

The Sociology of Race and Ethnicity: www.trinity.edu/~mkearl/race.html

Endnotes

1. "For 7 Million, One Census Race Category Wasn't Enough," *The New York Times,* March 13, 2001, pp. A1 and A14.

2. Jodi Wilgoren, "Swell of Minority Students Is Predicted at Colleges," *The New York Times,* May 24, 2000, p. A16.

3. Sheryl McCarthy, *Why Are the Heroes Always White?* Kansas City, MO: Andrews and McMeel, 1995, p. 188.

4. "Campus Killings Fall, but Some Crimes Rise," *The New York Times,* January 21, 2001, p. A25.

5. Martin Luther King, Jr., from his sermon, "A Tough Mind and a Tender Heart," *Strength in Love.* Philadelphia: Fortress Press, 1986, p. 14.

6. Sheryl McCarthy, *Why Are the Heroes Always White?*, p. 137.

7. Claude Steele, Ph.D., Professor of Psychology, Stanford University.

8. Louis E. Boone, David L. Kurtz, and Judy R. Block, *Contemporary Business Communication.* Englewood Cliffs, NJ: Prentice Hall, 1994, pp. 49–54.

9. Much of the information in this section is from Tina Kelley, "On Campuses, Warnings About Violence in Relationships," *The New York Times,* February 13, 2000, p. 40.

10. Information in this section from Tina Kelley, "On Campuses, Warnings About Violence in Relationships," *The New York Times,* February 13, 2000, p. 40.

11. U.S. Department of Justice, Bureau of Justice Statistics, "Sex Offenses and Offenders," 1997, and "Criminal Victimization," 1994.

12. Adapted by Richard Bucher, Professor of Sociology, Baltimore City Community College, from Paula Rothenberg, William Paterson College of New Jersey.

JOURNAL

name   date

10

340

*W*ellness and stress management

AS RANDY UST (see next page) realizes, the ability to manage the stress of adjusting to college can mean the difference between a positive or negative college experience. How healthy you are in mind and body has a significant impact on how well you do in school. In this chapter, you examine both the physical and mental aspects of wellness, with particular attention paid to stress management. You learn approaches for maintaining your health and identifying and working through common health problems that students face. You also explore substance use and abuse and sexuality as they relate to your personal wellness.

IN THIS CHAPTER

taking care of yourself

Randy Ust, University of Mary, Bismarck, North Dakota

Tracy Ust, St. Cloud State University, St. Cloud, Minnesota

How can I deal with adjusting to college?

I started high school with my best friend since seventh grade, and our big plan was to star on the freshman basketball team. The after-school workouts paid off, and when we made the final cuts, we envisioned future NBA contracts. We started our sophomore year with the same dreams, ready for the next step toward stardom. After weeks of conditioning sessions, we felt like invincible heroes.

Our mortality hit me when in October of that year my friend went into cardiac arrest and passed away. For a while I isolated myself and didn't let friends get close, fearing that they, too, would leave me. After more than two years, I've opened up to people again, and my two best friends and I are like brothers. Now that we've graduated, though, the fear is back. It scares me to think that when we get to new places in life, we could grow apart. I know I will soon be in a new place meeting new friends. How do I adapt to the stress of being away from old friends and fitting into my college community?

Get involved . . . broaden your horizons and talk to people

Weeks before students move into their new residence hall rooms, a group of individuals (the Resident Advisors, or RAs) gather for comprehensive training. I am an RA. In training, we learn how to deal with any situation that may arise in the residence halls: fire alarms, alcohol and drug situations, roommate conflicts, and most importantly, making college feel like home for the residents. One of my first duties as an RA is to hold a floor meeting where I meet my residents, and they meet each other. I share with them these tips to help them reduce the stress of being in a new situation.

The most important thing I tell them is to get involved. Most colleges have hundreds of clubs and sports that anyone can join. Look for the clubs that interest you most. Playing a sport, whether at the intramural, club, or collegiate level, helps you meet people and get active. Try a couple of different things to see what you like most, but try not to overload yourself with activities and let your studies slack.

Another way to begin to fit in is to reach out to the people with whom you live. Keep your room doors open, go to planned activities together, and be friendly—others will be friendly back! You can also meet great people on campus. Talk to people while you are in line at the cafeteria, get to know your chemistry lab partners, sit next to someone new in the student union and introduce yourself. Broaden your horizons and talk to people different from yourself.

There are new things all around you in college—give them a try. Remember that your old friends are no more than a mouse click or a phone call away. They'll be there for you any time of the day—or night! Make sure you all make the effort to continue to be friends—it'll pay off. Finally, you can always ask your RA or other older students for advice. They will help you find ways to reduce stress and to feel a part of your new community, while you still keep in touch with friends from home.

How can you maintain a
healthy body?

M ake your health a priority. The healthier you are,
the more energy you'll have. Eating right, exercising,
getting enough sleep, being up to date on your vaccinations, and taking steps to stay safe will help keep you well. Start by
knowing yourself, and then apply critical thinking to your health and
wellness choices.

Eating Right

If you eat well, you are more likely to be strong and healthy. If you
take in too much fat, sugar, and calories, your body operates at reduced
power. Learning to make healthier choices about what you eat can lead
to more energy, better general health, and a better quality of life.

Medical and nutritional experts in the federal government publish
Dietary Guidelines for Americans, which lists seven important rules of
healthy eating:

1. Eat a variety of foods.
2. Maintain a healthy weight.
3. Choose a diet low in fat and cholesterol.
4. Choose a diet with plenty of vegetables, fruits, and grain products.
5. Use sugars in moderation.
6. Use salt and sodium only in moderation.
7. If you drink alcoholic beverages, do so in moderation.

Try to vary your diet by targeting different food groups—meats and
meat substitutes, dairy, breads and grains, and fruits and vegetables.
Figure 10.1 shows the servings recommended by the U. S. Department
of Agriculture.

Eat in Moderation to Avoid Obesity

Obesity is a problem of epidemic proportion in the United States. A common measure to determine obesity is the body mass index, which is
based on weight and height. If you have an index of 25, you are considered *overweight*. If your index is 30 or greater, you are probably carrying
30 or more extra pounds, and are considered *obese*. Government statistics indicate how widespread—and serious—obesity is[1]:

- The obese and the overweight make up the majority of the population with 55 percent of women and 63 percent of men currently
falling into these two groups.

- Between 1991 and 1999, obesity was up a startling 57 percent.
Twenty percent of Americans are now considered obese compared to
12 percent in 1991.

Figure 10.1 **Food guide pyramid.**

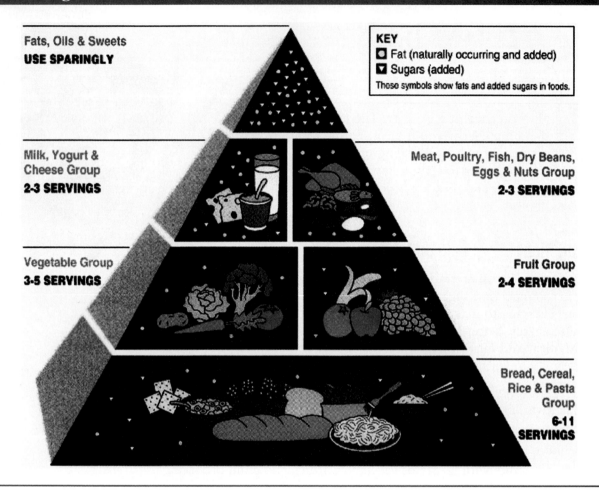

Fats, Oils & Sweets
USE SPARINGLY

KEY
☐ Fat (naturally occurring and added)
▼ Sugars (added)
These symbols show fats and added sugars in foods.

Milk, Yogurt &
Cheese Group
2-3 SERVINGS

Meat, Poultry, Fish, Dry Beans,
Eggs & Nuts Group
2-3 SERVINGS

Vegetable Group
3-5 SERVINGS

Fruit Group
2-4 SERVINGS

Bread, Cereal,
Rice & Pasta
Group
**6-11
SERVINGS**

Source: U. S. Department of Agriculture and the U. S. Department of Health and Human Services.

In most cases, obesity is caused by consuming more calories than your body needs. The tendency to gain weight increases if you spend too much time sitting—in front of the computer, in your car, on your couch—and if you eat foods loaded with calories and fat. Many college students, pressed for time, eat fast, fried, and fatty foods on the run. A daily diet like this quickly adds extra pounds.

Health officials have sounded the alarm on obesity because it is linked to an estimated 300,000 deaths a year. Obesity is a major risk factor in the development of adult-onset diabetes, coronary heart disease, high blood pressure, stroke, cancer, gallbladder disease, osteoarthritis, and sleep apnea and other respiratory conditions. *After smoking, obesity is the second leading cause of preventable death.* In addition, obese people may suffer social and employment discrimination and may find daily life difficult.

Whether you need to lose weight or not, you will benefit from paying attention to how you eat. Here are some tips to avoid gaining weight or to take off weight.

Keep a daily food log of everything you eat for a week. Your goal is a low-fat, low-calorie balanced diet (see Figure 10.1). Your food log will point to patterns that may explain a lack of energy or a weight gain.

Set specific, small goals that help you lose weight. Pledge to stop drinking soda and to give up French fries. Record your goals on paper so they become real.

Reduce portion size. A serving of cooked pasta is about one-half cup, for example, and cheddar cheese about 1.2 ounces. (The U.S. Department of Agriculture defines portion sizes based on a daily diet of 2,000 calories.) At restaurants, ask for a half portion or take home what you don't finish.

Read nutrition labels, focusing on calories as well as fat. Even if a product is described as "low fat" it may be loaded with sugar and therefore high in calories.

Make smart choices. Avoid fried foods, bake chicken without the skin, and use oils sparingly when you cook. If you have to eat out, choose foods like grilled chicken or salad, and limit your portions. Choose snacks with under 200 calories such as a frozen fruit juice bar or a container of low-fat fruit yogurt.

Plan your meals. Eat regularly and at the dining table, if possible. Try to minimize late-night eating sprees during study sessions. Avoid skipping meals—this may make you more likely to overeat later.

Move more. Studies have shown that people who are physically active while dieting lose up to seven pounds more than couch potatoes and are less likely to regain the weight. So, climb stairs instead of taking an elevator, park in the lot farthest from your classroom, and walk for pleasure.

Identify "emotional triggers" for your eating. If you eat for reasons other than physical hunger—for example, to relieve stress or handle disappointment—try substituting a positive activity. If you are upset about a course, spend more time studying, talk with your instructor, or write in your journal.

Don't expect perfection. If you sometimes indulge a craving for chocolate, for example, don't stress about it. Just refocus your energies on your goal.

"To keep the body in good health is a duty . . . Otherwise we shall not be able to keep our mind strong and clear."

BUDDHA

Set maintenance goals. Losing weight the healthy way takes time and patience; there are no quick fixes that last. Start by aiming to lose 5 to 10 percent of your current weight; for example, if you now weigh 200 pounds, your weight-loss goal is 10 to 20 pounds. Work toward your goal at a pace of approximately 1–2 pounds a week. When you reach it, set a new goal if you need to lose more, or begin a maintenance program.

As you diet, visualize success. See yourself making smart choices and being at a healthy weight. Finally, remember that your ultimate goal is to keep the weight off, not to lose it again and again.

Exercising

Being physically fit makes you healthier, adds energy for things that matter, and helps you handle stress. During physical activity, the brain releases endorphins, chemical compounds that have a positive and calming effect on the body.

For maximum benefit, make regular exercise a way of life. If you don't currently exercise, walking daily is a good way to begin. If you exercise frequently and are already in good shape, you may prefer an intense workout. Always check with a physician before beginning an exercise program, and adjust your program to your physical needs and fitness level.

Types of Exercise

There are three general categories of exercises. The type you choose depends on your exercise goals, available equipment, your time and fitness level, and other factors.

- *Cardiovascular training* strengthens your heart and lung capacity. Examples include running, swimming, in-line skating, aerobic dancing, and biking.
- *Strength training* strengthens different muscle groups. Examples include using weight machines and free weights and doing pushups and abdominal crunches.
- *Flexibility training* increases muscle flexibility. Examples include stretching and yoga.

Some exercises, such as lifting weights or biking, fall primarily into one category. Others combine elements of two or all three. For maximum benefit and a comprehensive workout, try alternating exercise methods through cross-training. For example, if you lift weights, also use a stationary bike for cardiovascular work. If possible, work with a fitness consultant to design an effective program.

CROSS-TRAINING
Alternating types of exercise and combining elements from different types of exercise.

Making Exercise a Priority

Student life, both in school and out, is crammed with responsibilities. You can't always spend two hours a day at the gym, and you may not have the money to join a health club. The following suggestions will help you make exercise a priority, even in the busiest weeks and on the tightest budgets:

- Walk to classes and meetings on campus. When you reach your building, use the stairs.
- Find out about using your school's fitness center.
- Do strenuous chores such as shoveling snow, raking, or mowing.
- Play team recreational sports at school or at a local YMCA.
- Use home exercise equipment such as weights, a treadmill, or a stair machine.
- Work out with a friend or family member to combine socializing and exercise.

Exercise is a key component of a healthy mind and body, as is adequate rest.

Getting Enough Sleep

During sleep, your body repairs itself while your mind sorts through problems and questions. A lack of sleep, or poor sleep, causes poor concentration and irritability, which can mean a less-than-ideal performance at school and at work. Irritability can also put a strain on personal relationships. Making up for lost sleep with caffeine may raise your stress level and leave you more tired than before.

On average, adults need about seven hours of sleep a night, but people in their late teens and early twenties may need eight to nine hours. Gauge your needs by how you feel. If you are groggy in the morning or doze off during the day, you may be sleep-deprived.

Barriers to a Good Night's Sleep

College students often get inadequate sleep. Long study sessions may keep you up late, and early classes get you up early. Socializing, eating, and drinking may make it hard to settle down. Some barriers to sleep are within your control, and some are not.

What is out of your control? Barriers such as outside noise may keep you up. Earplugs, playing relaxing music, or moving away from the noise (if you can) may help.

What is within your control? Late nights out, what you eat and drink, and your study schedule are often (although not always) within your power to change. Schedule your studying so that it doesn't pile up at the last minute. Avoid a late dinner the night before a big test. Respectfully ask the people you live with to keep the noise down when you need to rest. Be willing to do the same for them.

Tips for Quality Sleep

Sleep expert Gregg D. Jacobs recommends the following steps to better sleep:[2]

- *Reduce consumption of alcohol and caffeine.* Caffeine may keep you awake. Alcohol causes you to sleep lightly, making you feel less rested when you awaken.
- *Exercise regularly.* Regular exercise, especially in the afternoon or early evening, promotes sleep.
- *Complete tasks an hour or more before you sleep.* Getting things done well before you turn in gives you a chance to wind down.
- *Establish a comfortable sleeping environment.* Take a shower, change into comfortable sleepwear, turn down the lights and noise, find a comfortable blanket and pillow.

Adequate sleep also helps fight illnesses. Another way to prevent illness is to make sure your immunizations are up to date.

Reviewing Your Immunizations

Immunizations are not just for kids; adults often need them to prevent diseases in particular circumstances or because they didn't receive a full course of shots as children. Following is immunization information that may prevent major illness or literally save your life. If you think you need these vaccines, check with your doctor or the college health service:

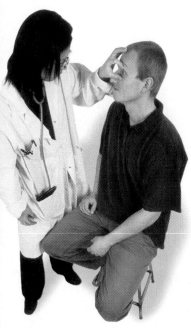

- Many colleges recommend that freshmen receive the *meningococcal meningitis vaccine* to prevent the spread of bacteria that can lead to permanent, serious disability and even death. Meningococcal bacteria are spread through direct contact (such as sharing a glass) or indirect contact (such as sneezing) with infected individuals. Outbreaks are linked to close living situations common in college.

- A *tetanus booster* is recommended every 10 years to protect you from bacterial infections related to certain wounds.

- Three shots to prevent *hepatitis B* are recommended in childhood. Vaccinations are recommended in college if you have not been immunized. Homosexuals and intravenous drug users are at increased risk.

- The *chicken pox vaccine* is recommended for any adult who did not have this illness as a child and who risks exposure. Chicken pox can be severe in adults.

A common illness, not protected by immunization, is *mononucleosis.* "Mono" is caused by a virus passed in saliva and is related to kissing and sharing glasses. Major symptoms, which can last for a few days or a few months, are fever, sore throat, swollen lymph glands, and fatigue. The only treatment is rest, fluids, and a balanced diet. Try to protect yourself by being careful in your close relationships with friends, family, and roommates.

Staying Safe

Staying safe is another part of staying well. Take steps to prevent incidents that jeopardize your well-being.

Avoid situations that present clear dangers. Don't walk or exercise alone at night or in neglected areas—travel with one or more people. Don't work or study alone in a building. If a person looks suspicious, contact someone who can help.

Avoid drugs or overuse of alcohol. Anything that impairs judgment makes you more vulnerable to assault. Avoid driving while impaired or being a passenger with someone who has taken drugs or alcohol.

Avoid people who make you uneasy. If a fellow student or coworker gives you bad vibrations, avoid situations that place you alone together. Speak to an instructor or supervisor if you feel threatened.

Communicate. Be clear about what you want from friends and acquaintances. Don't assume that others want what you want or even know what you want.

It is not enough to have a healthy body. Your well-being also depends on your mental health and, specifically, on your ability to manage stress.

How do you *manage stress?*

I f you are feeling more stress in your everyday life as a student, you are not alone.[3] Stress levels among college students have increased dramatically, according to an annual survey conducted at the University of California at Los Angeles. More than 30 percent of the freshmen polled at 683 two- and four-year colleges and universities nationwide reported that they frequently felt overwhelmed, almost double the rate in 1985.

Stress at College

What is responsible for the increased perception of stress among college freshmen? Here are some factors suggested by the UCLA researchers and others:

- *Being in a new environment,* where you may know few people and where you may be living away from home for the first time.

- *Facing increased work* compared to high school. The academic stakes have increased, instructors are often less "user friendly," and there is little room for coasting.

- *Facing critical decisions*—what courses to take, what to major in, your career focus, activities to join, whom to be friends with, how to evaluate the new ideas you are exposed to in school.

- *Juggling schoolwork and a job.* Nearly one in four students in the UCLA survey said that they expected to work full-time during school—a survey record. Many other students work part-time.

- *Concern about the future.* Many students realize that they will have to repay thousands of dollars in educational loans.

The Nature of Stress—It's About Change

Stress refers to the way in which your mind and body react to pressure— that is, increased workloads (a week of final exams), excitement (being a finalist for the lead in a play), change (new school, new courses), time pressure (spending 20 hours a week working and finding the time to study), illness (having a head cold that wipes you out for a week), or happiness (getting an A in a course when you expected a C).

More than 30 years ago, psychologists T. H. Holmes and R. H. Rahe developed a Social Readjustment Scale to measure the intensity of people's reaction to change and the level of stress related to it (see Table 10.1). They found that people perceive both good and bad events as stressors. For example, while some events, like going to jail or the death of a parent, are clearly negative, others, like starting or finishing school or even taking a vacation, are positive.

Everyone handles stress differently—the strategies linked to your stronger intelligences help you improve your coping skills.

INTELLIGENCE	SUGGESTED STRATEGIES	WHAT WORKS FOR YOU? WRITE NEW IDEAS HERE
Verbal–Linguistic	■ Keep a journal of what makes you stressed. ■ Make time to write letters or e-mail friends or talk with them.	
Logical–Mathematical	■ Think through problems critically using a problem-solving process and devise a plan. ■ Analyze possible positive effects that may result from the stress.	
Bodily–Kinesthetic	■ Choose a physical activity that helps you release tension—running, yoga, team sports—and do it regularly. ■ Plan fun physical activities for your free time—go for a hike, take a bike ride, go dancing with friends.	
Visual–Spatial	■ Take as much time as you can to enjoy beautiful things—art, nature, etc. Visit an exhibit, see an art film, shoot a roll of film with your camera. ■ Use a visual organizer to plan out a solution to a stressful problem.	
Interpersonal	■ Spend time with people who care about you and are very supportive. ■ Practice being a good listener to others who are stressed.	
Intrapersonal	■ Schedule down time when you can think through what is stressing you. ■ Allow yourself five minutes a day for visualizing a positive way in which you want a stressful situation to evolve.	
Musical	■ Play music that "feeds your soul." ■ Write a song about what stresses you out—or about anything that transports your mind.	
Naturalistic	■ Spend as much time as possible in your most soothing places in nature. ■ Listen to tapes of outdoor sounds to help you relax.	

Table 10.1	The Holmes–Rahe scale of life events that create stress.			
EVENT	**VALUE**	**EVENT**	**VALUE**	
Death of spouse or partner	100	Son or daughter leaving home	29	
Divorce	73	Trouble with in-laws	29	
Marital separation	65	Outstanding personal achievement	28	
Jail term	63	Spouse begins or stops work	26	
Personal injury	53	Starting or finishing school	26	
Marriage	50	Change in living conditions	25	
Fired from work	47	Revision of personal habits	24	
Marital reconciliation	45	Trouble with boss	23	
Retirement	45	Change in work hours, conditions	20	
Change in family member's health	44	Change in residence	20	
Pregnancy	40	Change in schools	20	
Sex difficulties	39	Change in recreational habits	19	
Addition to family	39	Change in religious activities	19	
Business readjustment	39	Change in social activities	18	
Change in financial status	38	Mortgage or loan under $10,000	17	
Death of a close friend	37	Change in sleeping habits	16	
Change to different line of work	36	Change in number of family gatherings	15	
Change in number of marital arguments	35	Change in eating habits	15	
Mortgage or loan over $10,000	31	Vacation	13	
Foreclosure of mortgage or loan	30	Christmas season	12	
Change in work responsibilities	29	Minor violation of the law	11	

Source: Reprinted with permission from *Journal of Psychosomatic Research,* 11(2), T. H. Holmes and R. H. Rahe, "The social readjustment rating scale," 1967. Elsevier Science Inc.

This scale is still valid today, and you can use it to find your personal stress score. Simply add the values of the events that you experienced in the past year. The higher the number on the scale, the greater the stress. Scoring over 300 points puts you at high risk for developing a stress-related problem. A score between 150 and 299 reduces your risk by 30 percent, and a score under 150 means that you have only a small chance of a problem.

The Stress Reaction

At their worst, stress reactions can make you physically ill. Your heart may race, your blood pressure may climb, your stomach may feel sick, and you may even experience back pain. You may feel tense, irritable, tired, or

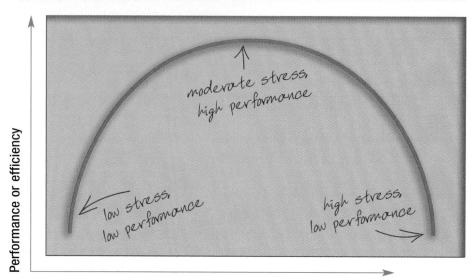

Figure 10.2 | Yerkes–Dodson law: Stress levels affect performance.

moderate stress, high performance

low stress, low performance

high stress, low performance

Performance or efficiency

Stress or anxiety

Source: From *Your Maximum Mind* by Herbert Benson, M. D., Copyright © 1987 by Random House, Inc. Used by permission of Time Books, a division of Random House, Inc.

depressed, and you may not be able to study or make decisions. But stress can also supply the heightened readiness you need to do well on tests, finish assignments on time, prepare for a class presentation, or meet new people. Because too little stress may actually create boredom and inactivity, your goal is not to eliminate stress altogether, but to find a balance so that you can manage it. Figure 10.2, based on research conducted by Drs. Robert M. Yerkes and John E. Dodson, shows that stress can be helpful or harmful, depending on how much you experience.

Managing Stress

The following strategies will help you avoid overload. Experiment with various techniques until you find those that work best for you.

- *Exercise, eat right, relax, and get enough sleep.* A healthy body will help you deal with stress.

- *Learn the power of positive thinking.* Think of all you have to do as challenges, not problems.

- *Seek balance.* A balanced life includes time by yourself—for your thoughts, hopes, and plans.

- *Address issues specifically.* Think through stressful situations and decide on a specific plan of action. For example, if you are having a hard time in English literature class, make an appointment to talk with your instructor about ways to get ahead.

- *Develop a schedule, and then stick to it.* Time pressure is one of the primary causes of stress. Use the techniques you learned in Chapter 3 to schedule time for all the things you have to accomplish and to avoid procrastination. If you feel overwhelmed by your schedule, rethink it.

- *Set reasonable goals.* Goals seem more manageable when approached as a series of small steps.
- *Set boundaries and learn to say "no."* Don't take responsibility for everyone and everything; learn to delegate. Review obligations regularly and let go of activities that have become burdens.
- *Evaluate assumptions.* A nursing student is stressed after getting a C on a biology paper. She needs at least a B in the course to be accepted as a major and assumes the grade means the end to her plans. Ironically, the assumption is her problem, not the grade itself. Assuming that things will go from bad to worse limits her ability to turn things around.
- *Surround yourself with people who are good for you.* Choose friends who are good listeners and who will support you when things get rough.
- *Avoid comparing yourself to others.* Each person has strengths and weaknesses. Comparing your weaknesses to the strengths of others is a losing game that makes you feel inadequate.
- *Avoid striking out in anger at those who are trying to help.* When you encounter frustration, it is human—and destructive—to displace your anger onto others. Try to keep focused on the problem. (For specific anger-management techniques see Chapter 9.)
- *Avoid destructive stress relievers.* Drinking too much, taking illegal drugs, smoking, or overeating will not solve your problems and may place you in physical and legal jeopardy.

If no matter what you do, stress still overwhelms you, consider talking with a trained counselor from your school's health services or your advisor. Table 10.2 shows how students in different circumstances can use stress-management techniques to avoid burnout.

Feeling overwhelmed by stress is sometimes related to mental health problems such as depression and eating disorders. It is important to recognize these problems and get help if you need it.

Beyond Stress: Recognizing Mental Health Problems

Emotional disorders limit your ability to enjoy life and to cope with its ups and downs. They affect people in all walks of life.

Depression

Almost everyone has experienced sadness or melancholy after the death of a friend or relative, the end of a relationship, or a setback such as a job loss. However, as many as 10 percent of Americans will experience a major depression at some point in their lives, and their reaction is more than temporary blues. A depressive disorder is an illness; it is not a sign of weakness or a mental state that can be escaped by just trying to "snap out of it." This illness requires a medical evaluation and is treatable.

A depressive disorder is "a 'whole-body' illness, involving your body, mood, and thoughts."[4] Among the symptoms of depression are the following:

Table 10.2	Techniques to avoid burnout.		
If you are in this situation . . .	**and encounter these stresses . . .**	**try these stress relievers.**
You share a room with two freshmen.	Your roommates stay up late every night. Their music keeps you awake and sets your nerves on edge.	Talk with your roommates right away and brainstorm solutions. Offer to wear a sleeping blindfold if they will use stereo headphones when you go to bed.
During your first semester, you join the tennis team, write for the school paper, and pledge a fraternity in addition to carrying a full course load.	You miss deadlines, fall asleep in class, and fail a test. Your stress level is high, but you are not sure what to do.	Use the prioritizing skills you learned in Chapter 3 to decide how much you can handle. Then, write a schedule that focuses on your academics and also allows time for activities and relaxation.
You live with your parents and commute to school.	Your parents make it hard to be independent. They question your schedule and even your friends. Your insides feel tight as a drum.	If you explain your feelings and your parents still treat you like a kid, reevaluate your plan. Consider working part- or full-time and renting an apartment with a friend near school.
You carry a full course load and work part-time to pay your bills.	There's no balance in your life. All you do is work—at your studies and your job. You feel overwhelmed so you drink every night.	Consider dropping a course or cutting back your work hours. Ask the financial aid office about loans that will help you meet expenses. Finally, cut back on your drinking.

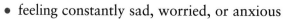

- feeling constantly sad, worried, or anxious
  - difficulty with decisions or concentration
    - no interest in classes, people, or activities
    - frequent crying
    - hopeless feelings and thoughts of suicide
    - constant fatigue
    - sleeping too much or too little
    - low self-esteem
    - eating too much or too little
    - physical aches and pains
    - low motivation

Depression can have a genetic, psychological, physiological, or environmental cause, or a combination of causes. Table 10.3 describes these causes along with strategies for fighting depression.

If you recognize any of these feelings in yourself, seek help. Start with your school's counseling office or student health program. You may be referred to a specialist who will help you sort through your symptoms and determine treatment. For some people, adequate sleep, a regular exercise program, a healthy diet, and stress decompression are the solution. For others, medication is important. If you are diagnosed with depression, know that your condition is common, even among college students. Be proud that you have taken a step toward recovery.

Suicide prevention. At its worst, depression can lead to suicide. SA\VE (Suicide Awareness\Voices of Education), an organization dedicated to suicide prevention education, lists these suicide warning signs:

- Statements about hopelessness or worthlessness: "The world would be better off without me."
- Loss of interest in people, things, or activities.
- Preoccupation with suicide or death.
- Making final arrangements such as visiting or calling family and friends and giving things away.
- Sudden sense of happiness or calm. (A decision to commit suicide often brings a sense of relief, making others believe that the person "seemed to be on an upswing.")

If you recognize these symptoms in someone you know, do everything you can to get the person to a doctor. Be understanding and patient as you urge action. If you recognize these symptoms in yourself, be your own best friend by reaching out for help.

Eating Disorders

Millions of people develop serious and sometimes life-threatening eating disorders every year. The most common disorders are anorexia nervosa, bulimia, and binge eating.

Table 10.3	Important information about depression.

POSSIBLE CAUSES OF DEPRESSION	HELPFUL STRATEGIES IF YOU FEEL DEPRESSED
• A genetic trait that makes depression more likely	• Do the best you can and don't have unreasonable expectations of yourself.
• A chemical imbalance in the brain	• Try to be with others rather than alone.
• Seasonal Affective Disorder, which occurs when a person becomes depressed in reaction to reduced daylight during autumn and winter	• Don't expect your mood to change right away; feeling better takes time.
• Highly stressful situations such as financial trouble, school failure, a death in the family	• Try to avoid making major life decisions until your condition improves.
• Illnesses, injuries, lack of exercise, poor diet	• Remember not to blame yourself for your condition.
• Reactions to medications	

Source: National Institutes of Health Publication No. 94-3561, National Institutes of Health, 1994.

Anorexia nervosa. This condition, occurring mainly in young women, creates an intense desire to be thin, which leads to self-starvation. People with anorexia become dangerously thin through restricting food intake, constant exercise, and use of laxatives, all the time believing they are overweight. An estimated 5 to 7 percent of college undergraduates in the United States suffer from anorexia.[5] The causes of anorexia are not fully known. The desire to emulate an "ideal" body type is one factor. In addition, eating disorders tend to run in families. Effects of anorexia-induced starvation include loss of menstrual periods in women, impotence in men, organ damage, heart failure, and death.

Bulimia. People who binge on excessive amounts of food, usually sweets and fattening foods, and then purge through self-induced vomiting have bulimia. They may also use laxatives or exercise obsessively. Bulimia can be hard to notice because bulimics are often able to maintain a normal appearance. The causes of bulimia, like those of anorexia, can be rooted in a desire to fulfill a body-type ideal or can come from a chemical imbalance. Bulimics often suffer from depression or other psychiatric illnesses. Effects of bulimia include damage to the digestive tract and even heart failure due to the loss of important minerals.

> "God grant me the serenity to accept things I cannot change, courage to change things I can, and wisdom to know the difference."
>
> **REINHOLD NIEBUHR**

Binge eating. Like bulimics, people with binge eating disorder eat large amounts of food and have a hard time stopping. However, they do not purge afterwards. Binge eaters are often overweight and feel that they cannot control their eating. As with bulimia, depression and other psychiatric illnesses may contribute to the problem. Binge eaters may suffer from all of the health problems associated with obesity.

Because eating disorders are a common problem on college campuses, most student health centers and campus counseling centers can provide both medical and psychological help. Treatment may involve psychotherapy, drug therapy, and even hospitalization or residence in a treatment center.

Mental health issues, stress, and other pressures may lead to substance abuse. Following is an exploration of the use and abuse of potentially addictive substances.

How are alcohol, tobacco, and drugs used and *abused?*

A lcohol, tobacco, and drug users are from all educational levels, racial and cultural groups, and areas of the country. Substance abuse can cause financial struggles, emotional traumas, health problems, and even death. Think critically as you read the following sections. Carefully consider the potential positive and negative effects of your actions, and take the time to make decisions that are best for you.

Alcohol

People receive mixed messages about alcohol: "Alcohol is fun," "alcohol is dangerous," "alcohol is for adults only." These conflicting ideas can make drinking appear glamorous, secretive, and exciting.

The National Institute on Alcohol Abuse and Alcoholism (NIAAA) offers these statistics about college students and alcohol:[6]

- An overwhelming majority of college students—88 percent—have used alcohol.
- Greater alcohol use is connected to sexual aggression. Among binge drinkers, there is an increased incidence of assault and unwanted sexual advances as a result of drinking.
- Drinking with a group and serving one's own drinks may contribute to greater consumption of alcohol. Both situations are common at large gatherings such as fraternity parties.

Of all alcohol consumption, binge drinking is associated with the greatest problems. Here are statistics from a recent survey:[7]

> BINGE DRINKING
>
> Having five or more drinks at one sitting.

- Forty-three percent of the students surveyed said they are binge drinkers, and 21 percent said that they binge drink frequently.
- Of students who do not binge drink, 80 percent surveyed reported experiencing one or more secondhand effects of binge drinking (e.g., vandalism, sexual assault or unwanted sexual advances, interrupted sleep or study).[8]
- Students who binge drink are more likely to miss classes, be less able to work, have hangovers, become depressed, engage in unplanned sexual activity, and ignore safe sex practices.[9]

The bottom line is that heavy drinking causes severe problems. The NIAAA estimates that alcohol contributes to the deaths of 100,000 people every year through both alcohol-related illnesses and accidents involving drunk drivers.[10] Heavy drinking can damage the liver, the digestive system, and brain cells and can impair the central nervous system. Prolonged use also leads to addiction, making it seem impossible to quit. Figure 10.3, a self-test, will help you determine if your drinking habits are a problem.

> ADDICTION
>
> Compulsive physiological need for a habit forming substance.

Figure 10.3 Substance use and abuse self-test.

Even one "yes" answer may indicate a need to evaluate your substance use. Answering "yes" to three or more questions indicates that you may benefit from discussing your use with a counselor.

WITHIN THE LAST YEAR:

(Y) (N)   1. Have you tried to stop drinking or taking drugs but found that you couldn't do so for long?

(Y) (N)   2. Do you get tired of people telling you they're concerned about your drinking or drug use?

(Y) (N)   3. Have you felt guilty about your drinking or drug use?

(Y) (N)   4. Have you felt that you needed a drink or drugs in the morning—as an "eye-opener"—in order to improve a hangover?

(Y) (N)   5. Do you drink or use drugs alone?

(Y) (N)   6. Do you drink or use drugs every day?

(Y) (N)   7. Have you found yourself regularly thinking or saying, "I need" a drink or any type of drug?

(Y) (N)   8. Have you lied about or concealed your drinking or drug use?

(Y) (N)   9. Do you drink or use drugs to escape worries, problems, mistakes, or shyness?

(Y) (N)   10. Do you find you need increasingly larger amounts of drugs or alcohol in order to achieve a desired effect?

(Y) (N)   11. Have you forgotten what happened while drinking or using drugs (had a blackout)?

(Y) (N)   12. Have you been surprised by how much you were using alcohol or drugs?

(Y) (N)   13. Have you spent a lot of time, energy, or money getting alcohol or drugs?

(Y) (N)   14. Has your drinking or drug use caused you to neglect friends, your partner, your children, or other family members, or caused other problems at home?

(Y) (N)   15. Have you gotten into an argument or a fight that was alcohol- or drug-related?

(Y) (N)   16. Has your drinking or drug use caused you to miss class, fail a test, or ignore schoolwork?

(Y) (N)   17. Have you rejected planned social events in favor of drinking or using drugs?

(Y) (N)   18. Have you been choosing to drink or use drugs instead of performing other activities or hobbies you used to enjoy?

(Y) (N)   19. Has your drinking or drug use affected your efficiency on the job or caused you to fail to show up at work?

(Y) (N)   20. Have you continued to drink or use drugs despite any physical problems or health risks that your use has caused or made worse?

(Y) (N)   21. Have you driven a car or performed any other potentially dangerous tasks while under the influence of alcohol or drugs?

(Y) (N)   22. Have you had a drug- or alcohol-related legal problem or arrest (possession, use, disorderly conduct, driving while intoxicated, etc.)?

Source: Compiled and adapted from the Criteria for Substance Dependence and Criteria for Substance Abuse in the *Diagnostic and Statistical Manual of Mental Disorders,* Fourth Edition, published by the American Psychiatric Association, Washington, D.C., and from materials entitled "Are You An Alcoholic?" developed by Johns Hopkins University.

Tobacco

The National Institute on Drug Abuse (NIDA) found that 38.8 percent of college students reported smoking at least once in the year before they were surveyed, and 24.5 percent had smoked once within the month before. Nationally, about 60 million people are habitual smokers.[11]

When people smoke they inhale nicotine, a highly addictive drug found in all tobacco products. Nicotine's immediate effects may include an increase in blood pressure and heart rate, sweating, and throat irritation. Long-term effects may include high blood pressure, bronchitis, emphysema, stomach ulcers, and heart conditions. Pregnant women who smoke increase their risk of having infants with low birth weight, premature births, or stillbirths.

Inhaling tobacco smoke damages the cells that line the air sacs of the lungs and can cause lung cancer. Lung cancer causes more deaths in the United States than any other type of cancer. Smoking also increases the risk of mouth, throat, and other cancers.[12]

Smoking also creates a danger to nonsmokers. "Secondhand smoke" causes about 3,000 lung cancer deaths per year in nonsmokers.[13] It is especially harmful to children, who are exposed to smoke in the nearly 50 percent of U.S. homes that house at least one smoker.

If you smoke regularly, you can quit through motivation and perseverance. Half of all people who have ever smoked have quit. Suggestions for quitting include the following:[14]

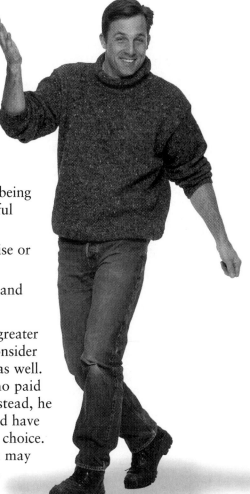

- Try a nicotine patch or nicotine gum, and be sure to use them consistently.

- Get support and encouragement from a health care provider, a "quit smoking" program, a support group, and friends and family.

- Avoid situations that cause you to want to smoke, such as being around other smokers, drinking alcohol, and highly stressful encounters or events.

- Find other ways of lowering your stress level such as exercise or other activities you enjoy.

- Set goals. Set a quit date and tell friends and family. Make and keep medical appointments.

The positive effects of quitting—increased life expectancy, greater lung capacity, and more energy—may inspire any smoker to consider making a lifestyle change. Quitting provides financial benefits as well. In fact, one study reports that if a one-pack-a-day smoker who paid $1.75 a pack for 50 years had put that money in the bank instead, he or she would have $169,325. A three-pack-a-day smoker would have saved $507,976.[15] Weigh your options and make a responsible choice. In order to evaluate the level of your potential addiction, you may want to take the self-test in Figure 10.3, replacing the words "alcohol" or "drugs" with "cigarettes" or "smoking."

Drugs

The NIDA reports that 31.4 percent of college students have used illicit drugs at least once in the year before being surveyed, and 16 percent in the month before.[16] If drug users were to think through the implications of their decision to take drugs, they might realize that many of the so-called "rewards" of drug use are empty. Drug-using peers may accept you for your drug use and not for who you are. Problems and responsibilities may multiply when you emerge from a high. Long-term drug use can damage your body and mind. Table 10.4 shows commonly used drugs and their potential effects.

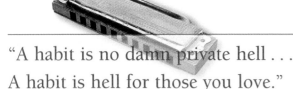

"A habit is no damn private hell . . . A habit is hell for those you love."

BILLIE HOLIDAY

One drug that doesn't fit cleanly into a particular category is MDMA, better known as Ecstasy. The use of this drug, a combination stimulant and hallucinogenic, is on the rise at college parties, raves, and concerts. Its immediate effects include diminished anxiety and relaxation. When the drug wears off, nausea, hallucinations, shaking, vision problems, anxiety, and depression replace these highs. Long-term users risk permanent brain damage in the form of memory loss, chronic depression, and other disorders.[17]

You are responsible for thinking critically about what to introduce into your body. Ask questions like the following: Why do I want to do this? What positive and negative effects might my behavior have? Why do others want me to take drugs? What do I really think of these people? How would my drug use affect the people in my life? The more critical analysis you do, the more likely you will make choices that are in your own best interest.

Drug use violates federal, state, and local laws. You can jeopardize your reputation, your student status, and your employment possibilities if you are caught using drugs or if drug use impairs your school performance. Today, many companies test employees and applicants for drug use. One report indicates that alcohol and

*W*hat seems at first like a minor wellness issue can gradually turn into a major problem that makes everything seem hopeless. However, Chip Case found that getting help and looking outside himself to help others can turn a life around and grant newfound perspective.

On the day that I found out I had been awarded the prestigious James R. Gilliam Scholarship from my college, Piedmont Virginia Community College, everything seemed alive. From where I stood in the campus garden, I could see the sun on the bald top of Brown's Mountain above Monticello. Ever since I was a boy, I had dreamed of going to the University of Virginia. I've come a long way to be this close to that dream.

As a child, I was an enthusiastic student, but by the time I was a junior in high school, I became a classic underachiever, smoking pot and going to parties instead of studying. I was arrested for possession of marijuana when I was 17 and for being drunk in public when I was 18, and I failed out of Radford University a year later. At 19, I got my first DUI. During the years following, I worked a series of jobs while continuing to drink. In 1994, I came home from a weekend away to find the apartment I shared with my girlfriend empty and abandoned. Deciding it was time to rededicate myself to the dream of attending UVA, I moved to Charlottesville and enrolled at PVCC. However, after two months, I withdrew from all my classes. I was drinking and depressed. I got my second DUI in 1997.

Two years later, after a second girlfriend broke up with me, I started taking Valium and really drinking. I got a medical leave of absence from work and had a nervous breakdown. The night I went to find her, I got my third DUI and ended up in jail. However, something changed in the subsequent two-and-a-half months I spent locked up. As I watched other inmates

leaving, I saw that they had nothing and I had the world. I realized I had taken for granted things like a hug from my Mom, a phone call, toothpaste.

I started a 12-step program. I decided to admit not only that I was an alcoholic, but that my whole life was out of control. Quitting drinking was easy. It was dealing with the problems inside that was the challenge.

I still visit that empty place within me. When things get rough, I sometimes want to get drunk to escape. I continue reworking the 12 steps; right now I'm on step number 2. I know I am always one day away from being where I was. I'm really focusing on not worrying, knowing it's going to be OK. I reenrolled at PVCC in August 2000, and celebrated my second year of sobriety in February 2001. Currently I am president of PVCC's Phi Theta Kappa chapter and active in community service.

Becoming happy again and finally being able to help myself has made me want to help others. Alcoholism is a selfish disease. Trying to help makes me forget about myself. When I share my experiences, it in turn helps me. It's a circle.

I'm definitely interested in teaching as a career, also in some sort of service. I'm not sure what route I will take. I do plan, however, to major in government and religious studies when I transfer to a four-year college. Recently I applied to UVA. Even if it doesn't go well, faith, family, and friends are the three most important things in my life. All else is a byproduct of these.

Take a moment to consider . . .

- What your most difficult personal wellness issue is, and what you plan to do to overcome it.
- What you would say are your "three most important things" in life.

drug use combined costs employers over $40 billion a year in reduced productivity.[18]

Identifying and Overcoming Addiction

People with addictions have lost control of their lives. Many addicts hide their addictions well because they continue to function. Although they are less likely to be substance abusers, women tend to conceal substance problems more carefully than men do.[19] If you think you may be addicted, realize that you are the only one who can take the initiative to change.

Facing Addiction

Because substances often cause physical and chemical changes, quitting may involve guiding your body through a painful withdrawal. Even substances that don't cause chemical changes create a psychological dependence that is tough to break. Asking for help isn't an admission of failure but a courageous move to reclaim your life.

Using the self-test in Figure 10.3, evaluate your behavior to see if you may need help. Even one "yes" answer may indicate that you need to evaluate your alcohol or drug use and to monitor it more carefully. If you answered yes to three or more questions, you may benefit from talking to a professional about your use and the problems it may be causing you.

Working Through Addiction

If you need to make some changes, there are many resources that can help you along the way.

Counseling and medical care. You can find help from school-based, private, government-sponsored, or workplace-sponsored resources. Ask your school's counseling or health center, your personal physician, or a local hospital for a referral.

Detoxification ("detox") centers. If you have a severe addiction, you may need a controlled environment in which to separate yourself completely from drugs or alcohol. Some are outpatient facilities. Other programs provide a 24-hour environment until you get through the withdrawal period.

Table 10.4 How drugs affect you.

DRUG CATEGORY	DRUG TYPES	HOW THEY MAKE YOU FEEL	PHYSICAL EFFECTS	DANGER OF PHYSICAL DEPENDENCE	DANGER OF PSYCHOLOGICAL DEPENDENCE
Stimulants	Cocaine, amphetamines	Alert, stimulated, excited	Nervousness, mood swings, stroke or convulsions, psychoses, paranoia, coma at large doses	Relatively strong	Strong
Depressants	Alcohol, Valium-type drugs	Sedated, tired, high	Cirrhosis; impaired blood production; greater risk of cancer, heart attack, and stroke; impaired brain function	Strong	Strong
Opiates	Heroin, codeine, other pain pills	Drowsy, floating, without pain	Infection of organs, inflammation of the heart, hepatitis	Yes, with high dosage	Yes, with high dosage
Cannabinols	Marijuana, hashish	Euphoria, mellowness, little sensation of time	Impairment of judgment and coordination, bronchitis and asthma, lung and throat cancers, anxiety, lack of energy and motivation, reduced ability to produce hormones	Moderate	Relatively strong
Hallucinogens	LSD, mushrooms	Heightened sensual perception, hallucinations, confusion	Impairment of brain function, circulatory problems, agitation and confusion, flashbacks	Insubstantial	Insubstantial
Inhalants	Glue, aerosols	Giddiness, lightheadedness	Damage to brain, heart, liver, and kidneys	Insubstantial	Insubstantial

Source: Compiled and adapted from *Educating Yourself about Alcohol and Drugs: A People's Primer* by Marc Alan Schuckit, M.D., Plenum Press, 1995.

Support groups. Alcoholics Anonymous (AA) is the premier support group for alcoholics. Based on a 12-step recovery program, AA membership costs little or nothing. AA has led to other support groups for addicts such as Overeaters Anonymous and Narcotics Anonymous. Many schools have AA, NA, or other group sessions on campus.

When people address their problems directly instead of avoiding them through substance abuse, they can begin to grow and improve. Working through substance-abuse problems can lead to a restoration of health and self-respect.

How can you make *smart* decisions about *sex?*

Sexual relationships involve body and mind on many levels. Being informed about sexual decision making, birth control options, and sexually transmitted diseases will help you make decisions that are right for you.

Sex and Critical Thinking

What sexuality means to you and the role it plays in your life are your own business. However, the physical act of sex goes beyond the private realm. Individual sexual conduct can have consequences such as unexpected pregnancy and the transmission of sexually transmitted diseases (STDs). These consequences affect everyone involved in the sexual act and, often, their families.

Your self-respect depends on making choices that maintain your health and safety, as well as those of the person with whom you are involved. Think critically about sexual issues, weighing the positive and negative effects of your choices. Among the questions to ask are the following:

- Is this what I really want? Does it fit with my values?
- Do I feel ready?
- Is this the right person/moment/situation? Does my partner truly care for me and not just for what we might be doing? Will this enhance our emotional relationship or cause problems later?
- Do I have what I need to prevent pregnancy and exposure to STDs? If not, what may be the consequences (pregnancy or disease)? Are they worth it?

Birth Control

Using birth control is a choice, and it is not for everyone. For some, using any kind of birth control is against their religious beliefs. Others may want to have children. Many sexually active people, however, choose one or more methods of birth control.

In addition to preventing pregnancy, some birth control methods also protect against sexually transmitted diseases. Table 10.5 describes the most established methods of birth control, with effectiveness percentages and STD prevention based on proper and regular use.

Evaluate the pros and cons of each method for yourself as well as for your partner. Consider cost, ease of use, reliability, comfort, and protection against STDs. Communicate with your partner and together make a choice that is comfortable for both of you. For more information, check your library, the Internet, or a bookstore; talk to your doctor; or ask a counselor at the student health center.

Table 10.5 Methods of birth control.

METHOD	APPROXIMATE EFFECTIVENESS	PREVENTS STDS?	DESCRIPTION
Abstinence	100%	Only if no sexual activity occurs	Just saying no. No intercourse means no risk of pregnancy. However, alternative modes of sexual activity can still spread STDs.
Condom (male)	94%	Yes, if made of latex	A sheath that fits over the penis and prevents sperm from entering the vagina.
Condom (female)	90%	Yes	A sheath that fits inside the vagina, held in place by two rings, one of which hangs outside. Can be awkward. It is relatively new and may not be widely available.
Diaphragm or cervical cap	85%	No	A bendable rubber cap that fits over the cervix and pelvic bone inside the vagina (the cervical cap is smaller and fits over the cervix only). Both must be fitted initially by a gynecologist and used with a spermicide.
Oral contraceptives (the pill)	97%	No	A dosage of hormones taken daily by a woman, preventing the ovaries from releasing eggs. Side effects can include headaches, weight gain, and increased chances of blood clotting. Various brands and dosages; must be prescribed by a gynecologist.
Spermicidal foams, jellies, inserts	84% if used alone	No	Usually used with diaphragms or condoms to enhance effectiveness, they have an ingredient that kills sperm cells (but not STDs). They stay effective for a limited period of time after insertion.
Intrauterine device (IUD)	94%	No	A small coil of wire inserted into the uterus by a gynecologist (who must also remove it). Prevents fertilized eggs from implanting in the uterine wall. Possible side effects include bleeding.
Norplant	Nearly 100%	No	A series of up to five small tubes implanted by a gynecologist into a woman's upper arm, preventing pregnancy for up to five years. Can be tough to remove. Possible side effects may resemble those of oral contraceptives. Must be removed by a doctor.
Depo-Provera	Nearly 100%	No	An injection that a woman must receive from a doctor every few months. Possible side effects may resemble those of oral contraceptives.
Tubal ligation	Nearly 100%	No	Surgery for women that cuts and ties the fallopian tubes, preventing eggs from traveling to the uterus. Difficult and expensive to reverse. Recommended for those who do not want any more children.
Vasectomy	Nearly 100%	No	Surgery for men that blocks the tube that delivers sperm to the penis. Like tubal ligation, difficult to reverse and only recommended for those who don't want children.
Rhythm method	Variable	No	Abstaining from intercourse during the ovulation segment of the woman's menstrual cycle. Can be difficult to time and may not account for cycle irregularities.
Withdrawal	Variable	No	Pulling the penis out of the vagina before ejaculation. Unreliable, because some sperm can escape in the fluid released prior to ejaculation. Dependent on a controlled partner.

Sexually Transmitted Diseases

Sexually transmitted diseases spread through sexual contact (intercourse or other sexual activity that involves contact with the genitals). All are highly contagious. The only birth control methods that offer protection are the male and female condoms (latex or polyurethane only), which prevent skin-to-skin contact. Most STDs can also spread to infants of infected mothers during birth. Have a doctor examine any irregularity or discomfort as soon as you detect it. Table 10.6 describes common STDs.

Table 10.6 Sexually transmitted diseases.

DISEASE	SYMPTOMS	HEALTH PROBLEMS IF UNTREATED	TREATMENTS
Chlamydia	Discharge, painful urination, swollen or painful joints, change in menstrual periods for women	Can cause pelvic inflammatory disease (PID) in women, which can lead to sterility or ectopic pregnancies; infection; miscarriage or premature birth.	Curable with full course of antibiotics; avoid sex until treatment is complete.
Gonorrhea	Discharge, burning while urinating	Can cause PID, swelling of testicles and penis, arthritis, skin problems, infections.	Usually curable with antibiotics; however, certain strains are becoming resistant to medication.
Genital herpes	Blisterlike itchy sores in the genital area, headache, fever, chills	Symptoms may subside and then reoccur, often in response to high stress levels; carriers can transmit the virus even when it is dormant.	No cure; some medications, such as Acyclovir, reduce and help heal the sores and may shorten recurring outbreaks.
Syphilis	A genital sore lasting one to five weeks, followed by a rash, fatigue, fever, sore throat, headaches, swollen glands	If it lasts over four years, it can cause blindness, destruction of bone, insanity, or heart failure; can cause death or deformity of a child born to an infected woman.	Curable with full course of antibiotics.
Human Papilloma Virus (HPV, or genital warts)	Genital itching and irritation, small clusters of warts	Can increase risk of cervical cancer in women; virus may remain in body even when warts are removed and cause recurrences.	Treatable with drugs applied to warts or various kinds of wart removal surgery.
Hepatitis B	Fatigue, poor appetite, vomiting, jaundice, hives	Some carriers will have few symptoms; others may develop chronic liver disease that may lead to other diseases of the liver.	No cure; some will recover, some will not. Bed rest may help ease symptoms. Vaccine is available.

Figure 10.4　20 years of AIDS in the United States: 1981–2001.

- Since the AIDS epidemic began in the United States, 774,467 cases of AIDS have been reported to the Centers for Disease Control (CDC), and approximately 450,000 Americans have died of AIDS.

- Since the epidemic began, well over one million Americans have been infected with HIV.

- Between 500,000 and 600,000 people in the United States are currently HIV-positive, and another 320,000 people are living with AIDS.

- CDC data show a high rate of infection among young gay and bisexual men. In a six-city study conducted between 1998 and 2000, the CDC found that 4.4 percent of 23- to 29-year-old men who have sex with men are being infected annually. Among African-American gays and bisexuals in this age group, the annual rate of new infections is an alarming 14.7 percent.

- HIV has hit minority communities hardest. Whereas in 1985 there were only 3,078 reported cases of African- and Hispanic-Americans with HIV, by 1999 that number had skyrocketed to 406,584.

- Women are now prime targets of HIV. Among 13 to 19 year olds, more than six out of ten HIV-positives are female.

Source: Centers for Disease Control, National Center for HIV, STD and TB Prevention, Press Release: "20 Years of AIDS: 450,000 Americans Dead, Over 1 million Have Been Infected," May 31, 2001.

AIDS and HIV

The most serious of the STDs is AIDS (acquired immune deficiency syndrome), which is caused by the human immunodeficiency virus (HIV). Not everyone who tests positive for HIV will develop AIDS, but AIDS has no cure and results in eventual death. Figure 10.4 shows some alarming statistics on AIDS on the twentieth anniversary of the first identified case.

HIV can lie undetected in the body for up to 10 years before surfacing, and a carrier can spread it during that time. Medical science continues to develop drugs to combat AIDS and its related illnesses. However, the drugs can cause severe side effects, many have not been thoroughly tested, and none are cures.

HIV is transmitted through two types of bodily fluids: fluids associated with sex (semen and vaginal fluids) and blood. People have acquired HIV through sexual relations, by sharing hypodermic needles for drug use, and by receiving infected blood transfusions. You cannot become infected unless one of those fluids is involved. Therefore, it is unlikely you can contract HIV from toilet seats, hugging, kissing, or sharing a glass.

The best defense against AIDS is not having sex. The U.S. Department of Health and Human Services reports:

THERE'S ABSOLUTELY NO GUARANTEE EVEN WHEN YOU USE A CONDOM. But most experts believe that the risk of getting AIDS and other sexually transmitted diseases can be greatly reduced if a condom is used properly. . . . Sex with condoms ISN'T totally "safe sex," but it IS "less risky" sex.[20]

Always use a latex condom, because natural skin condoms may let the virus pass through. If a lubricant is used, use K-Y Jelly or a spermicide because petroleum jelly can destroy the latex in condoms and diaphragms. Although some people dislike using condoms, it's a small price for preserving your life.

To be safe, have an HIV test done at your doctor's office or at a government-sponsored clinic. Your school's health department may also administer HIV tests, and home HIV tests are available over the counter. If you are infected, first inform all sexual partners and seek medical assistance. Then, contact support organizations in your area or call the National AIDS Hotline at 1-800-342-AIDS.

joie de vivre

The French have a phrase that is commonly used in the English language as well: *joie de vivre*, which literally means "joy of living." A person with *joie de vivre* finds joy and optimism in all parts of life, is able to enjoy life's pleasures, and can find something positive in its struggles. Without experiencing challenges, people might have a hard time recognizing and experiencing happiness and satisfaction. Think of this concept as you examine your personal wellness. If you focus on the positive, your attitude can affect all areas of your life.

Building Skills

FOR COLLEGE, CAREER, AND LIFE SUCCESS

Critical Thinking *Applying Learning to Life*

Health Habits

Put your critical-thinking skills to work in improving your physical health. The two key steps to take when making choices for your version of healthy living are as follows:

1. Ask questions to determine the options available to you.
2. Consider what you know about yourself (personality type, multiple intelligences, habits, abilities, etc.) to determine which of these options will work best for you.

For each of the following issues—food, exercise, and sleep—follow these two steps.

FOOD. Think critically about your eating habits. What could change for the better? Below, write three options available to you for changes you could make. Broaden your thinking to cover all kinds of changes—you could change when you eat, where you eat, the combination of foods you take in at a meal, the type of foods you eat (meat, vegetarian foods, etc.), the balance of food groups, whether you cook or not, how much sugar, caffeine, or fat you take in, and so on.

1. _____

2. _____

3. _____

Next, considering your self-knowledge, choose one option that you feel you can carry out, and circle it.

What about who you are makes this a good choice?

_____

_____

_____

What positive effects might this change have on you?

_____

_____

_____

EXERCISE. Now consider your exercise habits. Brainstorming all the possibilities—kinds of exercise, when and where you exercise, with whom you exercise, how long you exercise—come up with three possible changes.

_1._ _____

_2._ _____

_3._ _____

Then, considering your self-knowledge, choose one option that makes sense and is doable. Circle it.

What about who you are makes this a good choice?

_____

_____

_____

What positive effects might this change have on you?

_____

_____

_____

SLEEP. Finally, think critically about your sleep habits—when you sleep, where you sleep, for how long, and so on. Name three possible changes you could make in how you approach sleep.

_1._ _____

_2._ _____

_3._ _____

Then, considering your self-knowledge, choose an option you feel you could handle, and circle it.

What about who you are makes this a good choice?

_____

_____

_____

What positive effects might this change have on you?

_____

_____

_____

Early Warning Signs of Stress

STEP 1. Check any items that you have experienced at least once in the last three months. Under the Behavioral column, "compulsive behaviors" are behaviors that are repeated excessively, such as constant handwashing.

PHYSICAL	PSYCHOLOGICAL	BEHAVIORAL
☐ Indigestion	☐ Irritability	☐ Forgetfulness
☐ Diarrhea/constipation	☐ Excessive anger	☐ Poor concentration
☐ Nausea or vomiting	☐ Worry	☐ Distorted perception
☐ Appetite problems	☐ Depression	☐ Compulsive behaviors
☐ Headaches	☐ Excessive crying	☐ Decrease in productivity
☐ Neck or back pain	☐ Aggressiveness	☐ Decrease in creativity
☐ Allergies	☐ Isolation	☐ Living in the past
☐ Hair loss	☐ Boredom	☐ Drinking more
☐ Colds, flu, cold sore	☐ Decreased sense of humor	☐ Smoking more
☐ Teeth grinding	☐ Critical of self/others	☐ Decreased sex drive
☐ Problems sleeping	☐ Decreased motivation	☐ Acting "antsy"
☐ Fatigue	☐ Decreased self-esteem	☐ Accident prone

STEP 2. Circle the three items that usually occur as early warning signs of stress for you.

STEP 3. From what you know about relieving stress, describe the steps you plan to take when you experience any of the three items you circled as early warning signs.

_____

_____

_____

Note: Discuss any early warning signs with a doctor or counselor. Some of the symptoms listed above could also signify a condition that requires medical treatment.

Staying Safe

Consider your current personal safety habits and the effects they have on your life. Some may help keep you safe—others may put you in unnecessary danger. List two of each below.

Habits that have positive effects on your safety:

1. _____

2. _____

_____

Habits that have negative effects on your safety:

1. _____

_____

2. _____

_____

Choose to make one change that would increase your personal safety—either adding a positive habit or changing or eliminating a negative one. Write the change you will make below and list one or more positive effects it will have.

_____

_____

_____

_____

_____

_____

_____

_____

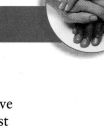

Teamwork *Combining Forces*

ACTIVELY DEALING WITH STRESS. By yourself, make a list of stressors—whatever events or factors cause you stress. As a class, discuss the stressors you have listed. Choose the five most common. Divide into five groups according to who would choose what stressor as his or her most important (redistribute some people if the group sizes are unbalanced). Each group should discuss its assigned stressor, brainstorming solutions and strategies. List your best coping strategies and present them to the class. Groups may want to make extra copies of the lists so that every member of the class has five, one for each stressor.

Writing *Discovery Through Journaling*

To record your thoughts, use a separate journal or the lined page at the end of the chapter.

ADDICTION. Describe how you feel about the concept of addiction in any form—to alcohol, drugs, food, a person, the Internet, gambling. How has it touched your life, if at all? How did you deal with it? If you have never faced an addiction or been close to someone who did, describe how you would face it if it ever happened to you.

YOUR HEALTH RECORD. Just as your health affects your success at school, it also affects how productive you are at work. You will benefit from being aware of your health status and working to improve your overall health and specific medical problems.

On a separate sheet of paper, draw up a "medical record" for yourself that will highlight your health status and the medical professionals you turn to for help. Include the following:

- health insurance plan and policy numbers
- phone numbers of physicians and clinics; phone numbers for medical emergencies
- immunizations: ones you have completed and any you have yet to receive
- surgical procedures you have had (include reasons)
- hospital stays (include reasons)
- illnesses and/or diseases
- family health history (parents, grandparents, siblings)
- chronic health problems (arthritis, diabetes, high blood pressure, etc.)
- vision and/or hearing status, if applicable
- prescriptions used regularly and why
- other

Highlight any conditions you feel you could improve with work or treatment. Choose one and draw up a problem-solving plan for making that improvement a reality.

Consider the positive side of your health as well. Make a list of the areas in which you enjoy very good health and the beneficial health habits you practice. For each, describe briefly how you maintain it.

Keep these lists up to date so you can monitor your health and communicate effectively with medical professionals. If you are transferred to a job in another city, you will also be changing doctors. You need to know your medical history in order to answer your new doctor's questions. This information is also needed before hospital admission.

If you have access to the CD-ROM Strategies for Success, use the following questions to assess your thoughts and enhance your understanding of the chapter. The questions below represent only some of the activities provided on the CD for the chapter topics—try others if you have time.

Click on the Personal Wellness bookmark. Use the following activities to boost your ability to live and work in healthy ways:

1. Take the pre-assessment to get an initial idea of your perspective on health and wellness.

2. Click on Activity Two: Test Your AIDS Knowledge. Making sure your computer is on-line, click on the link provided and take the test you will find there. Then complete the remaining questions in the activity.

3. Click on Activity Three: Journal Reflections. Type your response to the first question, regarding binge drinking in college.

4. Staying in Activity Three, scroll to the third journal question, about maintaining a healthy weight and diet while in college. Type your response to the question.

uggested Readings

Beattie, Melody. *Codependent No More: How to Stop Controlling Others and Start Caring for Yourself*. San Francisco, CA: Harper San Francisco, 1996.

Duyff, Roberta Larson. *The American Dietetic Association's Complete Food and Nutrition Guide*. Minneapolis, MN: Chronimed Publishing, 1998.

Grayson, Paul A., Phil Meilman, and Philip W. Meilman. *Beating the College Blues*. New York: Checkmark Books, 1999.

Johnson, Earvin "Magic." *What You Can Do to Avoid AIDS*. New York: Random House, 1996.

Mayo Clinic Family Health Book: The Ultimate Home Medical Reference, 2nd ed. New York: William Morrow, 1996.

McMahon, Susanna. *The Portable Problem Solver: Coping with Life's Stressors*. New York: Dell Publishing, 1996.

The New Wellness Encyclopedia. Edited by the Editors of the University of California at Berkeley Wellness Letter. Boston, MA: Houghton Mifflin, 1995.

The Physician's Desk Reference. *The Physician's Desk Reference Family Guide Encyclopedia of Medical Care*. New York: Ballantine Books, 1999.

Schuckit, Marc Alan. *Educating Yourself about Alcohol and Drugs: A People's Primer*. New York: Plenum Press, 1995.

Selkowitz, Ann. *The College Student's Guide to Eating Well on Campus*. Bethesda, MD: Tulip Hill Press, 2000.

Vedral, Marthe Simone and Joyce L. Vedral. *The College Dorm Workout: Fight the Freshman Fifteen in Twenty Minutes a Day without Starving to Death*. New York: Warner Books, 1994.

nternet Resources

Prentice Hall Student Success Supersite (fitness and well-being information): www.prenhall.com/success

American Cancer Society (general information, prevention, and early detection tips): www.cancer.org

Columbia University's Health Education Program: www.alice.columbia.edu

Federal Centers for Disease Control and Prevention (disease prevention and health information): www.cdc.gov

It's Your (Sex) Life: www.itsyoursexlife.com/

MayoClinic.com (medical information from this world-renowned medical center): www.mayohealth.org

E ndnotes

1. The sources used in this section include Jane E. Brody, "Added Sugars Are Taking a Toll on Health," *The New York Times*, September 12, 2000, p. F8; "Diabetes as Looming Epidemic," *The New York Times*, January 30, 2001, p. F8; "Extra Soft Drink Is Cited As Major Factor in Obesity," *The New York Times*, February 16, 2001, p. A12; Josh Stroud, "No more fast forward," *Dallas Business Journal*, January 21, 2000, p. 10C; "U.S. Favors Traditional Weight-Loss Plans," *The New York Times*, January 16, 2001, p. F12.

2. Herbert Benson, M.D., and Eileen M. Stuart, R.N. C. M.S., et al., *The Wellness Book*. New York: Simon & Schuster, 1992, p. 292.

3. The following articles were used as sources in this section: Glenn C. Altschuler, "Adapting to College Life in an Era of Heightened Stress," *The New York Times*, *Education Life*, Section 4A, August 6, 2000, p. 12; Carol Hymowitz and Rachel Emma Silverman, "Can Workplace Stress Get Worse? *The Wall Street Journal*, January 16, 2001, p. B1; Robert M. Sapolsky, "Best Ways to Reduce Everyday Levels of Stress . . . Bad Ol' Stress," *Bottom Line Personal*, January 15, 2000, p. 13; Kate Slaboch, "Stress and the College Student: A Debate," www.jour.unr.edu/outpost/voices/voi.slaboch.stress.htm, April 4, 2001; University of South Florida, The Counseling Center for Human Development, "Coping with Stress in College," http://usfweb.usf.edu/counsel/self-hlp/stress.htm, April 4, 2001; Jodi Wilgoren, "Survey Shows High Stress Levels in College Freshmen," *The New York Times*, January 23, 2000, p. NA.

4. National Institutes of Health Publication No. 94-3561, National Institutes of Health, 1994.

5. Kim Hubbard, Anne-Marie O'Neill, and Christina Cheakalos, "Out of Control," *People*, April 12, 1999, p. 54.

6. National Institute on Alcohol Abuse and Alcoholism, No. 29 PH 357, July 1995.

7. H. Wechsler et al., "Changes in Binge Drinking and Related Problems Among American College Students Between 1993 and 1997," *Journal of American College Health*, vol. 47, September 1998, p. 57.

8. Ibid, pp. 63–64.

9. National Institute on Alcohol Abuse and Alcoholism, No. 29 PH 357, July 1995.

10. J. McGinnis and W. Foege, "Actual Causes of Death in the United States," *Journal of the American Medical Association* (JAMA) 270.18, American Medical Association, Nov. 10, 1993, p. 2208.

11. National Institute on Drug Abuse, Capsule Series C-83-08, "Cigarette Smoking," Bethesda, MD: National Institutes of Health, 1994.

12. David Stout, "Direct Link Found Between Smoking and Lung Cancer," *The New York Times*, October 18, 1996, pp. A1, A19.

13. *Chicago Tribune*, February 26, 1997, "Secondhand Smoke Blamed in 3,000 Yearly Cancer Deaths." [on-line]. Available at http://archives.chicago.tribune.com (April 1997).

14. National Institutes of Health, Agency for Health Care Policy and Research, "Nicotine: A Powerful Addiction."

15. Anne R. Carey and Bob Laird, "USA Snapshots," "Dollars Up in Smoke," *USA Today*, February 20, 1997, p. D1. Source: Demotech, Inc.

16. National Institute on Drug Abuse, "National Survey Results on Drug Abuse from Monitoring the Future Study," Bethesda, MD: National Institutes of Health, 1994.

17. www.usdoj.gov/dea/concern/mdma/mdmaindex.htm; U.S. Department of Justice, Drug Enforcement Administration.

18. D. P. Rice, S. Kelmen, et al., "The Economic Costs of Alcohol and Drug Abuse and Mental Illness: Report Submitted to the Office of Financing and Coverage Policy of the Alcohol, Drug Abuse and Mental Health Administration," U.S. Department of Health and Human Services, 1990, p. 26.

19. Kim Painter, "Drinking: Loving and Leaving It," *USA Today*, June 4, 1996, p. D1.

20. U.S. Department of Health and Human Services, "A Condom Could Save Your Life," Publication # 90-4239.

JOURNAL

name   date

Managing
career and money

MONEY ISSUES are a big deal for college students, and Brett Cross (see next page) is experiencing one of the most common—credit card concerns. Career exploration, a job-hunting strategy, and money management can work together to help you find and maximize a career, whether it is being a teacher in Minnesota, an attorney in Manhattan, an archaeologist in Egypt, or anything else you dream of. In this chapter, you look at career exploration, how to balance work and school, and how to manage your money so that you can make the most of what you earn.

reality resources

Brett Cross, University of
Washington, Seattle, Washington

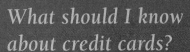

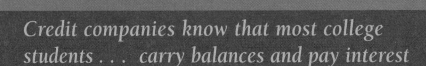

Tim Short,
Washington State University, Pullman, Washington

What should I know about credit cards?

Credit companies know that most college students . . . carry balances and pay interest

I am a pre-engineering student at the University of Washington. Recently, I have been receiving a number of credit card applications offering a low interest rate. In fact, I get at least one offer a week. I've been thinking it would be nice to establish credit, but I'm not sure if getting a credit card right now is a good idea. Even though I have a part-time job and have financial aid, it seems like there's never enough to make it to the end of the semester. Should I apply for one of these credit cards? It would be really great to have some extra cash every now and then.

Dealing with financial hardships while in college is a part of life for many people these days. Credit card offers are in abundance for college students, and for good reason. Credit companies know that most college students won't be able to pay off their cards until after they graduate, and that they tend to carry balances and pay interest and hefty fees until they are solvent. Believe me, I know. Throughout my past four years at college, I have acquired several credit cards. On them I have charged things such as books, car repairs, auto insurance, and other personal items. I am still paying interest on these cards monthly and will not be able to pay them off until after I graduate.

My suggestion is that you not use a credit card for anything other than easily covered expenses. If you have bigger expenses and can take out student loans or borrow from your parents, do that instead. Most academic loans have a 6–8 percent interest rate that is much lower than the 18–21 percent that most credit card companies charge. Don't be fooled by offers for a card with a low rate. These invariably expire after one year and then the rate jumps up. If you miss a payment during that year, some companies raise your rates immediately. Rationalizing that you will pay the card off before that time frame is up is also not a good idea. Unless you are on the verge of graduation, you probably will not have any more cash in a year than you do now.

Overall, my advice is this: Do what you can to limit your borrowing from credit card companies to what you can afford to pay back right away. You will be a lot happier in the long run.

How can you prepare for a
successful career?

S tudents are in different stages when it comes to thinking about careers. Like many people, you may not have thought too much about it yet. You may have had a career for years and are looking for a change. You may have decided on a particular career but are now having second thoughts. Regardless of your starting point, now is the time to make progress.

Everything in this book is geared toward workplace success. Critical thinking, teamwork, writing skills, and long-term planning all prepare you to thrive in any career. Use the following strategies to start getting more specific in your preparation for career success.

Investigate Career Paths

What's happening in the working world changes all the time. You can get a good idea of what's out there—and what you think of it all—by exploring potential careers and building knowledge and experience.

Explore Potential Careers

Career possibilities extend far beyond what you can imagine. Brainstorm about career areas. Ask instructors, relatives, mentors, and fellow students about careers they are familiar with. Check your library for books on careers or biographies of people who worked in fields that interest you. Explore careers you discover through movies, newspapers, novels, or nonfiction.

Use your critical-thinking skills to broaden your investigation. Look at Table 11.1 for some of the kinds of questions you might ask as you talk to people or investigate materials. You may discover that:

A wide array of job possibilities exists for most career fields. For example, the medical world consists of more than doctors and nurses. Emergency medical technicians respond to emergencies, administrators run hospitals, researchers test new drugs, pharmacists prepare prescriptions, and so on.

"Whatever you think you can do or believe you can do, begin it. Action has magic, grace, and power in it."

JOHANN WOLFGANG VON GOETHE

Within each job, there is a variety of tasks and skills. You may know that an instructor teaches, but you may not see that instructors also often write, research, study, design courses, give presentations, and counsel. Push past your first impression of any career and explore what else it entails.

Table 11.1 Critical-thinking questions for career exploration.

What can I do in this area that I like and do well?	Do I respect the company or the industry? The product or service?
What are the educational requirements (certificates or degrees, courses)?	Does this company or industry accommodate special needs (child care, sick days, flex time)?
What skills are necessary?	Do I have to belong to a union?
What wage or salary and benefits can I expect?	Are there opportunities near where I live (or want to live)?
What kinds of personalities are best suited to this kind of work?	What other expectations exist (travel, overtime, etc.)?
What are the prospects for moving up to higher-level positions?	Do I prefer the service or production end of this industry?

Common assumptions about salaries don't always hold. Finance, medicine, law, and computer science aren't the only high-paying careers. According to data from the U.S. Labor Department, other careers with high earnings include electricians, public administrators, aircraft mechanics, and more.[1] Don't jump to conclusions until you have investigated. And remember to place earnings in perspective: Even if you earn an extraordinary salary, you may not be happy unless you truly enjoy and learn from what you are doing.

Your school's career center may offer job listings, occupation lists, assessments of skills and personality types, questionnaires to help you pinpoint areas that may suit you, and information about different careers and companies. Visit the center early in your college career and work with a counselor there to develop a solid career game plan.

Build Knowledge and Experience

Having knowledge and experience specific to the career you want to pursue is valuable on the job hunt. Courses, internships, jobs, and volunteering are four great ways to build both.

Courses. When you narrow your career exploration to a couple of areas of interest, try to take a course or two in those areas. How you react to the material gives you clues as to how you feel about the area in general. Find out what courses you have to take to major in the field, what jobs are available in the field, what credentials (degrees or training) you need for particular jobs, and so on.

Internships. Companies that offer internships are looking for people who will work hard in exchange for experience they can't get in the classroom. An internship may or may not offer pay. Your career center may be able

INTERNSHIP

A temporary work program in which a student can gain supervised practical experience in a particular professional field.

to help you explore summer internship opportunities or those during the school year. Stick to areas that interest you, and look for an internship that you can handle while still being able to fulfill your financial obligations. An internship is a great way to gain real-world experience and show initiative.

Jobs. No matter what you do to earn money while you are in college, whether it is in your area of interest or not, you may discover career opportunities that appeal to you. Someone who takes a third-shift legal proofreading job to make extra cash might discover an interest in law. Someone who answers phones for a newspaper company might be drawn into journalism. Be open to the possibilities around you.

Volunteering. Offering your services to others in need can introduce you to careers and increase your experience. Some schools have programs to help you find volunteering opportunities. Include volunteer activities on your résumé. Many employers look favorably on volunteering.

Even after you've completed a college degree, training program, course, book, or job, the key is to continually build on what you know. With the world's fast-paced changes in mind, today's employers value those who seek continual improvement in their skills and knowledge.

Know What Employers Want

When you look for a job in a particular career area, your technical skills, work experience, and academic credentials that apply to that career are important. Beyond those basics, though, other skills and qualities make you an excellent job candidate in any career.

Important Skills

Particular skills and qualities tell an employer that you are likely to be an efficient and effective employee. Table 11.2 describes these skills.

These skills appear throughout this book, and they are as much a part of your school success as they are of your work success. The more you develop them now, the more employable and promotable you will be. You may already use them on the job if you are a student who works.

Emotional Intelligence

Another quality employers seek is emotional intelligence. In his book *Working with Emotional Intelligence*, psychologist Daniel Goleman states that emotional intelligence can be even more important than IQ and knowledge. He defines emotional intelligence as a combination of these factors:[2]

- *Personal competence.* This includes self-awareness (knowing your internal states, preferences, resources, intuitions), self-regulation (being able to manage your internal states, impulses, and resources), and motivation (the factors that help you reach your goals).
- *Social competence.* This includes empathy (being aware of the feelings, needs, and concerns of others) and social skills (your ability to create desirable responses in those with whom you interact).

Table 11.2	Skills employers seek.
SKILLS	**WHY?**
Communication	Both good listening and effective communicating are keys to workplace success, as is being able to adjust to different communication styles.
Critical thinking	An employee who can assess workplace choices and challenges critically and recommend appropriate actions stands out.
Teamwork	All workers interact with others on the job. Working well with others is essential for achieving work goals.
Goal setting	Teams fail if goals are unclear or unreasonable. Benefit is gained from setting realistic, specific goals and achieving them reliably.
Acceptance	The workplace is becoming increasingly diverse. A valuable employee is able to work with, and respect all kinds of people.
Leadership	The ability to influence others in a positive way earns you respect and helps advance your career.
Creativity	The ability to come up with new concepts, plans, and products is valuable in the workplace.
Positive attitude	If you show that you have a high level of commitment to all tasks, you may earn the right to tackle more challenging projects.
Integrity	Acting with integrity at work—communicating promptly, being truthful and honest, following rules, giving proper notice, respecting others—enhances your value.
Flexibility	The most valuable employees understand the constancy of change and have developed the skills to adapt to its challenge.
Continual learning	The most valuable employees stay current on changes and trends by reading up-to-the-minute media and taking workshops and seminars.

The current emphasis on teamwork has made emotional intelligence very important in the workplace. The more adept you are at working comfortably and productively with others (i.e., the more emotionally intelligent you are and the more you use this intelligence), the more likely you are to succeed.

Stay Current

The working world is always in flux, responding to technological developments, global competition, and other changes. Reading newspapers and magazines, scanning business sites on the Internet, and watching television news all help you keep abreast of what you face as you make

Table 11.3	Fastest growing occupations 1998–2008.	
OCCUPATION	**PROJECTED GROWTH IN NUMBERS OF JOBS**	**THIS OCCUPATION WILL GROW BY . . .**
Computer engineer	323,000	108 percent
Computer support specialist	439,000	102 percent
Systems analyst	577,000	94 percent
Database administrator	67,000	77 percent
Desktop publishing specialist	19,000	73 percent
Paralegal/legal assistant	84,000	62 percent
Medical assistant	146,000	58 percent
Personal care/home health aide	433,000	58 percent
Social and human service assistant	141,000	53 percent
Physician assistant	32,000	48 percent

Source: U.S. Bureau of Labor. Table 1: Fastest growing occupations covered in the 2000–01 *Occupational Outlook Handbook,* 1998–2008. Accessed online 6/14/01. Available at http://stats.bls.gov/news.release/ooh.t01.htm.

career decisions. Spend your time staying on top of two issues: growing and declining career areas and workplace trends.

Growing and Declining Career Areas

Try to stay on top of what careers are growing most rapidly. Rapid workplace change means that a growth area today may be declining tomorrow —witness the sudden drop in Internet company jobs and fortunes in 2001. The U.S. Bureau of Labor keeps updated statistics on the status of various career areas. Table 11.3 shows projected job growth from 1998–2008 for the 10 fastest growing occupations. Note that the top five are all computer-related occupations.

You can keep tabs on these important statistics by checking the *Occupational Outlook Handbook,* published by the Bureau of Labor every two years. You will find it in your library, or you can look up highlights on the Internet at http://stats.bls.gov/ocohome.htm.

Workplace Trends

Following are two current workplace trends that may be important for you in your career investigation.

More temporary employment. To save money, corporations are hiring more temporary employees (temps) and fewer full-time employees (the number of temps increased from 800,000 in 1986 to more than 2.5 million in 1997).[3] When considering whether to take a permanent job or a temporary job, consider the effects of each. Permanent jobs offer benefits (employer contribution to pension plan, paid vacations, and health insurance) and stability, but less flexibility. Temporary jobs offer flexibility, few obligations, and often more take-home pay, but have limited benefits.

New variety in benefits. Companies are responding to the changing needs of the modern workforce, where workers often have to care for children or aging parents. This response often involves "quality of life" benefits such as the following:

- *telecommuting* (working from home via telephone, fax, and Internet access)
- *job sharing* (two employees working part-time to fulfill the duties of one full-time position)
- *personal services* such as medical care, psychological counseling, and financial planning
- *flextime* (the ability to adjust work time in response to school or family needs)
- *child care* on-site or nearby, often at reduced rates

Both workers and companies benefit from these alternatives to traditional work arrangements. Workers enjoy greater quality of life, and companies are able to promote loyalty and keep employee turnover low in an age where changing jobs is common. These benefit offerings are likely to increase in the years ahead (see Figure 11.1 for growth of particular benefits).

Expect Change

As you learned in Chapter 1, rapid change in the workplace means that workers are changing jobs and careers often. Today's workers have to be prepared to go back to the drawing board should jobs not work out. When you experience the stress of job and career shifts, look for the positive in the change. Even difficult changes can open doors that you never even imagined were there. For example:

- Susan Davenny Wyner, a successful classical singer, was hit by a car while biking. The accident damaged her vocal cords beyond repair. She later discovered that conducting held an opportunity for her to express herself musically in a way she didn't think she could ever do again.
- Jimmy Carter, once a peanut farmer, became President of the United States. After losing his bid for reelection, he has used his personal reputation to gather funds and attention for Habitat for Humanity, an organization that builds affordable homes for families in need.

As these people and many others have demonstrated, if you think creatively about your marketable skills and job possibilities, you will be able to find new ways to achieve. What you know about your learning style should play an important role in your thinking.

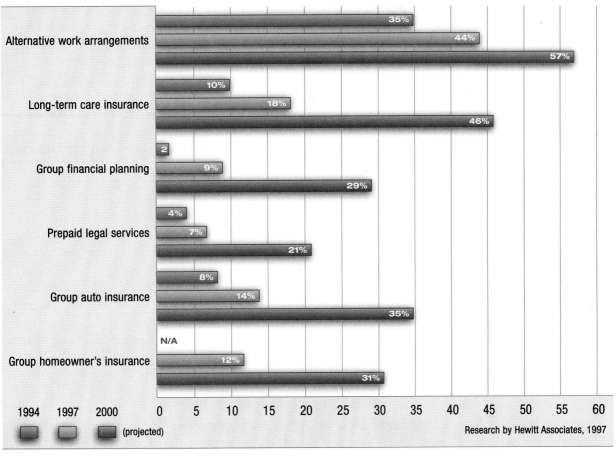

Figure 11.1 Modern benefits.

Percentage of 509 companies surveyed that offer these benefits to employees

Alternative work arrangements
35%
44%
57%

Long-term care insurance
10%
18%
46%

Group financial planning
2
9%
29%

Prepaid legal services
4%
7%
21%

Group auto insurance
8%
14%
35%

Group homeowner's insurance
N/A
12%
31%

0 5 10 15 20 25 30 35 40 45 50 55 60

1994 1997 2000 (projected)

Research by Hewitt Associates, 1997

Source: "Perks That Work," *Time,* Nov. 9, 1998. © 1998 Time Inc. Reprinted by permission.

What does your *learning style* mean for your *career?*

I f you don't know exactly what you want to do, you are not alone. Many students who have not been in the workplace—and even some who have—aren't sure what career to pursue. Start with what you know about yourself. In your initial exploration, you might ask yourself questions like the following:

- What do I know best, do best, and enjoy best?
- Out of the jobs I have had, what did I like and not like to do?
- What kinds of careers could make the most of everything I am?

You may not realize it, but with what you know about your learning style from your work in Chapter 2, you already have a head start on the self-knowledge that will help you find the right career. You can use each half of your learning style profile in a different way. Because the Multiple Intelligences assessment gives you information about your innate learning strengths and weaknesses, your results can help point you toward areas that take advantage of your abilities and involve your interests.

Your Personality Spectrum assessment results are perhaps even more significant to career success because they provide insight on how you work best with others. Nearly every aspect of the search process—looking for, interviewing for, and winning a job—involves dealing with people. Succeeding in your chosen job depends, in large part, on your ability to communicate and function in a team.

Table 11.4 focuses the four dimensions of the Personality Spectrum on career ideas and strategies. Look for your strengths and decide what you may want to keep in mind as you search. Look also at your weaknesses because even the most ideal job involves some tasks that may not be in your area of comfort. Identifying ways to boost your abilities in those areas will help you succeed.

Keep in mind a few important points as you consider the information in this table.

Use information as a guide, not a label. You may not necessarily have all the strengths and challenges that your dominant areas indicate. Chances are, though, that thinking through them will help you narrow your focus and clarify your abilities and interests.

Avoid thinking that challenges are weaknesses. Work challenges describe qualities that may cause issues in particular work situations. They aren't necessarily weaknesses in and of themselves. For example, not many people would say that a need for structure and stability (a challenge of the Giver) is a weakness. However, it can be a challenge in a workplace that operates in an unstructured manner. Look at items that may be challenges for you. Then, looking at the careers or jobs you are considering, see if you think you will encounter situations that will bring your challenges into play.

Know that you are capable of change. What you know about how you learn now will help you develop the ability to make positive changes in college and in your career. Use ideas about strengths and challenges as a starting point and make some decisions about how you would like to progress as a working person.

Now that you've done your homework, it's time to get to the search. What you know, along with the strategies that follow, will help you along the path to a career that works for you.

			LOOK FOR JOBS/CAREERS
DIMENSION	**STRENGTHS ON THE JOB**	**CHALLENGES ON THE JOB**	**THAT FEATURE . . .**
Thinker	• Problem solving • Development of ideas • Keen analysis of situations • Fairness to others • Efficiency in working through tasks • Innovation of plans and systems • Ability to look strategically at the future	• A need for private time to think and work • A need, at times, to move away from established rules • A dislike of sameness— systems that don't change, repetitive tasks • Not always open to expressing thoughts and feelings to others	• Some level of solo work/think time • Problem solving • Opportunity for innovation • Freedom to think creatively and to bend the rules • Technical work • Big-picture strategic planning
Organizer	• High level of responsibility • Enthusiastic support of social structures • Order and reliability • Loyal • Able to follow through on tasks according to require-ments • Detailed planning skills with competent follow-through • Neatness and efficiency	• A need for tasks to be clearly, concretely defined • A need for structure and stability • A preference for less rapid change • A need for frequent feedback • A need for tangible appreciation • Low tolerance for people who don't conform to rules and regulations	• Clear, well-laid-out tasks and plans • Stable environment with consistent, repeated tasks • Organized supervisors • Clear structure of how employees interact and report to one another • Value of, and reward for, loyalty
Giver	• Honesty and integrity • Commitment to putting energy toward close relationships with others • Finding ways to bring out the best in self and others • Peacemaker and mediator • Able to listen well, respect opinions, and prioritize the needs of coworkers	• Difficulty in handling conflict, either personal or between others in the work environment • Strong need for apprecia-tion and praise • Low tolerance for perceived dishonesty or deception • Avoidance of people perceived as hostile, cold, or indifferent	• Emphasis on teamwork and relationship building • Indications of strong and open lines of communication among workers • Encouragement of personal expression in the workplace (arrangement of personal space, tolerance of personal celebrations, and so on)
Adventurer	• Skillfulness in many different areas • Willingness to try new things • Ability to take action • Hands-on problem-solving skills • Initiative and energy • Ability to negotiate • Spontaneity and creativity	• Intolerance of being kept waiting • Lack of detail focus • Impulsiveness • Dislike of sameness and authority • Need for freedom, constant change, and constant action • Tendency not to consider consequences of actions	• A spontaneous atmosphere • Less structure, more freedom • Adventuresome tasks • Situations involving change • Encouragement of hands-on problem solving • Travel and physical activity • Support of creative ideas and endeavors

Table 11.4 Personality Spectrum in the working world.

How can you find a *career* that's *right for you?*

Many different routes can lead to satisfying jobs and careers. In the career areas that interest you, explore what's possible and evaluate potential positive and negative effects so that you can make an educated decision about what suits you best. Maximize your opportunities by using the resources available to you, making a strategic search plan, and knowing some basics about résumés and interviews.

Use Available Resources

Use your school's career planning and placement office, your networking skills, classified ads, on-line services, and employment agencies to help you explore possibilities both for jobs you need right away and for post-graduation career opportunities.

Your School's Career Planning and Placement Office

Generally, the career planning and placement office deals with postgraduation job placements, whereas the student employment office, along with the financial aid office, has more information about working while in school. At either location you might find general workplace information, listings of job opportunities, sign-up sheets for interviews, and contact information for companies.

The career office may hold frequent informational sessions on different topics. Your school may also sponsor job or career fairs that give you a chance to explore job opportunities. Start exploring your school's career office early in your college life. The people and resources there can help you at every stage of your career and job exploration process.

Networking

NETWORKING
The exchange of information or services among individuals, groups, or institutions.

Networking is one of the most important job-hunting strategies. With each person you get to know, you build your network and tap into someone else's. With whom can you network?

- Friends and family members
- Instructors, administrators, or counselors
- Personnel at employment or career offices
- Alumni
- Employers or coworkers

CONTACT
A person who serves as a carrier or source of information.

Try to develop personal relationships with your networking **contacts.** They may be willing to answer your questions regarding job hunting, challenges and tasks of their jobs, and salary expectations. Thank your contacts for their help and be ready to help others who may need advice from you.

Classified Ads

Some of the best job listings are in newspapers. Individual ads describe the kind of position available and give a telephone number or post office box for you to contact. Some ads include additional information such as job requirements, a contact person, and the salary or wages offered. You can run your own classified ads if you have a skill to advertise.

On-Line Services

The Internet has exploded into one of the most fruitful sources of job listings. There are many different ways to hunt for a job on the Web:

- Look up career-focused and job listing Web sites such as CareerBuilder.com, CareerMosaic, Monster.com, hotjobs .com, JobsOnline, or futurestep.com. In addition to listing and describing different jobs, sites like these offer resources on career areas, résumés, on-line job searching, and more.

- Access job search databases such as the Career Placement Registry and U.S. Employment Opportunities.

- Check the Web pages of individual associations and companies, which may post job listings and descriptions.

- If nothing happens right away, keep at it. New job postings appear; new people sign on to look at your résumé. Plus, sites change all the time. Do a general search using the keywords "hot job sites" or "job search sites" to stay current on what sites are up and running.

Employment Agencies

Employment agencies are organizations that help people find full-time, part-time, or temporary work. Most employment agencies put you through a screening process that consists of an interview and one or more tests in your area of expertise. If you pass the tests and interview well, the agency tries to place you in a job. Most employment agencies specialize in particular careers or skills such as medicine, legal, computer operation, graphic arts, child care, or food services.

Employment agencies are a great way to hook into job networks. However, they usually require a fee that either you or the employer has to pay. Ask questions so that you know as much as possible about how the agency operates.

Make a Strategic Job Search Plan

After you've gathered enough information to narrow your career goals, plan strategically to achieve them by mapping out your long-term time line and keeping track of specific actions.

Figure 11.2 **Career time line.**

1 month	—	Enter community college on a part-time schedule
6 months	—	Meet with advisor to discuss desired major and required courses
1 year	—	
	—	Declare major in secondary education
2 years	—	Switch to full-time class schedule
3 years	—	Graduate with associate's degree
	—	Transfer to 4-year college
4 years	—	Work part-time as a classroom aide
5 years	—	Student teaching
	—	Graduate with bachelor's degree and teaching certificate
6 years	—	Have a job teaching high school

Make a Big-Picture Time Line

Make a career time line that illustrates the steps toward your goal, as shown in Figure 11.2. Mark years and half-year points (and months for the first year), and write in the steps when you think they should happen. If your plan is five years long, indicate what you plan to do by the fourth, third, and second years, and then the first year, including a six-month goal and a one-month goal for that first year.

Using what you know about strategic planning, fill in the details about what you will do throughout your plan. Set goals that establish who you will talk to, what courses you will take, what skills you will work on, what jobs or internships you will investigate, and any other research you need to do. Your path may change, of course; use your time line as a guide rather than as an inflexible plan.

The road to a truly satisfying career can be long. Seek support as you work toward goals. Confide in supportive people, talk positively to yourself, and read books about career planning such as those listed at the end of this chapter.

Keep Track of Details

After you establish your time frame, make a plan for pursuing the jobs or careers that have piqued your interest. Organize your approach according to what you need to do and how much time you have to do it. Do you plan to make three phone calls per day? Will you fill out three job applications a week for a month? Keep a record—on 3 × 5 cards, in a computer file, or in a notebook—of the following:

- people you contact
- companies to which you apply
- jobs you rule out (e.g., jobs that become unavailable or that you find don't suit your needs)
- responses to your communications (phone calls to you, interviews, written communications), information about the person who contacted you (name, title), and the time and the dates of contact

Keeping accurate records enables you to both chart your progress and maintain a clear picture of the process. You never know when information might come in handy again. If you don't get a job now, another one could open up at the same company in a couple of months. In that case, well-kept records enable you to contact key personnel quickly and efficiently. Figure 11.3 illustrates a sample file card.

Your Résumé and Interview

Information on résumés and interviews fills many books. Therefore, your best bet is to consult some that go into more detail, such as *The Resume Kit* by Richard H. Beatty or *Job Interviews for Dummies* by Joyce Lain Kennedy. You'll find these sources and other suggestions listed at the end of the chapter.

Figure 11.3   **Sample file card.**

Job/company:	Child-care worker at Morningside Day Care
Contact:	Sally Wheeler, Morningside Day Care,
	17 Parkside Rd, Silver Spring, MD 20910
Phone/fax/e-mail:	(301) 555-3353 phone, (301) 555-3354 fax,
	no e-mail
Communication:	Saw ad in paper, sent résumé & cover letter on Oct. 7
Response:	Call from Sally to set up interview
	—Interview on Oct. 15 at 2 p.m., seemed to get a positive
	response, said she would contact me again by end of the week
Follow-up:	Sent thank-you note on Oct. 16

Here are a few basic tips to get you started on giving yourself the best possible chance at a job.

Résumé. Your résumé should always be typed or printed on a computer. Design your résumé neatly, using an acceptable format (books or your career office can show you some standard formats).

Fill your résumé with keywords that a computer is likely to pick when a prospective employer scans the document. Proofread it for errors and have someone else proofread it as well. Type or print it on a heavier bond paper than is used for ordinary copies. Use white or off-white paper and black ink.

Interview. Be clean, neat, and appropriately dressed. Choose a nice pair of shoes—people notice. Bring an extra copy of your résumé and any other materials that you want to show the interviewer, even if you have already sent a copy ahead of time. Avoid chewing gum or smoking. Offer a confident handshake. Make eye contact. Show your integrity by speaking honestly about yourself. After the interview is over, no matter what the outcome, send a formal but pleasant thank-you note right away as a follow-up.

Having a job may not only be a thought for the future; it may be something you are concerned about right now. Many students need to work and take classes at the same time to fund their education. Although you may not necessarily work in an area that interests you, you can hold a job that helps you pay the bills and still make the most of your school time.

What will help you juggle *work* and *school?*

W hat you are studying today can prepare you to find a job when you graduate. In the meantime, though, you can make work a part of your student life to make money, explore a career, and increase your future employability through contacts or résumé building.

As the cost of education continues to rise, more and more students are working and taking classes at the same time. In the school year 1995–96, 79 percent of undergraduates—four out of five—reported working while in school. Most student workers 23 years of age or younger held part-time jobs (about 36 percent). Of students over the age of 23, the majority had full-time jobs (nearly 55 percent).[4] Figure 11.4 shows statistics related to working for both community college and four-year college students.

Being an employed student isn't for everyone. Adding a job to the list of demands on your time and energy may create problems if it sharply reduces study time or family time. However, many people want to work and many need to work to pay for school. Weigh the potential positive and negative effects of working so that you can make the most beneficial choice.

Effects of Working While in School

Working while in school has many different positive and negative effects, depending on the situation. Evaluate any job opportunity by looking at these effects. Potential positive effects include:

- money earned
- general and career-specific experience
- being able to keep a job you currently hold
- enhanced school and work performance (working up to 15 hours a week may encourage students to manage time more effectively and build confidence)

    Potential negative effects include:

- demanding time commitment
- reduced opportunity for social and extracurricular activities
- having to shift gears mentally from work to classroom

    If you consider the effects and decide that working will help you, consider what you need from a job.

Establishing Your Needs

Think about what you need from a job before you begin your job hunt. Table 11.5 shows questions you may want to consider. Evaluate any potential job in terms of your needs.

In addition, be sure to consider how any special needs you have might be accommodated. If you have a hearing or vision impairment, reduced mobility, children for whom you need day care, or any other particular need, you may want to find an employer who can and will accommodate them.

Your experiences in exploring careers and working are closely tied to your experiences with money. An important part of becoming a working person is earning the money you need to live. For that reason, investigating your financial needs and your particular strategies of dealing with money is important as you move toward the career for you. With what you learn about your finances, you are able to find the job and career that fit your needs.

No matter where your money comes from—financial aid or paychecks from one or more jobs—you can take steps to help it stretch as far as it can go. Using budgeting skills and strategic planning, you can more efficiently cover your expenses and still have some left over for savings and fun.

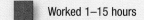

Figure 11.4

Working students.

Community college students

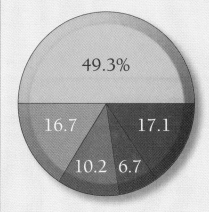

- Not employed
- Worked 1–15 hours
- Worked 16–20 hours
- Worked 21–34 hours
- Worked 35 hours or more

Four-year college students

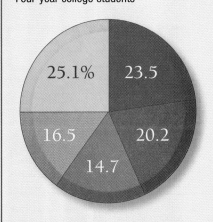

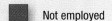

Source: U.S. Department of Education, National Center for Educational Statistics, *Profile of Undergraduates in U.S. Postsecondary Education Institutions: 1995–1996* (NCES 98-084), May 1998.

Table 11.5 Evaluate what you need from a job you take when in school.

NEED	EVALUATION QUESTIONS
Salary or wage level	How much do I need to make for the year? How much during the months when I am paying tuition? What amount of money justifies the time my job takes?
Time of day	When is best for me? If I take classes at night, can I handle a day job? If I take day classes, would I prefer night or weekend work?
Hours per week (part-time vs. full-time)	If I take classes part-time, can I handle a full-time job? If I am a full-time student, is part-time work best?
Duties performed	Do I want hands-on experience in my chosen field? Is the paycheck the priority over choosing what I do? What do I like and dislike doing?
Location	Does location matter? Will a job near school save me a great deal of time? What does my commute involve?
Flexibility	Do I need a job that offers flexibility, allowing me to shift my working time when I have an academic or family responsibility?
Affiliation with school or financial aid program	Does my financial aid package require me to take work at the school or a federal organization?

How can you create a
budget that *works?*

BUDGETING

Making a plan for the coordination of resources and expenditures; setting goals regarding money.

For the vast majority of students, college is not a time to be "rolling in money." Even if you are a fully independent adult who has returned to school after years of working, money is probably tight, perhaps making it necessary to skimp in order to meet expenses. Similarly, if you depend on money from relatives or financial aid, not having enough to meet your monthly expenses can add stress to your daily life.

Every time you have to figure out whether the money in your pocket will pay for what you want at a store, you are **budgeting** your money. It is a process that considers your resources (money flowing in) and expenditures (money flowing out) and adjusts the flow so that you come out even or perhaps even ahead. Being able to budget effectively relieves money-related stress and helps you feel more in control.

Your biggest expense right now is probably the cost of your education, including tuition and room-and-board. However, that expense may not hit you fully until after you graduate and begin to pay back your student loans. For now, include in your budget only the part of the cost of your education you are paying while you are in school.

The Art of Budgeting

Budgeting involves a few basic steps: Determining spendable income (how much money you have after taxes), determining how much money you spend, subtracting what you spend from your after-tax income, evaluating the result, and deciding how to adjust your spending or earning based on that result. Budgeting regularly, using a specified time frame, is easiest. Most people budget on a month-by-month basis.

Determine Your Spendable Income

Add up all of the money you receive during the year—the actual after-tax money you have to pay your bills. You may earn some of this money every month—from a part-time, after-school job, for example—while other income may come from summer and holiday employment that you have saved and then prorated for your monthly expenses. Common sources of income include:

- Your take-home pay from a regular full-time or part-time job during the school year.
- Your take-home pay from summer and holiday employment.
- Money you earn as part of a work-study program.
- Money you receive from your parents or other relatives for your college expenses.
- Scholarships or grants that provide spending money.

If you have savings specifically earmarked for your education, decide how much you will withdraw every month for your school-related expenses.

Figure Out How Much You Spend

If you have never paid much attention to how you spend, examine your patterns. Start by recording every check you write for fixed expenses like rent and telephone. Then, over the next month, record personal expenditures in a small notebook. Indicate any expenditure over five dollars, making sure to count smaller expenditures if they are frequent (e.g., a bus pass for a month, soda or newspaper purchases per week).

"Money can't buy you happiness. It just helps you look for it in more places."

MILTON BERLE

Some expenses, like insurance, are billed only a few times a year. In these cases, convert the expense to monthly by dividing the yearly cost by 12. Be sure to count only *current* expenses, not expenses that you will pay after you graduate:

- rent or mortgage
- tuition that you are paying right now (the portion remaining after all forms of financial aid, including loans, scholarships and grants, are taken into account)
- books, lab fees, and other educational expenses
- regular bills (electric, gas, oil, phone, water)
- food, clothing, toiletries, and household supplies
- child care
- transportation and auto expenses (gas, maintenance)
- credit cards and other payments on credit (car payments)
- insurance (health, auto, homeowner's or renter's, life)
- entertainment and related items (cable television, movies, restaurants, books and magazines)
- computer-related expenses, including the cost of your on-line service
- miscellaneous unplanned expenses

Use the total of all your monthly expenses as a baseline for other months, realizing that your expenditures will vary depending on what is happening in your life.

Evaluate the Result

Focusing again on your current situation, subtract your monthly expenses from your monthly income. Ideally, you have money left over—to save or to spend. However, if you are spending more than you take in, your first job is to analyze the problem by looking carefully at your budget, your spending patterns, and priorities. Use your critical-thinking skills to ask some focused questions.

Question your budget. Did you forget to budget for recurring expenses such as the cost for semiannual dental visits? Or was your budget derailed by an emergency expense that you did not foresee, such as the cost of a new transmission for your car? Is your budget realistic? Is your income sufficient for your needs?

Question your spending patterns and priorities. Did you spend money wisely during the month? Did you go to too many restaurants or movies? Can you afford the luxury of your own car? Are you putting too many purchases on your credit card and being hit by high interest payments?

When you are spending more than you are taking in during a "typical month," you may need to adjust your budget over the long term.

Make Decisions About How to Adjust Spending or Earning

Look carefully at what may cause you to overspend and brainstorm possible solutions that address those causes. Solutions can involve either increasing resources or decreasing spending. To deal with spending, prioritize your expenditures and trim the ones you really don't need to make. Cut out unaffordable or wasteful extras. For example, you can save a lot

Looking into the strategies associated with your strongest intelligences helps you identify effective ways to manage your money.

INTELLIGENCE	SUGGESTED STRATEGIES	WHAT WORKS FOR YOU? WRITE NEW IDEAS HERE
Verbal–Linguistic	■ Talk over your budget with someone you trust. ■ Write out a detailed budget outline. If you can, keep it on a computer where you can change and update it regularly.	
Logical–Mathematical	■ Focus on the numbers; using a calculator and amounts as exact as possible, determine your income and spending. ■ Calculate how much money you'll have in 10 years if you start now to put $2,000 in an IRA account each year.	
Bodily–Kinesthetic	■ Consider putting money, or a slip with a dollar amount, each month in different envelopes for various budget items—rent, dining out, etc. When the envelope is empty or the number is reduced to zero, your spending stops.	
Visual–Spatial	■ Set up a budgeting system that includes color-coded folders and colored charts. ■ Create color-coded folders for papers related to financial and retirement goals—investments, accounts, etc.	
Interpersonal	■ Whenever budgeting problems come up, discuss them right away. ■ Brainstorm a solid five-year financial plan with one of your friends.	
Intrapersonal	■ Schedule quiet time and think about how you want to develop, follow, and update your budget. Consider financial-management software, such as Quicken. ■ Think through the most balanced allocation of your assets—where you think your money should go.	
Musical	■ Include a category of music-related purchases in your budget—going to concerts, buying CDs—but keep an eye on it to make sure you don't go overboard.	
Naturalistic	■ Remember to include time and money in your budget to enjoy nature. ■ Sit in a spot you like. Brainstorm how you will achieve your short- and long-term financial goals.	

of money each month by renting movies at your local video rental store instead of going to the theater. You can save even more if you borrow movies from your local library, which are often free.

As for resources, investigate ways to take in more money. Start your summer job search early so you have the choice of the highest-paying positions. Taking a part-time job, hunting down scholarships or grants, or increasing hours at a current job may also help. You may also want to look for a job that pays more than you are currently making.

A Sample Budget

Table 11.6 shows a sample budget of an unmarried student living with two other students in off-campus housing with no meal plan. Included are all regular and out-of-pocket expenses with the exception of tuition expenses, which the student will pay back after graduation in student loan payments. In this case, the student is $164 over budget. How would you make up the shortfall?

Table 11.6	A student's sample monthly budget.

- Wages: $10 an hour (after taxes) x 20 hours a week = $200 a week x 4 1/3 weeks (one month) = $866
- Withdrawals from savings (from summer earnings) = $200
- Total income per month: $1,066

MONTHLY EXPENDITURES:

School-related expenses (not covered by student loans, grants, scholarships—including books and supplies)	$150
Public transportation	$90
Phone	$40
Food	$450
Credit card payments	$100
Rent (including utilities)	$200
Entertainment	$100
Miscellaneous expenses, including clothes and toiletries	$100
Total monthly spending	$1,230

$1,066 (income) − $1,230 (spending) = $−164 ($164 over budget)

Not everyone likes the work involved in keeping a budget. For example, whereas logical–mathematical learners may take to it easily, visual learners may resist the structure and detail of the budgeting process (see Chapter 2). Visual learners may want to create a budget chart such as the one in the example or use strategies that make budgeting more tangible, such as dumping receipts into a big jar and tallying them at the end of the month. Even if you have to force yourself to use a budget, you will discover that the process can reduce stress and help you take control of your finances and your life.

Savings Strategies

Your challenge is to figure out ways to save money and still enjoy life. This involves being honest with yourself about your *needs* versus your *wants*. If your current sneakers are falling apart, you certainly *need* a new pair. However, your decision to buy an especially expensive pair is a *want* because other equally serviceable brands may cost far less.

Here are some savings suggestions for cutting corners. Small amounts can eventually add up to big savings and may keep you out of debt.

Share living space with one or more roommates.

Rent or borrow movies.

Eat at home more often than at restaurants.

Use your local library.

Use coupons, take advantage of sales, buy store brands, and buy in bulk.

Find discounted play and concert tickets (students often receive discounts).

Walk or use public transport.

Bring your lunch from home.

Shop in secondhand stores.

Use e-mail or write letters.

Ask a relative to help you with child care.

Add your own suggestions here:

_____

_____

_____

Make Strategic Financial Decisions

Every budgetary decision you make has particular effects, often involving a trade-off among options. When you spend $80 for that new pair of sneakers, for example, you may not have enough for movie tickets and dinner with friends that weekend. That is, there is an *opportunity cost* in addition to money. In this case, the new sneakers deprive you of the chance to attend the movie and go to dinner. Although buying the sneakers may be the right decision for you, look at the whole picture before you spend your money.

Being strategic with your money primarily means taking that big-picture look before making any financial decision, large or small. Use what you know about decision making to make the decisions that work best for you.

1. *Establish your needs.* Be honest about what you truly need and what you just want. Do you really need a new bike? Or can the old one serve while you pay off some credit card debt?

2. *Brainstorm available options.* Think about what you can do with your money and evaluate the positive and negative effects of each option.

3. *Choose an option and carry it out.* Spend it—save it—invest it—whatever you decide.

4. *Evaluate the result.* This crucial step builds knowledge that you can use in the future. What were the positive and negative effects of what you chose? Would you make that choice again?

Often, making some short-term sacrifices in order to save money can help you a great deal in the long run. However, this doesn't mean you should never spend money on things that bring you immediate satisfaction. The goal is to make choices that provide both short-term satisfaction and long-term money growth.

"It is thrifty to prepare today for the wants of tomorrow."

AESOP

Following are two final pointers for being strategic with your hard-earned money:

- *Live beneath your means.* Spend less than you make. This strategy helps you create savings. Any amount of savings gives you a buffer zone that can help with emergencies or bigger expenditures.

- *Pay yourself.* After you pay your monthly bills, put whatever you can save in an account. Paying yourself helps you store

*L*ife's twists and turns, including the demands of family and financial issues, can put stubborn roadblocks in your path. Sometimes you just have to push them away over and over. With perseverance, Carol Comlish kept clearing the road that led to her goal of a college degree.

The author Jack London once said, "You can't wait for inspiration. You have to go after it with a club." After pursuing my bachelor's degree for 29 years, London's statement keeps reminding me that, indeed, there were many times I had to flog myself for inspiration to persevere.

When I was in high school, I chose a business curriculum because I knew I had no means to attend college. My mother, a single parent of six, was left ill-equipped to provide the encouragement or the funds to help steer me toward a college education. After high school, I worked as a government secretary in Washington, D.C., and later as a flight attendant. Every penny I earned paid for much-needed dental work and for shoes and clothing my mother was unable to provide. There was no money left for schooling.

During those years, I married and had four children. I had much of what I had always wanted, but I still felt the drive to get an education. So, when my youngest child was two years old, I enrolled in my first college course—15 years after high school. I had not taken college prep courses to prepare me, and it was tough. Soon, another baby appeared on the scene, and I quit school. Two years later, I had yet another baby. School and studying were out of the question. I could barely hold my head above water.

Then, when my youngest child began kindergarten, I tried school again. But it was so difficult to maintain a balance between the constant demands of the family and the demands of schoolwork that, after a couple of years of that grueling routine, I dropped out again.

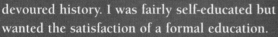

Carol Comlish, graduate of the University of Alabama, Tuscaloosa, Alabama

Over the next 10 years, my desire for learning was exceptionally intense. Everything interested me. I learned to speak French, I read Shakespeare, and I devoured history. I was fairly self-educated but wanted the satisfaction of a formal education.

When my sixth child was in junior high, I began working to help pay for college expenses for my brood. But, in time, my personal desire to get a degree led me to the University of Alabama External Degree program. The program was difficult because it required that I complete assignments without the benefit of classroom lectures and the help of professors. For six years, I toiled in the program while working full-time and trying to maintain equilibrium in a household with two remaining children whose needs still had to be met.

The most difficult aspect of the program was cramming assignments into every single weekend. There was no time for leisure—not if I wanted to achieve my goal. However, with all my other responsibilities, I have to admit that I was not always as motivated as I might have been. I would burn out periodically and not open a book for months.

When the end was finally in sight, I was unable to continue my studies due to a particularly discouraging experience with one of my courses. I was ready to quit for good. But I soon realized that because so much was invested, I had to go on. I pushed harder than ever. At last, on May 19, 2001, at the University of Alabama in Tuscaloosa, I received my B.A. degree in Humanities, with high honors.

Take a moment to consider . . .

- *Which of your life's goals so far has required the most effort and perseverance.*

- *What you plan to do to come up with the resources to pay for college.*

money in your savings where it can grow. Make your payment to yourself a high priority so that you honor it as you do your other bills.

One final part of keeping an accurate, useful budget is being a strategic consumer of banking services.

Use Bank Accounts Wisely

Paying your bills and saving require that you form your own relationship with a financial institution such as a bank. Choose a bank with convenient locations, hours that fit your schedule, account fees that aren't too high, and a convenient network of automatic teller machines (ATMs).

Most banks issue debit cards that look like credit cards but take money directly out of your checking account immediately (unlike checks, which clear after one or more days). Many banks now have phone or on-line payment services that help you bank from your home, as well as services that allow you to set up the automatic payment of bills directly from your account each month.

The two specific services you need when you use a bank are checking and savings accounts.

Checking Accounts

Most banks offer more than one checking plan. Some accounts include check-writing fees, a small charge on every check you write or on any checks above a certain number per month. Some accounts have free checking, meaning unlimited check writing without extra fees—but you often have to maintain a minimum balance in your account to qualify. Some accounts charge a monthly fee that is standard or varies according to your balance. Interest checking pays you a low rate of interest, although you may have to keep a certain balance or have a savings account at the same bank.

Savings Accounts

The most basic savings account, the interest savings account, pays a rate of interest to you determined by the bank. Many interest savings accounts do not have a required balance, but the interest rate they pay is very low. A certificate of deposit (CD) pays greater interest, but your money is "locked in" for a specific period of time—often six months or a year—and you pay a penalty if you withdraw part or all of your money. Money market accounts allow you to withdraw your money without penalty. However, interest rates are generally lower than the rates offered by CDs and may rise or fall as the economy changes.

How can you *manage* your *credit cards?*

It is common for college students to receive dozens of credit card offers from different financial institutions issuing VISA and MasterCard. These offers—and the cards that go along with them—are a double-edged sword: They have the power to help you manage your money, but they also can plunge you into a hole of debt that may take you years to dig out of. Some recent statistics from a Nellie May survey of undergraduates illustrate the challenging situation:[5]

- Average number of credit cards per student—3.2
- Average credit card debt per student—$1,843
- Average available credit card limit—$3,683
- Percentage of students with debt between $3,000 and $7,000—9 percent
- Percentage of students with more than $7,000 in credit card debt—5 percent

When used properly, credit cards are a handy alternative to cash. They give you the peace of mind of knowing that you always have money for emergencies and that you have a record of all your purchases. In addition, if you pay your bills on time, you will be building a strong credit history that will affect your ability to take out future loans including auto loans and mortgages.

However, it takes self-control to avoid overspending, especially because it is so easy to hand over your credit card when you see something you like. To avoid excessive debt, ask yourself these questions before charging anything: Would I buy it if I had to pay cash? Can I pay off the balance in full at the end of the first billing cycle? If I buy this, what purchases will I have to forgo? If I buy this, do I have enough to cover emergencies?

How Credit Cards Work

When you make purchase on credit—everything from your textbooks to holiday presents for friends and family—the merchant accepts immediate payment from the credit card issuer and you accept the responsibility to pay the money back. *Every time you charge, you are creating a debt that must be repaid.* The credit card issuer earns money by charging interest on your unpaid balance. With rates that are often higher than 20 percent, you may soon find yourself wishing that you had paid cash.

Here's an example of how quickly credit card debt can mount. Say you have a $3,000 unpaid balance on your credit card at an annual interest rate of 18 percent. If you make the $60 minimum monthly payment every month, it will take you 8 long years to pay off your debt, assuming that you make no other purchases. The math—and the effect on your wallet—is staggering:

- Original debt—$3,000
- Cost to repay credit card loan at an annual interest rate of 18 percent for 8 years—$5,760
- Cost of credit—$2,760

By the time you finish, you will repay nearly twice your original debt.

To avoid unmanageable debt that can lead to a personal financial crisis, learn as much as you can about credit cards, starting with the important concepts in Table 11.7.

Learn to use credit wisely while you are still in school. The habits you learn today can make a difference to your financial future.

Managing Debt

The majority of American citizens have some level of debt, and many people go through periods when they have a hard time keeping up with their bills. Falling behind on payments, however, could result in a poor credit rating that makes it difficult for you to make large purchases or take out loans. Particular resources can help you solve credit problems; see Figure 11.5 for some ideas.

The most basic way to stay in control is to pay bills regularly and on time. On credit card bills, pay at least the minimum amount due. If you get into trouble, deal with it in three steps. First, admit that you made a mistake, even though you may be embarrassed. Then, address the problem immediately to minimize damages. Call the creditor and see if you can pay your debt gradually using a payment plan. Finally, examine what got you into trouble and avoid it in the future if you can. Cut up a credit card or two if you have too many. If you clean up your act, your credit history will gradually clean up as well.

CREDITOR
A person or company to whom a debt is owed, usually money.

Figure 11.5

Credit help resources.

Consumer Credit Counseling Service (credit counseling)
1-800-338-2227
Spanish 1-800-682-9832

Money Matters for College Students (free booklet from Citibank)
1-800-833-9666

Genus Credit Management (free debt counseling)
1-888-436-8715

National Foundation for Credit Counseling (tips on credit management)
www.nfcc.org

Springboard Non-profit Consumer Credit Management
www.ncfe.org

Table 11.7	Learn to be a smart credit consumer.

WHAT TO KNOW ABOUT . . .	. . . AND HOW TO USE WHAT YOU KNOW
Account balance—a dollar amount that includes any unpaid balance, new purchases and cash advances, finance charges, and fees. Updated monthly on your card statement.	Charge only what you can afford to pay at the end of the month. Keep track of your balance. Hold onto receipts and call customer service if you have questions about recent purchases.
Annual fee—the yearly cost some companies charge for owning a card.	Look for cards without an annual fee or, if you've paid your bills on time, ask your current company to waive the fee.
Annual percentage rate (APR)—the amount of interest charged on your unpaid balance, meaning the cost of credit if you carry a balance in any given month. The higher the APR, the more you pay in finance charges.	Credit card companies compete by charging different APRs. Shop around, especially on the Web. Two sites with competitive APR information are www.studentcredit.com and www.bankrate.com. Also, watch out for low, but temporary, introductory rates that skyrocket to over 20 percent after a few months. Look for *fixed* rates (guaranteed not to change).
Available credit—the unused portion of your credit line. Determine available credit by deducting your current card balance from your credit limit.	It is important to have credit available for emergencies, so avoid charging to the limit.
Billing cycle—the number of days between the last statement date and the current statement date.	Knowledge of your billing cycle can help you juggle funds. For example, if your cycle ends on the 3rd of the month, holding off on a large purchase until the 4th gives you an extra month to pay without incurring finance charges.
Cash advance—an immediate loan, in the form of cash, from the credit card company. You are charged interest immediately and may also pay a separate transaction fee.	Use a cash advance only in emergencies because the finance charges start as soon as you complete the transaction. It is a very expensive way to borrow money.
Credit limit—the debt ceiling the card company places on your account (e.g., $1,500). The total owed, including purchases, cash advances, finance charges, and fees, cannot exceed this limit.	Credit card companies generally set low credit limits for college students. Many students get around this limit by owning more than one card, which increases the credit available but most likely increases problems as well.
Credit line—a revolving amount of credit that can be used, paid back, then used again for future purchases or cash advances.	Work with the credit line of one card, paying the money you borrow back at the end of each month so you can borrow again.
Delinquent account—an account that is not paid on time or for which the minimum payment has not been met.	Avoid having a delinquent account at all costs. Not only will you be charged substantial late fees, but you also risk losing your good credit rating, affecting your ability to borrow in the future. Delinquent accounts remain part of your credit record for many years.
Due date—the date your payment must be received and after which you will be charged a late fee.	Avoid late fees and finance charges by mailing your payment a week in advance.

Table 11.7   Continued.

WHAT TO KNOW ABOUT . . .	. . . AND HOW TO USE WHAT YOU KNOW
Finance charges—the total cost of credit, including interest and service and transaction fees.	Your goal is to incur no finance charges. The only way to do that is to pay your balance in full by the due date on your monthly statement.
Grace period—the interest-free time period between the date of purchase and the date your payment for that purchase is due once it appears on your statement. For example, a purchase on November 4 may first appear on your November 28 statement with payment due 25 days later.	It is important to know that interest-free grace periods only apply if you have no outstanding balance. If you carry a balance from month to month, all new purchases are immediately subject to interest charges.
Minimum payment—the smallest amount you can pay by the statement due date. The amount is set by the credit card company.	Making only the minimum payment each month can result in disaster if you continue to charge more than you can realistically afford. When you make a purchase, think in terms of total cost, not monthly payments.
Outstanding balance—the total amount you owe on your card.	If you carry a balance over several months, additional purchases are immediately hit with finance charges. Pay cash instead.
Past due—your account is considered "past due" when you fail to mail the minimum required payment on schedule.	Three credit bureaus note past due accounts on your credit history: Experian, Trans Union, and Equifax. You can contact each bureau for a copy of your credit report to make sure there are no errors.

sacrifici

In Italy, parents often use the term *sacrifici*, meaning "sacrifices," to refer to tough choices that they make to improve the lives of their children and family members. They may sacrifice a larger home so that they can afford to pay for their children's sports and after-school activities. They may sacrifice a higher-paying job so that they can live close to where they work. They give up something in exchange for something else that they have decided is more important to them.

Think of the concept of *sacrifici* as you analyze the sacrifices you can make to get out of debt, reach your savings goals, and prepare for a career that you find satisfying. Many of the short-term sacrifices you are making today will help you do and have what you want in the future.

Building Skills

FOR COLLEGE, CAREER, AND LIFE SUCCESS

Critical Thinking *Applying Learning to Life*

Career Possibilities

Choose one of the career areas you have listed as an interest in any other exercise in this book. Follow up on it by using the following leads. List two or three specific possibilities found using each of the sources below.

Help wanted listings in newspapers, magazines, or Internet databases:

_____

_____

_____

Listings of job opportunities/company contact information at your career center, student employment office, or independent employment agency:

_____

_____

_____

Contacts from friends or family members:

_____

_____

_____

Contacts from instructors, administrators, or counselors:

_____

_____

_____

Current or former employers or coworkers:

_____

_____

_____

Your Budget

PART ONE: WHERE YOUR MONEY GOES. Estimate your current expenses in dollars per month, using the table below. This may require tracking expenses for a month, if you don't already keep a record of your spending. The grand total is your total monthly expenses.

EXPENSE	AMOUNT SPENT
Rent/mortgage or room and board payment	$
Utilities (electric, heat, gas, water)	$
Food (shopping and eating out)	$
Telephone	$
Books, lab fees, or other educational expenses	$
Loan payments (education or bank loans)	$
Car (repairs, insurance, monthly payments)	$
Gasoline/public transportation	$
Clothing/personal items	$
Entertainment	$
Child care (caregivers, clothing/supplies, etc.)	$
Medical care/insurance	$
Miscellaneous/unexpected	$
Other	$
GRAND TOTAL	$

PART TWO: WHERE YOUR MONEY COMES FROM. Calculate your average monthly income from earnings/grants/other sources. If it's easiest to come up with a yearly figure, divide by 12 to derive the monthly figure.

INCOME SOURCE	AMOUNT EARNED
Regular work salary/wages (full-time or part-time)	$
Grants or work-study payments	$
Scholarships	$
Assistance from family members	$
Any independent contracting work	$
Other	$
GRAND TOTAL	$

Now, subtract the grand total of your monthly expenses (Part one) from the grand total of your monthly income (Part two):

Income per month	$
Expenses per month	–$
CASH FLOW	$

Choose one:	○ I have $ +	○ I have $ –	○ I pretty much break even

PART THREE: ADJUSTING YOUR BUDGET. If you have a negative cash flow, you can increase your income, decrease your spending, or do both. Go back to your list of current expenses to determine where you may be able to save. Look also at your list of income sources to determine what you can increase.

My current expenses	$	per month
I want to spend	$	less per month
My current income	$	per month
I want to earn	$	more per month

Evaluating your situation, describe here what you think are the two most workable ideas about how to adjust your budget. Making smart decisions now will earn you long-term financial gain.

1. _____

2. _____

Teamwork *Combining Forces*

SAVINGS BRAINSTORM. As a class, brainstorm areas that require financial management (e.g., funding an education, running a household, or putting savings away for the future) and write them on the board. Divide into small groups. Each group should choose one area to discuss (make sure all areas are chosen). In your group, brainstorm strategies that can help with the area you have chosen. Think of savings ideas, ways to control spending, ways to earn more money, and any other methods of relieving financial stress. Agree on a list of possible ideas for your area and share it with the class.

Writing *Discovery Through Journaling*

To record your thoughts, use a separate journal or the lined page at the end of the chapter.

CREDIT CARDS. Describe how you use credit cards. What do you buy? How much do you spend? Do you pay in full each month or run a balance? How does using a credit card make you feel? If you would like to change how you use credit, discuss changes you want to make and what effects they might have.

Career Portfolio *Charting Your Course*

FINANCIAL HISTORY. Create for yourself a detailed picture of your financial history. First, put your budget exercises, or copies of them, in your portfolio so that you have a record of your spending habits. Then compile the following pieces of information on a separate sheet and keep your work. Keeping accurate financial records is vital in making intelligent financial decisions.

1. *Financial aid.* List school, federal, and personal loans; scholarship funds; grants; and the amount that you pay out of pocket. Indicate all account numbers, payment plans, and records of payment including dates and check numbers if applicable.

2. *Bank accounts.* For any account to which you have access, list all names on the accounts, bank name, type of account, and account number. Include any restrictions on the accounts such as minimum balances or time frames during which you will receive a penalty for removing funds.

3. *Loans.* List any nonacademic loans you are currently repaying, noting bank names, account numbers, loan types, repayment schedule, payment amounts, and dates of payments made.

4. *Credit cards.* List major credit cards (American Express, Visa, MasterCard, Discover, etc.), as well as cards for gas stations or department stores. For each card, include the following:

   - Name on the card, card number, and expiration date
   - Typical payment style (pay in full, pay minimum each month, etc.)
   - Problems (late payments, lost cards, card fraud, etc.)

   Keep a copy of important credit card numbers separate from your wallet or purse so that you have records should you lose your cards. For your protection, any record of personal identification numbers (PINs) should be kept separate from credit cards or credit card numbers.

5. *Earning history.* List the jobs you have had or currently have. Include the following for each:

   - name of the company or business
   - job title and duties
   - wages or salary
   - dates of your employment

   Store this information in your portfolio. Update it when you have new entries.

6. *References.* First, create a list of people who have served or could serve as references for you. Brainstorm names from all areas of your human resources:

Instructors	Fellow students
Friends	Administrators
Present/former employers	Mentors
Counselors	Present/former coworkers
	Family members

   For each potential reference, list the name, contact information (phone number and address), and how you know the person. Update the information as you meet potential references or lose touch with old ones. Keep it on hand for the time that you need a new letter or want to cite a reference on a résumé. When references write letters of recommendation for you, be sure to thank them right away for their help and to keep them up-to-date on your activities. Always let a reference know when you have sent a letter out, so that he or she may be prepared to receive a call from the person/company/program to which you have applied.

Assess Yourself *Student Success Strategies*

If you have access to the CD-ROM Strategies for Success, *use the following questions to assess your thoughts and enhance your understanding of the chapter. The questions below represent only some of the activities provided on the CD for the chapter topics—try others if you have time.*

Click on the Managing Your Money bookmark. Use the following activities to expand your money management skills:

1. Take the pre-assessment to evaluate your money management knowledge.

2. Watch the video and consider the consequences of your financial actions and decisions. In the field provided, answer the question about how you currently handle your finances.

3. Click on Activity Two: Credit Cards. Answer the questions (the second screen will require that your computer be on-line) to assess your credit card knowledge.

4. Click on Activity Three: Journal Reflections. Scroll to the third question regarding critical thinking and money planning. In the field provided, type a critical-thinking plan for a purchase you want to make.

Suggested Readings

Adams, Robert Lang, et al. *The Complete Résumé and Job Search Book for College Students.* Holbrook, MA: Adams Publishing, 1999.

Beatty, Richard H. *The Resume Kit, 4th ed.* New York: John Wiley & Sons, Inc., 2000.

Boldt, Laurence G. *Zen and the Art of Making a Living: A Practical Guide to Creative Career Design.* New York: Arkana, 1999.

Bolles, Richard Nelson. *What Color Is Your Parachute? 2001: A Practical Manual for Job Hunters and Career Changers.* Berkeley, CA: Ten Speed Press, 2000.

Detweiler, Gerri. *The Ultimate Credit Handbook.* New York: Plume, 1997.

Goleman, Daniel. *Emotional Intelligence.* New York: Bantam Books, 1997.

Goleman, Daniel. *Working With Emotional Intelligence.* New York: Bantam Books, 1998.

Kennedy, Joyce Lain. *Job Interviews for Dummies.* Foster City, CA: IDG Books Worldwide, Inc., 2000.

Tyson, Eric. *Personal Finance for Dummies.* Foster City, CA: IDG Books Worldwide, Inc., 2000.

Internet Resources

Student Advantage—information on discounts: www.studentadvantage.com

Monster.com (online job search): www.monster.com

Tripod—Money/Business (financial and career advice, budget counseling): www.tripod.com/money_business/

1st Steps in the Hunt: Daily News for Online Job Hunters (advice on finding a job via an online search): www.interbiznet.com/hunt/

College Grad Job Hunter (advice on resumes, interviews, and a database of entry-level jobs): www.collegegrad.com

Women's Wire (helping women target a career and juggle work and family): www.womenswire.com/work

JobWeb (career information site for college students): www.jobweb.org

Prentice Hall Student Success Supersite—Money Matters: www.prenhall.com/success/MoneyMat/index.html

Career Path: www.prenhall.com/success/CareerPath/index.html

Endnotes

1. Peter Passell, "Royal Blue Collars," *The New York Times,* March 22, 1998, p. 12.

2. Daniel Goleman, *Working with Emotional Intelligence.* New York: Bantam Books, 1998, pp. 26–27.

3. Steven Greenhouse, "Equal Work, Less-Equal Perks," *The New York Times,* March 30, 1998, pp. D1, D6.

4. U.S. Department of Education, National Center for Education Statistics, *Profile of Undergraduates in U.S. Postsecondary Education Institutions: 1995–96,* NCES 98-084, by Laura J. Horn, Jennifer Berktold, Andrew G. Malizio, Project Officer, and MPR Associates, Inc. Washington, DC: U.S. Government Printing Office, 1998, pp. 4, 31.

5. Laura A. Bruce, "College Kids' Credit Card Use Can Leave Them Drowning in High-Interest Debt," Bankrate.com (www.bankrate. com/brm/news/cc/20000815.asp), downloaded March 2, 2001.

JOURNAL

name   date

GROW

12

414

Moving ahead

IN THIS CHAPTER

In this chapter you explore answers to the following questions:

- How does what you've learned translate into success? • How can you be flexible in the face of change? • Why should you be an active citizen?

- How can you live your mission?

AS YOU COME TO THE END of your work in this course, you have built up a wealth of knowledge. Like Morgan Packard (see next page), you are facing important decisions about what direction you want your life to take and how you can find a place in the working world. This chapter helps you realize how what you've learned can fuel your success. You explore how flexibility can help you adjust to change. You consider what is important about being an active citizen. Finally, you revisit your personal mission, exploring how to keep it in sync with life's changes.

building a flexible future

Morgan Packard, Tulane University, New Orleans, Louisiana

Ramona Z. Locke, Vice President, Senior Financial Consultant, Merrill Lynch Private Client Group, Dallas, Texas

How can I find a career I will enjoy?

Use college to discover what you do well; then . . . find the job you are most suited for

I have always had varied interests. Through high school, my extracurricular activities ranged from piano and voice lessons to spending my summers acting in a Renaissance Fair and everything in between. I was also continually motivated to keep a high grade point average; though I love my activities, school is my top priority. So, when it came time to choose a college, I looked for one whose reputation in academics, particularly the English department, was balanced by opportunities to participate in the arts.

Now attending college and majoring in English, I am faced with a problem. Since I was little, one of my favorite escapes has been reading. When I chose my major, I did so based on a subject that interested me and that would prepare me to participate in a profession that I would like to turn into my career, editing and publishing. I'm wondering how I can apply my major along with my interests to allow me to stay flexible in my studies, and how I can use those tools to find and maintain a career I will enjoy.

I think that some of your biggest strengths when you graduate and look for a job will be not only your school affiliation and grades, but those other activities and strengths you acquired along the way. People who strictly adhere to the academic route don't necessarily acquire the skills associated with those activities; they may not have worked in a team environment, which is important in the job market. What is important to businesses today is not your grade point average or your major, but what skills you bring to the table, how flexible you can be to mold and grow into the position for which that company is looking.

I think one of the greatest attributes a person can acquire is to be able to get up in front of a crowd. I've been in the business world long enough to know that you do not have to be brilliant to be a success; however, if you can communicate your ideas, you *will* be successful. I think that your other activities, such as acting, singing, and dancing, will be important and helpful to you down the road. There are so many nontraditional career paths open today. You need to stay flexible and active so that you can be available when the right choice comes along.

Life doesn't work within the bounds of a rigid focus. To be successful and happy, you must learn to take life's curve balls. You must assimilate all of those situations that come your way and find the benefit in them. My analytical background and nature have helped me the most in my current career; I have a bachelor's degree in science and a master's in biochemistry and biophysics. I love what I do now, but that doesn't mean that I couldn't do seven other careers and be happy in them too. Try to come to grips with what you do best and do that because if you are good at it you will enjoy it. Use college to discover what you do well; then, when it comes time to leave, you can find the job you are most suited for and be happy in it, staying flexible and always open to the next opportunity that comes your way.

Figure 12.1   **Examples of changes people experience.**

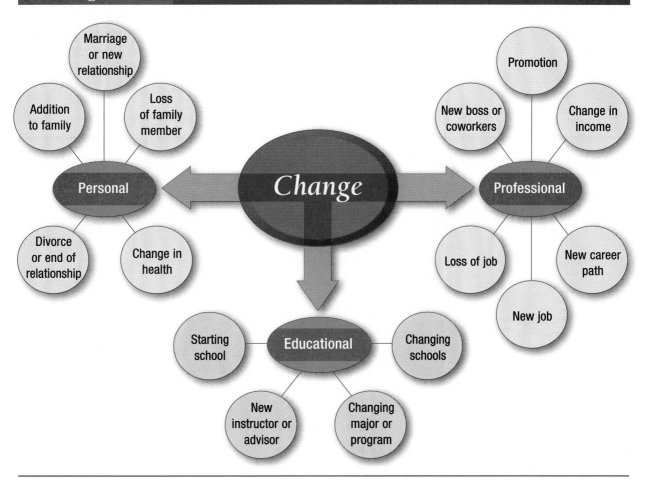

by surprise, such as losing a job. Some changes that shift your needs occur within a week or even a day; for example, an instructor may inform you that you have an end-of-week quiz. Even the different times of year bring different needs; for example, a need for extra cash around the holidays or additional child care when your children are home for the summer.

Different needs may lead to changing priorities. Table 12.2 shows how this can happen.

Flexibility is the key to navigating change successfully. When change affects your needs, flexibility helps you acknowledge the change, address different needs, and shift priorities. Flexibility also helps you open your mind to the hidden positive effects of change. For example, a loss of a job can lead you to reevaluate your abilities and look for a job that suits you better.

Although being flexible won't always be easy, inflexibility—not acknowledging a shift in needs—has the potential to cause serious problems. For example, if you lose your job and continue to spend as much money as you did before, ignoring your need to live more modestly, you can drive yourself into debt and make the situation worse.

How can you maximize your flexibility? Knowing how to adjust your goals, being open to unpredictability, and thinking creatively will help.

Table 12.2	Change produces new priorities.	
CHANGE	**POTENTIAL EFFECTS/NEW NEEDS**	**NEW PRIORITIES**
Started school	Fewer hours for personal time; responsibility for classes and assignments; need to plan semesters ahead of time	Careful scheduling to provide adequate class and study time; strategic planning of classes and of career goals
Changed major	Shift in courses and in academic goals; need to rework schedule and change academic focus	Course scheduling; meeting with advisor to determine requirements; reevaluation of academic time line
New job	Change in daily/weekly schedule; need for increased contribution of household help from others	Time and energy commitment, maintaining confidence, learning new skills
Relationship/marriage	Responsibility toward your partner; merging of your schedules and perhaps finances and belongings	Time and energy commitment to relationship
New baby	Increased parenting responsibility; need money to pay for baby's needs or if you had to stop working; need help with other children	Child care; flexible employment; increased commitment from a partner or other supportive people

Adjust Your Goals

Goals need adjusting for many reasons. Some don't pose enough of a challenge. Others may be unhealthy for the goal setter or harmful to others. Some turn out to be unreachable; for example, a goal to graduate in four years may not be reasonable if economic constraints take you out of school for a while. Use what you know about goal setting from Chapter 3 to reevaluate and, if necessary, modify your goals as your life changes.

Step One: Reevaluate

Before making adjustments in response to change, take time to reevaluate both the goals themselves and your progress toward them.

The goals. First, determine whether your goals still fit the person you have become in the past week or month or year. Circumstances can change quickly. For example, an unexpected health problem might cause a student to take a semester off, short-circuiting a goal to graduate by a particular date.

Your progress. If you feel you haven't gotten far, determine whether the goal is out of your range or simply requires more stamina than you had anticipated. As you work toward any goal, alternating periods of progress and stagnation ("hills and valleys") are normal. You may want to seek the support and perspective of a friend or counselor as you evaluate your progress.

Step Two: Modify

If, after your best efforts, it becomes clear that a goal is out of reach, modifying your goal may bring success. Perhaps the goal doesn't suit you. For example, an active interpersonal learner might become frustrated while pursuing a detailed, desk-bound career such as computer programming. Based on your reevaluation, you can modify a goal in two ways.

Adjust the existing goal. To adjust a goal, change one or more aspects that define it—the schedule, due dates, or expectations. For example, a student needing to take a semester off for health reasons could set a new graduation date goal, taking an extra semester or even a year to complete necessary course work.

Replace it with a more compatible goal. If you find that a particular goal does not make sense, try to find another that works better for you at this time. For example, a couple who wants to buy a house but can't afford it can choose to work toward the goal of making improvements in their current living space. You and your circumstances never stop changing—your goals should reflect those changes.

Considering this method of adjustment, think back to goals you set for yourself earlier in the semester after reading Chapter 3. Do any of them need to be adjusted? Why? Take some time to make sure your goals still fit after the changes you may have gone through in the last couple of months.

Be Open to Unpredictability

Life is unpredictable. If you consider the course of your life up until this point, you are likely to find that much of what you do and who you are is not as you imagined it would be.

In their article "A Simpler Way," Margaret J. Wheatley and Myron Kellner-Rogers discuss how the unpredictability of life can be a gift that opens up new horizons. They say that people "often look at this unpredicta-bility with resentment, but it's important to notice that such unpredictability gives us the freedom to experiment. It is this unpredictability that welcomes our creativity."[3] Wheatley and Kellner-Rogers offer the following suggestions for making the most of unpredictability.

Look for what happens when you meet someone or something new. Be aware of new feelings or insights when you interact with a new person, class, project, or event. Instead of accepting or rejecting them based on whether they fit into your idea of life, follow a bit. See where they lead you.

Be willing to be surprised. Great creative energies can come from the force of a surprise. Instead of turning back to familiar patterns after a surprise throws you off balance, see what you can discover.

Use your planning as a guide rather than a rule. Planning helps you focus your efforts, shape your path, and gain a measure of control over your world. Life, however, won't always go along with your plan. If you see your plans as a guide, allowing yourself to follow new paths when changes occur, you are able to grow from what life gives you.

Focus on what is rather than what is supposed to be. Often people are unable to see what's happening because they are too focused on what they feel *should* be happening. When you put all your energy into your future plans, you may miss out on some incredible occurrences happening right now. Planning for the future works best as a guide when combined with an awareness of the changes that the present brings.

Think Creatively

Being flexible demands creative thinking. Only through creativity can you come up with the alternatives—the different ideas, options, goals, and paths—that flexibility requires. When you come up against a big change in your life, take time to allow your creative mind to work through possibilities. Skim through the creativity strategies in Chapter 4 and see what spurs your thinking.

Creativity is important, too, because many more options are available to you now than ever before. The speed of change in the world has given rise to all kinds of ways to get an education and fulfill the duties of a job. Table 12.3 shows some examples.

Not so long ago, such options weren't imaginable. College almost always involved a full-time commitment to classes and homework; a job almost always meant being at a particular location 9 to 5 every weekday.

Table 12.3	Creative educational and career options are growing.	
YOU CAN . . .	**WHERE?**	**WHEN?**
Get an education	• In the classroom • At home over the Internet or watching a video or special telecast	• During weekday hours • At night • On weekends • On your own time, if you use video or Internet • Part-time or full-time, depending on your schedule
Perform your job	• At the workplace site • At home, via phone, Internet, and fax • On the road, using a computer and e-mail to communicate	• Daytime hours during the week • On flextime—working a particular number of hours each week, according to a schedule you and your employer agree on • On your own time, if you work at home, provided you meet goals • Half-time, at a part-time job • Half-time, sharing a job description with another employee

Now, thanks to computers and Internet technology, colleges and employers have adapted to make the most of what the changing population has to offer. Older citizens are working longer; mothers often need to work, but want to spend time with their children as well; working people want to continue to learn as they work, and want to leave different career options open. Creative thinking helps you evaluate your changing life, look at the options available to you, and plan a path that fits.

"The word impossible is not in my dictionary."

NAPOLEON

When you think creatively, you become an explorer, open to every experience that crosses your path. Having this awareness helps you understand that there are always others around you who are in need of your help. Giving what you can of your time, energy, and resources is part of being a citizen of your community and of the world.

Why should you be an active *citizen?*

E veryday life is demanding. You can become so caught up in the issues of your own life that you neglect to look outside your immediate needs. However, your ability to make a difference extends beyond your personal life. You have spent time in this course working to improve yourself; now, explore how you can make positive differences in the lives of others.

Your Imprint on the World

Sometimes you can evaluate your own hardships more reasonably when you look at them in light of what is happening elsewhere in the world. You have something to give, and in giving you affirm that you are part of a world community of people who depend on each other.

Your perspective may change after tutoring a fellow student. Your appreciation of those close to you may increase after you volunteer at a shelter or soup kitchen. Your view of your living situation may change after you help people improve their housing conditions.

What you do for others has enormous impact. Giving another human being hope, comfort, or help can improve his or her ability to cope. That person in turn may be able to offer help to someone else, which generates a cycle of positive effects. For example, Helen Keller, blind and deaf

Table 12.4	Organizations that can use your help.		
AIDS-related organizations	Educational support organizations	Nursing homes
American Red Cross	Environmental awareness/support organizations such as Greenpeace	Planned Parenthood
Amnesty International		School districts
Audubon Society	Hospitals	Scouting organizations
Battered women shelters	Hotlines	Share Our Strength/other food donation organizations
Big Brothers and Big Sisters	Kiwanis/Knights of Columbus/Lions Club/Rotary	
Churches, synagogues, temples, and affiliated organizations such as the YM/WCA or YM/WHA	Libraries	Shelters and organizations supporting the homeless
	Meals on Wheels	Sierra Club/World Wildlife Fund

from the age of two, was educated through the help of her teacher Annie Sullivan, and then spent much of her life lecturing to raise money for the teaching of the blind and deaf. Another example is Betty Ford, who was helped in her struggle with alcoholism and founded the Betty Ford Center to help others with addiction problems.

How can you make a difference? Look for some kind of volunteering activity that you can fit in your schedule. Many schools, realizing the importance of community involvement, have service learning programs or committees that find and organize volunteering opportunities. Table 12.4 lists organizations that provide volunteer opportunities; you might also look into more local efforts or private clearinghouses that set up a number of different smaller projects.

SERVICE LEARNING

A program whereby students can earn credits in particular subjects through specific volunteering activities.

Reaching out to others can also be a plus for your career. Being involved in causes and the community shows caring and an awareness of how people's needs interconnect, and companies look for these qualities in people they hire. Many companies now encourage, and reward, community involvement.

Volunteerism is also getting attention on the national level. In an effort to stress the importance of community service as part of being a good citizen, the government has developed AmeriCorps, which provides financial awards for education in return for community service. If you work for AmeriCorps, you can use the funds you receive to pay current tuition expenses or repay student loans. You may work either before, during, or after your college education. You can find more information on AmeriCorps by contacting The Corporation for National and Community Service, 1201 New York Avenue NW, Washington, DC 20525, 1-800-942-2677.

Sometimes it's hard to find time to volunteer when so many responsibilities compete for your attention. One solution is to combine other activities with volunteer work. Get exercise while helping to improve conditions at a local school, or bring the whole family to sing at a nursing home on a weekend afternoon. Whatever you do, your actions will have a positive impact on those you help and those they encounter in turn.

Getting Involved Locally and Nationally

Being an active citizen is another form of involvement. On a local level, you might take part in your community's debate over saving open space from developers. On a state level, you might contact legislators about building sound barriers along an interstate highway that runs through your town. On a national level, you might write letters to your congressional representative to urge support of an environmental, energy, or patients' rights bill. Work for political candidates who espouse the views you support, and consider running for office yourself—in your district, city, state, or nationally.

Most importantly, vote in every election. Despite the problems in the 2000 presidential election, every vote counts, and governments around the country are improving voting machines and systems to reduce the likelihood of error. It is important to remember that men and women have died in many wars to protect your right to vote. Having this right places you in a privileged minority among people around the world who have no voice in how they live. Your votes and your actions can make a difference—and getting involved will bring you the power and satisfaction of being a responsible citizen.

Valuing Your Environment

Your environment is your home. When you value it, you help to maintain a clean, safe, and healthy place to live. What you do every day has an impact on others around you and on the future of the planet. One famous slogan says that if you are not part of the solution, you are part of the problem. Every environmentally aware person, saved bottle, and reused bag is part of the solution. Take responsibility for what you can control—your own habits—and develop sound practices that contribute to the health of the environment.

Recycle anything that you can. What can be recycled varies with the system set up in your area. You may be able to recycle any combination of plastics, aluminum, glass, newspapers, and magazines. Products that use recycled materials are often more expensive, but if they are within your price range, try to reward the company's dedication by purchasing them.

Trade and reuse items. Instead of throwing away clothes or other items that are in good condition but that you don't use, find a home for them. Shop consignment or used clothing and goods stores for bargains. Trade clothes and items with friends. When your children have grown too old for the crib, baby clothes, and toys, give away whatever is still usable. Organizations like Goodwill may pick up used items in your neighborhood on certain days or through specific arrangements.

Respect the outdoors. Use products that reduce chemical waste. Pick up after yourself. Through volunteering, voicing your opinion, or making monetary donations, support the maintenance of parks and the preservation of natural, undeveloped land. Be creative: One young woman planned a cleanup of a local lakeside area as the main group activity for the guests at her birthday party (she joined them, of course). Everyone benefits when each person takes responsibility for maintaining the fragile earth.

Remember that valuing yourself is the base for valuing all other things. Improving the earth is possible when you value yourself and think you deserve the best living environment possible. Part of valuing yourself is doing whatever you can to create the life you want to live. Developing, revisiting, and revising your personal mission is how you make a map to guide yourself to that life.

How can you *live your mission?*

Whatever changes occur in your life, your continued learning will give you a greater sense of security in your choices. Recall your mission statement from Chapter 3. Think about how it may change as you develop. It will continue to reflect your goals, values, and strengths if you live with integrity, create personal change, observe role models, broaden your perspective, and work to achieve your personal best.

Live with Integrity

You've spent time exploring who you are, how you learn, and what you value. In Chapter 1, you learned about academic integrity and what it means to your education. Expand that idea to all areas of your life—personal and professional, as well as educational. Living with integrity will bring you great personal and professional rewards.

Having integrity puts your *ethics*—your sense of what is right and wrong—into day-to-day action. When you act with integrity, you earn trust and respect from others. If people can trust you to be honest, to be sincere in what you say and do, and to consider the needs of others, they will be more likely to encourage you, support your goals, and reward your work.

Think of situations in which a decision made with integrity has had a positive effect. Have you ever confessed to an instructor that your paper is late without a good excuse, only to find that despite your mistake, you have earned the instructor's respect? Have you chosen not to look at a copy of an exam before taking it? Have extra efforts in the workplace ever helped you gain a promotion or a raise? Have your kindnesses toward a friend or spouse moved the relationship to a deeper level? When you decide to act with integrity, you can improve your life and the lives of others.

Most important, living with integrity helps you believe in yourself and in your ability to make good choices. A person of integrity isn't a perfect person, but is one who makes the effort to live according to values and principles, continually striving to learn from mistakes and to improve. Take responsibility for making the right moves, and you will follow your mission with strength and conviction.

Create Personal Change

How has your idea of who you are and where you want to be changed since you first opened this book? What have you learned about your values, your goals, and your styles of communication and learning? If you make the effort to grow and develop, your values, goals, and style will shift in response. Responding with awareness to these developments and shifts means making some courageous changes in your life.

Stephen Covey, in *The Seven Habits of Highly Effective People,* says: "Change—real change—comes from the inside out. It doesn't come from hacking at the leaves of attitude and behavior with quick fix personality ethic techniques. It comes from striking at the root—the fabric of our thought, the fundamental essential **paradigms** which give definition to our character and create the lens through which we see the world."[4] For example, imagine that a student has a bias against an instructor because of a cultural difference. The "quick fix" is for the student to just try to ignore the bias in order to focus on passing the course successfully. On the other hand, the "striking at the root," inspiring real change, happens if the student examines the bias and its source, considers its potential negative effects, and perhaps tries to overcome it by getting to know the instructor on a more personal level.

PARADIGM
An especially clear pattern or typical example.

There are two steps to creating personal change. First, you must ask yourself honest questions to decide what you want to change. Ask yourself, "What really matters to me? How am I doing with making those things part of my life? How am I developing as a person? Am I on the path I want to be on?" Examining yourself deeply in that way is a real risk, demanding courage and strength of will. Questioning your established beliefs and facing the unknown are much more difficult than staying with how things are.

Once you have some idea of what you want to do, the second and toughest step—but most rewarding—is to make the changes. When you face the consequences of trying something unfamiliar, admitting failure, or challenging what you thought you knew, you open yourself to learning opportunities. When you foster personal changes and make new choices based on those changes, you grow.

Learn from Role Models

People often derive high motivation and inspiration from learning how others have struggled through the ups and downs of life and achieved their goals. Somehow, seeing how a **role model** went through difficult situations can give you hope for your own struggles. The positive effects

ROLE MODEL
A person whose behavior in a particular role is imitated by others.

of being true to oneself become more real when a person has earned them.

Learning about the lives of people who have achieved their own version of success can teach you what you can accomplish. For example, Elizabeth (Bessie) and Sadie Delany, African-American sisters born in the late 1800s, are two valuable role models. They took risks, becoming professionals in dentistry and teaching at a time when women and African-Americans were often denied both respect and opportunity. They worked to fight prejudice and taught others what they learned. They believed in their intelligence, beauty, and ability to give, and lived without regrets. In their *Book of Everyday Wisdom,* Sadie Delany says: "If there's anything I've learned in all these years, it's that life is too good to waste a day. It's up to you to make it sweet."[5]

Broaden Your Perspective

Look wide, beyond the scope of your daily life. You are part of an international community. In today's media-saturated world, people are becoming more aware of, and dependent on, each other. What happens to the Japanese economy affects the prices of goods in your neighborhood. A music trend that starts in New York spreads to Europe. When human rights are violated in one nation, other nations become involved. You are as important a link in this worldwide chain of human connection as any other person. Together, all people share an interest in creating a better world for future generations.

In the early part of the twentieth century, intense change took place. The Industrial Revolution changed the face of farming, and inventions, such as the telephone and television, fostered greater communication. Labor unions organized, the civil rights movement struggled against inequality, and women fought for the right to vote. Now, at the turn of this century, major shifts are happening once again. Computer technology is drastically changing every industry. The media spread information to people all over the world at a rapid rate. Many people continue to strive for equal rights. You are part of a world that is responsible for making the most of such devel-

PERSONAL TRIUMPH

g *rowing up around people who've been hampered by difficulties can inspire a person to make different choices. Joe Martin made the effort to achieve as a student—but that wasn't enough for him. His main focus now is his life mission to use his abilities to help and inspire others.*

I grew up in the housing projects of Miami, Florida. My mother didn't finish high school, and no one in my family even considered going to college, including me. My low GPA and SAT scores seemed to indicate I wasn't "college material."

While I was in high school, six of my friends died as a result of crime, drugs, or murder. At least 12 people I knew were in prison, five from my own family. I made a vow that if I survived the projects, I would do something constructive with my life and give something back to the community. I initially wanted to join the military, but after the recruiter told me I wasn't smart enough to go to college, I decided to prove him wrong.

I enrolled in college and, given my academic background, was shocked by my success. I ended up graduating at the top of my class, with a bachelor's degree in public relations, and was voted "Student of the Year" among 10,000 students. Competing against more than 400 other candidates, I landed a job right out of college working for the federal government. Within a year, I was able to move my mother out of the projects and afford almost anything I wanted. Life was great, but I didn't like my job and the person I was becoming.

Around that time, I heard a motivational speaker talk about the need for young professionals to give back to the community. I suddenly realized that I hadn't kept my vow. I was indulging myself, but I didn't have any passion or purpose for what I was doing with my life.

After his presentation, I asked the speaker for advice. I jotted down his suggestions on a napkin and began to implement his ideas. I discovered that I could make money doing what I

Joe A. Martin, Jr., Professor of Communications, University of West Florida, Tallahassee, Florida

do best—talking. I became a motivational speaker for students and found that my true passion was teaching. Through teaching, whether on stage or in the classroom, I discovered that I could make a difference in the lives of students who were growing up in poverty as I had.

I've given over 300 presentations and spoken to more than a quarter of a million people about student success. I've written books, recorded audio and video tapes of my programs, and have my own television show. However, my biggest accomplishment so far has been the creation of a Web site called "RealWorld University." With the Web site, I'm now able to reach more than 100,000 students a month in 26 different countries.

I believe the reason many students fail is because they have no clue about their gifts and talents or about how they can use those gifts and talents to serve others. Many people are on what I call the "Treadmill Trench" of life—motivated to stay busy, but too scared to live their dreams.

My two main questions to students are: "If you knew you couldn't fail, what would you attempt to do professionally?" and "What kind of work would you be willing to do for free if you never had to worry about money?" The answers to those two questions can help anyone find their purpose and passion in life. I also stress to students the importance of meeting a model of success—not someone you'll probably never meet, like Michael Jordan, but someone who is doing what you love to do. Then, spend time with that person to find out how they did it. Once students have a clear vision of what they want to become, they're destined to succeed.

Take a moment to consider . . .

- *What you think you'd like to give back to others in the community.*

- *What you feel is missing in your life, and how you plan to find the missing piece and fill the gap.*

opments. In making the choices that allow you to achieve your potential, you make the world a better place.

Aim for Your Personal Best

Your personal best is simply the best that you can do, in any situation. It may not be the best you have ever done. It may include mistakes, for nothing significant is ever accomplished without making mistakes and taking risks. It may shift from situation to situation. As long as you aim to do your best, though, you are inviting growth and success.

In Figure 12.2 you see a blank Wheel of Life. Without looking at your Chapter 1 wheel, evaluate yourself as you are right now, after completing this course: Where would you rank yourself in the eight categories? After you have finished, compare this wheel to your previous wheel. Look at the changes: Where have you grown? How has your self-perception changed? Let what you learn from this new wheel inform you about what you have accomplished and what you plan for the future.

"And life is what we make it, always has been, always will be."

GRANDMA MOSES

Aim for your personal best in everything you do. As a lifelong learner, you will always have a new direction in which to grow and a new challenge to face. Seek constant improvement in your personal, educational, and professional life, knowing that you are capable of such improvement. Enjoy the richness of life by living each day to the fullest, developing your talents and potential into the achievement of your most valued goals.

Figure 12.2 Your new wheel of life.

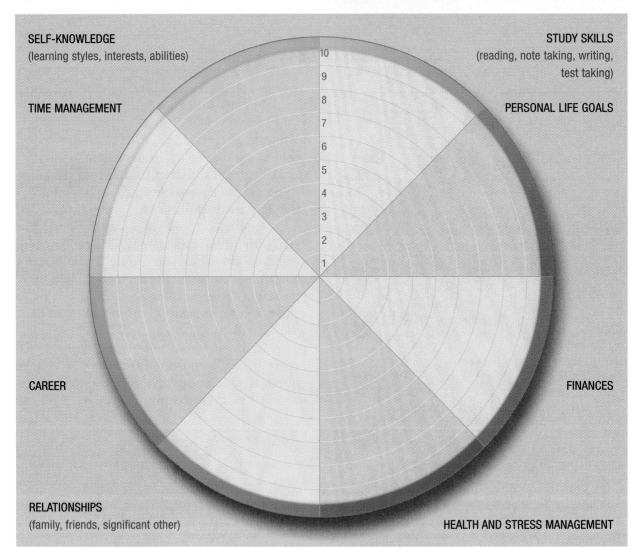

SELF-KNOWLEDGE
(learning styles, interests, abilities)

STUDY SKILLS
(reading, note taking, writing, test taking)

TIME MANAGEMENT

PERSONAL LIFE GOALS

CAREER

FINANCES

RELATIONSHIPS
(family, friends, significant other)

HEALTH AND STRESS MANAGEMENT

Source: Based on "The Wheel of Life" model developed by the Coaches Training Institute, © Co-Active Space 2000.

Kaizen is the Japanese word for "continual improvement." Striving for excellence, finding ways to improve on what already exists, and believing that you can effect change are at the heart of the industrious Japanese spirit. The drive to improve who you are and what you do provides the foundation of a successful future.

Think of this concept as you reflect on yourself, your goals, your life-long education, your career, and your personal pursuits. Create excellence and quality by continually asking yourself, "How can I improve?" Living by *kaizen* helps you to be a respected friend and family member, a productive and valued employee, and a truly contributing member of society. You can change the world.

Building Skills

FOR COLLEGE, CAREER, AND LIFE SUCCESS

Critical Thinking *Applying Learning to Life*

Changes in Goals

As changes occur in your life, your goals change and need reevaluation. Think about what may have changed in your school, career, and life goals over the past semester. For each category name an old goal, name the adjusted new goal, and briefly state why you think the change occurred.

SCHOOL.

Old: _____

New: _____

Why the change? _____

_____

_____

CAREER.

Old: _____

New: _____

Why the change? _____

_____

_____

PERSONAL LIFE.

Old: _____

New: _____

Why the change? _____

_____

_____

Looking at Change, Failure, and Success

Life can go by so fast that you don't take time to evaluate what changes have taken place, what failures you could learn from, and what successes you have experienced. Take a moment now to answer the following questions about your experiences in the past year.

LIFE CHANGES. Name a change that you feel you handled well. What shifts in priorities or goals did you make?

_____

_____

_____

Name a change that you could have handled better. What happened? What else could you have done?

_____

_____

_____

SUCCESSES. Describe a recent success of which you are proudest.

_____

_____

_____

How did this success affect your self-perception?

_____

_____

_____

FAILURES. Name an experience, occurring this year, that you would consider a failure. What happened?

_____

_____

_____

How did you handle it—did you ignore it, blame it on someone else, or admit and explore it?

_____

_____

_____

What did you learn from experiencing this failure?

_____

_____

_____

Lifelong Learning

Review the strategies for lifelong learning on pages 417–420. Which do you think you can do, or can plan to do, in your life now and when you are out of school? Name the three that mean the most to you and briefly state why.

1. _____

2. _____

3. _____

Teamwork *Combining Forces*

GIVING BACK. In your group, research volunteering opportunities in your community. Each group member should choose one possibility to research. Answer questions such as the following: What is the situation or organization? What are its needs? Do any volunteer positions require an application, letters of reference, or background checks? What is the time commitment? Is there any special training involved? Are there any problematic or difficult elements to this experience?

When you have the information, meet together so that each group member can describe each volunteering opportunity to the rest of the members. Choose one that you feel you will have the time and ability to try next semester. Name your choice and tell why you selected it.

Writing *Discovery Through Journaling*

To record your thoughts, use a separate journal or the lined page at the end of the chapter.

FIFTY POSITIVE THOUGHTS. Make a list. The first 25 items should be things you like about yourself. You can name anything—things you can do, things you think, things you've accomplished, things you like about your physical self, and so on. The second 25 items should be things you'd like to do in your life. These can be of any magnitude—anything from trying Vietnamese food to traveling to the Grand Canyon to keeping your room neat to getting to know someone. They can be things you'd like to do tomorrow or things that you plan to do in 20 years. Be creative. Let everything be possible.

Career Portfolio | *Charting Your Course*

REVISED MISSION STATEMENT. Retrieve the mission statement you wrote at the end of Chapter 3. Give yourself a day or so to read it over and think about it. Then, revise it according to the changes that have occurred in you. Add new priorities and goals and delete those that are no longer valid. Continue to update your mission statement so that it reflects your growth and development, helping to guide you through the changes that await you in the future.

Assess Yourself | *Student Success Strategies*

If you have access to the CD-ROM Strategies for Success, use the following questions to assess your thoughts and enhance your understanding of the chapter. The questions below represent only some of the activities provided on the CD for the chapter topics—try others if you have time.

Click on the Managing Your Career bookmark. Use the following activities to clarify your vision of what you want for your future:

1. Take the pre-assessment to explore your views on career planning while in college.

2. Click on Activity One: Investigate Yourself. Making sure your computer is on-line, click on the links provided and take the Emotional Intelligence assessment and the Keirsey Sorter assessment. Then connect your results with potential career plans by answering the rest of the questions in the activity.

3. Click on Activity Three: Journal Reflections. Scroll to the second question, which asks you about what employers value in the people they hire. Type your answer in the field provided.

4. Take the post-assessment to see how ready you are to put your best foot forward in the working world.

Suggested Readings

Delany, Sarah and Elizabeth Delany with Amy Hill Hearth. *Book of Everyday Wisdom.* New York: Kodansha International, 1994.

Moore, Thomas. *Care of the Soul: How to Add Depth and Meaning to Your Everyday Life.* New York: HarperCollins, 1998.

Internet Resources

AmeriCorps: www.americorps.org

Campus Compact site for citizenship and community service: www.compact.org

Hearts and Minds clearinghouse for volunteer opportunities and civic involvement: www.heartsandminds.org/index.htm

Queendom.com Soul Search (self-tests, personal exploration and growth): www.queendom.com/portals/soulsearch.html

Endnotes

1. Linton Weeks, "The No-Book Report: Skim It and Weep," *The Washington Post*, May 14, 2001, p. C8.

2. Thomas Moore, *The Care of the Soul.* New York: Harper Perennial, 1992, pp. xi–xx.

3. Margaret J. Wheatley and Myron Kellner-Rogers, "A Simpler Way," *Weight Watchers Magazine* 30.3 (1997), pp. 42–44.

4. Stephen Covey, *The Seven Habits of Highly Effective People.* New York: Simon & Schuster, 1989, pp. 70–144, 309–318.

5. Sarah Delany and Elizabeth Delany with Amy Hill Hearth, *Book of Everyday Wisdom.* New York: Kodansha International, 1994, p. 123.

JOURNAL

name   date

Part III
CREATING SUCCESS

Becoming a Better Test Taker

MULTIPLE CHOICE. Circle or highlight the answer that seems to fit best.

1. Students who experience stereotype vulnerability may
   A. call attention to themselves as members of a minority group.
   B. be self-conscious because they see themselves as underachievers.
   C. feel superior to others because of their minority status.
   D. distance themselves from the qualities they think others associate with their group and avoid asking for help because they fear perpetuating a group stereotype.

2. The goal of stress management is to
   A. eliminate all stress from your life.
   B. focus only on school-related stress.
   C. learn to blame all stressful situations on others.
   D. develop strategies for handling the stresses that are an inevitable part of life.

3. Emotional intelligence, as defined by Daniel Goleman, is a combination of
   A. empathy and social skills.
   B. self-regulation and motivation.
   C. Thinker qualities and Giver qualities.
   D. personal competence and social competence.

4. *Networking* can be defined as
   A. visiting your instructor during office hours.
   B. the exchange of information or services among individuals, groups, or institutions.
   C. discovering your ideal career.
   D. making a strategic plan.

5. Being flexible in the face of change involves
   A. changing your direction when you encounter obstacles in your life and work.
   B. acknowledging the change and assessing what new needs it brings.
   C. reacting in a way that you have seen work for others.
   D. focusing on an aspect of your life not affected by the change.

6. To be open to unpredictability,
   A. put your energy into building existing relationships.
   B. make a plan and stick with it even in the face of change.
   C. focus on what is rather than on what is supposed to be.
   D. don't let surprises throw you off.

FILL-IN-THE-BLANK. Complete the following sentences with the appropriate word(s) or phrase(s) that best reflect what you have learned. Choose from the items that follow each sentence.

1. _____ factors play an important role in how _____ are interpreted. (Personal/body movements, Biological/verbal cues, Cultural/nonverbal cues)

2. _____ criticism involves goodwill suggestions for improvement. (Nonconstructive, Direct, Constructive)

3. The three most common eating disorders are _____, _____, and _____. (anorexia nervosa/food allergies/binge drinking, anorexia nervosa/bulimia/binge eating, constant dieting/eating too much fat/bulimia)

4. Two effective ways to build career knowledge and experience are _____ and _____. (job hunting/networking, internships/volunteering, learning style/critical thinking)

5. The debt ceiling a credit card company places on your account is called a _____. (cash advance, account balance, credit limit)

6. _____ is a government agency that provides financial awards for education in return for community service. (U.S. Bureau of Labor, AmeriCorps, Red Cross)

ESSAY QUESTIONS. The following essay questions will help you organize and communicate your ideas in writing, just as you must do on an essay test. Before you begin answering a question, spend a few minutes planning (brainstorm possible approaches, write a thesis statement, jot down main thoughts in outline or think link form). To prepare yourself for actual test conditions, limit writing time to no more than 30 minutes per question.

1. Discuss the mind–body connection—specifically, the impact of diet, exercise, sleep, and medical care on the development and management of stress. Describe the changes you hope to make in your stress-management plan as a result of the information you have read in this textbook.

2. Choose three important skills you have developed during this course. Explain how they will contribute to your success both in the remainder of your college experience and beyond.

PERSONAL TRIUMPH

Wilma Rudolph, Olympic champion

i n some situations, particular life goals may seem out of reach. Wilma Rudolph is proof that the unthinkable is possible. A polio victim not expected to walk, she determinedly and steadily became an Olympic runner—and a humanist with a mission to bring about social change.

Wilma Rudolph was born in Bethlehem, Tennessee, on June 23, 1940, the seventeenth of 19 children in her family. At an early age, Wilma survived polio, as well as bouts of scarlet fever and pneumonia. However, the polio left her with the use of only one of her legs. With the help of daily massages administered by her parents and siblings, Rudolph eventually was able to walk with the help of leg braces that she wore until age 11. Through the aid of backyard battles with her siblings in basketball and other sports, Wilma eventually progressed from just being able to participate to becoming a bona fide athlete.

As a sophomore at Burt High School, Wilma excelled as a basketball player, where she set several state high school girls' records in the sport. As successful as Wilma was on the basketball court, however, her performance there paled in comparison to her achievements in track and field. Throughout her entire high school career, Rudolph never lost a single race. She had gone from being unable to walk without the aid of leg braces to being the fastest young woman in the state of Tennessee. Her achievements on the track led her to a full scholarship at Tennessee State University, where she enrolled in 1957. Despite her successes on the collegiate level, including the world record in the 200-meter dash, it was not enough for Wilma. She soon set her sights on the 1960 Olympics in Rome.

Rudolph's performance in the Olympics led her to be recognized as "the world's fastest woman." She won three gold medals, still a record for female Olympians, in the 100-meter and 200-meter dash as well as the 4 x 100-meter relay. Her performance led to the Associated

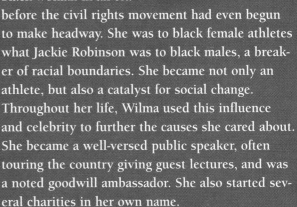

Press naming her the Female Athlete of the Year for 1960.

Wilma Rudolph's story, however, transcends the world of sports. Aside from being an accomplished athlete, Wilma was a celebrated and respected black woman in an era before the civil rights movement had even begun to make headway. She was to black female athletes what Jackie Robinson was to black males, a breaker of racial boundaries. She became not only an athlete, but also a catalyst for social change. Throughout her life, Wilma used this influence and celebrity to further the causes she cared about. She became a well-versed public speaker, often touring the country giving guest lectures, and was a noted goodwill ambassador. She also started several charities in her own name.

Wilma Rudolph's life was marked by amazing achievements despite almost impossible odds. She overcame near crippling illnesses to become one of the greatest athletes of the twentieth century. Her story serves as a shining example that no matter how many obstacles may appear in one's path, anything is possible as long as you try your hardest and never give up. After years of dedicated service to her causes, Wilma finally succumbed to a malignant brain tumor on November 12, 1994. Although she is now gone, the legacy she leaves behind as both an accomplished athlete and a dedicated humanitarian lives on.

Take a moment to consider . . .

- *What personal deficiency has inspired you to work harder.*
- *What causes you would fight for if you were in the public eye.*

Sources: www.gale.com/freresrc/blkhstry/Rudolph.htm, www.espn.go.com.

The Prentice Hall Supersite (www.prenhall.com/success) has a Career Path tab. Click on it and take the quiz to see what it says about your career possibilities.

1. What group number did you most closely associate with? What in the description of that group describes you well?

2. Which group would be your second choice, and what about that description suits you?

3. Select two professions that interest you from those listed as suiting your group type. Use a search engine to find sites on the Web that might have information about those professions. Write down the URLs for those sites so that you can return to them.

Next, visit the Career Assessments section and click on the "What are my values?" assessment. Copy or print the value lists and complete the assessment as directed.

1. What are your most important terminal values?

2. What are your most important instrumental values?

3. Think about it—what careers do you think suit the values that are most important to you? If you are already involved with or interested in one or more particular careers, how well do you think those careers suit your values?

Finally, use a search engine to locate a number of career-related Web sites that you can use as resources in your quest for a career. They might be general job-search sites, career information sites, or sites run by specific companies that list jobs or other job-related information (some potential sites are listed at the end of Chapter 11). Note the URLs of these sites so that you can use them again during the course of your exploration.

Answer Key

FOR BECOMING A BETTER TEST TAKER

PART I: DEFINING YOURSELF AND YOUR GOALS

Multiple Choice

1. D
2. A
3. D
4. A
5. C
6. A

Fill-in-the-Blank

1. commitment
2. initiative
3. learning preferences/personality traits
4. interests/abilities
5. mission
6. flexible

PART II: DEVELOPING YOUR LEARNING SKILLS

Multiple Choice

1. D
2. B
3. A
4. D
5. B
6. C

Fill-in-the-Blank

1. taking in information/asking questions about information/using information
2. creativity
3. context
4. cue column
5. mnemonic device
6. Freewriting/uncensored/planning

PART III: CREATING SUCCESS

Multiple Choice

1. D
2. D
3. D
4. B
5. B
6. C

Fill-in-the-Blank

1. Cultural/nonverbal cues
2. Constructive
3. anorexia nervosa/ bulimia/ binge eating
4. internships/volunteering
5. credit limit
6. Americorps

Index